America's ★ Best

Low Carb
Recipes

compiled and edited by
Anne C. Cain, M.S., M.P.H., R.D.

©2005 by Oxmoor House, Inc.
Book Division of Southern Progress Corporation
P.O. Box 2463, Birmingham, Alabama 35201

ISBN: 0-8487-2863-7

Printed in the United States of America
First printing 2005

Be sure to check with your health-care provider before making any changes in your diet.

Oxmoor House, Inc.
Editor in Chief: Nancy Fitzpatrick Wyatt
Executive Editor: Katherine M. Eakin
Art Director: Cynthia R. Cooper
Copy Chief: Allison Long Lowery

America's Best Low Carb Cookbook
Editor: Anne C. Cain, M.S., M.P.H., R.D.
Senior Designer: Melissa Jones Clark
Editorial Assistant: Terri Laschober
Director, Test Kitchens: Elizabeth Tyler Luckett
Assistant Director, Test Kitchens: Julie Christopher
Test Kitchens Staff: Kristi Carter, Nicole L. Faber, Kathleen Royal Phillips,
   Elise Weis, Kelley Self Wilton
Senior Photographer: Jim Bathie
Photographer: Brit Huckabay
Senior Photo Stylist: Kay Clarke
Photo Stylist: Amy Wilson
Publishing Systems Administrator: Rick Tucker
Director of Production: Phillip Lee
Books Production Manager: Theresa L. Beste
Production Assistant: Faye Porter Bonner

Contributors:
Copy Editor: Dolores Hydock
Indexer: Mary Ann Laurens

To order additional copies of this book or others, call 1-800-765-6400.
For more books to enrich your life, visit oxmoorhouse.com

Cover: clockwise from top center: Ice Cream Sandwich Dessert (page 408), Polynesian Beef Kebabs (page 241), Marinated Strawberries (page 384), and Spicy Chicken Finger Salad (page 294)

contents

dear friends,

New research shows that following a low-carbohydrate diet can result in weight loss, but it was my husband's 65-pound weight loss that convinced me that a sensible low-carb plan can really work. And we have that plan to share with you.

At last! A new cookbook and a new plan for low-carb eaters who love great food.

America's Best Low Carb Recipes provides the tools you'll need to lose weight the low-carb way. Our Carbo-Rater system is an easy way to keep up with your carbs and helps you choose the right kinds of carbs. The plan and the recipes can be used alone, or in conjunction with any of the other low- or modified-carb plans on the market. One of the biggest complaints I hear from folks who are following a low-carb diet is that they're tired of eating the same things, day after day. So we're offering a book packed full of recipes for main dishes, low-carb breakfasts, soups and sandwiches, snacks, and desserts.

America's Best Low Carb Recipes is more than just a cookbook. In addition to the new Carbo-Rater system, here are just a few of the other benefits you'll get from this book:
• over 500 kitchen-tested, dietitian-approved recipes
• complete nutrient breakdown for every recipe including carbs, fiber, calories, fat, protein, and sodium
• 80 mouthwatering color photographs
• 3 weeks of low-carb menus
• over 35 best-bet breakfasts
• low-carb grocery shopping list
• recipe tips and shortcuts
• strategies for eating on the run
• sugar substitute guide
• practical tips from people who have had successful weight loss on a low-carb diet

When it gets down to it, the basic question everyone asks when they start a weight-loss program is "What can I eat?" *America's Best Low Carb Recipes* gives answers that will please you.

In health,

Anne Cain

Anne Cain, R.D., Editor

the carbo-rater system

Lose weight and improve your health with this plan that gives you an easy way to keep track of carbohydrates and offers a wide variety of great-tasting, good-for-you recipes.

Carbo Rating

Our Carbo-Rater system is a simple way to keep up with your grams of carbohydrate and to help you eat the right kind and amounts of carbohydrate. The carbo rating is a whole number based on the total grams of carbohydrate minus the grams of fiber in one serving of food.

Total Carbohydrate (grams) – Fiber (grams) = Carbo Rating

When you subtract the grams of fiber from the total carbohydrate, that's the amount of carbohydrate that will actually be absorbed by your body. That's the amount of carbohydrate that can raise blood sugar or be stored as fat if it's not burned for energy. The carbo rating per serving for each recipe is printed just above the recipe title.

▶ carbo rating: 1

Pick Your Carb Level

The recipes in this book are organized according to carbo rating, starting with the lowest ratings. If you're looking for recipes with the least amount of carbohydrate, turn to the beginning of each recipe chapter.

> Much like a car relies on the carburetor for the proper mix of fuel and air so that the car can run, our bodies rely on the proper mix of fuel for energy.

Nutrient Guarantee

Even though the focus of the carbo rating is on carbohydrate and fiber, calories, fat, and sodium should be considered in any healthy recipe. Here's what you can count on in our recipes:

- **low-carb recipes without an excessive amount** of saturated fat or cholesterol
- **the use of fish, lean meats, and poultry** without an excessive amount of protein
- **moderate amounts** of sodium
- **recipes featuring heart-healthy fats** such as the type of fat in olive oil, nuts, and salmon
- **reasonable portions** based on the serving sizes recommended by leading health organizations
- **complete nutrient analysis** with every recipe
- **high-fiber, high-nutrient sources** of carbohydrate

the carburetor connection

Your body operates in a manner similar to your car. In your car, the fuel mixes with air in the carburetor where it combusts, creating energy for the car to move. A similar process goes on in your body. Much like a car relies on the carburetor for the proper mix of fuel and air so that the car can run, our bodies rely on the proper mix of fuel for energy.

The preferred fuel for the body is carbohydrate (units of carbon, hydrogen, and oxygen—the same elements in gasoline, just arranged differently). The foods you eat are digested and converted into a form of carbohydrate called glucose that your body uses for energy.

And, like our cars' engines, how well our body runs depends on the proper mix of fuel, particularly carbohydrates.

guide to carbs

Not all carbs are bad. Our Carbo-Rater system shows you how to pick the right kind of carbs in the right amounts so that you can lose weight.

Carbohydrate is your body's preferred source of fuel. The brain depends exclusively on carbohydrate for its energy when that fuel is available. If there is no carbohydrate available (either from the foods that are eaten or in storage in the liver or muscles), the body will convert protein and/or fat to glucose (the form of carbohydrate the body uses for energy).

But if you eat more carbohydrate than your body needs for fuel, a small amount of it is stored in the liver or the muscles to be used later for energy. The rest of it gets changed into fat.

Ideal Carbohydrate Level
There's no specific recommended amount of carbohydrate. The amount of carbohydrate you need depends on many factors, including the following:
• current weight and height
• physical activity level
• gender
• health status

Preferred Carbohydrate
Our Carbo-Rater plan doesn't completely restrict carbohydrate—it allows a specific amount of the right kinds of carbohydrate. The ideal carbohydrates in terms of weight loss and disease prevention have the following characteristics:
• high in fiber
• absorbed slowly
• do not cause rapid increases in blood glucose

The carbs in fruits and vegetables are good for you because when you eat them, you get a whole package

preferred carb list

These are some of the "good carbs" that you can include in your low-carb plan.
Vegetables: leafy green vegetables; spinach and other greens; tomatoes; yellow squash; zucchini
Fruits: fresh berries, melons, citrus fruits
Dairy products: low and reduced-fat milk, yogurt with no added sugar; low-carb and no-added-sugar ice creams; sugar-free puddings
Breads: low-carb bread; 100 percent whole wheat or whole-grain breads
Cereals and grains: brown rice, barley, oats; bulgur, wheat germ; whole-grain or bran ready-to-eat cereals with no added sugars

of disease-fighting vitamins and minerals. Fruits and vegetables, as well as whole grains and cereals, also contain carbohydrate in the form of fiber. Since fiber isn't digested by the body, these foods are absorbed slowly, so they don't cause a rapid rise in blood glucose. When the blood glucose rises slowly, the carbohydrate isn't stored as fat as easily.

See the list above of some carbohydrate-containing foods that you can include in the Carbo-Rater Eating Plan. The number of servings that you can have will depend on your particular level of carbohydrate intake. (Detailed information about the carbohydrate level at each phase of the plan is provided in the left column of each weekly menu plan.)

Our Carbo-Rater plan doesn't completely restrict carbohydrate—it allows a specific amount of the right kinds of carbohydrate.

carbo-rater eating plan

If you're already on a low-carbohydrate diet, you can use the recipes in this book with that plan. If you need one to go by, use our Carbo-Rater Eating Plan to lose weight and keep it off.

This easy-to-understand plan has three phases based on gradually increasing amounts of carbs, but always emphasizing the right kind of carbs.

Phase 1: No-Carb carbo rating of 20–25 per day (approximately 1300 calories)

Phase 2: Low-Carb carbo rating of 60–70 per day (approximately 1600 calories)

Phase 3: Go-Carb carbo rating of 90–120 per day (approximately 1800 calories)

Getting Started

If you want to lose weight, start with the No-Carb phase (phase 1), then move up to the Low-Carb and Go-Carb phases as you lose the desired amount of weight. If you simply want to eat in a more heart-healthy fashion, start with the Low-Carb or Go-Carb plan.

Here's what we suggest if weight loss is your goal:

1. Start with phase 1, No-Carb, to lose weight initially. Follow this plan for at least one week.
2. Move to phase 2, Low-Carb, and stay on this plan until you've lost the amount of weight you want to lose.
3. When you have reached your weight-loss goal, you can move on to phase 3, Go-Carb, which is more liberal in total amount of carbohydrate, but is all about eating the right kind of carbs for health and weight maintenance. (See the "preferred carb list" on the previous page.) If you start gaining weight, you can move back to either the No-Carb or Low-Carb phase.

Menu Plans

To follow the plan, start with the sample menus on the next six pages. There is a one-week menu plan for each of the three phases, featuring recipes in this cookbook. Since each meal has its own carbo rating, you can mix and match meals as you wish.

Create even more menus by using other recipes in the cookbook. See the carbo rating at the top of each recipe, then simply add up your carbo rating for each meal. For each phase, we give you a basic pattern, then you can adapt that pattern to suit your particular lifestyle and your food preferences.

The key to almost any weight-loss plan is portion control.

Serving Sizes

On any of the phases, if you need to add calories, you can eat more than one serving of the low-carb menu items, especially the fish, poultry, and meat entrées. The portion sizes for meats, poultry, and fish in this book are based on 6-ounce portions raw weight for poultry and fish, and 4-ounce portions for meats.

"I am so excited about this book! One of the other low-carb diets worked for me, but with my family's history of heart disease, I just didn't feel comfortable being on it because of all the fat. This healthier approach puts my mind at ease."
Melissa Clark

no-carb plan: carbo rating 20–25

	day 1	day 2	day 3
breakfast	**Cheesy Zucchini Frittata,** page 28 Bacon, 3 slices ► **carbo rating: 3**	Scrambled eggs with cheese (2 eggs, 1 oz. shredded Cheddar cheese) Whole wheat low-carb toast, 1 slice Light butter, 1 T. ► **carbo rating: 6**	**Spinach Frittata,** page 28 Bacon, 3 slices Cantaloupe, 1 wedge ► **carbo rating: 8**
lunch	Deli-roasted chicken, 6 oz. **Sliced Tomato Salad with Capers and Basil,** page 279 Sugar-free gelatin dessert, 1 c. ► **carbo rating: 3**	**Shrimp Rémoulade,** page 126 Mixed salad greens, 2 c. Oil and vinegar dressing, 2 T. ► **carbo rating: 4**	**Shrimp Salad,** page 279 Sliced tomato drizzled with olive oil and sprinkled with pepper (4 slices tomato, 1 T. oil) Cucumber slices, 10 Sugar-free gelatin dessert, 1 c. ► **carbo rating: 8**
dinner	**Sesame Salmon,** page 100 Steamed snow peas, 1 c. Angel hair cabbage with sesame vinaigrette (1 c. shredded cabbage, 1 T. sesame oil, 1 T. rice wine vinegar) ► **carbo rating: 7**	**Southwestern Grilled Flank Steak,** page 188 **Cumin-Scented Squash,** page 322 **Orange-Avocado Salad,** page 277 ► **carbo rating: 6**	**Greek Chicken with Lemon and Mint,** page 249 Sautéed zucchini, ½ c. (sautéed in 1 tsp. olive oil) Mixed salad greens, 2 c. Olive oil vinaigrette, 2 T. ► **carbo rating: 3**
snack	**Snappy Spinach Dip,** page 49, ½ c. Swiss cheese, 1 oz. Whole wheat crackers, 2 ► **carbo rating: 9**	**Garlic-Herb Cheese Spread,** page 52, 2 T. Cucumber slices, 10 Almonds, ¼ c. ► **carbo rating: 6**	Cheddar cheese, 1 oz. Almonds, ¼ c. ► **carbo rating: 3**
total	**total carbo rating: 22** **total calories: 1327**	**total carbo rating: 22** **total calories: 1352**	**total carbo rating: 22** **total calories: 1303**

no-carb phase:
• Not completely carb-free, but the only carb comes from vegetables, fruits, small amounts of dairy products, and whole wheat bread or crackers
• Corresponds with the 20-gram carbohydrate level in the induction phase of the Atkins plan
• Provides approximately 1300 calories per day, which may be too low for men and for physically active women (talk to a registered dietitian or physician about calories needed for weight loss; you may be able to start with the Low-Carb plan [phase 2] and still lose weight)
• Contributes 5 percent or less of daily calories from carbohydrate

Note: For all recipe items, the amount is the serving size listed for the recipe, unless otherwise noted. The carbo rating listed at the end of each meal is the total for all of the items listed in that particular menu. The total carbo rating at the bottom of each column is the total for the whole day.

c.= cup   T.= tablespoon   tsp.= teaspoon   oz.= ounce

	day 4	day 5	day 6	day 7	
breakfast	**Salsa Omelet with Roasted Red Peppers and Cheese,** page 27 Reduced-fat sausage, 2 oz. ▶ carbo rating: 4	**Cinnamon Toast,** page 34, 1 slice Bacon, 3 slices ▶ carbo rating: 7	**Cheese Toast,** page 34, 1 slice Reduced-fat sausage, 2 oz. ▶ carbo rating: 8	Whole wheat low-carb toast with peanut butter (1 slice, 2 T. natural peanut butter) Hard-cooked egg, 1 ▶ carbo rating: 9	
lunch	Chef Salad (2 c. torn lettuce, 2 tomato slices, 2 oz. cheese, 2 oz. chopped ham, 2 oz. chopped turkey, 2 T. bacon pieces, 1 hard-cooked egg, chopped) Blue cheese dressing, 2 T. ▶ carbo rating: 5	**Cold Poached Salmon with Summer Tomato Dressing,** page 115 Spinach Salad (1 c. chopped fresh spinach, 2 T. onion, 2 T. oil and vinegar dressing) ▶ carbo rating: 6	**Crustless Spinach Quiche,** page 140 Mixed green salad, 2 c. Oil and vinegar dressing, 2 T. Tomato slices, 4 ▶ carbo rating: 8	**Lemon-Herb Roasted Chicken,** page 246 Steamed yellow squash, ½ c. Steamed broccoli, ½ c. Light butter, 2 T. ▶ carbo rating: 4	
dinner	**Dijon Sirloin,** page 196 **Roasted Snap Beans,** page 327 Steamed yellow squash, ½ c. Light butter, 1 T. ▶ carbo rating: 8	**Roasted Turkey Breast,** page 244 **Sesame Steamed Broccoli,** page 321 Mixed salad greens, 2 c. Blue cheese dressing, 2 T. ▶ carbo rating: 4	**Grilled Sirloin Steak with Stilton Sauce,** page 190 **Lemon Roasted Asparagus,** page 304 Sugar-free gelatin dessert, 1 c. ▶ carbo rating: 3	**Pork Tenderloin with Rosemary and Garlic,** page 195, 2 servings **Garlicky Sautéed Spinach,** page 322 Sugar-free gelatin dessert, 1 c. ▶ carbo rating: 4	
snack	**Pimiento Cheese Dip,** page 51, 4 T. Whole wheat crackers, 2 Celery sticks, 4 ▶ carbo rating: 7	Almonds, ¼ c. Cheddar cheese, 2 oz. ▶ carbo rating: 3	Roasted turkey, 3 oz. Swiss cheese, 1 oz. Whole wheat crackers, 2 ▶ carbo rating: 4	**Spiced Pecans,** page 58, ¼ c. String cheese, 1 oz. ▶ carbo rating: 5	
total	total carbo rating: 24 total calories: 1352	total carbo rating: 20 total calories: 1334	total carbo rating: 23 total calories: 1379	total carbo rating: 22 total calories: 1317	

low-carb plan: carbo rating 60–70

day 1   day 2   day 3

low-carb phase:
- May add additional fruits and vegetables and small amounts of whole-grain products
- Provides about 15 percent of daily calories from carbohydrate
- Plan provides approximately 1600 calories

Note: For all recipe items, the amount is the serving size listed for the recipe, unless otherwise noted. The carbo rating listed at the end of each meal is the total for all of the items listed in that particular menu. The total carbo rating at the bottom of each column is the total for the whole day.

breakfast

day 1
Multigrain Pancakes, page 88, 1 pancake
Hard-cooked egg, 1
Light butter, 1 T.
Bacon, 3 slices
▶ carbo rating: 12

day 2
Cheesy Zucchini Frittata, page 28
Oatmeal, ½ c.
Light butter, 1 T.
Bacon, 3 slices
▶ carbo rating: 14

day 3
Whole Wheat Buttermilk Pancakes, page 88, 1 pancake
Light butter, 1 T.
Canadian bacon, 4 oz.
Grapefruit, ½
▶ carbo rating: 21

lunch

day 1
Turkey Club Salad, page 292
Whole wheat crackers, 4
Fat-free milk, ½ c.
▶ carbo rating: 28

day 2
Tuna-Cheese Melt, page 354
Celery sticks with peanut butter (4 celery sticks, 2 T. peanut butter)
Strawberries, ½ c.
Fat-free milk, ½ c.
▶ carbo rating: 21

day 3
Chicken Salad, page 289
Tomato slices, 4
Cucumber slices, 10
Whole wheat crackers, 4
Cheddar cheese, 2 oz.
▶ carbo rating: 20

dinner

day 1
Creole Shrimp Stew, page 348
Zucchini with Garlic, page 326, 2 servings
Mixed salad greens, 2 c.
Oil and vinegar dressing, 2 T.
▶ carbo rating: 15

day 2
Peppery Mushroom Burgers, page 201
Garlicky Sautéed Spinach, page 322
Sliced tomato drizzled with olive oil and sprinkled with pepper (4 slices tomato, 1 T. oil)
Whole wheat crackers, 4
▶ carbo rating: 19

day 3
Grilled Pesto Salmon, page 100
Mediterranean Tossed Salad, page 281
Whole-grain roll, 1 small
Light butter, 1 T.
▶ carbo rating: 17

snack

day 1
Turkey-cheese sandwich (1 slice whole wheat low-carb bread, 2 oz. turkey, 2 oz. cheese, 1 T. mayonnaise)
▶ carbo rating: 5

day 2
Sugar-free fruitsicle, 1
Almonds, ¼ c.
▶ carbo rating: 6

day 3
Deviled Eggs, page 49, 2 halves
Whole wheat crackers, 4
Swiss cheese, 1 oz.
▶ carbo rating: 4

total

day 1
total carbo rating: 60
total calories: 1626

day 2
total carbo rating: 60
total calories: 1681

day 3
total carbo rating: 62
total calories: 1628

c.= cup   T.= tablespoon   tsp.= teaspoon   oz.= ounce

breakfast

day 4	day 5	day 6	day 7
Omelet with Zucchini and Onion, page 29	**Spanish Breakfast Scramble,** page 30	All-Bran cereal with extra fiber, ½ c.	**Crawfish Omelet,** page 31
Reduced-fat sausage, 2 oz.	Whole wheat low-carb toast, 1 slice	Fat-free milk, ½ c.	Whole wheat low-carb toast, 1 slice
Whole wheat low-carb toast, 1 slice	Butter, 1 T.	Sausage links, 3	Butter, 1 T.
Butter, 1 T.	Tomato juice, ½ c.		Grapefruit, ½
▶ carbo rating: 10	▶ carbo rating: 18	▶ carbo rating: 14	▶ carbo rating: 19

lunch

day 4	day 5	day 6	day 7
Deli-roasted chicken, 6 oz.	**White Bean Chicken Chili,** page 358	**Chicken Salad with Asparagus,** page 291	Chef Salad (2 c. torn lettuce, 2 tomato slices, 2 oz. cheese, 3 oz. lean chopped ham, 3 oz. lean chopped turkey, 2 T. bacon pieces, 1 hard-cooked egg, chopped)
Mozzarella-Tomato Salad, page 290	Monterey Jack cheese, 2 oz.	Whole-grain roll, 1	
Strawberries, ½ c.	Apple, 1 small	Butter, 1 T.	Blue cheese dressing, 2 T.
Yogurt with no-added-sugar, 8 oz.		Orange, 1 medium	Apple, 1 small
▶ carbo rating: 31	▶ carbo rating: 33	▶ carbo rating: 35	▶ carbo rating: 23

dinner

day 4	day 5	day 6	day 7
Grilled Caribbean Chicken, page 244	**Southwestern Pork Chops,** page 193	**Blackened Catfish Fillets,** page 101	**Tenderloin Steaks with Garlic Sauce,** page 197
Orange-Avocado Salad, page 277	**Green Beans with Cilantro,** page 325	**Roasted Asparagus,** page 323	Steamed broccoli, ½ c.
Black beans sprinkled with Monterey Jack cheese (½ c. beans, 1 oz. cheese)	Shredded lettuce, 2 c.	Steamed yellow squash, ½ c.	Sautéed mushrooms, 1 c.
	Ranch dressing, 2 T.	Butter, 1 T.	Butter, 1 T.
▶ carbo rating: 13	▶ carbo rating: 7	▶ carbo rating: 7	▶ carbo rating: 7

snack

day 4	day 5	day 6	day 7
Blue Cheese Spread, page 53, 2 T.	String cheese, 2 oz.	Cheese toast (1 slice whole wheat low-carb bread, 2 oz. Cheddar cheese)	**Pimiento Cheese Dip,** page 51, 4 T.
Celery sticks, 4	Almonds, ¼ c.		Celery sticks, 4
Whole wheat crackers, 2		Deli-roasted chicken, 3 oz.	Whole wheat crackers, 4
▶ carbo rating: 7	▶ carbo rating: 5	▶ carbo rating: 5	▶ carbo rating: 11

total

day 4	day 5	day 6	day 7
total carbo rating: 61 total calories: 1626	total carbo rating: 63 total calories: 1611	total carbo rating: 61 total calories: 1681	total carbo rating: 60 total calories: 1634

go-carb plan: carbo rating 90–120

	day 1	day 2	day 3
breakfast	**Cinnamon Toast,** page 34, 2 slices Scrambled egg, 1 Strawberries, ½ c. ▶ **carbo rating: 19**	Oatmeal, 1 c. Butter, 1 T. Bacon, 4 slices ▶ **carbo rating: 22**	**Rise-and-Shine Sandwiches,** page 40 Blueberries, ½ c. Fat-free milk, ½ c. ▶ **carbo rating: 29**
lunch	Deli-roasted chicken, 6 oz. **Greek Salad Bowl,** page 288 Whole wheat pita (6-inch), ½ Grapes, ½ c. ▶ **carbo rating: 37**	**Fresh Tomato Soup with Cilantro,** page 348 **Grilled Three-Cheese Sandwich,** page 351 Apple, 1 small ▶ **carbo rating: 33**	**Smoked Turkey Mango Salad,** page 297 Almonds, ½ c. Whole-grain roll, 1 small Butter, 1 T. ▶ **carbo rating: 31**
dinner	**Flank Steak with Horseradish Cream,** page 216 Sweet potato, baked, 1 small Steamed broccoli, 1 c. Butter, 1 T. ▶ **carbo rating: 33**	**Shrimp with Feta,** page 124 Steamed spinach, ½ c. Mixed salad greens, 2 c. Olive oil vinaigrette, 4 T. ▶ **carbo rating: 9**	**Sirloin Tips with Vegetables,** page 209 Brown rice, ½ c. Whole-grain roll, 1 small Butter, 1 T. Mixed salad greens, 2 c. Olive oil vinaigrette, 2 T. ▶ **carbo rating: 27**
snack	**Homemade Peanut Butter,** page 62, 2 T. Whole wheat crackers, 4 ▶ **carbo rating: 12**	**Ice Cream Sandwich Dessert,** page 408 Almonds, ¼ c. ▶ **carbo rating: 29**	**Ham and Cheese Ball,** page 52, 4 T. Whole wheat crackers, 4 ▶ **carbo rating: 12**
total	**total carbo rating: 101** **total calories: 1888**	**total carbo rating: 93** **total calories: 1882**	**total carbo rating: 99** **total calories: 1827**

go-carb phase:

• Promotes a more liberal amount of carbohydrate, but the focus is on adding "good carbs" (fruits, vegetables, whole grains)

• Provides a daily carbo rating of about 90 each day, and approximately 1800 calories

• For weight maintenance, you may want to increase to a carbo rating of about 120 and approximately 2000 calories

• Approximately 20 percent of calories are from carbohydrate, so this phase is still relatively low in carbohydrate, compared to some low-fat diets that have as much as 55 to 60 percent daily calories from carbohydrate

Note: For all recipe items, the amount is the serving size listed for the recipe, unless otherwise noted. The carbo rating listed at the end of each meal is the total for all of the items listed in that particular menu. The total carbo rating at the bottom of each column is the total for the whole day.

c.= cup   T.= tablespoon   tsp.= teaspoon   oz.= ounce

day 4	day 5	day 6	day 7	
French Toast, page 35	**Crunchy Granola,** page 44	**Toasted PB&J,** page 37, 2 slices	**Sausage-Egg Casserole,** page 36	breakfast
Sausage links, 3	**Raspberry Smoothie,** page 409	Strawberries, ½ c.	Grapefruit, ½	
Grapefruit, ½		Sausage links, 3	Tomato juice, ½ c.	
▶ carbo rating: 22	▶ carbo rating: 60	▶ carbo rating: 30	▶ carbo rating: 27	
Tuna Salad Sandwich, page 366	**Chicken Salad with Asparagus,** page 291	**Quick Vegetable Soup,** page 356	**Tuna-Cheese Melt,** page 354	lunch
Sliced tomatoes drizzled with olive oil and sprinkled with pepper (4 slices tomato, 2 T. oil)	Swiss cheese, 2 oz.	Cheddar cheese, 2 oz.	Celery sticks with peanut butter (4 celery sticks, 4 T. peanut butter)	
	Whole wheat crackers, 4	Whole wheat crackers, 4		
Cantaloupe, 1 wedge			Apple, 1 small	
▶ carbo rating: 34	▶ carbo rating: 18	▶ carbo rating: 22	▶ carbo rating: 38	
Grecian Pork Tenderloin Salad, page 295	**Tuna Steaks with Salsa,** page 112	**Spicy Chicken Finger Salad,** page 294	**Turkey Sausage with Peppers,** page 272	dinner
Whole-grain roll, 1 small	Steamed broccoli, 1 c.	Celery sticks, 4	**Caraway Coleslaw,** page 283	
Butter, 1 T.	Butter, 1 T.	Blue cheese dressing, 2 T.	Whole-grain roll, 1 small	
	Pineapple, ½ c.	Steamed yellow squash, ½ c.	Butter, 1 T.	
		Orange, 1 medium		
▶ carbo rating: 25	▶ carbo rating: 16	▶ carbo rating: 28	▶ carbo rating: 29	
Peanut butter sandwich (2 slices whole wheat low-carb bread, 3 T. peanut butter)	Turkey-cheese sandwich (1 slice whole wheat low-carb bread, 2 oz. turkey, 2 oz. cheese, 1 T. mayonnaise)	**Banana-Nut Cookies,** page 375, 2 cookies	**Raspberry Tea Spritzer,** page 48	snack
		Almonds, ¼ c.	Peanuts, ½ c.	
▶ carbo rating: 16	▶ carbo rating: 5	▶ carbo rating: 19	▶ carbo rating: 4	
total carbo rating: 97 total calories: 1858	total carbo rating: 99 total calories: 1850	total carbo rating: 99 total calories: 1863	total carbo rating: 98 total calories: 1821	total

label guide

To find out about the carbohydrate in packaged food, look for clues on the package label.

Learning Label Terms

When you're trying to limit carbohydrate, check out the Nutrition Facts panel for specific information about the product. Plus, pay attention to the standard package label terms listed below.

• **Calorie-free:** less than 5 calories

• **Sugar-free:** less than 0.5 grams sugars per serving

• **Reduced sugar** or **less sugar:** at least 25 percent less sugar or sugars per serving (as compared with a standard serving size of the traditional food)

• **No added sugars, without added sugar,** or **no sugar:** no sugars added during processing or packing including ingredients that contain sugar such as juice or dry fruit

> There are no current legal definitions of the terms "low-carb" or "net carbs." When you see food labels with these terms, they have no specific meaning and are mainly used as a marketing strategy.

ingredients list

By looking at the ingredients list, you can see what types of carbohydrate and sugar are actually in the food. Although this part of the label doesn't state the amount of each ingredient, the ingredients are listed from most to least. This list will tell you what type(s) of sugar is in the product. Check the ingredient list for any of the sweeteners below.

- Anything ending in "-ose"—sucrose, maltose, dextrose, sucrose
- Anything ending in "ol"—these are sugar alcohols that are sometimes used for low-calorie sweetening (sorbitol, manitol, xylitol)
- Beet sugar
- Brown sugar
- Cane sugar
- Corn sweeteners
- Corn syrup
- Crystallized cane sugar
- Dextrin
- Evaporated cane juice
- Fruit juice concentrate
- High-fructose corn syrup (HFCS)
- Honey
- Invert sugar
- Malt
- Maple syrup
- Molasses
- Powdered sugar
- Raw sugar
- Turbinado sugar

Sugar Alcohols

A sugar alcohol (also called polyol) is a type of carbohydrate used to sweeten foods and to provide bulk. Some sugar alcohols that are used often in low-carb products are isomalt, lactitol, malitol, mannitol, sorbitol, and xylitol. Because only part of the sugar alcohol is absorbed, most of these sweeteners provide about half the calories of sugars and other carbohydrates. And because they're only partially absorbed, they cause less of a rise in blood glucose than other sugars and starches.

When you see the term "net carb" or "impact carb" or "net effective carb" on a label, that number is usually derived by subtracting the fiber and the sugar alcohol from the Total Carbohydrate (see the label guide on the next page), based on the assumption that the fiber and the sugar alcohol aren't absorbed by the body. **However, this is a bit misleading because although it's true that fiber isn't absorbed, some of the sugar alcohol will be absorbed.** Keep in mind that sugar alcohols may cause cramping, gas, or diarrhea.

Here are some things to consider when you use food labels to select low-carb items:

1. Serving size: Values are for one serving of the food. A portion may be more or less than what you expect, so pay attention to the amount given.

2. Total Carbohydrate: Total Carbohydrate is just that—the total amount of carbohydrate in one serving. This value doesn't indicate what specific type of carbohydrate the food contains, simply a total amount.

3. Dietary Fiber: Fiber is a type of carbohydrate, so even though it's listed separately, the value is included in the amount of Total Carbohydrate.

4. Carbo Rating: Calculate the carbo rating by subtracting the grams of fiber from the grams of Total Carbohydrate. For the product label on the right, you would subtract 1 from 16 for a carbo rating of 15.

5. Sugars: The value for sugars is also part of the amount of Total Carbohydrate. This value refers to both natural sugars and added sugars, but you need to look on the ingredients list panel to determine the types of sugar. You cannot tell from this value what types of sugar are in the food, only the amount of sugars. It may be one type of sugar, or it may be a mix of sugars. **The value for sugars gives part of the picture, but the main number to look at is the Total Carbohydrate.**

6. Sugar Alcohol: Some foods contain sweeteners in the form of sugar alcohols such as sorbitol, manitol, and xylitol. You won't see the specific name of the sugar alcohol listed on the Nutrition Facts panel; they're listed generally as Sugar Alcohol.

We haven't subtracted Sugar Alcohol from Total Carbohydrate to calculate the carbo rating, but if you choose to do so, subtract only half the amount.

Nutrition Facts

Serving Size 2 Cookies (24g)
Servings Per Container about 6

Amount Per Serving

Calories 110   Calories from Fat 60

	% Daily Value*
Total Fat 6g	**10%**
Saturated Fat 4g	**19%**
Polyunsaturated Fat 0g	
Monounsaturated Fat 1g	
Cholesterol 0mg	**0%**
Sodium 80mg	**3%**
Total Carbohydrate 16g	**5%**
Dietary Fiber 1g	**4%**
Sugars 0g	
Sugar Alcohol 6g	
Protein 1g	

Vitamin A 0% • Vitamin C 0% • Calcium 0% • Iron 4%

* Percent Daily Values are based on a 2,000 calorie diet. Your daily values may be higher or lower depending on your calorie needs:

	Calories:	2,000	2,500
Total Fat	Less than	65g	80g
Sat Fat	Less than	20g	25g
Cholesterol	Less than	300mg	300mg
Sodium	Less than	2,400mg	2,400mg
Total Carbohydrate		300g	375g
Dietary Fiber		25g	30g

g = grams   mg = milligrams

quick & easy grocery shopping strategy

Shopping for low-carb foods can actually be very quick and easy because there are a lot of aisles you don't even need to go down. Basically, you can zoom around the outside sections and get everything you need without ever getting trapped in the middle of the store. And all the items in the chart will help you get a low-carb meal on the table in minutes.

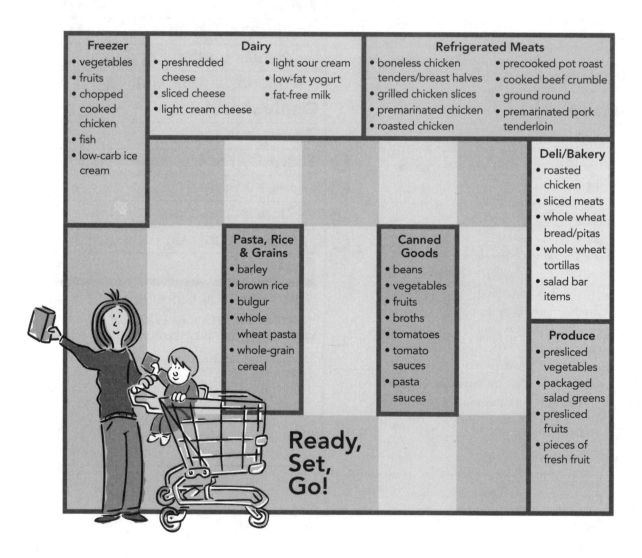

Freezer
- vegetables
- fruits
- chopped cooked chicken
- fish
- low-carb ice cream

Dairy
- preshredded cheese
- sliced cheese
- light cream cheese
- light sour cream
- low-fat yogurt
- fat-free milk

Refrigerated Meats
- boneless chicken tenders/breast halves
- grilled chicken slices
- premarinated chicken
- roasted chicken
- precooked pot roast
- cooked beef crumble
- ground round
- premarinated pork tenderloin

Deli/Bakery
- roasted chicken
- sliced meats
- whole wheat bread/pitas
- whole wheat tortillas
- salad bar items

Pasta, Rice & Grains
- barley
- brown rice
- bulgur
- whole wheat pasta
- whole-grain cereal

Canned Goods
- beans
- vegetables
- fruits
- broths
- tomatoes
- tomato sauces
- pasta sauces

Produce
- presliced vegetables
- packaged salad greens
- presliced fruits
- pieces of fresh fruit

Ready, Set, Go!

carbo-rater grocery list

If you keep these items on hand, you'll always be able to put together a delicious low-carb meal.

▶ fresh produce

- ❑ asparagus
- ❑ avocado
- ❑ bell peppers
- ❑ celery
- ❑ cucumbers
- ❑ fresh herbs
- ❑ garlic cloves
- ❑ green beans
- ❑ mushrooms
- ❑ onions, green
- ❑ onion, red
- ❑ salad greens, mixed
- ❑ spinach leaves, baby
- ❑ tomatoes

▶ fruits

- ❑ apples
- ❑ blueberries
- ❑ cantaloupe
- ❑ grapes, green and red
- ❑ lemons and limes
- ❑ oranges
- ❑ strawberries

▶ deli/bakery

- ❑ English muffins, whole wheat
- ❑ pita bread, whole wheat
- ❑ whole wheat low-carb bread, sliced

▶ refrigerated meats

- ❑ bacon
- ❑ beef, ground round
- ❑ beef, sirloin
- ❑ beef tenderloin
- ❑ Canadian bacon
- ❑ chicken breast halves
- ❑ chicken breast strips, grilled
- ❑ chicken breast tenders
- ❑ lean ham/lower-sodium ham
- ❑ pork tenderloin
- ❑ sausage
- ❑ turkey breast, roasted

▶ canned goods

- ❑ black beans
- ❑ chicken broth, less-sodium
- ❑ chickpeas (garbanzo beans)
- ❑ mushrooms, sliced
- ❑ olives, ripe and kalamata
- ❑ pasta sauce
- ❑ tuna

▶ pasta/rice

- ❑ brown rice
- ❑ whole wheat pasta

▶ cereals/nuts/snacks

- ❑ high-fiber bran or whole-grain cereal
- ❑ nuts: almonds, peanuts, pecans
- ❑ whole wheat crackers

▶ dairy/eggs

- ❑ Cheddar cheese
- ❑ cream cheese, fat-free
- ❑ eggs
- ❑ milk, fat-free
- ❑ Monterey Jack cheese
- ❑ mozzarella cheese, part-skim (string cheese)
- ❑ Parmesan cheese
- ❑ sour cream, reduced-fat
- ❑ Swiss cheese
- ❑ yogurt, no-sugar-added
- ❑ yogurt, plain fat-free

▶ freezer

- ❑ chicken, chopped cooked
- ❑ ice cream, low-carb or no-sugar-added
- ❑ vegetables: broccoli, green beans, cauliflower, spinach

▶ staples

- ❑ butter or margarine
- ❑ calorie-free sweetener
- ❑ cooking spray
- ❑ dried spices
- ❑ fruit spread or low-sugar jam
- ❑ garlic, bottled minced
- ❑ maple syrup, reduced-calorie
- ❑ mayonnaise, light
- ❑ olive oil
- ❑ olive oil vinaigrette
- ❑ peanut butter
- ❑ salad dressings
- ❑ salt

sugar substitute guide

The following sugar substitutes are measured like sugar, so when you use them in recipes, you can use the same amount of substitute as you would use of sugar.

Sugar Substitute	Description	Amount to equal ½ cup sugar
Equal Spoonful	Contains aspartame; no aftertaste; loses some sweetness in high heat	½ cup
Splenda	Contains sucralose, a modified sugar molecule that isn't absorbed by the body; no aftertaste; extremely heat stable; also available in packets	½ cup
Sugar Twin	Contains saccharin; some aftertaste; heat stable	½ cup
DiabetiSweet	Contains a combination of acesulfame-K (Sunette) and isomalt; no aftertaste; looks like sugar; heat stable	½ cup

These sugar substitutes are in more concentrated form, so you don't use as much of these as you would use of sugar in order to get the same sweetness.

Sugar Substitute	Description	Amount to equal ½ cup sugar
Equal for Recipes	Contains aspartame; no aftertaste; the bulk form of Equal packets; loses some sweetness in high heat	3½ teaspoons
Equal Packets	Contains aspartame; no aftertaste; same as Equal for Recipes, but in packets; loses some sweetness in high heat	12 packets
Sweet'N Low	Contains saccharin; some aftertaste; available in bulk form or in packets; heat stable	1 tablespoon or 12 packets
Sweet One	Contains acesulfame-K (Sunette); no aftertaste; heat stable	12 packets

Liquid sugar substitutes blend easily with other ingredients and work well in sauces and marinades.

Sugar Substitute	Description	Amount to equal ½ cup sugar
Sweet'N Low	Contains saccharin; some aftertaste; heat stable	1 tablespoon
Sweet-10	Contains saccharin; some aftertaste; heat stable	1 tablespoon

This list includes the sugar substitutes that we use most often in our Test Kitchens but is not an all-inclusive list and not meant as an endorsement of any particular product.

What's in a Name?

There are several sugar substitutes and calorie-free sweeteners on the market, and the best one to use is really a personal preference. However, we've found that some types of sweeteners work better in baked goods than others.

Here's a list of the sweeteners we have used in this book and what they're called in the recipes.

- **Splenda:** "measures-like-sugar" calorie-free sweetener
- **Equal:** calorie-free sweetener with aspartame
- **Equal Spoonful:** "measures-like-sugar" calorie-free sweetener with aspartame
- **Brown Sugar Twin:** "measures-like-sugar" brown sugar calorie-free sweetener

Aspartame Safety

The Food and Drug Administration (FDA) approved the use of aspartame (sold under the trade names Equal and Nutrasweet) in all foods and beverages in 1996. Although this sweetener has come under a lot of scrutiny due to reports that it caused symptoms such as headaches, dizziness, nausea, memory loss, and seizures, and was responsible for the increased incidence of brain tumors, there is no scientific research to support these complaints. None of the leading health organizations in the United States has found a causal relationship between aspartame and the adverse effects listed above.

> Both The American Dietetic Association and the American Diabetes Association consider **FDA-approved sugar substitutes a safe part of a calorie- or carbohydrate-controlled diet.**

Using Sugar Substitutes on a Low-Carb Diet

When you love sweets and are trying to cut back on carbohydrate, calorie-free sweeteners and sugar substitutes can help you enjoy sweet treats without excess carbs. **Both the Atkins and the South Beach Diets allow limited intake of sugar substitutes, although there are some diet book authors who believe that sugar substitutes intensify the craving for sweets rather than satisfy that desire.**

In our Carbo-Rater recipes, you'll see that we use small amounts of a variety of sweeteners: calorie-free sweeteners and sugar substitutes, honey, fruit juices, and even real sugar. The important thing to remember about any type of sweet food is to look at the total grams of carbohydrate in one serving and see how that fits into your plan.

more options for sweeteners

In addition to the calorie-free sweeteners in the chart on the opposite page, there are some other products that you can use to add sweetness to your recipes.

Equal Sugar Lite: This new product is a blend of sugar and calorie-free sweeteners and has half the calories and carbohydrate of granulated sugar (8 calories and 2 grams of carbohydrate per teaspoon). It measures cup-for-cup like sugar, and can be used in most recipes that call for sugar. It bakes, browns, and provides volume to baked goods better than some of the calorie-free sweeteners.

Stevia: This herbal sweetener is derived from the plant *stevia rebaudiana* and is said to be 100–300 times sweeter than granulated sugar. Stevia extract is available in health-food stores in bulk powdered form, liquid extract, and single-serving packets. One teaspoon of powdered stevia extract has 0 grams of carbohydrate and 0 calories. It's most often used in the powdered form and stirred into beverages. See the package instructions or contact the manufacturer for specific instructions on baking with stevia. Go to www.nowfoods.com for more information or to order.

restaurant guide

Eating low-carb when you're traveling, or simply out and about in town, is easy when you keep these strategies in mind. We've rated each type of restaurant based on the variety of low-carb items on the menu (see the middle column of the chart). No restaurant is really "off limits"; some are just more of a challenge than others. Look under "Strategies" for specific information about what to order when you go into the specific type of restaurant.

low-carb restaurant guide

Type of restaurant	Variety of low-carb menu items	Strategies for making low-carb selections
Fast-Food Burgers	limited	• Many fast-food restaurants now sell low-carb items such as burgers wrapped in lettuce instead of a bun. If not, just order a burger and take off the bun. • Order a grilled chicken sandwich and remove the bun. • Order a salad. • If you order a sugar-free soft drink, make sure that's what you get. Sometimes the servers get confused, or the lines get crossed in the soda machines. • Leave off the fries.
Fast-Food Chicken	limited	• Order grilled or rotisserie chicken if they have it on the menu. • Remove the breading from fried chicken if that is all they have. • Generally, the coleslaw has added sugar, so it's best to avoid the slaw and order a salad. • Order green beans instead of sweet baked beans.
Pizza	limited	• If you're eating pizza, you're eating carbs unless you eat only the toppings. But you can reduce your carbs by eating thin-crust rather than thick. • Order a salad.
Casual Family-Style	good selection	• If you're ordering soup, make sure that it's one without a lot of high-carb ingredients such as pasta, rice, or potatoes. • Order a main-dish salad such as a Cobb Salad or Chicken Caesar Salad. • If you're going to the salad bar, steer clear of the macaroni salads and sweet fruit salads. Leave off the crackers and the croutons. • Ask for a salad or steamed vegetables instead of a baked potato or fries.

Type of restaurant	Variety of low-carb menu items	Strategies for making low-carb selections
Steak & Seafood	good selection	• Instead of a baked potato or fries, request steamed vegetables. • Ask about the sauce that comes on any meat to make sure it's not a sweet sauce or glaze. • Order a salad and request that they leave off the croutons. • Order grilled or broiled meats and seafood with savory seasonings instead of sweet sauces, marinades, and glazes.
Asian-Style	limited	• Since the rice is usually served separately, it's not hard to leave it off and just eat the meat and vegetables in a stir-fry. • Pay attention to portion size. Even if you're eating a meat and vegetable stir-fry and leaving off the rice, stir-fry mixtures are often thickened with cornstarch, so the carbohydrate content may be higher than you think. • Order individual stir-fry items instead of combination plates with fried rice and egg rolls. (Egg rolls have about 25 grams of carbohydrate per roll.) • Eat only small amounts of dipping sauces such as plum or ginger sauce; they generally have a good bit of sugar. • Avoid items with "sweet and sour" in the title.
Italian	limited	• Select menu items that aren't pasta dishes. If it's a dish such as veal piccata that is served with pasta, request that the pasta be left off. • Keep in mind that all Italian food isn't pasta. If you're eating at a restaurant that specializes in northern Italian cuisine, there may be plenty of selections that feature meat, poultry, or seafood in a tomato-based sauce, but not served over pasta. • Read the menu description carefully, or ask your server to describe the dish. • Tomato sauces often have a little sugar added; ask the server to describe the sweetness of the tomato sauce at that particular restaurant. • Pasta is often served as a side dish; ask the server if there are other side dish options such as a vegetable, soup, or salad.
Mexican	limited	• Ask the server not to bring the basket of chips to the table. Or move to the end of the table as far away from the chips as you can. • Order fajitas and don't eat the tortillas. • Order a taco salad, but don't eat the fried tortilla shell. • Keep the beans. Although beans have carbohydrate, it's complex carbohydrate and very high in fiber. • Steer clear of the margaritas—they're high in sugar.

Type of restaurant	Variety of low-carb menu items	Strategies for making low-carb selections
Breakfast	good selection	• Order eggs (fried, poached, scrambled) or egg dishes such as omelets or frittatas. If you're trying to cut down on fat and/or cholesterol, order egg items made with an egg substitute or egg whites if that choice is available. • Order bacon or sausage as a side item instead of potatoes or grits. • Request whole wheat toast. • Order fresh fruit instead of fruit juice, or tomato juice instead of orange juice. • If you don't want eggs, you can order oatmeal or whole-grain bran cereal. • Avoid sweet pastries and doughnuts. • Avoid pancakes and waffles unless there is a whole-grain choice. • Request sugar-free syrup.
Delicatessen	limited	• Order a sandwich on 100 percent whole wheat or whole-grain bread. • Order a sandwich with sandwich-sliced bread rather than a hoagie roll, submarine roll, bagel, or bun. • Ask for a salad or fruit side dish instead of chips (or some delis may have soy chips as another option). • Request a plain or spicy mustard instead of honey mustard. • Request dill pickles rather than sweet pickle relish. • Plain meats and cheeses may be slightly lower in carbohydrate than chicken or tuna salad, especially if the salad contains sweet pickle relish. • If you're ordering soup, order chili or a vegetable-based soup without potatoes. • Ask if the coleslaw has a lot of added sugar. Some slaws are much sweeter than others. Some delis will substitute shredded lettuce for slaw if you ask. • Order a Chef's Salad with deli meats instead of a sandwich.

flavor guarantee

To make sure that the recipes in this book really are America's Best, we invited readers just like you to sample them and tell us what they thought.

Not only have the recipes in this book been evaluated by our food editors, registered dietitians, and Test Kitchens staff, we also put them to the test with a group of "real life low-carbers." We wanted to make sure that these were the kind of recipes that people following low-carb plans could use and enjoy.

We recruited a group of people, men and women, age ranging from 25 to 60, who had lost weight on a low-carb diet, or were just starting a low-carb program. They came to our Test Kitchens and sampled recipes from every chapter of the book. We asked them to rate the recipes (see the rating scale on the right) and give us feedback on flavor, texture, and appearance, as well as whether this would be a recipe they would include in their low-carb plan.

> "Is this really low-carb? It's too good to be low-carb!"
>
> *Heather Winslett*

We were delighted with their response—and you'll see their comments throughout the book. Because the recipes were such a hit with our sample panel, we feel sure that they'll be a hit with you and your family, too.

recipe rating scale

To objectively evaluate the recipes, we use a simple system, and invited our panel to rate the recipes using this same scale. Some dishes simply fail, while those that pass receive a numerical rating:

1   OK recipe

1+ good overall

2   very good overall

2+ high-quality recipe

3   superior in all aspects

We asked our test panel members to think about the following questions as they rated each recipe:
- Would I do anything to make this better?
- Does this fit into my low-carb eating plan?
- Would my family eat this, even if they weren't following a low-carb diet?
- Would I make this tonight? Would I make it again and again?
- Is it better than other versions of the dish I've had?
- Does it taste "low-carb"?
- Would I tell my friends to make this?
- Would I be proud to serve this to guests?

> "This is good. I would definitely make this again."
>
> *Brenda Howe*

best-bet breakfasts

Breakfast breakthrough: Bagels and sugar-coated cereals are not your only options for the morning meal dash. Try the *Rise-and-Shine Sandwiches* (page 40) or the *Strawberry-Banana Soy Smoothies* (page 41).

▶ **carbo rating: 1**
Basic Scrambled Eggs

This tried-and-true method is the way to get perfect scrambled eggs every time.

4 large eggs
2 tablespoons water
¼ teaspoon salt
Dash of pepper
1 tablespoon butter

1. Combine first 4 ingredients; stir briskly with a fork until blended.
2. Melt butter in an 8-inch nonstick skillet over medium heat, tilting pan to coat bottom; pour in egg mixture.
3. Cook, without stirring, until mixture begins to set on bottom. Draw a spatula across bottom of pan to form large curds. Continue cooking until eggs are set but still moist (do not stir constantly). Yield: 2 servings (serving size: 2 eggs).

CALORIES 197; FAT 15.6 (sat 6g); PROTEIN 12.7g; CARBOHYDRATE 0.8g; FIBER 0g; CHOLESTEROL 438mg; IRON 1.9mg; SODIUM 471mg; CALCIUM 55mg

Microwave Directions: Combine eggs, water, salt, and pepper; stir briskly with a fork until blended. Place butter in a shallow 1-quart casserole. Microwave at HIGH 20 seconds or until melted; rotate casserole to coat bottom of dish. Pour in egg mixture. Microwave at HIGH 1 minute. Break up set portions of egg with a fork, and push toward center of dish. Microwave at HIGH 1 to 2 minutes or until eggs are almost set (eggs will be soft and moist), stirring gently after 1 minute. Cover and let stand 2 minutes or until set.

scrambled egg stir-ins

If you're tired of plain ol' scrambled eggs for breakfast, but don't have time to make an omelet or frittata, try these simple additions to perk up Basic Scrambled Eggs (left). Stir any one of these into the eggs just before they're almost set.

With any of the following variations, the carbo rating of Basic Scrambled Eggs will remain a 1.

- ¼ cup sliced mushrooms and 1 tablespoon chopped green onions
- ¼ cup chopped red or green bell pepper
- 1 tablespoon chopped fresh herb (basil, oregano, dill)
- 1 tablespoon chopped green onions and 1 ounce Brie
- 1 ounce shredded reduced-fat Cheddar cheese
- 3 tablespoons salsa (top eggs with salsa after cooking)
- 2 tablespoons packaged bacon pieces (such as Hormel)
- 2 slices bacon, cooked and crumbled
- 2 to 3 tablespoons chopped pepperoni
- ¼ cup chopped cooked ham
- ¼ cup chopped cooked turkey

▶ **carbo rating: 3**

Vegetable-Cheddar Omelet

Use any type of reduced-fat cheese you choose—the carbo rating will not change.

Cooking spray
⅓ cup chopped zucchini
¼ cup chopped green onions
¼ cup chopped tomato
2 large egg whites
¾ cup egg substitute
2 tablespoons water
¼ teaspoon celery seeds
¼ teaspoon pepper
⅛ teaspoon salt
¼ cup (1 ounce) shredded reduced-fat Cheddar or Swiss cheese

1. Coat a 6-inch skillet with cooking spray. Place over medium-high heat until hot. Add zucchini and onions; sauté until tender. Add tomato; cook 1 minute. Transfer vegetables to a small bowl; cover, and keep warm. Set aside.
2. In a medium bowl, beat egg whites with a mixer at high speed until stiff peaks form. Combine egg substitute and next 4 ingredients in a large bowl. Fold egg whites into egg substitute mixture.
3. Wipe pan dry, and coat with cooking spray. Place over medium heat until hot. Spread half of egg mixture in pan. Cover; reduce heat to low. Cook 5 minutes or until puffy. Turn omelet; cook 3 minutes or until golden. Slide omelet onto a serving plate. Spoon half of vegetables over half of omelet; sprinkle with 2 tablespoons cheese. Fold omelet in half. Repeat procedure with remaining ingredients. Serve immediately. Yield: 2 servings (serving size: 1 omelet).

CALORIES 155; FAT 6.4g (sat 2.7g); PROTEIN 19.6g; CARBOHYDRATE 4.3g; FIBER 0.9g; CHOLESTEROL 11mg; IRON 2.5mg; SODIUM 391mg; CALCIUM 198mg

▶ **carbo rating: 3**

Salsa Omelet with Roasted Peppers and Cheese

Substitute one (2-ounce) jar of sliced pimiento if you don't have roasted red bell peppers. The carbo rating will remain the same.

2 large eggs
2 large egg whites
2 tablespoons 1% low-fat milk
¼ teaspoon salt
⅛ teaspoon black pepper
2 tablespoons chopped bottled roasted red bell pepper
1 teaspoon butter
¼ cup (1 ounce) shredded reduced-fat Cheddar cheese
2 tablespoons salsa
½ teaspoon finely chopped fresh cilantro

1. Combine first 5 ingredients in a bowl, stirring with a whisk. Stir in roasted red bell pepper.
2. Melt butter in an 8-inch nonstick skillet over medium heat. Add egg mixture, and cook 3 to 5 minutes or until set (do not stir). Sprinkle with cheese. Loosen omelet with a spatula; fold in half. Cut omelet in half. Slide halves onto plates.
3. Top with salsa; sprinkle with cilantro. Yield: 2 servings (serving size: ½ omelet).

CALORIES 166; FAT 10.2g (sat 4.9g); PROTEIN 14.1g; CARBOHYDRATE 3g; FIBER 0.3g; CHOLESTEROL 228mg; IRON 1mg; SODIUM 641mg; CALCIUM 152mg

▶ carbo rating: 3

Spinach Frittata

Look at the labels to find the marinara sauce with the least carbohydrate. Most will be between 9 and 14 grams of carbohydrate per ½-cup serving, depending on the amount of sugar that is added. You can also use a tomato pasta sauce in place of the marinara.

2	teaspoons butter or margarine
½	cup chopped onion
1	garlic clove, minced
1½	cups egg substitute
¼	teaspoon salt
¼	teaspoon pepper
⅛	teaspoon ground nutmeg
1	(10-ounce) package frozen chopped spinach, thawed, drained, and squeezed dry
½	cup (2 ounces) shredded Swiss cheese
1	cup marinara sauce, warmed

1. Melt butter in a large nonstick skillet with sloped sides over medium-high heat. Add onion and garlic, and sauté until tender.
2. Combine egg substitute and next 4 ingredients; add onion mixture, stirring well. Pour egg mixture into pan. Cover; cook over medium-low heat 10 minutes or until mixture is set. Remove from heat; sprinkle with cheese. Cover; let stand 5 minutes or until cheese melts. Cut into 8 wedges, and serve with warm marinara sauce. Yield: 4 servings (serving size: 2 wedges and ¼ cup sauce).

CALORIES 154; FAT 5.1g (sat 2.3g); PROTEIN 15.9g; CARBOHYDRATE 6.9g; FIBER 3.7g; CHOLESTEROL 10mg; IRON 3.5mg; SODIUM 580mg; CALCIUM 223mg

(pictured on page 65)

▶ carbo rating: 3

Cheesy Zucchini Frittata

If you need to make breakfast in a hurry, chop the vegetables and separate the eggs the night before and keep them covered in the refrigerator until morning.

6	large egg whites
2	large eggs
½	cup (2 ounces) shredded part-skim mozzarella cheese
½	cup finely chopped green onions
¼	cup (1 ounce) grated fresh Parmesan cheese
¼	cup chopped fresh basil
¼	teaspoon black pepper
⅛	teaspoon salt
1	teaspoon olive oil
1½	cups thinly sliced zucchini
½	cup chopped green bell pepper

1. Preheat oven to 475°.
2. Combine first 8 ingredients in a bowl; stir well with a whisk.
3. Heat oil in an ovenproof medium skillet over medium-high heat. Add zucchini and bell pepper; sauté 5 minutes. Add egg mixture. Reduce heat to low; cook 5 minutes or until set around edges. Remove pan from heat.
4. Bake at 475° for 8 minutes or until center is set. Cut into 4 wedges. Yield: 4 servings (serving size: 1 wedge).

CALORIES 155; FAT 8g (sat 3.7g); PROTEIN 15.4g; CARBOHYDRATE 4.6g; FIBER 1.3g; CHOLESTEROL 119mg; IRON 0.8mg; SODIUM 381mg; CALCIUM 215mg

▶ **carbo rating: 4**
Vegetable-Swiss Omelet

Swiss cheese adds a rich, mild cheese flavor to the omelet; if you want a sharper flavor, use reduced-fat Cheddar.

Cooking spray
⅓ cup finely chopped zucchini
¼ cup chopped green onions
¼ cup chopped seeded peeled tomato
Dash of pepper
2 large egg whites
¾ cup egg substitute
2 tablespoons water
¼ teaspoon dried basil
¼ teaspoon celery seeds
¼ teaspoon salt
⅛ teaspoon pepper
½ cup (2 ounces) shredded reduced-fat Swiss cheese

1. Coat a 6-inch heavy skillet with cooking spray; place over medium heat until hot. Add zucchini, green onions, and tomato; sauté 2 to 3 minutes or until tender. Stir in dash of pepper. Remove vegetables from pan; set aside, and keep warm.
2. Beat egg whites until stiff peaks form; set aside.
3. Combine egg substitute and next 5 ingredients in a small bowl; stir well. Gently fold egg whites into egg substitute mixture.
4. Place pan over medium heat until hot enough to sizzle a drop of water. Spread half of egg mixture in pan. Cover, reduce heat to low, and cook 5 minutes or until puffy and golden on bottom, gently lifting omelet at edge to judge color. Turn omelet, and cook 3 minutes or until golden. Carefully slide omelet onto a warm plate. Spoon half of vegetable mixture over half of omelet; sprinkle with ¼ cup cheese, and fold in half. Repeat procedure with remaining egg mixture, vegetable mixture, and cheese. Yield: 2 servings (serving size: 1 omelet).

CALORIES 124; FAT 1.6g (sat 1g); PROTEIN 21.3g; CARBOHYDRATE 5.1g; FIBER 0.9g; CHOLESTEROL 10mg; IRON 2.2mg; SODIUM 611mg; CALCIUM 326mg

(pictured on page 66)

▶ **carbo rating: 4**
Omelet with Zucchini and Onion

Hearty omelets aren't limited to a breakfast assignment—they make a filling meal any time.

Cooking spray
1 teaspoon olive oil
1 cup finely chopped zucchini (about 1 large)
3 tablespoons chopped onion
2 large eggs
2 large egg whites
1 tablespoon shredded fresh Parmesan cheese
¼ teaspoon salt
⅛ teaspoon pepper
⅛ teaspoon dried oregano

1. Heat oil over medium heat in an 8-inch nonstick skillet coated with cooking spray. Add zucchini and onion; sauté 7 minutes or until tender. Set aside; cool slightly.
2. Combine eggs, egg whites, and next 4 ingredients in a medium bowl, stirring with a whisk until well blended. Stir in zucchini and onion.
3. Coat pan with cooking spray; return to medium heat. Add egg mixture; cook 4 to 5 minutes or until center is set (do not stir). Loosen omelet with spatula; fold in half. Cut omelet in half. Slide halves onto plates. Yield: 2 servings (serving size: ½ omelet).

CALORIES 144; FAT 8.4g (sat 2.5g); PROTEIN 11.9g; CARBOHYDRATE 5g; FIBER 1.4g; CHOLESTEROL 215mg; IRON 1.1mg; SODIUM 471mg; CALCIUM 86mg

▶ carbo rating: 4
Spanish Breakfast Scramble

Why settle for plain scrambled eggs when you can pump them up with hot sauce and veggies?

Cooking spray
¾ cup chopped seeded tomato
¼ cup chopped green bell pepper
¼ cup sliced green onions
3 large eggs
1½ cups egg substitute
¼ cup fat-free milk
¼ teaspoon salt
⅛ teaspoon black pepper
⅛ teaspoon hot sauce

1. Coat a large nonstick skillet with cooking spray; place over medium-high heat until hot. Add tomato, bell pepper, and onions; sauté until tender, stirring occasionally. Remove mixture from pan, and set aside.
2. Combine eggs and next 5 ingredients in a large bowl; beat well with a whisk. Pour mixture into pan, and cook over low heat, stirring occasionally. Cook until eggs are set but still moist. Remove from heat. Stir in reserved vegetable mixture. Transfer to serving plates, and serve immediately. Yield: 4 servings (serving size: about ¾ cup).

CALORIES 116; FAT 3.9g (sat 1.2g); PROTEIN 14.7g; CARBOHYDRATE 4.8g; FIBER 0.7g; CHOLESTEROL 159mg; IRON 2.6mg; SODIUM 397mg; CALCIUM 75mg

▶ carbo rating: 5
Confetti Cheese Omelet

Change the cheese to whatever your heart desires. Almost any kind (other than very soft varieties) will work and the carbo rating will remain the same. The total fat will vary depending on the cheese, and will increase if you use a full-fat cheese.

Cooking spray
¼ cup chopped red bell pepper
¼ cup chopped green or orange bell pepper
¼ cup sliced green onions
1 cup egg substitute
¼ teaspoon salt
¼ teaspoon freshly ground black pepper
½ cup (2 ounces) shredded reduced-fat sharp Cheddar cheese

1. Coat a 10-inch nonstick skillet with cooking spray; place over medium heat until hot. Add bell peppers and onions; cook 4 minutes, stirring occasionally.
2. Pour egg substitute into pan; sprinkle with salt and pepper. Cook, without stirring, 2 to 3 minutes or until golden brown on bottom. Sprinkle with cheese. Loosen omelet with a spatula; fold in half. Cook 2 minutes or until egg mixture is set and cheese begins to melt.
3. Cut omelet in half. Slide halves onto serving plates. Yield: 2 servings (serving size: ½ omelet).

CALORIES 159; FAT 5.9g (sat 3.2g); PROTEIN 20.7g; CARBOHYDRATE 5.3g; FIBER 0.7g; CHOLESTEROL 19mg; IRON 2.4mg; SODIUM 680mg; CALCIUM 247mg

Crawfish Omelet

If you live too far away from the bayou to have fresh crawfish on hand, you can use frozen. See the information on the right about ordering crawfish, or you can substitute shrimp.

4	large egg whites
2	large eggs
1	tablespoon chopped fresh chives
1	tablespoon water
¼	teaspoon hot sauce
¼	cup cooked crawfish tail meat, chopped
1	tablespoon salt-free Creole seasoning
1	teaspoon fat-free sour cream
¼	teaspoon salt

Cooking spray

⅓	cup sliced mushrooms
¼	cup finely diced reduced-fat ham (about 1½ ounces)
2	tablespoons shredded light processed cheese (such as Velveeta Light)

1. Combine first 5 ingredients, stirring with a whisk.
2. Combine crawfish, Creole seasoning, sour cream, and salt.
3. Heat a small nonstick skillet coated with cooking spray over medium-high heat. Add mushrooms and ham; sauté 3 minutes. Pour egg mixture into pan; let egg mixture set slightly. Tilt pan, and carefully lift edges of omelet with a spatula; allow uncooked portion to flow underneath cooked portion. Cook 3 minutes; flip omelet. Spoon crawfish mixture onto half of omelet. Carefully loosen omelet with a spatula; fold in half. Gently slide omelet onto a plate; top with cheese. Cut omelet in half. Yield: 2 servings (serving size: ½ omelet).

CALORIES 185; FAT 7.3g (sat 2.5g); PROTEIN 23.3g; CARBOHYDRATE 5.4g; FIBER 0.7g; CHOLESTEROL 254mg; IRON 1.6mg; SODIUM 909mg; CALCIUM 98mg

If you're not familiar with crawfish, you need to know that **all the meat's in the tail,** and there's not much there. You have to peel a whole pound of crawfish to get just 2½ ounces of meat.

where to find crawfish

If live crawfish aren't available in your area, order them by telephone or via the Internet for next-day delivery.

among the best sources we've found:
- Simply Seafood, 877-706-4022 or www.simplyseafood.com
- Marlin Seafood, 504-466-1824 or www.crawfish.com
- Louisiana Crawfish Company, 888-522-7292 or www.lacrawfish.com

like shrimp, crawfish come in grades based on their size:
Peelers: 21 to 30 crawfish per pound
Medium or restaurant grade: 16 to 20 crawfish per pound; these offer the highest percentage of meat
Jumbos: 10 to 15 crawfish per pound; these are the most prized, although they're sometimes hard to peel

Most sources sell live crawfish by the 30- or 40-pound sack. Some also sell fresh boiled crawfish, crawfish tail meat, and parboiled crawfish. You can find frozen crawfish tail meat in some supermarkets.

▶ carbo rating: 6
Salsa Eggs

The three types of peppers in this egg dish will certainly help wake up your taste buds.

  6   large eggs, lightly beaten
  1   (4.5-ounce) can chopped green chiles
  1   jalapeño pepper, seeded and minced
  ¼   teaspoon salt
Dash of ground red pepper
  2   teaspoons butter
  ½   cup finely chopped red bell pepper
  6   tablespoons salsa
  3   tablespoons reduced-fat sour cream

1. Combine first 5 ingredients, stirring well with a whisk.
2. Melt butter in a large nonstick skillet over medium-high heat, tilting pan to coat bottom. Add bell pepper; sauté 3 minutes or until tender. Reduce heat to medium-low. Add egg mixture; cook, without stirring, until mixture begins to set on bottom. Draw spatula across bottom of pan to form large curds. Continue cooking until eggs are set but still moist. Top each serving with 2 tablespoons salsa and 1 tablespoon sour cream. Yield: 3 servings (serving size: about ¾ cup).

CALORIES 223; FAT 14.5g (sat 5.6g); PROTEIN 15.5g; CARBOHYDRATE 8.1g; FIBER 2.1g; CHOLESTEROL 437mg; IRON 2.3mg; SODIUM 532mg; CALCIUM 90mg

▶ carbo rating: 7
Baby Vidalia Onion Frittata

If you substitute green onions for the baby Vidalias, be sure to use 1½ cups instead of 2 because green onions are so much stronger than mild, sweet baby Vidalia onions.

  1   tablespoon light butter, melted
  1   (¾-pound) bunch baby Vidalia onions, thinly sliced with some green tops (about 2 cups), or 1½ cups chopped green onions
  1   garlic clove, minced
  1   (16-ounce) carton egg substitute
  ¼   teaspoon salt
  ¼   teaspoon pepper
  ⅛   teaspoon hot sauce
  ¾   cup (3 ounces) shredded reduced-fat sharp Cheddar cheese

1. Melt butter in a 10-inch ovenproof skillet over medium heat. Add onions and garlic; cook 5 minutes or until tender, stirring occasionally.
2. Arrange onion mixture evenly in bottom of pan. Combine egg substitute and next 3 ingredients; pour evenly over onion mixture. Reduce heat to medium-low; cook, uncovered, 8 minutes or until almost set (mixture will still be wet on top).
3. Preheat broiler.
4. Broil frittata 3 minutes; sprinkle with cheese, and broil 1 minute or until cheese melts. Let stand 5 minutes before cutting into 8 wedges. Yield: 4 servings (serving size: 2 wedges).

CALORIES 161; FAT 5.7g (sat 3.4g); PROTEIN 18.7g; CARBOHYDRATE 8.7g; FIBER 1.4g; CHOLESTEROL 19mg; IRON 2.2mg; SODIUM 494mg; CALCIUM 209mg

(pictured on page 66)

▶ carbo rating: 7

Sweet Pepper and Basil Frittata

Balsamic vinegar is a low-carb "secret ingredient."
A little splash of this vinegar adds a sweet, rich layer
of flavor without adding carbohydrate.

6	large eggs, lightly beaten
½	cup (2 ounces) shredded fontina cheese
¼	cup (1 ounce) shredded fresh Parmesan cheese
¼	cup thinly sliced fresh basil
½	teaspoon salt, divided
½	teaspoon black pepper, divided
1	tablespoon olive oil
1	yellow onion, thinly sliced
4	garlic cloves, minced
4	red bell peppers, thinly sliced (about 4 cups)
1	bay leaf
3	tablespoons balsamic vinegar

1. Preheat oven to 375°.

2. Combine eggs, cheeses, basil, ¼ teaspoon salt, and ¼ teaspoon black pepper in a large bowl; stir well. Set aside.

3. Heat oil in a 12-inch nonstick skillet over medium-high heat until hot. Add onion, garlic, ¼ teaspoon salt, and ¼ teaspoon black pepper; sauté until tender. Add bell pepper and bay leaf to pan; sauté until very tender. Discard bay leaf. Spread bell pepper evenly in bottom of pan. Reduce heat to medium-low. Stir egg mixture, and pour over bell pepper in pan. Cook 3 to 5 minutes or until edges begin to set. Wrap handle of pan with foil. Transfer pan to oven, and bake, uncovered, at 375° for 6 to 8 minutes or until eggs are completely cooked.

4. Loosen sides and bottom of frittata with a spatula. Turn out onto a plate. Brush bottom and sides with balsamic vinegar. Cut into 6 wedges, and serve immediately. Yield: 6 servings (serving size: 1 wedge).

CALORIES 191; FAT 12.2g (sat 4.8g); PROTEIN 11.8g; CARBOHYDRATE 9.2g;
FIBER 1.8g; CHOLESTEROL 226mg; IRON 1.1mg; SODIUM 338mg; CALCIUM 138mg

incredible eggs

• Brown and white eggs are alike inside.

• A large egg has 76 calories: 17 from the white and 59 from the yolk. The whites are generally more health-friendly, containing more than half the total protein of a whole egg and none of the fat. The yolk is tasty, nutrient-rich, and useful in cooking. It has 213 milligrams of cholesterol and 5 grams of fat, 1.6 of which are saturated.

• It is nearly impossible to hard-cook an egg at an altitude of more than 10,000 feet (in case you're planning a trek).

• The white ropelike strands in the egg white, called the chalazae (kuh-LAY-zee), hold the yolk in place and are not, contrary to popular belief, the beginnings of an embryo. In fact, the more prominent the chalazae are, the fresher the egg.

• We don't recommend eating raw eggs. Cook them to a temperature of 160° to make sure they're safe to eat.

• Eggs keep for three to five weeks in your refrigerator. It's best to keep them in the carton (whether made of foam or pulp) because it insulates the eggs and helps maintain moisture.

• Egg substitutes are simply egg whites combined with corn oil, water, flavorings, and preservatives. Because of these additives, they can't be beaten to peak stage.

bread bites

There are many new low-carb breads on the market, and most of these breads are lower in carbohydrate and higher in fiber than regular whole-grain breads.

We've tested the recipes in this chapter with a variety of breads, and most of the dishes will work with any whole-grain sliced bread. The nutrient analysis and carbo rating will vary slightly depending on the bread that is used, so we've noted which type of bread was used for each recipe.

How do you figure out which is the best bread to use? If you're eating low-carb or reduced-carb, the first thing to look for is a bread that is 100 percent whole wheat or whole grain. Many breads labeled "wheat bread" are basically white bread with brown coloring.

carbo rating

To find the bread with the lowest carbo rating, read the label and find the one with the lowest total carbohydrate and the highest fiber content. Then subtract the grams of fiber from the grams of total carbohydrate for the carbo rating. The carbohydrate values of bread vary greatly, depending on the thickness of the slice and whether the bread has additional types of flour, or added grains, nuts, or seeds. The breads with nuts and seeds will be higher in fat than the plain breads, but the fats from these ingredients are the "good-for-you" kind.

▶ carbo rating: 7
Cheese Toast

Use whatever cheese you happen to have on hand.

2   teaspoons light butter
1   (1-ounce) slice reduced-carb whole wheat bread (such as Arnold)
¼   cup (1 ounce) shredded reduced-fat Cheddar cheese

1. Preheat broiler.
2. Spread butter over bread. Top with cheese. Broil 2 to 3 minutes or until cheese melts and bread is lightly toasted. Yield: 1 serving (serving size: 1 slice).

Note: The bread we analyzed for in this recipe has 9 grams of carbohydrate and 3 grams of fiber per slice.

CALORIES 183; FAT 11.5g (sat 6.7g); PROTEIN 11.7g; CARBOHYDRATE 10g; FIBER 3g; CHOLESTEROL 33mg; IRON 72mg; SODIUM 417mg; CALCIUM 240mg

▶ carbo rating: 7
Cinnamon Toast

If you eat cinnamon toast regularly, go ahead and mix a "batch" of calorie-free sweetener and cinnamon and keep it on hand to sprinkle on toast as well as oatmeal or other whole-grain hot cereals.

2   teaspoons light butter
1   (1-ounce) slice reduced-carb whole wheat bread (such as Arnold)
2   teaspoons "measures-like-sugar" calorie-free sweetener
⅛   teaspoon ground cinnamon

1. Preheat broiler.
2. Spread butter over bread. Sprinkle with sweetener and cinnamon. Broil 2 to 3 minutes or until bread is lightly toasted. Yield: 1 serving (serving size: 1 slice).

Note: The bread we analyzed for in this recipe has 9 grams of carbohydrate and 3 grams of fiber per slice.

CALORIES 98; FAT 5.5g (sat 2.7g); PROTEIN 4.7g; CARBOHYDRATE 10.2g; FIBER 3.1g; CHOLESTEROL 13mg; IRON 72mg; SODIUM 177mg; CALCIUM 43mg

> "Some people think that when you're on a low-carb diet, the only breakfast choices are eggs and bacon, every single day. That's just not the case!"
>
> *Lynn Mays*

▶ carbo rating: 8
Southwestern Omelet

To vary this omelet, use kidney beans and Monterey Jack cheese with jalapeños.

4   large egg whites
1   large egg
2   tablespoons chopped fresh cilantro
¼   teaspoon salt
½   cup canned black beans, rinsed and drained
¼   cup chopped green onions
¼   cup (1 ounce) shredded reduced-fat Cheddar
       cheese
¼   cup bottled salsa
Cooking spray

1. Combine first 4 ingredients in a medium bowl, stirring with a whisk. Combine beans, onions, cheese, and salsa in a medium bowl.
2. Heat a nonstick skillet coated with cooking spray over medium heat. Pour egg mixture into pan; let egg mixture set slightly. Tilt pan and carefully lift edges of omelet with a spatula; allow uncooked portion to flow underneath cooked portion. Cook 3 minutes; flip omelet. Spoon bean mixture onto half of omelet. Carefully loosen omelet with a spatula; fold in half. Cook 1 minute or until cheese melts. Slide omelet onto a plate; cut in half. Yield: 2 servings (serving size: ½ omelet).

CALORIES 181; FAT 5.5g (sat 2.3g); PROTEIN 20.2g; CARBOHYDRATE 13.8g; FIBER 6g; CHOLESTEROL 116mg; IRON 2.1mg; SODIUM 822mg; CALCIUM 184mg

▶ carbo rating: 11
French Toast

This French toast is lower in carbs than a traditional version because it has reduced-carb whole wheat bread and is topped with sugar-free syrup instead of powdered sugar.

3   tablespoons fat-free milk
1   large egg
½   teaspoon vanilla extract
¼   teaspoon ground cinnamon
⅛   teaspoon salt
2   (1-ounce) slices reduced-carb whole wheat bread
       (such as Arnold)
1   tablespoon light butter
2   tablespoons sugar-free maple-flavored syrup

1. Combine first 5 ingredients in a shallow dish, stirring well with a whisk. Add bread to dish; let stand 5 minutes, turning once.
2. Melt butter in a large nonstick skillet over medium heat. Add bread slices; cook 3 to 4 minutes on each side or until browned and crisp. Serve with sugar-free syrup. Yield: 2 servings (serving size: 1 slice French toast and 1 tablespoon syrup).

Note: The bread we analyzed for in this recipe has 9 grams of carbohydrate and 3 grams of fiber per slice.

CALORIES 144; FAT 7.1g (sat 2.8g); PROTEIN 8.6g; CARBOHYDRATE 13.9g; FIBER 3.1g; CHOLESTEROL 117mg; IRON 1.1mg; SODIUM 382mg; CALCIUM 88mg

▶ carbo rating: 11
Vegetable Frittata

Frittatas are Italian omelets that are round, rather than folded like a traditional omelet. Typically, they are cooked on the stovetop and then finished under the broiler in the oven. We simplified the cooking procedure in this recipe by using only the oven.

1   (14-ounce) can quartered artichoke hearts, drained
2   plum tomatoes, seeded and finely chopped
2   tablespoons sliced green onions
1   garlic clove, minced
1   tablespoon light butter, melted
2   (8-ounce) cartons egg substitute
¼   teaspoon pepper
⅛   teaspoon hot sauce
Cooking spray
½   cup (2 ounces) grated fresh Parmesan cheese
½   (8-ounce) package ⅓-less-fat cream cheese, quartered

1. Preheat oven to 350°.
2. Press artichoke hearts between layers of paper towels to remove excess moisture. Combine tomato and green onions in a small bowl; set aside.
3. Cook artichoke hearts and garlic in butter in a small nonstick skillet over medium-high heat 2 minutes. Set aside.
4. Combine egg substitute, pepper, and hot sauce in a bowl. Pour about ½ cup egg substitute mixture into each of 4 individual ovenproof au gratin dishes coated with cooking spray. Sprinkle with Parmesan cheese. Dot each with cream cheese, and sprinkle with tomato mixture.
5. Bake on top shelf of oven at 350° for 5 to 7 minutes or until edges begin to set, but center is still soft. Turn oven to broil. Top evenly with artichoke mixture. Broil 3 to 4 minutes or until browned and set. Serve immediately. Yield: 4 servings (serving size: 1 frittata).

CALORIES 244; FAT 12.3g (sat 7.6g); PROTEIN 21.9g; CARBOHYDRATE 12.9g; FIBER 2.2g; CHOLESTEROL 36mg; IRON 3.3mg; SODIUM 592mg; CALCIUM 261mg

(pictured on page 67)

turkey sausage

We used turkey sausage in this recipe because it is lower in fat than pork sausage. Look for ground turkey sausage or turkey breakfast sausage in the fresh-meat or freezer section of the supermarket. Turkey sausage has about the same amount of protein and sodium as pork sausage, but 6 grams of fat for a 2-ounce portion compared to 15 grams for pork sausage.

▶ carbo rating: 11
Sausage-Egg Casserole

You can assemble this casserole a day ahead and store it, covered, in the refrigerator.

1   pound turkey breakfast sausage
3   cups (½-inch) cubed whole wheat bread (about 6 [1-ounce] slices)
2   cups fat-free milk
1½   cups egg substitute
½   cup (2 ounces) shredded reduced-fat sharp Cheddar cheese
1   teaspoon dry mustard
Cooking spray

1. Preheat oven to 350°.
2. Cook sausage in a large nonstick skillet over medium-high heat until browned, stirring to crumble. Drain well.
3. Combine sausage and next 5 ingredients in a 13 x 9-inch baking dish coated with cooking spray; stir well.
4. Bake at 350° for 45 minutes or until a wooden pick inserted in center comes out clean. Yield: 9 servings (serving size: about 1½ cups).

CALORIES 194; FAT 8g (sat 2.9g); PROTEIN 17.9g; CARBOHYDRATE 12.6g; FIBER 1.3g; CHOLESTEROL 47mg; IRON 2.2mg; SODIUM 571mg; CALCIUM 158mg

► carbo rating: 13

Horseradish Cheese Toast with Tomatoes

This open-faced broiled sandwich is also a great choice for lunch or a light dinner. Pair it with a tossed green salad to round out the meal.

4	slices turkey bacon, cut in half crosswise
½	small onion, quartered
½	cup (2 ounces) shredded reduced-fat sharp Cheddar cheese
2	teaspoons prepared horseradish
2	teaspoons plain fat-free yogurt

Dash of pepper

4	(1-ounce) slices whole wheat French bread (¾ inch thick), lightly toasted
1	small tomato
2	tablespoons thinly sliced green onions

1. Preheat broiler.
2. Partially cook bacon 3 minutes in a nonstick skillet; drain and set aside.
3. Place quartered onion in a food processor; process until finely chopped. Add cheese and next 3 ingredients; process until onion is minced, scraping sides of processor bowl occasionally. Set aside.
4. Place toasted bread slices on a baking sheet; spread cheese mixture evenly over slices, spreading to edges of bread. Cut tomato into 4 slices. Top each bread slice with a tomato slice and 2 bacon pieces. Broil 2 to 2½ minutes or until cheese melts and bacon is crisp. Sprinkle with green onions. Yield: 4 servings (serving size: 1 slice).

CALORIES 165; FAT 6.8g (sat 2.8g); PROTEIN 9.4g; CARBOHYDRATE 15.4g; FIBER 2.1g; CHOLESTEROL 23mg; IRON 1mg; SODIUM 435mg; CALCIUM 117mg

"I like to make my own peanut butter because **the freshly ground flavor of the peanuts can't be beat!**"

Anne Cain
(See recipe on page 76.)

► carbo rating: 13

Toasted PB&J

Use your favorite flavor of commercial sugar-free jelly or jam, or make your own with the recipes on pages 38-39. We analyzed for Smucker's sugar-free preserves, with 5 grams of carbohydrate per tablespoon.

1	tablespoon natural peanut butter
1	(1-ounce) slice reduced-carb whole wheat bread (such as Arnold)
1	tablespoon sugar-free preserves or jelly

1. Preheat broiler.
2. Spread peanut butter over bread. Broil 2 to 3 minutes or until bread is lightly toasted and peanut butter melts slightly. Top with preserves. Yield: 1 serving (serving size: 1 slice).

Note: The bread we analyzed for in this recipe has 9 grams of carbohydrate and 3 grams of fiber per slice.

CALORIES 163; FAT 9.5g (sat 1.1g); PROTEIN 7.8g; CARBOHYDRATE 17.4g; FIBER 4.1g; CHOLESTEROL 0mg; IRON 72.4mg; SODIUM 170mg; CALCIUM 49mg

making jams & jellies

Try some of these "pick-of-the-season" jams and jellies and taste the goodness of summer in a jar. To make sugar-free jams and jellies, use a pectin that's for low-sugar recipes or a recipe that calls for unflavored gelatin.

The Right Pectin

If you're using pectin, you must use a low-methoxyl pectin (no-sugar-needed pectin), a special kind of pectin that helps fruit to gel without sugar. Look for Ball No-Sugar-Needed Fruit Jell Pectin, Slimset, Mrs. Wages, Jamit, or Walnut Acres. The product should have a statement on the label that says the product is "for making homemade jams and jellies with low or no sugar."

Since this type of pectin does not need sugar to form a gel, the sweetness will come from the fruit, fruit juice, and/or sugar substitute.

Sugar aids in gel formation, so jams and jellies made without sugar tend to have a soft set. Refrigerate the spread if you want a firmer product.

Canning Procedures

Follow the manufacturer's directions for processing that are enclosed in the package of pectin. Don't use old recipes or procedures from old cookbooks; canning methods have changed over the years and the old methods may not be safe. If properly processed and sealed, sugar-free jams and jellies can be stored in a cool, dry, dark area up to one year. Or store them in the refrigerator.

Safety Tips for Jams & Jellies

1. Wash and rinse jars, and examine for nicks and cracks.
2. Sterilize jars in a boiling water bath at least 10 minutes. Keep jars warm in the dishwasher or in hot water until ready to fill.
3. Wash and rinse lids and bands. Place lids in a small saucepan of water. Bring to a simmer; remove from heat (do not boil). Keep lids in warm water until ready to use.
4. Check lids for seal by pressing down on the center of lid. If lid springs up, it hasn't sealed, so jars must be stored in the refrigerator.

▶ **carbo rating: 2**
Peach-Orange Jam

12	cups sliced fresh peaches
1	(1¾-ounce) package no-sugar-needed pectin
1¾	cups "measures-like-sugar" calorie-free sweetener
2	(0.3-ounce) tubs orange-flavored sugar-free drink mix (such as Crystal Light)

1. Process peaches in a food processor until chopped. Transfer peaches to a Dutch oven; stir in pectin. Let stand 10 minutes. Bring to a boil over medium-high heat; cook 15 minutes, stirring constantly. Remove from heat.
2. Stir in sweetener and drink mix. Pour into hot sterilized jars, leaving ¼ inch at the top of jar; wipe jar rims. Cover at once with metal lids, and screw on bands. Process in boiling water bath 5 minutes. Yield: 8 cups (serving size: 1 tablespoon).

CALORIES 9; FAT 0.4 (sat 0g); PROTEIN 0.2g; CARBOHYDRATE 2.1g; FIBER 0g; CHOLESTEROL 0mg; IRON 0mg; SODIUM 4mg; CALCIUM 1mg

▶ **carbo rating: 4**
Raspberry Jam

8	cups fresh raspberries
2	tablespoons granulated sugar
1½	cups unsweetened apple juice, divided
¾	cup "measures-like-sugar" calorie-free sweetener
1	tablespoon lemon juice
2	envelopes unflavored gelatin

1. Process raspberries in a food processor until chopped. Place raspberries, sugar, 1 cup apple juice, sweetener, and lemon juice in a Dutch oven. Bring to a boil over medium-high heat; reduce heat, and simmer, uncovered, 20 minutes or until mixture is slightly thickened, stirring often. Strain raspberry mixture, and discard seeds.

2. Sprinkle gelatin over ½ cup apple juice; let stand 5 minutes. Stir gelatin mixture into berry mixture; cook 1 to 2 minutes or until gelatin dissolves.

3. Pour into hot sterilized jars, leaving ¼ inch at the top of jar; wipe jar rims. Cover at once with metal lids, and screw on bands. Process in boiling water bath 5 minutes. Yield: 4 cups (serving size: 1 tablespoon).

CALORIES 19; FAT 0.1 (sat 0g); PROTEIN 1g; CARBOHYDRATE 5.2g; FIBER 1g; CHOLESTEROL 0mg; IRON 0.1mg; SODIUM 2mg; CALCIUM 5mg

▶ **carbo rating: 4**
Strawberry Jam

    8   cups fresh strawberries
 1½   cups unsweetened apple juice, divided
    ¾   cup "measures-like-sugar" calorie-free sweetener
    1   tablespoon lemon juice
    2   envelopes unflavored gelatin

1. Wash and hull strawberries. Process in a food processor until chopped. Place berries, 1 cup apple juice, sweetener, and lemon juice in a Dutch oven. Bring to a boil over medium-high heat; reduce heat, and simmer, uncovered, 20 minutes or until mixture is slightly thickened, stirring often.

2. Sprinkle gelatin over ½ cup apple juice; let stand 5 minutes. Stir gelatin mixture into berry mixture; cook 1 to 2 minutes or until gelatin dissolves.

3. Pour into hot sterilized jars, leaving ¼ inch at the top of jar; wipe jar rims. Cover at once with metal lids, and screw on bands. Process in boiling water bath 5 minutes. Yield: 4 cups (serving size: 1 tablespoon).

CALORIES 16; FAT 0.1 (sat 0g); PROTEIN 0.9g; CARBOHYDRATE 4.4g; FIBER 0.4g; CHOLESTEROL 0mg; IRON 0.1mg; SODIUM 2mg; CALCIUM 4mg

▶ **carbo rating: 4**
Grape Jelly

    2   (11.5-ounce) cans no-sugar-added frozen concentrated grape juice, thawed (such as Welch's 100% Grape Juice)
 1½   cups water
    1   (1¾-ounce) package no-sugar-needed pectin
    ¾   cup "measures-like-sugar" calorie-free sweetener

1. Combine grape juice concentrate and water in a 2-quart glass measuring cup. Gradually add pectin, stirring well. Let mixture stand 5 minutes. Microwave at HIGH until mixture comes to a rolling boil, stirring after 4 minutes. Boil 1 minute. Remove from heat; skim foam if necessary. Add sweetener, stirring until sweetener is completely dissolved.

2. Pour into hot sterilized jars, leaving ¼ inch at the top of jar; wipe jar rims. Cover at once with metal lids, and screw on bands. Process in boiling water bath 5 minutes. Yield: 4⅓ cups (serving size: 1 tablespoon).

CALORIES 19; FAT 0.1 (sat 0g); PROTEIN 0.2g; CARBOHYDRATE 4.4g; FIBER 0g; CHOLESTEROL 0mg; IRON 0.1mg; SODIUM 8mg; CALCIUM 3mg

jammin'

Compare the carbohydrate content of these jams, jellies, preserves, and fruit spreads.

Product	Calories	Carbohydrate (grams)	Carbo Rating
Smucker's light sugar-free preserves and jams (1 tablespoon)	10	5	5
Knott's Berry Farm light preserves (1 tablespoon)	20	5	5
Smucker's low-sugar orange marmalade (1 tablespoon)	25	6	6
Smucker's low-sugar strawberry preserves (1 tablespoon)	25	6	6
Polaner's All-Fruit spread (all flavors) (1 tablespoon)	40	10	10

▶ **carbo rating: 14**

Rise-and-Shine Sandwiches

Because of the cheese and cold cuts, the sodium content of this sandwich is higher than some of the other breakfast items in this chapter. If you need to reduce your sodium, you can use reduced-sodium ham or cheese.

 2   teaspoons reduced-calorie margarine, divided
 4   (1-ounce) slices turkey ham, chopped
 1   cup egg substitute
 4   (¾-ounce) slices reduced-fat American cheese
 2   whole wheat English muffins, split and toasted

1. Melt 1 teaspoon margarine in a large nonstick skillet over medium heat. Add turkey ham, and cook 2 minutes or until lightly browned. Remove from pan; set aside, and keep warm.
2. Melt 1 teaspoon margarine in pan over medium heat. Add egg substitute; cook 45 seconds or until set, stirring occasionally. Place 1 cheese slice on each of 4 muffin halves. Spoon egg substitute mixture evenly over cheese, and top with turkey ham. Yield: 4 servings (serving size: 1 muffin half).

CALORIES 188; FAT 5.9g (sat 2.8g); PROTEIN 19.1g; CARBOHYDRATE 16.6g; FIBER 2.2g; CHOLESTEROL 29mg; IRON 2.3mg; SODIUM 1,002mg; CALCIUM 262mg

▶ **carbo rating: 15**

Farmhouse Strata

This layered casserole has a little less bread than a traditional strata. We used whole wheat bread, which increased the fiber content and decreased the carbo rating.

 8   ounces turkey Italian sausage
 2   cups egg substitute
 1   cup fat-free milk
 ½   cup (2 ounces) shredded reduced-fat Cheddar cheese
 ½   teaspoon dry mustard
 ¼   teaspoon dried rubbed sage
Dash of salt
Dash of ground red pepper
 ¼   cup chopped green onions
 6   (1-ounce) slices whole wheat bread, cut into ½-inch cubes
Cooking spray

1. Cook sausage in a nonstick skillet over medium-high heat until browned, stirring to crumble.
2. Combine egg substitute and next 6 ingredients in a medium bowl; stir well with a whisk. Stir in sausage, green onions, and bread cubes. Pour mixture into an 11 x 7-inch baking dish coated with cooking spray; cover and chill at least 8 hours.
3. Preheat oven to 350°.
4. Bake, uncovered, at 350° for 45 minutes or until set and lightly browned. Cut into 6 squares. Yield: 6 servings (serving size: 1 [3½-inch] square).

CALORIES 217; FAT 6.9g (sat 2.7g); PROTEIN 21.4g; CARBOHYDRATE 17.1g; FIBER 2.1g; CHOLESTEROL 39mg; IRON 2.9mg; SODIUM 711mg; CALCIUM 168mg

▶ **carbo rating: 15**

Strawberry-Banana Soy Smoothies

For a quick breakfast when you're running out the door, whip up this super soy smoothie and grab a couple of packages of low-fat string cheese.

- 2 cups fresh strawberries, stemmed and halved (about 10 strawberries)
- 1½ cups vanilla low-fat soy milk
- 1½ tablespoons honey
- ½ teaspoon vanilla extract
- 1 banana, sliced
- 1 cup frozen fat-free whipped topping, thawed

1. Combine first 5 ingredients in a blender; process until smooth. Top each serving with ¼ cup whipped topping. Serve immediately. Yield: 4 servings (serving size: 1 cup).

CALORIES 74; FAT 0.6g (sat 0.1g); PROTEIN 1.2g; CARBOHYDRATE 16.2g; FIBER 1.3g; CHOLESTEROL 0mg; IRON 0.2mg; SODIUM 24mg; CALCIUM 22mg

soy milk smarts

Soy products are excellent sources of isoflavones, which are thought to prevent breast cancer and heart disease. However, soy products (including soy milk) are not good natural sources of calcium. If you're replacing cow's milk with soy milk, select a soy milk that is fortified with calcium.

▶ **carbo rating: 16**

Nutty Cinnamon Oatmeal

Cinnamon is a spice that offers the perception of sweetness when it's added to foods.

- 1 (1-ounce) package instant oatmeal
- 1 tablespoon chopped pecans
- 2 teaspoons "measures-like-sugar" calorie-free sweetener

Dash of ground cinnamon

1. Prepare instant oatmeal with water, according to package directions. Stir pecans into prepared oatmeal, and sprinkle with sweetener and cinnamon. Yield: 1 serving (serving size: ½ cup).

CALORIES 160; FAT 7.1g (sat 0.8g); PROTEIN 5.1g; CARBOHYDRATE 20.2g; FIBER 3.8g; CHOLESTEROL 0mg; IRON 6.5mg; SODIUM 285mg; CALCIUM 169mg

▶ **carbo rating: 23**

Cinnamon-Raisin Oatmeal

If you want to leave out the raisins, add 1 teaspoon light butter along with the cinnamon and sweetener. The carbo rating will decrease to 16 without the raisins.

- 1 (1-ounce) package instant oatmeal
- 1 tablespoon raisins
- 2 teaspoons "measures-like-sugar" calorie-free sweetener

Dash of ground cinnamon

1. Prepare instant oatmeal with water, according to package directions. Stir raisins into prepared oatmeal, and sprinkle with sweetener and cinnamon. Yield: 1 serving (serving size: ½ cup).

CALORIES 136; FAT 1.8g (sat 0.3g); PROTEIN 4.7g; CARBOHYDRATE 26.3g; FIBER 3.4g; CHOLESTEROL 0mg; IRON 6.5mg; SODIUM 286mg; CALCIUM 169mg

▶ carbo rating: 23

Savory Breakfast Casserole

The vegetarian sausage adds a lot of sage flavor to the casserole and doesn't need to be precooked. The sausage is usually located in the refrigerated area of the produce section, near the tofu. Although we call this dish a breakfast casserole, you can serve it for dinner with sautéed greens or a salad.

    2   cups 2% reduced-fat milk
    1   cup (4 ounces) shredded reduced-fat Cheddar
         cheese, divided
    ½   cup chopped green onions
    ½   teaspoon dry mustard
    ¼   teaspoon salt
    ¼   teaspoon freshly ground black pepper
    8   large egg whites, lightly beaten
    4   large eggs, lightly beaten
    14   ounces meatless fat-free sausage, crumbled (such
         as Gimme Lean!)
    4   cups (½-inch) cubed whole wheat bread
         (about 4½ ounces)
    Cooking spray

1. Preheat oven to 350°.
2. Combine milk, ½ cup Cheddar cheese, green onions, and next 5 ingredients, stirring with a whisk.
3. Divide sausage and bread evenly between 2 (8 x 4-inch) loaf pans coated with cooking spray. Pour egg mixture evenly into pans. Top each pan with ¼ cup cheese.
4. Cover each pan with foil. Bake at 350° for 20 minutes. Uncover and bake an additional 40 minutes or until a wooden pick inserted in center comes out clean. Yield: 2 casseroles, 3 servings per pan (serving size: ⅓ of loaf pan).

CALORIES 316; FAT 9.2g (sat 4.3g); PROTEIN 30g; CARBOHYDRATE 26.7g;
FIBER 4.1g; CHOLESTEROL 162mg; IRON 3.2mg; SODIUM 864mg; CALCIUM 347mg

▶ carbo rating: 23

Mountain Peak Granola

This is not only a great jump-start breakfast when served with milk or yogurt, but also a great snack on the trail or in the office.

    3   cups regular oats
    2   cups puffed-wheat cereal
    ½   cup wheat bran
    2   tablespoons slivered almonds
    ½   cup applesauce
    ¼   cup honey
    1   tablespoon vegetable oil
    ½   teaspoon ground cinnamon
    ¼   teaspoon ground ginger
    ½   cup chopped dried apricots
    ½   cup sweetened dried cranberries or raisins

1. Preheat oven to 375°.
2. Combine first 4 ingredients in a large bowl.
3. Combine applesauce, honey, oil, cinnamon, and ginger in a small saucepan; cook over medium heat 2 minutes or until honey melts, stirring occasionally.
4. Pour applesauce mixture over oat mixture, stirring to coat. Place mixture in a jelly roll pan, and bake at 375° for 20 minutes. Gently stir granola; bake an additional 15 minutes or until dry. Cool; stir in apricots and cranberries. Store in an airtight container. Yield: 14 servings (serving size: ½ cup).

CALORIES 141; FAT 3g (sat 0.3g); PROTEIN 3.8g; CARBOHYDRATE 26.7g;
FIBER 3.4g; CHOLESTEROL 0mg; IRON 1.4mg; SODIUM 2mg; CALCIUM 17mg

▶ **carbo rating: 24**
Eggs Sardou

Eggs Sardou is a specialty of Antoine's Restaurant in New Orleans and is often served over English muffins. We used whole wheat muffins, and each serving has just one muffin half. To reduce the carb content even more, just serve the poached eggs and sauce over the spinach mixture. If you leave off the muffins, the carbo rating is 13.

1   (10-ounce) package frozen creamed spinach, thawed
1   (14-ounce) can artichoke hearts, drained, rinsed, and chopped
⅛   teaspoon ground nutmeg
4   large eggs
1½ tablespoons (½ package) hollandaise sauce mix (such as Knorr)
½   cup fat-free milk
2   tablespoons light butter
2   whole wheat English muffins, halved

1. Prepare creamed spinach according to package microwave directions. Stir in artichoke hearts and nutmeg. Microwave at HIGH 4 to 5 minutes or until thoroughly heated.
2. Add water to a large saucepan to a depth of 2 inches. Bring to a boil; reduce heat, and maintain a simmer. Break eggs, 1 at a time, into water. Simmer 7 to 9 minutes or until internal temperature of eggs reaches 160°. Remove eggs with a slotted spoon, and keep warm.
3. Prepare ½ package hollandaise sauce mix according to package directions, using ½ cup milk and 2 tablespoons light butter.
4. Top muffin halves evenly with spinach mixture. Top each with an egg. Spoon 2 tablespoons sauce over each egg. Yield: 4 servings (serving size: 1 muffin half, about ⅔ cup spinach mixture, 1 egg, and 2 tablespoons sauce).

CALORIES 262; FAT 10.7g (sat 4.7g); PROTEIN 14.8g; CARBOHYDRATE 28.4g; FIBER 4.3g; CHOLESTEROL 222mg; IRON 3mg; SODIUM 964mg; CALCIUM 217mg

▶ **carbo rating: 28**
Frittata with Leeks, Spaghetti, and Zucchini

This is a great recipe to use if you happen to have leftover whole wheat spaghetti.

1   tablespoon butter, divided
2   cups thinly sliced leek
1½ cups diced zucchini
⅓   cup 1% low-fat milk
2   teaspoons chopped fresh basil
¼   teaspoon salt
¼   teaspoon pepper
4   large egg whites
3   large eggs
2   cups hot cooked whole wheat spaghetti (about 4 ounces uncooked pasta)
⅓   cup (about 1½ ounces) shredded Swiss cheese

1. Heat 1½ teaspoons butter in a large skillet over medium heat. Add leek and zucchini; sauté 6 minutes or until leek mixture is lightly browned.
2. Combine milk and next 5 ingredients in a bowl; stir with a whisk. Stir in leek mixture and spaghetti.
3. Preheat broiler.
4. Heat 1½ teaspoons butter in pan over low heat. Add egg mixture. Cover; cook 10 minutes or until almost set. Top with cheese. Wrap handle of pan with foil. Broil 5 minutes or until cheese melts. Yield: 4 servings (serving size: 1 wedge).

CALORIES 298; FAT 11.3g (sat 5.3g); PROTEIN 17.1g; CARBOHYDRATE 31.9g; FIBER 3.6g; CHOLESTEROL 186mg; IRON 3mg; SODIUM 337mg; CALCIUM 199mg

the scoop on granola

Compare the carbohydrate, fiber, and fat in these different brands of granola. Some are much higher in sugar than others.

Granola (½ cup)	Carbohydrate (grams)	Fiber (grams)	Fat (grams)	Carbo Rating
Great Granola Cereal	36.0	10.0	8.0	26
Breadshop's Super Natural with Almonds and Raisins	31.0	3.0	9.0	28
Nature Valley Toasted Oats	30.4	2.8	8.1	28
Health Valley Almond Crunch	34.0	5.0	3.0	29
C.W. Post Hearty Granola	34.1	3.0	6.8	31
Sun Country Granola with Almonds	38.3	3.0	10.3	35
Heartland Granola Cereal	41.0	4.0	11.0	37
Heartland Granola Cereal with Raisins	42.0	4.0	10.0	38

▶ carbo rating: 32

Crunchy Granola

For those who have a higher carb allowance, here's a whole-grain granola to eat for breakfast or snacks. This recipe is comparable to some of the commercial granolas on the market, but still lower in carbs than a few of the brands. Sometimes it's easier just to make your own rather than search for the brands with the least amount of sugar and the most fiber.

2	cups regular oats
1	cup wheat germ
¼	cup flaxseed
1½	teaspoons ground cinnamon
½	teaspoon salt
⅓	cup "measures-like-sugar" calorie-free sweetener
⅓	cup vegetable oil
¼	cup apple juice
1	tablespoon honey
½	cup sliced almonds
⅓	cup flaked sweetened coconut
½	cup raisins

1. Preheat oven to 250°.

2. Combine first 5 ingredients in a large bowl; stir well. Combine sweetener, oil, juice, and honey. Pour over dry mixture, stirring well to coat. Spoon mixture onto a jelly roll pan; spread evenly. Bake at 250° for 45 minutes.

3. Stir in almonds and coconut; bake an additional 30 minutes. Cool; stir in raisins. Store in an airtight container. Yield: 10 servings (serving size: ½ cup).

CALORIES 325; FAT 15.4g (sat 2.2g); PROTEIN 10.6g; CARBOHYDRATE 38.9g; FIBER 6.9g; CHOLESTEROL 0mg; IRON 3mg; SODIUM 127mg; CALCIUM 50mg

"I like to make my own granola because I think **it tastes better than store-bought brands.**"

Lynn Mays

▶ carbo rating: 35

Cheesy Bacon and Tomato Strata

This colorful breakfast casserole is a great dish to serve at a brunch because you can make it a day ahead. If you have some left over, reheat it in the microwave for a quick breakfast.

3	bacon slices
½	cup coarsely chopped onion
2	garlic cloves, minced
1	cup fat-free milk
3	large eggs
3	large egg whites
¼	cup thinly sliced fresh basil
¼	teaspoon salt
¼	teaspoon dried thyme
¼	teaspoon pepper
12	(1-ounce) slices reduced-carb multi-grain bread, cut into ½-inch cubes

Cooking spray

2	cups (8 ounces) shredded reduced-fat sharp Cheddar cheese, divided
4	plum tomatoes, sliced into ½-inch-thick slices

1. Cook bacon in a large nonstick skillet over medium heat until crisp. Remove bacon from pan; crumble, and set aside. Add onion to drippings in pan; sauté 4 minutes. Add garlic, and sauté 1 minute. Remove from heat.
2. Combine milk and next 6 ingredients in a large bowl; stir well with a whisk. Add bread cubes to milk mixture, tossing to coat bread cubes.
3. Arrange half of bread cubes in bottom of an 11 x 7-inch baking dish coated with cooking spray. Top with ⅔ cup cheese and half of onion mixture. Add remaining bread cubes, ⅔ cup cheese, and remaining onion mixture. Top with tomato slices and crumbled bacon. Cover and chill at least 8 hours.
4. Preheat oven to 325°.
5. Bake, uncovered, at 325° for 55 minutes. Sprinkle with remaining cheese; bake an additional 5 minutes or until cheese melts. Let stand 5 minutes before serving. Yield: 8 servings (serving size: ⅛ of casserole).

CALORIES 344; FAT 11.6g (sat 5.1g); PROTEIN 21g; CARBOHYDRATE 39.9g; FIBER 5.1g; CHOLESTEROL 115mg; IRON 2.8mg; SODIUM 707mg; CALCIUM 485mg

▶ carbo rating: 44

Mediterranean Muesli

Muesli *is the German word for mixture and usually refers to a mixture of raw or toasted cereals, dried fruits, and milk. You can eat this cereal right away, or store it 1 or 2 days in the refrigerator. It's higher in carbohydrate than some of the other breakfast items, but the carbs come from whole grains and fruits. It does have honey, but it's less than 1 tablespoon per serving.*

1	cup regular oats
1	cup plain low-fat yogurt
1	cup 1% low-fat milk
½	cup coarsely chopped walnuts
¼	cup honey
¼	cup oat bran
3	tablespoons chopped dried apricots
3	tablespoons chopped dried figs
3	tablespoons chopped pitted dates

Raspberries or other fresh berries (optional)

1. Combine first 9 ingredients in a bowl, stirring well. Cover and chill 2 hours.
2. Garnish with fresh berries, if desired (berries not included in nutrient analysis). Yield: 5 servings (serving size: ½ cup).

CALORIES 303; FAT 9.9g (sat 1.5g); PROTEIN 11.2g; CARBOHYDRATE 48.6g; FIBER 4.5g; CHOLESTEROL 5mg; IRON 2mg; SODIUM 62mg; CALCIUM 187mg

snacks & beverages

If chips and margaritas are your biggest downfall when it comes to living low-carb, try the *Quick Pita Chips* (page 63), *Creamy Lime Guacamole* (page 57), and *Tangy Cranberry Coolers* (page 83).

► carbo rating: 0
Raspberry Tea Spritzer

There's no point in using up all of your carb allowance in a beverage when you can sip on a refreshing sugar-free spritzer. You can make this sparkling tea with any flavored tea bags. And since one serving has less than 1 gram of carbohydrate, you don't have to count it in your meal plan.

2   cups boiling water
4   raspberry zinger herb tea bags
2   cups sugar-free ginger ale, chilled

1. Pour boiling water over tea bags; cover and steep 5 minutes.
2. Remove tea bags, squeezing gently; cool tea. Stir in chilled ginger ale.
3. Serve over ice. Yield: 4 servings (serving size: 1 cup).

CALORIES 0; FAT 0g (sat 0g); PROTEIN 0g; CARBOHYDRATE 0.1g; FIBER 0g; CHOLESTEROL 0mg; IRON 0.1mg; SODIUM 18mg; CALCIUM 5mg

► carbo rating: 0
Moroccan Mint Tea

Fresh mint adds a bright sweet flavor to beverages with or without any additional sweeteners.

2½   cups boiling water
2   teaspoons "measures-like-sugar" calorie-free sweetener
2   teaspoons loose Chinese gunpowder green tea or green tea
6   mint leaves, crushed

1. Combine all ingredients in a medium bowl; cover and steep 5 minutes. Strain tea mixture through a fine sieve into a bowl; discard solids. Yield: 2 servings (serving size: 1 cup).

Note: When you get loose tea from tea bags, one regular green tea bag will yield 1 teaspoon loose tea leaves.

CALORIES 2; FAT 0g (sat 0g); PROTEIN 0g; CARBOHYDRATE 0.5g; FIBER 0g; CHOLESTEROL 0mg; IRON 0mg; SODIUM 0mg; CALCIUM 0mg

sugar substitutes

If you use packets of calorie-free sweetener instead of a "measures-like-sugar" brand, here are some helpful conversions:

Sugar	"Measures-like-sugar" calorie-free sweetener	Packets of calorie-free sweetener
2 teaspoons	2 teaspoons	1 packet (¼ teaspoon)
1 tablespoon	1 tablespoon	1½ packets (½ teaspoon)
¼ cup	¼ cup	6 packets (1¾ teaspoons)
½ cup	½ cup	12 packets (3½ teaspoons)
1 cup	1 cup	24 packets (7¼ teaspoons)

▶ carbo rating: 0

Snappy Spinach Dip

Be sure to drain and press the spinach well, or the dip will be too runny.

1   (10-ounce) package frozen chopped spinach, thawed, drained, and squeezed dry
1   cup 1% low-fat cottage cheese
¼   cup reduced-fat sour cream
2   tablespoons light mayonnaise
2   tablespoons minced fresh parsley
2   teaspoons extraspicy salt-free herb and spice blend
2   teaspoons lemon juice
¼   teaspoon garlic powder

1. Press spinach between layers of paper towels to remove excess moisture.
2. Combine cottage cheese and sour cream in a food processor. Process until smooth, stopping once to scrape down sides. Add spinach, mayonnaise, and remaining 4 ingredients; process until smooth.
3. Transfer dip to a bowl. Serve with assorted fresh vegetables (vegetables not included in analysis). Yield: 2 cups (serving size: 1 tablespoon).

CALORIES 13; FAT 0.6g (sat 0.2g); PROTEIN 1.2g; CARBOHYDRATE 0.8g; FIBER 0.3g; CHOLESTEROL 1mg; IRON 0.2mg; SODIUM 44mg; CALCIUM 17mg

"I love spinach dip! Now, instead of just serving it as a dip, I serve it as a vegetable side. For a ½-cup portion, the carbo rating will be 4."

Jenni LuQuire

▶ carbo rating: 0

Deviled Eggs

Most deviled eggs are low in carbohydrate (the only bit of carbohydrate comes from the pickle relish and the mayonnaise). But these are even lower in carbs because we use dill relish instead of sweet. Plus, they have the advantage of being lower in fat than traditional deviled eggs.

6   hard-cooked large eggs, peeled
2½   tablespoons light mayonnaise
1   tablespoon dill pickle relish, drained
1   tablespoon grated onion
1   teaspoon prepared mustard
⅛   teaspoon salt
Dash of ground white pepper
Paprika

1. Slice eggs in half lengthwise. Scoop out yolks, and place 4 yolks in a small bowl. (Reserve remaining yolks for another use.) Set whites aside.
2. Mash yolks with a fork. Add mayonnaise, pickle relish, onion, mustard, salt, and pepper; stir well.
3. Spoon mixture evenly into egg whites; sprinkle with paprika. Yield: 12 servings (serving size: 1 filled egg half).

CALORIES 29; FAT 1.7g (sat 0.5g); PROTEIN 2.7g; CARBOHYDRATE 0.4g; FIBER 0g; CHOLESTEROL 71mg; IRON 0.2mg; SODIUM 69mg; CALCIUM 9mg

perfect hard-cooked eggs

Place eggs in a single layer in a saucepan. Add enough cold water to measure at least 1 inch above eggs. Cover and quickly bring to a boil. Remove from heat. Let stand, covered, in hot water 15 minutes. Pour off water. Immediately run cold water over eggs or place them in ice water until completely cooled.

► carbo rating: 0
Party Shrimp

Steamed shrimp is a great item for an appetizer buffet—party guests love it whether they're eating low-carb or not.

⅓ cup finely chopped fresh parsley
3 tablespoons finely chopped green onions
3 tablespoons minced red onion
2 tablespoons fresh lemon juice
1 tablespoon extravirgin olive oil
¼ teaspoon salt
⅛ teaspoon ground red pepper
1 pound large shrimp, cooked and peeled

1. Combine first 7 ingredients; add shrimp, tossing well. Cover and chill at least 3 hours. Yield: 12 servings (serving size: approximately 3 shrimp).

Note: To save time, purchase fresh steamed and peeled shrimp from your grocery.

CALORIES 37; FAT 1.4g (sat 0.2g); PROTEIN 5.1g; CARBOHYDRATE 0.6g; FIBER 0.1g; CHOLESTEROL 47mg; IRON 0.8mg; SODIUM 103mg; CALCIUM 10mg

(pictured on page 68)

► carbo rating: 0
Tandoori Chicken Saté

*A **saté** (or **satay**) is a popular Indonesian dish of small marinated cubes of meat or poultry threaded on skewers and grilled or broiled. Satés are usually served with a spicy, sweet peanut sauce, but in this tandoori version, the chicken is marinated in a spiced yogurt mixture.*

¼ cup plain low-fat yogurt
¼ cup coarsely chopped onion
1 tablespoon extravirgin olive oil
½ teaspoon ground coriander
½ teaspoon chopped peeled fresh ginger
¼ teaspoon salt
¼ teaspoon ground cumin
¼ teaspoon ground turmeric
¼ teaspoon ground red pepper
¼ teaspoon black pepper
1 garlic clove
1½ pounds skinless, boneless chicken breast halves, cut into ½-inch-wide strips
Cooking spray
Lemon wedges (optional)
Cilantro sprigs (optional)

1. Place first 11 ingredients in a food processor; process until smooth, scraping sides once. Combine yogurt mixture and chicken in a large heavy-duty zip-top plastic bag. Seal and marinate in refrigerator 2 hours, turning bag occasionally.
2. Preheat broiler.
3. Remove chicken from bag, discarding marinade. Thread chicken strips onto 24 (6-inch) skewers. Place skewers on a broiler pan coated with cooking spray; broil 5 minutes on each side or until chicken is done. Arrange skewers on a serving platter, and garnish with lemon wedges and cilantro sprigs, if desired. Yield: 24 servings (serving size: 1 skewer).

CALORIES 39; FAT 1g (sat 0.3g); PROTEIN 6.7g; CARBOHYDRATE 0.3g; FIBER 0g; CHOLESTEROL 18mg; IRON 0.2mg; SODIUM 36mg; CALCIUM 7mg

▶ carbo rating: 1

Pimiento Cheese Dip

This creamy cheese dip can do a second shift as a sandwich spread—a sandwich with whole wheat bread, that is.

¾ cup 1% low-fat cottage cheese
3 tablespoons light mayonnaise
½ teaspoon white wine vinegar
⅛ teaspoon pepper
Dash of hot sauce
¼ cup (1 ounce) shredded reduced-fat sharp Cheddar cheese
1 (2-ounce) jar diced pimiento, drained

1. Combine first 5 ingredients in a blender or food processor; process until smooth. Cover and chill. Stir in Cheddar cheese and pimiento. Serve with fresh vegetables (vegetables not included in analysis). Yield: 1¼ cups (serving size: 1 tablespoon).

CALORIES 18, FAT 1.2g (sat 0.4g); PROTEIN 1.6g; CARBOHYDRATE 0.6g; FIBER 0.1g; CHOLESTEROL 2mg; IRON 0.1mg; SODIUM 64mg; CALCIUM 18mg

▶ carbo rating: 1

Classic Onion Dip

There's no need to give up chips and dip when you're watching the carbs. It's just a matter of changing your chips.

1 (8-ounce) carton fat-free sour cream
½ cup finely chopped onion
2 teaspoons low-sodium soy sauce
¼ teaspoon garlic pepper

1. Combine all ingredients in a medium bowl; stir well. Cover and chill 1 hour.
2. Serve with assorted raw fresh vegetables, whole wheat Melba toast rounds, or reduced-carb chips (vegetables, toast rounds, and chips not included in analysis). Yield: 1 cup (serving size: 1 tablespoon).

CALORIES 12; FAT 0g (sat 0g); PROTEIN 1.1g; CARBOHYDRATE 1.4g; FIBER 0.1g; CHOLESTEROL 0mg; IRON 0mg; SODIUM 40mg; CALCIUM 21mg

dip in

Here's a list of good choices for low-carb dippers.

Food/Amount	Carbohydrate (grams)	Fiber (grams)	Carbo Rating
Celery sticks, 4-inch-long (4 sticks)	0.5	0	0
Zucchini slices (¼ cup)	0.7	0.3	0
Broccoli florets (4 florets)	2.3	1.3	1
Cauliflower florets (4 florets)	2.8	1.3	1
Yellow squash slices (¼ cup)	1.2	0	1
Cherry tomatoes (3 tomatoes)	2.0	0.5	2
Triscuits (5 crackers)	5.5	0.9	5
Kavli crispbread (1 sheet)	7.0	2.0	5
Whole wheat toast (1 slice)	9.0	3.0	6
Quick Pita Chips, recipe on page 63 (3 chips)	6.6	0.9	6
Wheat Melba toast (5 toasts)	7.6	0.7	7
Whole wheat pita bread (½ pita)	7.7	1.0	7

► **carbo rating: 1**
Ham and Cheese Ball

To vary the flavor, use another reduced-fat cheese and a spicy mustard.

1 (8-ounce) block ⅓-less-fat cream cheese, softened
¼ cup plain low-fat yogurt
1 cup (4 ounces) shredded reduced-fat sharp Cheddar cheese
¾ cup finely chopped lean cooked ham
2 tablespoons finely chopped green onions
2 teaspoons prepared horseradish
1 teaspoon country-style Dijon mustard
¼ cup chopped fresh parsley

1. Beat cream cheese and yogurt in a large bowl with a mixer at medium speed until smooth. Stir in Cheddar cheese, ham, onions, horseradish, and mustard. Cover and chill at least 1 hour.
2. Shape cheese mixture into a ball, and sprinkle with parsley. Press parsley gently into cheese ball. Wrap cheese ball in heavy-duty plastic wrap, and chill. Serve with sliced vegetables or whole wheat crackers (vegetables and crackers not included in analysis). Yield: 2 cups (serving size: 1 tablespoon).

CALORIES 35; FAT 2.6g (sat 1.5g); PROTEIN 2.5g; CARBOHYDRATE 0.6g; FIBER 0g; CHOLESTEROL 10mg; IRON 0.1mg; SODIUM 112mg; CALCIUM 41mg

► **carbo rating: 1**
Garlic-Herb Cheese Spread

Fresh garlic and herbs make this stir-and-chill dip taste garden fresh. The chilling time is important because it gives the flavors a chance to blend.

1½ cups fat-free sour cream
½ cup light cream cheese
1 tablespoon minced fresh chives
2 teaspoons minced fresh parsley
½ teaspoon salt
½ teaspoon pepper
1 small garlic clove, minced, or ½ teaspoon bottled minced garlic

1. Combine sour cream and cream cheese in a bowl; stir well. Stir in chives and remaining ingredients; cover and chill at least 1 hour.
2. Spoon into hollowed-out cherry tomatoes or mushroom caps (tomatoes and mushrooms not included in analysis). Or serve with fresh vegetable slices. To store, cover cheese spread, and refrigerate up to 4 days. Yield: 2 cups (serving size: 1 tablespoon).

CALORIES 16; FAT 0.6g (sat 0.4g); PROTEIN 1.2g; CARBOHYDRATE 1.1g; FIBER 0g; CHOLESTEROL 2mg; IRON 0mg; SODIUM 65mg; CALCIUM 18mg

► carbo rating: 1

Blue Cheese Spread

We could not get enough of this spread when we served it with apple slices. The creamy cheese mixture and crunchy pecans make a great combination with the sweetness of the apple. But if apples are too high in carbs for you, we loved it with crisp celery sticks, too.

    1   (8-ounce) package fat-free cream cheese,
         softened
    ½   cup crumbled blue cheese
    ¼   cup chopped pecans, toasted

1. Combine cream cheese and blue cheese in a food processor; process 20 seconds or until blended.
2. Line a 1-cup bowl with plastic wrap; press cheese mixture into bowl. Cover and chill at least 8 hours.
3. Unmold cheese, and remove plastic wrap. Roll outside edge of cheese in chopped pecans. Serve cheese spread with celery sticks and apple slices (celery and apple not included in analysis). Yield: 1 cup (serving size: 1 tablespoon).

CALORIES 41; FAT 2.7g (sat 1g); PROTEIN 3.1g; CARBOHYDRATE 1.2g; FIBER 0.2g; CHOLESTEROL 4mg; IRON 0.1mg; SODIUM 136mg; CALCIUM 50mg

"This full-flavored olive spread is great to keep in the refrigerator when you need a quick and satisfying low-carb snack or when you want to add extra flavor to grilled fish or chicken."

Holley Johnson

► carbo rating: 1

Olive and Onion Tapenade

A tapenade is a thick olive paste usually served on French bread. We recommend you serve this savory spread on either whole-grain crackers or fresh vegetable slices: fennel, radishes, celery, carrots, or bell pepper pieces.

    1   tablespoon olive oil
    1   cup chopped onion
    2   teaspoons chopped fresh or ½ teaspoon dried
         thyme
    4   garlic cloves, finely chopped
    ¼   cup dry white wine
    2   tablespoons white wine vinegar
    1⅔   cups chopped pitted green olives
    ⅓   cup pitted kalamata olives
    ¼   teaspoon freshly ground black pepper

1. Heat oil in a saucepan over medium heat. Add onion; cook 8 minutes or until soft, stirring frequently. Stir in thyme and garlic; cook 2 minutes, stirring frequently. Stir in wine and vinegar. Bring to a boil; reduce heat, and cook 8 minutes or until most of liquid evaporates, stirring occasionally.
2. Place onion mixture in a food processor. Add olives and black pepper; process until smooth, scraping down sides of bowl. Yield: 1¾ cups (serving size: 1 tablespoon).

CALORIES 19; FAT 1.7g (sat 0.1g); PROTEIN 0.2g; CARBOHYDRATE 1.1g; FIBER 0.2g; CHOLESTEROL 0mg; IRON 0.1mg; SODIUM 101mg; CALCIUM 7mg

▶ carbo rating: 1

Salmon Pâté

Generally, a **pâté** *(an elegant, seasoned ground meat spread) will be a good low-carb appetizer choice, but traditional ones are typically high in fat. This one is low-fat because it uses salmon and fat-free cream cheese instead of high-fat meat and cheese.*

2	(6-ounce) cans skinless, boneless pink salmon in water, drained
1	(8-ounce) block fat-free cream cheese, softened
2	tablespoons minced red onion
2	teaspoons minced fresh dill
2	teaspoons fresh lemon juice
2	teaspoons prepared horseradish
¼	teaspoon freshly ground black pepper
⅛	teaspoon salt

1. Combine all ingredients in a large bowl; beat with a mixer at medium speed until well blended. Cover and chill until ready to serve. Serve with whole wheat toasts, whole wheat crackers, or fresh vegetables (bread, crackers, and vegetables not included in analysis). Yield: 2 cups (serving size: 2 tablespoons).

CALORIES 44; FAT 1.5g (sat 0.5g); PROTEIN 6.3g; CARBOHYDRATE 1.1g; FIBER 0.1g; CHOLESTEROL 13mg; IRON 0.2mg; SODIUM 114mg; CALCIUM 72mg

▶ carbo rating: 1

Curried Deviled Eggs

Add a flavor twist, but no extra carbs, to deviled eggs with a splash of fresh lime juice and a sprinkle of curry and cumin. (See "Perfect Hard-Cooked Eggs" on page 49.)

6	hard-cooked large eggs
3	tablespoons fat-free mayonnaise
1½	tablespoons small-curd 2% low-fat cottage cheese
1	tablespoon freeze-dried chives
2	teaspoons fresh lime juice
1½	teaspoons curry powder
¼	teaspoon ground cumin
⅛	teaspoon ground red pepper
¼	teaspoon paprika

1. Peel and slice eggs in half lengthwise. Mash yolks; stir in mayonnaise and next 6 ingredients. Spoon about 1 tablespoon yolk mixture into each egg white half. Cover and chill 1 hour. Sprinkle with paprika. Yield: 12 servings (serving size: 1 filled egg half).

CALORIES 44; FAT 2.9g (sat 0.9g); PROTEIN 3.4g; CARBOHYDRATE 1.1g; FIBER 0.2g; CHOLESTEROL 106mg; IRON 0.4mg; SODIUM 67mg; CALCIUM 16mg

▶ **carbo rating: 1**
Stuffed Cherry Tomatoes

If you have some lean ham on hand, you can use it in place of the Canadian bacon. The carbo rating will be the same.

20	large cherry tomatoes
½	cup light cream cheese, softened
2	tablespoons reduced-fat ranch dressing
4	(½-ounce) slices Canadian bacon, finely chopped
3	tablespoons minced green onions
¼	teaspoon ground white pepper
⅛	teaspoon garlic powder
⅛	teaspoon hot sauce

Parsley sprigs (optional)

1. Cut top off each tomato; carefully scoop out pulp. Reserve pulp for another use. Invert tomato shells onto paper towels; let drain 30 minutes.
2. Combine cream cheese and dressing, stirring well. Add Canadian bacon and next 4 ingredients; stir. Spoon mixture evenly into tomato shells, or pipe into shells using a decorating bag fitted with a large round tip. Garnish with parsley, if desired. Yield: 20 servings (serving size: 1 filled tomato shell).

CALORIES 24; FAT 1.5g (sat 0.8g); PROTEIN 1.2g; CARBOHYDRATE 1.1g; FIBER 0.1g; CHOLESTEROL 5mg; IRON 0.1mg; SODIUM 75mg; CALCIUM 10mg

▶ **carbo rating: 1**
Italian Stuffed Mushrooms

For variety, use reduced-fat Cheddar in place of part-skim mozzarella; the carbo rating, as well as the fat and calories, will be about the same.

30	fresh mushrooms
½	cup (2 ounces) shredded part-skim mozzarella cheese
¼	cup minced fresh parsley
¼	cup reduced-fat Italian dressing

1. Preheat oven to 350°.
2. Clean mushrooms with damp paper towels. Remove mushroom stems, and finely chop; set caps aside.
3. Combine chopped mushroom stems, cheese, parsley, and Italian dressing in a medium bowl, stirring well. Spoon evenly into mushroom caps, and place in a shallow baking dish. Bake at 350° for 15 to 20 minutes or until thoroughly heated. Yield: 30 servings (serving size: 1 stuffed mushroom).

Microwave Instructions: Prepare mushroom mixture as directed above. Spoon chopped mushroom mixture evenly into mushroom caps. Arrange mushroom caps in a shallow baking dish. Microwave, uncovered, at HIGH 3 to 4 minutes or until cheese melts, rotating a quarter-turn every minute.

CALORIES 15; FAT 0.9g (sat 0.3g); PROTEIN 1.1g; CARBOHYDRATE 1g; FIBER 0.2g; CHOLESTEROL 1mg; IRON 0.2mg; SODIUM 27mg; CALCIUM 15mg

▶ carbo rating: 1

Salsa Meatballs

These appetizer meatballs have a low-carb salsa-sour cream sauce instead of a sweet glaze made with jelly.

1	pound ground turkey
½	cup salsa, divided
¼	cup whole wheat breadcrumbs
¼	cup (1 ounce) shredded reduced-fat Monterey Jack cheese
2	tablespoons finely chopped green onions
2	garlic cloves, minced
Cooking spray	
¾	cup reduced-fat sour cream

1. Preheat oven to 400°.
2. Combine turkey, ¼ cup salsa, breadcrumbs, and next 3 ingredients in a large bowl; stir well. Shape turkey mixture into 48 (¾-inch) balls. Place meatballs on a broiler pan coated with cooking spray. Bake at 400° for 20 to 25 minutes or until done. Drain on paper towels.
3. Combine sour cream and ¼ cup salsa, stirring well. Serve meatballs warm with sour cream sauce mixture. Yield: 16 servings (serving size: 3 meatballs and 1 tablespoon sauce).

CALORIES 70; FAT 4.5g (sat 2g); PROTEIN 6.2g; CARBOHYDRATE 1.5g; FIBER 0.2g; CHOLESTEROL 30mg; IRON 0.6mg; SODIUM 95mg; CALCIUM 36mg

---

make your own breadcrumbs

To make whole wheat breadcrumbs, toast 1 slice of whole wheat bread. Place toasted bread in a food processor or mini food chopper and process until you have fine crumbs. (You'll probably have about ⅔ cup of crumbs, so save remaining crumbs for another use.)

"The flavor of this dip reminds me a little of pimiento cheese. **It's easy to make, and even my kids love it!"**

Heather Winslett

▶ carbo rating: 1

Roasted Pepper Dip

Instead of roasting your own peppers, you can use a 12-ounce jar of roasted red bell peppers, drained well.

3	large red bell peppers
8	sun-dried tomatoes (packed without oil)
¾	cup boiling water
4	ounces light cream cheese, cubed and softened
½	cup light sour cream
2	tablespoons chopped fresh parsley
1	tablespoon lemon juice
¼	teaspoon salt
¼	teaspoon pepper
1	garlic clove, minced

1. Cut bell peppers in half lengthwise; discard seeds and membranes. Place peppers, skin sides up, on a baking sheet; flatten with hand. Broil peppers 5½ inches from heat 15 minutes or until blackened. Place peppers in a zip-top plastic bag, and seal; let stand 15 minutes. Peel and coarsely chop peppers; discard skins.
2. Combine tomatoes and boiling water in a small bowl; let stand 5 minutes. Drain.
3. Combine chopped peppers, tomatoes, cream cheese, and remaining 6 ingredients in a food processor. Process until smooth. Transfer mixture to a bowl. Serve with raw vegetables (vegetables not included in analysis). Yield: 2 cups (serving size: 1 tablespoon).

CALORIES 19; FAT 1.2g (sat 0.7g); PROTEIN 0.7g; CARBOHYDRATE 1.4g; FIBER 0.1g; CHOLESTEROL 4mg; IRON 0.1mg; SODIUM 40mg; CALCIUM 12mg

(pictured on page 69)

▶ **carbo rating: 2**

Creamy Lime Guacamole

Guacamole itself is a fairly low-carb dip; it's the chips that get you. Serve this reduced-fat version with raw vegetable slices.

1	ripe peeled avocado, seeded and coarsely mashed
¼	cup fat-free sour cream
2	tablespoons chopped fresh cilantro
2	tablespoons fresh lime juice
1	teaspoon Dijon mustard
½	teaspoon salt
½	teaspoon hot sauce
¼	teaspoon ground cumin

1. Combine all ingredients in a medium bowl. Cover and chill until ready to serve. Serve with raw vegetables (vegetables not included in analysis). Yield: 1 cup (serving size: 2 tablespoons).

CALORIES 48; FAT 3.7g (sat 0.6g); PROTEIN 0.8g; CARBOHYDRATE 3.5g; FIBER 1.2g; CHOLESTEROL 1mg; IRON 0.3mg; SODIUM 177mg; CALCIUM 15mg

low-carb chips

If you've given up corn tortilla chips, another dipping option is low-carb tortilla chips made with soy protein. They come in flavors such as Nacho Cheese and Fiesta Salsa. A 1-ounce serving (about 15 chips) has 12 grams of carbohydrate, 4 grams of fiber, and 8 grams of fat. The chips we tried are from Genisoy Products Co. (www.genisoy.com)

▶ **carbo rating: 2**

Marinated Cheese

You can serve this flavorful cheese on whole wheat crackers, but it's just as good all by itself. It's a great dish for holiday entertaining because of its festive colors and make-ahead instructions.

½	cup olive oil
½	cup white wine vinegar
1	(2-ounce) jar diced pimiento, drained
3	tablespoons chopped fresh parsley
3	tablespoons minced green onions
3	garlic cloves, minced
1	teaspoon "measures-like-sugar" calorie-free sweetener
¾	teaspoon dried basil
½	teaspoon salt
½	teaspoon freshly ground black pepper
1	(8-ounce) block reduced-fat sharp Cheddar cheese
1	(8-ounce) package light cream cheese, chilled

1. Combine first 10 ingredients, stirring with a whisk.
2. Cut block of Cheddar cheese in half lengthwise. Cut crosswise into ¼-inch-thick slices. Repeat procedure with cream cheese. Arrange cheese slices alternately in a shallow baking dish, standing slices on edge. Pour marinade over cheese slices. Cover and marinate in refrigerator at least 8 hours.
3. Transfer cheese slices to a serving platter in the same alternating fashion, reserving marinade. Spoon marinade over cheese slices. Serve with whole wheat crackers (crackers not included in analysis). Yield: 16 servings (serving size: 1 ounce cheese and 1 teaspoon marinade).

CALORIES 111; FAT 8.7g (sat 4g); PROTEIN 5g; CARBOHYDRATE 2.3g; FIBER 0.2g; CHOLESTEROL 17mg; IRON 0.2mg; SODIUM 261mg; CALCIUM 123mg

▶ carbo rating: 2

Spiced Pecans

Not only are these a sweet and crunchy snack, you can sprinkle them over low-sugar ice cream for a quick and easy dessert.

½ cup "measures-like-sugar" calorie-free sweetener
1½ teaspoons ground cinnamon
1 teaspoon ground nutmeg
¼ teaspoon salt
1 large egg white
4½ teaspoons water
2½ cups pecan halves
Cooking spray

1. Preheat oven to 300°.
2. Combine first 4 ingredients in a medium bowl, stirring well.
3. Beat egg white and water with a mixer at medium speed until foamy. Gradually add sweetener mixture, 1 tablespoon at a time, beating until stiff peaks form; fold in pecan halves.
4. Pour pecan mixture onto a jelly roll pan coated with cooking spray. Bake at 300° for 25 minutes, stirring every 10 minutes.
5. Cool completely in pan. Store in an airtight container. Yield: 20 servings (serving size: 2 tablespoons).

CALORIES 100; FAT 9.7g (sat 0.9g); PROTEIN 1.5g; CARBOHYDRATE 2.6g; FIBER 0.9g; CHOLESTEROL 0mg; IRON 0.3mg; SODIUM 32mg; CALCIUM 2mg

oh, nuts!

Nuts are great for low-carb snacking. Sure, they're high in fat, but it's a kind of fat that's good for you. Nuts have different amounts of fat, but, roughly speaking, ¼ cup of any nut contains about 20 grams of fat. And that fat is highly monounsaturated—the same form found in abundance in heart-healthy olive and canola oils. Nuts are also rich in polyunsaturated fat, the other form known to lower cholesterol levels. They contain relatively modest amounts of artery-clogging saturated fat. So the fat you're getting is quite different from the kind found in red meat.

▶ carbo rating: 2

Crab Mousse

Light and delicate in texture, this mousse gets its flavor punch from lemon juice, hot sauce, and dry mustard.

2 teaspoons unflavored gelatin
¼ cup cold water
1 cup fat-free milk
3 tablespoons fresh lemon juice
1 tablespoon grated onion
1 teaspoon dry mustard
½ teaspoon salt
¼ teaspoon paprika
¼ teaspoon hot sauce
1 (8-ounce) package light cream cheese, softened
8 ounces fresh crabmeat, drained
Cooking spray

1. Sprinkle gelatin over cold water in a 1-cup liquid measuring cup; let stand 1 minute.
2. Combine gelatin mixture, milk, and next 6 ingredients in a heavy saucepan; cook over low heat, stirring constantly, until gelatin dissolves (mixture may appear curdled). Add cheese, stirring until blended. Cover and chill until consistency of unbeaten egg white.
3. Flake crabmeat, removing any bits of shell; gently fold crabmeat into gelatin mixture, and spoon into a 4-cup mold coated with cooking spray. Cover and chill at least 8 hours. Unmold and serve with whole wheat crackers or toast (crackers and toast not included in analysis). Yield: 14 servings (serving size: ¼ cup).

CALORIES 61; FAT 2.6g (sat 1.8g); PROTEIN 6g; CARBOHYDRATE 2.4g; FIBER 0g; CHOLESTEROL 19mg; IRON 0.1mg; SODIUM 230mg; CALCIUM 58mg

► carbo rating: 2

Artichoke Squares

If you're serving these appetizers at a party, use a hot tray, griddle, or bun warmer to keep them warm at the serving table.

Cooking spray
- 3 tablespoons chopped green onions
- 1 (14-ounce) can artichoke hearts, drained and chopped
- ¼ cup chopped fresh parsley
- 2 large eggs
- 2 large egg whites
- ¾ cup (3 ounces) shredded reduced-fat Swiss cheese
- ½ cup plain fat-free yogurt
- ½ cup whole wheat breadcrumbs
- ¼ teaspoon salt

1. Preheat oven to 350°.
2. Heat a small nonstick skillet coated with cooking spray over medium-high heat. Add green onions; sauté 3 minutes or until tender. Remove from heat. Add artichoke hearts and chopped parsley; stir gently.
3. Beat eggs and egg whites in a large bowl with a whisk. Add cheese, yogurt, breadcrumbs, and salt; stir well. Stir in artichoke mixture.
4. Spread mixture in an 8-inch square baking pan coated with cooking spray. Bake at 350° for 20 minutes or until set. Cut into squares. Serve warm. Yield: 16 servings (serving size: 1 square).

Microwave Instructions: Prepare steps 1 and 2 as directed. Spread mixture in an 8-inch square baking dish coated with cooking spray. Place in microwave oven on an inverted saucer. Microwave, uncovered, at MEDIUM-HIGH (70% power) 11 to 12 minutes or until set, rotating a half-turn every 3 minutes. Let stand 5 minutes before serving.

CALORIES 42; FAT 1.6g (sat 0.7g); PROTEIN 4.2g; CARBOHYDRATE 2.4g; FIBER 0.2g; CHOLESTEROL 34mg; IRON 0.4mg; SODIUM 113mg; CALCIUM 79mg

"I love that these can be served at room temperature. They're **also great for breakfast,** especially on days when everyone isn't up at the same time."

Brad Sims

► carbo rating: 2

Mini Frittatas with Ham and Cheese

Bake these bite-sized frittatas in miniature muffin cups. They taste great hot or at room temperature, so you can make them in advance.

Cooking spray
- ½ cup finely chopped onion
- ⅔ cup chopped reduced-fat ham (about 2 ounces)
- ⅓ cup (about 1½ ounces) shredded reduced-fat extrasharp Cheddar cheese
- 2 tablespoons chopped fresh chives
- ⅛ teaspoon dried thyme
- ⅛ teaspoon black pepper
- 4 large egg whites
- 1 large egg

1. Preheat oven to 350°.
2. Heat a large nonstick skillet coated with cooking spray over medium-high heat. Add onion; sauté 2 minutes or until crisp-tender. Add ham; sauté 3 minutes. Remove from heat; cool 5 minutes. Combine cheese and remaining ingredients in a large bowl; stir with a whisk. Add ham mixture, stirring with a whisk. Spoon ham mixture into 24 miniature muffin cups coated with cooking spray. Bake at 350° for 20 minutes or until set. Yield: 8 servings (serving size: 3 frittatas).

CALORIES 39; FAT 1.3g (sat 0.5g); PROTEIN 4.4g; CARBOHYDRATE 2.3g; FIBER 0.4g; CHOLESTEROL 32mg; IRON 0.2mg; SODIUM 121mg; CALCIUM 80mg

(pictured on page 70)

▶ **carbo rating: 2**

Hot and Spicy Oysters

These broiled oysters are similar to Oysters Bienville, a traditional Creole appetizer. The red-hot flavor is characteristic of many Creole dishes.

12	oysters on the half shell
	Cooking spray
⅓	cup chopped green onions
½	cup whole wheat breadcrumbs
3	tablespoons grated Parmesan cheese
½	teaspoon black pepper
¼	teaspoon ground red pepper

1. Preheat broiler.
2. Place oysters on a baking sheet, and set aside.
3. Place a nonstick skillet coated with cooking spray over medium-high heat. Add green onions; sauté until tender. Add breadcrumbs and next 3 ingredients, stirring well.
4. Spoon breadcrumb mixture evenly over oysters. Broil 2 minutes or until golden. Serve immediately. Yield: 12 servings (serving size: 1 oyster).

CALORIES 20; FAT 0.7g (sat 0.3g); PROTEIN 1.5g; CARBOHYDRATE 1.9g; FIBER 0.2g; CHOLESTEROL 4mg; IRON 1mg; SODIUM 58mg; CALCIUM 27mg

▶ **carbo rating: 3**

Southwestern Shrimp Cocktail

If you don't want to cook your own shrimp, you can buy it steamed from the seafood department at the grocery store. The star of this appetizer is the sauce.

1½	pounds unpeeled medium shrimp
4	cups water
1	(8-ounce) can no-salt-added tomato sauce
¼	cup chopped fresh cilantro
1	tablespoon finely chopped onion
1½	tablespoons fresh lime juice
1	tablespoon prepared horseradish
½	teaspoon garlic powder
½	teaspoon onion powder
½	teaspoon salt
⅛	teaspoon hot sauce
1	jalapeño pepper, seeded and chopped

1. Peel and devein shrimp, if desired, leaving tails intact. Bring water to a boil in a large saucepan. Add shrimp; cook 3 to 5 minutes or until shrimp are done. Drain well. Cover and chill.
2. Combine tomato sauce and next 9 ingredients in a bowl; stir well. Cover and chill. Serve with shrimp. Yield: 8 servings (serving size: about 2 ounces shrimp and 2 tablespoons sauce).

CALORIES 82; FAT 1.2g (sat 0.2g); PROTEIN 13g; CARBOHYDRATE 3.6g; FIBER 0.4g; CHOLESTEROL 97mg; IRON 1.8mg; SODIUM 258mg; CALCIUM 36mg

> Serve this hearty bean spread with celery sticks or the Quick Pita Chips on page 63.

▶ **carbo rating: 3**
Cannellini Bean Spread

Beans are naturally low in fat and packed with protein, vitamins, and minerals. They're also very high in fiber, so the effect of the carbohydrate in beans on your blood sugar is minimal. In fact, some studies show that eating beans can actually help decrease blood sugar.

1 (15.5-ounce) can cannellini beans, rinsed and drained
1 garlic clove
2 tablespoons minced red onion
1 tablespoon finely chopped fresh flat-leaf parsley
1 tablespoon extravirgin olive oil
1 tablespoon water
2 teaspoons fresh lemon juice
¼ teaspoon salt
⅛ teaspoon pepper

1. Place all ingredients in a food processor; process to a spreadable consistency. Cover and chill until ready to serve. Serve with whole wheat pita chips or raw vegetables (chips and vegetables not included in analysis). Yield: 1¼ cups (serving size: 2 tablespoons).

CALORIES 35; FAT 1.5g (sat 0.2g); PROTEIN 1.1g; CARBOHYDRATE 4.1g; FIBER 1.1g; CHOLESTEROL 0mg; IRON 0.4mg; SODIUM 100mg; CALCIUM 9mg

▶ **carbo rating: 3**
Spicy Buffalo Wings

The wings you order at sports bars often have a sweet barbecue sauce covering the wings. The sauce for the recipe here contains mostly hot sauce, so the carbs stay low.

3 dozen chicken wings (about 3 pounds)
Cooking spray
½ cup hot sauce
¼ cup water
1 (1-ounce) envelope dry onion soup mix
1 to 3 teaspoons ground red pepper
1½ cups reduced-fat blue cheese dressing

1. Preheat oven to 375°.
2. Cut off and discard wing tips; cut wings in half at joint. Place chicken on a broiler pan coated with cooking spray.
3. Combine hot sauce, water, soup mix, and red pepper. Brush chicken with half of hot sauce mixture.
4. Bake, uncovered, at 375° for 30 minutes. Remove from oven; turn chicken, and brush with remaining hot sauce mixture. Bake an additional 10 to 15 minutes or until tender. Serve warm with dressing. Yield: 36 servings (serving size: 1 wing and 2 teaspoons dressing).

CALORIES 63; FAT 3.8g (sat 0.9g); PROTEIN 3.8g; CARBOHYDRATE 2.9g; FIBER 0.3g; CHOLESTEROL 16mg; IRON 0.3mg; SODIUM 193mg; CALCIUM 5mg

► carbo rating: 3
Almond Butter

Whole almonds have more oil than slivered almonds, so if you use whole you only need to process the butter for 2½ minutes.

1   cup slivered almonds, toasted

1. Place almonds in a food processor. Process 3½ minutes, stopping once to scrape down sides. Store in a covered jar or other airtight container in refrigerator. Yield: ½ cup (serving size: 2 tablespoons).

CALORIES 205; FAT 17.8g (sat 1.2g); PROTEIN 7.1g; CARBOHYDRATE 6.6g; FIBER 3.2g; CHOLESTEROL 0mg; IRON 1.3mg; SODIUM 4mg; CALCIUM 85mg

nut butters and creams

Homemade nut butter is more perishable than a commercial variety, so make a small batch. Store homemade butter covered in the refrigerator for up to a month. To make spreading easier, let the nut butter return to room temperature.

As a general rule, there is a 2 to 1 ratio of nuts used to the nut butter yield (1 cup nuts will make ½ cup nut butter, for example). To toast nuts, spread them on a baking sheet and bake at 350° for 6 to 8 minutes.

To make nut butter, grind nuts in a food processor until pasty. Some nut butters will be creamy; others, a bit grainy. The higher the fat, the smoother the butter will be.

To make nut creams, whisk 1 cup water into ¼ cup nut butter; nut creams are a good substitute for heavy cream in pasta sauces and desserts. Start with neutral-flavored cashew or almond butter, then branch out to more flavorful nuts.

There's just no better way
to get that freshly-roasted peanut taste than to make your own peanut butter.

► carbo rating: 4
Homemade Peanut Butter

We liked the flavor of unsalted peanuts in this recipe, but if salt is not a problem for you, you can make it with salted peanuts. To save time, you can start with shelled roasted peanuts.

1   pound unshelled, unsalted roasted peanuts
     (2½ cups shelled)

1. Shell peanuts; remove and discard skins.
2. Place peanuts in a food processor. Process 3 minutes, stopping once to scrape down sides. Store in a covered jar or other airtight container in refrigerator. Yield: 1¼ cups (serving size: 2 tablespoons).

CALORIES 192; FAT 16.4g (sat 2.5g); PROTEIN 7.8g; CARBOHYDRATE 7g; FIBER 2.6g; CHOLESTEROL 0mg; IRON 0.7mg; SODIUM 2mg; CALCIUM 21mg

(pictured on page 71)

► carbo rating: 6
Cashew Butter

Use this nut butter with vegetables in a whole wheat pita, or use it as a substitute for tahini when you make hummus.

1   cup cashews, toasted

1. Place cashews in a food processor. Process 2 minutes, stopping once to scrape down sides. Store in a covered jar or other airtight container in refrigerator. Yield: ½ cup (serving size: 2 tablespoons).

CALORIES 34; FAT 0.5g (sat 0.1g); PROTEIN 1.2g; CARBOHYDRATE 6.6g; FIBER 0.9g; CHOLESTEROL 0mg; IRON 0.4mg; SODIUM 64mg; CALCIUM 2mg

Although the calories and fat in different types of peanut butter are not that different, the carbohydrate content varies greatly. And the sodium content of homemade is much lower than that of most store-bought brands. Compare the nutrients in these different types of peanut butter:

Peanut Butter (2 tablespoons)	Calories	Carb	Fiber	Carbo Rating	Fat	Sodium
Homemade	192	7.0g	2.6g	4	16.4g	2mg
No-sugar-added (Fifty-50)	220	6.0g	2.0g	4	18.0g	15mg
Reduced-fat, creamy (Jif)	190	15.0g	2.0g	13	12.0g	250mg
Reduced-fat, crunchy (Jif)	190	15.0g	2.0g	13	12.0g	250mg
Regular, creamy (Jif)	190	7.0g	2.0g	5	16.0g	150mg
Regular, crunchy (Jif)	190	7.0g	2.0g	5	16.0g	150mg
Low-Carb Peanut Spread, chunky	190	5.0g	2.0g	3	17.0g	130mg

When you need a dipper, **crispy whole wheat pita chips are a great alternative** to potato or corn chips.

▶ carbo rating: 6
Quick Pita Chips

Store chips in a zip-lock plastic bag or other air-tight container to keep them crisp.

    3   whole wheat pita rounds, halved horizontally
Cooking spray

1. Preheat oven to 350°.
2. Cut each pita half into 8 wedges. Spray wedges with cooking spray, and place on an ungreased baking sheet. Bake at 350° for 8 minutes or until crisp. Yield: 16 servings (serving size: 3 chips).

CALORIES 34; FAT 0.5g (sat 0.1g); PROTEIN 1.2g; CARBOHYDRATE 6.6g;
FIBER 0.9g; CHOLESTEROL 0mg; IRON 0.4mg; SODIUM 64mg; CALCIUM 2mg

▶ carbo rating: 6
Bean, Bacon, and Blue Cheese Dip

Serve with warm whole wheat pita wedges or raw vegetables.

    ¼   cup chopped onion
    1   tablespoon chopped fresh parsley
    1   teaspoon chopped fresh or ¼ teaspoon dried thyme
    ¼   teaspoon salt
    ¼   teaspoon freshly ground black pepper
    1   (15-ounce) can navy beans, drained
    1   garlic clove, chopped
    ½   cup (2 ounces) crumbled blue cheese
    3   bacon slices, cooked and crumbled (drained)

1. Place first 7 ingredients in a blender; process until smooth. Combine bean mixture and remaining ingredients in a small bowl. Yield: 1½ cups (serving size: 2 tablespoons).

CALORIES 71; FAT 2.6g (sat 1.4g); PROTEIN 4.4g; CARBOHYDRATE 7.8g;
FIBER 1.9g; CHOLESTEROL 6mg; IRON 0.7mg; SODIUM 230mg; CALCIUM 49mg

▶ carbo rating: 6

Tomato Mocktail

Canned and bottled tomato products such as tomato juice are the top sources of lycopene, a substance in foods that may help prevent prostate cancer.

2	cups ice cubes
1½	cups no-salt-added tomato juice
¼	cup finely chopped celery
¼	cup canned tomato puree
1	tablespoon finely chopped green onions
1	tablespoon fresh lemon juice
¼	teaspoon salt
¼	teaspoon celery seeds
¼	teaspoon hot sauce

Dash of black pepper

4	celery stalks with leaves (optional)

1. Combine all ingredients except celery stalks in a blender; process until smooth. Garnish with celery stalks, if desired. Serve immediately. Yield: 4 servings (serving size: ¾ cup).

CALORIES 28; FAT 0.1g (sat 0g); PROTEIN 1.3g; CARBOHYDRATE 6.9g; FIBER 0.6g; CHOLESTEROL 0mg; IRON 0.8mg; SODIUM 229mg; CALCIUM 18mg

▶ carbo rating: 7

Crustless Smoked Salmon Quiche with Dill

Serve this warm from the oven as an appetizer or for breakfast. Leftovers are good served cold.

1¼	cups evaporated fat-free milk
¼	cup fat-free sour cream
1	teaspoon Dijon mustard
4	large egg whites
1	large egg
½	cup (2 ounces) shredded Gouda cheese
½	cup thinly sliced green onions
¼	cup thinly sliced smoked salmon, chopped (about 2 ounces)
2	tablespoons chopped fresh dill
½	teaspoon black pepper

Cooking spray

1. Preheat oven to 350°.

2. Combine first 5 ingredients in a large bowl, stirring with a whisk. Stir in cheese, onions, salmon, dill, and pepper. Pour egg mixture into a 9-inch pie plate coated with cooking spray. Bake at 350° for 35 minutes. Let stand 15 minutes. Cut into wedges. Yield: 8 servings (serving size: 1 wedge).

CALORIES 95; FAT 3g (sat 1.5g); PROTEIN 8.8g; CARBOHYDRATE 7.5g; FIBER 0.2g; CHOLESTEROL 37mg; IRON 0.3mg; SODIUM 223mg; CALCIUM 171mg

Spinach Frittata
▶ carbo rating: 3
page 28

Baby Vidalia Onion Frittata
▶ carbo rating: 7
page 32

Vegetable Frittata
▶ carbo rating: 11
page 36

Party Shrimp
▶ carbo rating: 0
page 50

Roasted Pepper Dip
► carbo rating: 1
page 56

69

Mini Frittatas with Ham and Cheese
▶ carbo rating: 2
page 59

Homemade Peanut Butter
▶ carbo rating: 4
page 62

Tangy Cranberry Coolers
▶ carbo rating: 11
page 83

Whole Wheat Buttermilk Pancakes
▶ carbo rating: 12
page 88

Banana Bread
▶ carbo rating: 14
page 90

Whole Wheat-Banana Muffins
▶ carbo rating: 16
page 91

Hazelnut-Apple Bread
▶ carbo rating: 30
page 95

Grouper Athenian
▶ carbo rating: 1
page 104

Flounder with Pimiento
▶ carbo rating: 1
page 102

Blackened Tuna with Orange-Zested Salsa
▶ carbo rating: 3
page 114

Tuna with Tapenade
▶ carbo rating: 2
page 108

Cold Poached Salmon with Summer Tomato Dressing
▶ carbo rating: 4
page 115

▶ carbo rating: 7
Garlicky Red Lentil Dal

*In India, a **dal** is a pureed mixture of legumes—usually lentils—that is often served with curried dishes. You can also serve it as a dip for fresh vegetables. This dip tastes best at room temperature. If you can't find red lentils, use brown or green instead.*

2½	cups water
1	cup dried small red lentils
1	bay leaf
1½	teaspoons cumin seeds, divided
1	teaspoon salt
½	teaspoon ground turmeric
½	teaspoon Hungarian sweet paprika
½	teaspoon ground red pepper
4	teaspoons olive oil, divided
¼	cup chopped onion
½	cup chopped seeded tomato
1	garlic clove, chopped
2	tablespoons fresh lemon juice
¼	teaspoon freshly ground black pepper
1	teaspoon chopped fresh mint

1. Combine first 3 ingredients in a medium saucepan; bring to a boil. Cover, reduce heat, and simmer 10 minutes or until tender. Drain; discard bay leaf. Place lentils in a small bowl.

2. Combine 1 teaspoon cumin seeds, salt, turmeric, paprika, and red pepper in a spice or coffee grinder; process until finely ground.

3. Heat 1 tablespoon oil in a medium nonstick skillet over medium-high heat. Add onion; sauté 2 minutes or until tender. Stir in spice mixture, tomato, and garlic; cook 2 minutes or until slightly thick. Remove pan from heat; stir in lentils, lemon juice, and black pepper. Place lentil mixture in a food processor; process until smooth.

4. Heat 1 teaspoon olive oil in a small nonstick skillet over medium heat, and add ½ teaspoon cumin seeds. Sauté seeds for 15 seconds, and drizzle over dal. Sprinkle with fresh mint. Yield: 9 servings (serving size: ¼ cup).

CALORIES 97; FAT 2.4g (sat 0.3g); PROTEIN 6.3g; CARBOHYDRATE 13.8g; FIBER 6.8g; CHOLESTEROL 0mg; IRON 2.3mg; SODIUM 265mg; CALCIUM 17mg

water: the ultimate low-carb beverage

Do you really need to drink eight glasses of water a day? Unless you live in a very warm climate or you're doing heavy aerobic exercise, you can probably get by with six or seven glasses of water—or another type of beverage—a day.

A recent study found no evidence supporting the eight-glasses-a-day rule. Some people report that their skin looks better, they have less pain from arthritis, and they have fewer migraines when they drink eight glasses a day. If that works for you, then do it, but most healthy adults probably don't need quite that much water every day. However, there are certainly no drawbacks to drinking as much water as you want.

▶ carbo rating: 7
Lavender Lemonade

Lavender adds a delightfully different dimension to this refreshing summer favorite.

4	cups water, divided
¼	cup chopped fresh lavender leaves
⅔	cup "measures-like-sugar" calorie-free sweetener
1	cup fresh lemon juice (about 6 lemons)

Lavender stems (optional)

1. Bring 1 cup water to a boil in a medium saucepan. Combine boiling water and lavender in a medium bowl; cover and steep 30 minutes. Strain lavender mixture through a fine sieve into a bowl; discard lavender leaves.

2. Combine 3 cups water and sweetener in pan. Bring mixture to a boil; cook 1 minute or until sweetener is dissolved. Combine lavender water, sweetened syrup, and lemon juice in a pitcher. Cover and chill. Serve over ice. Garnish lemonade with lavender stems, if desired. Yield: 5 servings (serving size: 1 cup).

CALORIES 27; FAT 0.1g (sat 0.1g); PROTEIN 0.2g; CARBOHYDRATE 7.8g; FIBER 0.4g; CHOLESTEROL 0mg; IRON 0.1mg; SODIUM 1mg; CALCIUM 9mg

► carbo rating: 8
Bellini Spritzers

Use 4 cups of frozen slices peaches, thawed, if fresh peaches are not in season. If you don't want to use Champagne, use 3 cups of sugar-free lemon-lime carbonated beverage (such as Diet 7-Up or sugar-free Sprite). The carbo rating will be 7 if you substitute with the carbonated beverage.

2 pounds fresh peaches, peeled and halved
1 (750-milliliter) bottle Champagne, chilled
2 cups sparkling mineral water, chilled

1. Place peaches in a food processor; process until smooth.
2. Combine puree, Champagne, and mineral water in a large pitcher; stir gently. Pour into chilled glasses. Serve immediately. Yield: 9 servings (serving size: 1 cup).

CALORIES 96; FAT 0.1g (sat 0g); PROTEIN 0.8g; CARBOHYDRATE 9.4g;
FIBER 1.2g; CHOLESTEROL 0mg; IRON 0.4mg; SODIUM 395mg; CALCIUM 19mg

how to peel a peach

1. First, cut an "X" in the bottom of each peach, carefully cutting just through the skin. Heat a large pot of water to boiling, and drop in the peaches. Cook for 20 seconds to 1 minute—the riper they are, the less time they need.
2. Remove the peaches from the water with a slotted spoon, and place them in a sink filled with ice water.
3. Pick them out of the water, and use a paring knife or your fingers to remove the skins, which should slip right off, leaving picture-perfect peaches.

► carbo rating: 9
Cheese Fondue with Apples

We recommend Pink Lady apples, which don't discolor as quickly as other apples, for this fondue. Use your favorite apple, or a combination of a few varieties; just toss the apple wedges with 2 teaspoons lemon juice to prevent browning.

¼ cup all-purpose flour
¾ cup (3 ounces) shredded Swiss cheese
⅛ teaspoon ground nutmeg
1 garlic clove, halved
¾ cup fat-free, less-sodium chicken broth
¼ cup dry white wine
3 Pink Lady apples, each cored and cut into 9 wedges

1. Lightly spoon flour into a dry measuring cup; level with a knife. Combine flour, cheese, and nutmeg, tossing well.
2. Rub cut sides of garlic on inside of a medium, heavy saucepan. Add broth and wine to pan; bring to a simmer over medium heat.
3. Add one-third cheese mixture to pan, stirring with a whisk until combined. Repeat procedure with remaining cheese mixture. Reduce heat to medium-low; cook 5 minutes or until smooth, stirring frequently.
4. Remove cheese mixture from heat. Pour mixture into a fondue pot. Keep warm over low flame. Serve with apple wedges. Yield: 9 servings (serving size: 3 apple wedges and about 2 tablespoons fondue).

CALORIES 84; FAT 3g (sat 1.8g); PROTEIN 3.4g; CARBOHYDRATE 9.9g;
FIBER 1.3g; CHOLESTEROL 9mg; IRON 0.3mg; SODIUM 80mg; CALCIUM 101mg

► carbo rating: 10
Wasabi Bloody Marys

Prepared horseradish typically adds heat to this drink, but we've opted for wasabi paste—the green, Japanese version of horseradish. Garnish with an asparagus stalk or green bean, or the more traditional stick of celery.

½ cup fresh lime juice
1½ tablespoons wasabi paste
6 cups low-sodium vegetable juice
3 tablespoons Worcestershire sauce
1¼ teaspoons hot pepper sauce
¾ teaspoon salt
1½ cups vodka

1. Combine lime juice and wasabi paste; stir with a whisk until wasabi dissolves.
2. Combine wasabi mixture, vegetable juice, Worcestershire, pepper sauce, and salt in a pitcher. Cover and chill thoroughly.
3. Stir in vodka. Serve over ice. Yield: 8 servings (serving size: about 1 cup).

CALORIES 166; FAT 0g (sat 0g); PROTEIN 1.6g; CARBOHYDRATE 11.3g; FIBER 1.8g; CHOLESTEROL 0mg; IRON 1.2mg; SODIUM 395mg; CALCIUM 43mg

► carbo rating: 11
Tangy Cranberry Coolers

Be sure to use a reduced-calorie cranberry juice; the regular cranberry juice cocktail has a lot of carbohydrate. And, instead of buying both cranberry juice and apple juice, you can use 1¼ cups of reduced-calorie cran-apple drink if it's available.

¾ cup reduced-calorie cranberry juice cocktail, chilled
½ cup apple juice, chilled
2 tablespoons fresh lime juice, chilled
1 tablespoon "measures-like-sugar" calorie-free sweetener
1 (6-ounce) can pink grapefruit juice, chilled
Lime slices (optional)

1. Combine first 5 ingredients in a small pitcher, stirring well. Serve juice mixture over crushed ice. Garnish with lime slices, if desired. Yield: 4 servings (serving size: ½ cup).

CALORIES 43; FAT 0g (sat 0g); PROTEIN 0.3g; CARBOHYDRATE 10.6g; FIBER 0.1g; CHOLESTEROL 0mg; IRON 0.2mg; SODIUM 3mg; CALCIUM 10mg

(pictured on page 72)

carb content of alcohol

Most alcoholic beverages have carbohydrate (even if it's a negligible amount) because they are all made from fruit or a grain. But the carb content varies depending on the source of the carbohydrate and the amount of added sugars.

Beverage (amount)	Calories	Carbohydrate (grams)	Carbo Rating
Beer (Budweiser), 12 ounces	145	10.6	11
Light beer (Budweiser), 12 ounces	110	6.6	7
Low-carb beer (Michelob), 12 ounces	95	2.6	3
Wine, red, 6 ounces	128	3.0	3
Wine, white, 6 ounces	120	1.4	1
Low-carb wine (Merlot), 5 ounces	125	1.9	2
Bourbon (100 proof), 1½ ounces	123	0.0	0
Gin (100 proof), 1½ ounces	123	0.0	0
Rum (100 proof), 1½ ounces	123	0.0	0
Vodka (100 proof), 1½ ounces	123	0.0	0

▶ **carbo rating: 11**

Eggplant and Chickpea Dip with Mint

Serve with toasted whole wheat pita wedges.

1   whole garlic head
1   (1-pound) eggplant, cut in half lengthwise
2   tablespoons sesame seeds, toasted
1   tablespoon chopped fresh mint
3   tablespoons fresh lemon juice
1   tablespoon extravirgin olive oil
1   teaspoon sea salt
¼   teaspoon ground red pepper
1   (15½-ounce) can chickpeas (garbanzo beans), drained

1. Preheat oven to 450°.
2. Remove white papery skin from garlic head (do not peel or separate the cloves); wrap in foil. Bake at 450° for 45 minutes, and cool 10 minutes. Separate cloves; squeeze to extract garlic pulp. Discard skins.
3. While garlic roasts, place eggplant, cut sides down, in a baking pan. Add water to a depth of ¼ inch. Bake at 450° for 30 minutes or until tender; cool 10 minutes.
4. Scrape pulp from eggplant skins; discard skins. Place eggplant, garlic pulp, sesame seeds, and remaining ingredients in a food processor; process until smooth, scraping sides of bowl. Yield: 2½ cups (serving size: ¼ cup).

CALORIES 84; FAT 1.9g (sat 0.2g); PROTEIN 2.5g; CARBOHYDRATE 12.3g; FIBER 1.7g; CHOLESTEROL 0mg; IRON 3.4mg; SODIUM 336mg; CALCIUM 25mg

▶ **carbo rating: 12**

Curried Crab Spread

This cold crab spread can be made up to a couple of days ahead. If you want to make the whole wheat crostini ahead, let the slices cool completely on a wire rack, then place them in a zip-top plastic bag.

½   cup minced celery
½   cup minced green bell pepper
½   cup minced red bell pepper
½   cup light cream cheese
⅓   cup light mayonnaise
1   teaspoon curry powder
1   teaspoon hot sauce
½   teaspoon salt
½   teaspoon grated lemon rind
¼   teaspoon dry mustard
¼   teaspoon black pepper
1   pound lump crabmeat, shell pieces removed
36   (¼-inch-thick) slices whole wheat French bread (about 18 ounces)
1   tablespoon olive oil

1. Combine first 11 ingredients in a large bowl, stirring until well combined. Gently fold in crabmeat.
2. Preheat broiler.
3. Place bread slices in a single layer on a baking sheet. Brush 1 side of bread slices evenly with olive oil. Broil 1 minute or until lightly browned. Serve with spread. Yield: 18 servings (serving size: about 2 tablespoons spread and 2 bread slices).

CALORIES 132; FAT 4.9g (sat 1.4g); PROTEIN 8.1g; CARBOHYDRATE 14.5g; FIBER 2.1g; CHOLESTEROL 25mg; IRON 1.2mg; SODIUM 362mg; CALCIUM 55mg

▶ **carbo rating: 15**

Baked Feta with Marinara

If you can find them, use fire-roasted diced tomatoes (such as Muir Glen); add a pinch of basil, a pinch of oregano, and a minced garlic clove.

1 (14.5-ounce) can diced tomatoes with basil, garlic, and oregano, drained
1 teaspoon fresh lemon juice
¼ teaspoon crushed red pepper
2 garlic cloves, minced
1 (4-ounce) package crumbled feta cheese
Cooking spray
32 (½-inch-thick) slices whole wheat French bread (about 1 pound), toasted

1. Preheat oven to 350°.
2. Combine first 4 ingredients in a bowl. Sprinkle feta evenly into a 6-inch gratin dish or small shallow baking dish coated with cooking spray. Top with tomato mixture. Bake at 350° for 20 minutes. Serve as a spread with bread slices. Yield: 16 servings (serving size: 2 bread slices and 2 tablespoons spread).

CALORIES 107; FAT 2.4g (sat 1.3g); PROTEIN 4.1g; CARBOHYDRATE 16.9g; FIBER 1.6g; CHOLESTEROL 6mg; IRON 1mg; SODIUM 352mg; CALCIUM 72mg

▶ **carbo rating: 15**

Mocha Punch

Serve this sweet, creamy punch at a holiday party— no one will ever suspect that it's low in carbs. A bonus is that the carbohydrate in this recipe comes from calcium-containing milk products.

1 (2-ounce) jar instant coffee granules
1 cup boiling water
¾ cup "measures-like-sugar" calorie-free sweetener
1 gallon fat-free milk
8 cups (½ gallon) chocolate no-sugar-added, reduced-fat ice cream, softened
8 cups (½ gallon) vanilla no-sugar-added, fat-free ice cream, softened
1 cup frozen fat-free whipped topping, thawed

1. Combine coffee granules and boiling water, stirring until coffee granules dissolve. Add sweetener, stirring until dissolved. Cover and chill.
2. Combine coffee mixture and milk in a large punch bowl; gently stir in ice creams. Spoon whipped topping onto ice cream mixture. Serve immediately. Yield: 40 servings (serving size: 1 cup).

CALORIES 87; FAT 0.3g (sat 0.2g); PROTEIN 5.5g; CARBOHYDRATE 15.3g; FIBER 0g; CHOLESTEROL 2mg; IRON 0.1mg; SODIUM 82mg; CALCIUM 159mg

breads

You don't have to give up bread forever to lose weight. It's simply a matter of switching to "smart carb" breads such as *Whole Wheat-Banana Muffins* (page 91) or *Sturdy Multigrain Bread* (page 97).

► carbo rating: 11
Multigrain Pancakes

Serve these multigrain pancakes with a small amount of melted butter or margarine or some sugar-free syrup.

½ cup all-purpose flour
½ cup whole wheat flour
¼ cup quick-cooking oats
2 tablespoons yellow cornmeal
2 tablespoons "measures-like-sugar" brown sugar calorie-free sweetener (such as Sugar Twin Brown)
1½ teaspoons baking powder
½ teaspoon salt
1 cup 2% reduced-fat milk
¼ cup plain fat-free yogurt
1 tablespoon vegetable oil
1 large egg
Cooking spray

1. Lightly spoon flours into dry measuring cups; level with a knife. Combine flours, oats, and next 4 ingredients, stirring well. Combine milk and next 3 ingredients, stirring with a whisk. Add milk mixture to flour mixture, stirring just until moist.

2. Heat a nonstick griddle or nonstick skillet coated with cooking spray over medium heat. Spoon about ¼ cup batter per pancake onto griddle. Turn pancakes over when tops are covered with bubbles and edges look cooked. Cook 1 minute. Yield: 12 servings (serving size: 1 pancake).

CALORIES 79; FAT 2.3g (sat 0.5g); PROTEIN 3.1g; CARBOHYDRATE 11.7g; FIBER 1g; CHOLESTEROL 22mg; IRON 1.4mg; SODIUM 170mg; CALCIUM 73mg

► carbo rating: 12
Whole Wheat Buttermilk Pancakes

Keep cooked pancakes warm in a 200° oven while preparing the remaining pancakes.

¾ cup all-purpose flour
¾ cup whole wheat flour
3 tablespoons "measures-like-sugar" calorie-free sweetener
1½ teaspoons baking powder
½ teaspoon baking soda
½ teaspoon salt
1½ cups low-fat buttermilk
1 tablespoon vegetable oil
1 large egg
1 large egg white
Cooking spray
Sugar-free maple-flavored syrup (optional)
Butter or margarine (optional)

1. Lightly spoon flours into dry measuring cups; level with a knife. Combine flours and next 4 ingredients in a large bowl, stirring with a whisk. Combine buttermilk, oil, egg, and egg white, stirring with a whisk; add to flour mixture, stirring just until moist.

2. Heat a nonstick griddle or nonstick skillet coated with cooking spray over medium heat. Spoon about ¼ cup batter per pancake onto griddle. Turn pancakes over when tops are covered with bubbles and edges look cooked. Serve with syrup or butter, if desired. Yield: 12 servings (serving size: 1 pancake).

CALORIES 87; FAT 2g (sat 0.4g); PROTEIN 3.7g; CARBOHYDRATE 13.3g; FIBER 1.1g; CHOLESTEROL 22mg; IRON 0.7mg; SODIUM 244mg; CALCIUM 72mg

(pictured on page 73)

make-ahead pancakes

To get a jump-start on breakfast, combine the dry and wet ingredients in separate bowls the night before and refrigerate. Combine them the next morning. Or mix the batter in a heavy-duty zip-top plastic bag and refrigerate until ready to cook. Snip off the bottom corner of the bag; squeeze batter into the measuring cup.

Another make-ahead option is to make a batch of pancakes and freeze them in an airtight container, placing wax paper between pancakes. You can store them in the freezer for up to 1 month. To reheat, place on a baking sheet and bake at 350° for 10 minutes.

flour facts

Compare the carbohydrate, fiber, and other nutrients in 1-cup portions of a variety of flours.

Type of Flour (1 cup)	Carbohydrate (grams)	Fiber (grams)	Protein (grams)	Fat (grams)
All-purpose	95.4	3.4	2.9	1.2
Buckwheat	84.7	12.0	15.1	3.7
Cake flour	74.9	1.6	7.9	0.8
Rye, dark	87.9	28.9	18.9	3.4
Rye, light	81.8	14.9	8.6	1.4
Soy, defatted	38.4	17.5	47.0	1.2
Soy, full-fat	29.6	8.1	29.0	17.4
Whole wheat	87.1	14.6	16.4	2.2

▶ **carbo rating: 14**

Buckwheat Pancake Mix

Keep a container of this pancake mix on hand for those mornings when you need a quick, hearty, hot breakfast.

Pancake mix:

1½ cups whole wheat flour
1 cup buckwheat flour
3 tablespoons sugar
2½ teaspoons baking powder
½ teaspoon baking soda
¼ teaspoon salt

Remaining ingredients:

2½ cups low-fat buttermilk
1 tablespoon butter or margarine, melted
1 teaspoon vanilla extract
1 large egg white
Cooking spray

1. To prepare pancake mix, lightly spoon flours into dry measuring cups; level with a knife. Combine flours and next 4 ingredients in a large bowl. Store mix in an airtight container until ready to use.

2. To prepare pancake batter, combine buttermilk and next 3 ingredients; add to pancake mix, stirring until smooth.

3. Heat a nonstick griddle or nonstick skillet coated with cooking spray over medium heat. Spoon ¼ cup batter per pancake onto griddle. Turn when tops are covered with bubbles and edges look cooked. Cook 1 minute. Yield: 18 servings (serving size: 1 pancake).

CALORIES 89; FAT 1.6g (sat 0.8g); PROTEIN 3.7g; CARBOHYDRATE 15.9g; FIBER 1.9g; CHOLESTEROL 2mg; IRON 0.7mg; SODIUM 163mg; CALCIUM 86mg

buckwheat flour

Buckwheat flour is made from the triangular seeds of buckwheat, which is not really a cereal, but an herb. Buckwheat flour has a more assertive flavor than whole wheat flour and has 12 grams of fiber per cup. (Whole wheat flour has 14.6 grams per cup.) Buckwheat groats are the hulled, crushed kernels of buckwheat and are usually cooked in a similar manner to rice. Kasha is roasted buckwheat groats.

Look for buckwheat flour in the organic foods section of the supermarket or in health-food stores. Because buckwheat flour and groats contain some fat from the germ of the grain, it's best to store them in airtight containers in the freezer or refrigerator so they won't become rancid.

▶ carbo rating: 14

Banana Bread

The sweetness in this whole wheat banana bread comes mostly from the four bananas.

1   cup whole wheat flour
½   cup all-purpose flour
1   teaspoon baking powder
1   teaspoon baking soda
⅛   teaspoon salt
¼   cup "measures-like-sugar" calorie-free sweetener
2   tablespoons margarine, melted
4   medium-sized very ripe bananas, peeled and mashed
1   large egg, lightly beaten
Cooking spray

1. Preheat oven to 350°.
2. Lightly spoon flours into dry measuring cups; level with a knife. Combine flours and next 3 ingredients in a large bowl. Combine sweetener and next 3 ingredients; add to flour mixture, stirring just until moist.
3. Pour batter into an 8 x 4-inch loaf pan coated with cooking spray. Bake at 350° for 50 to 55 minutes or until a wooden pick inserted in center comes out clean. Cool in pan on a wire rack 10 minutes; remove from pan, and cool completely on wire rack. Yield: 16 servings (serving size: 1 [½-inch] slice).

CALORIES 86; FAT 2.1g (sat 0.4g); PROTEIN 2.1g; CARBOHYDRATE 15.8g; FIBER 1.7g; CHOLESTEROL 13mg; IRON 0.6mg; SODIUM 125mg; CALCIUM 22mg

(pictured on page 74)

shortcut to ripe bananas

It's important to use very ripe bananas in this recipe—the ones with skins that have turned black. These are best for banana bread because they're softer and blend into the batter better, and they're sweeter than less ripe bananas.

If you can't wait for your bananas to ripen, you can take a shortcut and roast the bananas. Roast the number of bananas you need, unpeeled, at 350° for 10 minutes. Cool and proceed with the recipe.

▶ carbo rating: 14

Whole-Grain-Pumpkin Muffins

Pumpkin, whether canned or fresh, is packed with two disease-fighting nutrients: Vitamins A and C.

¾   cup bite-sized whole wheat cereal biscuits, crumbled (such as Shredded Wheat)
¾   cup low-fat buttermilk
½   cup canned pumpkin
¼   cup vegetable oil
1   large egg, lightly beaten
1   teaspoon grated orange rind
1   cup whole wheat flour
½   cup all-purpose flour
⅓   cup "measures-like-sugar" calorie-free sweetener
1   teaspoon ground cinnamon
¾   teaspoon baking powder
¼   teaspoon baking soda
⅛   teaspoon salt
Cooking spray
1   tablespoon "measures-like-sugar" calorie-free sweetener
¼   teaspoon ground cinnamon

1. Preheat oven to 400°.
2. Combine cereal and buttermilk in a medium bowl; let stand 10 minutes until soft. Add pumpkin and next 3 ingredients; stir well.
3. Lightly spoon flours into dry measuring cups; level with a knife. Combine flours and next 5 ingredients in a medium bowl, stirring with a whisk. Make a well in center of mixture. Add pumpkin mixture to flour mixture, stirring just until moist (batter with be thick). Spoon batter evenly into 12 muffin cups coated with cooking spray.
4. Combine 1 tablespoon sweetener and ¼ teaspoon cinnamon; sprinkle over muffins. Bake at 400° for 15 minutes or until golden. Yield: 12 servings (serving size: 1 muffin).

CALORIES 126; FAT 5.6g (sat 0.6g); PROTEIN 3.5g; CARBOHYDRATE 17g; FIBER 3g; CHOLESTEROL 18mg; IRON 1.5mg; SODIUM 132mg; CALCIUM 56mg

> "Sometimes a muffin is just the most convenient thing to grab for breakfast. But if I'm having one, **I make sure that it's a whole wheat muffin without a lot of sugar.**"
>
> *Hal Cain*

▶ carbo rating: 16
Whole Wheat-Banana Muffins

The toasted wheat germ not only adds nutty flavor to the muffins, but also a dose of Vitamin E—a vitamin that may prevent blood clots, strokes, and cancer, as well as protect against cataracts.

 1   cup all-purpose flour
 1   cup whole wheat flour
 ¼   cup toasted wheat germ
 1   teaspoon baking powder
 1   teaspoon baking soda
 ½   teaspoon salt
 1½   cups mashed very ripe banana (about 3 large)
 ⅓   cup "measures-like-sugar" calorie-free sweetener
 ¼   cup vegetable oil
 1   large egg, lightly beaten
Cooking spray

1. Preheat oven to 350°.
2. Lightly spoon flours into dry measuring cups; level with a knife. Combine flours and next 4 ingredients in a large bowl; make a well in center of mixture. Combine banana and next 3 ingredients; add to dry ingredients, stirring just until moist.
3. Spoon mixture into muffin cups coated with cooking spray, filling two-thirds full. Bake at 350° for 20 minutes. Serve warm. Yield: 16 servings (serving size: 1 muffin).

CALORIES 118; FAT 4.4g (sat 0.5g); PROTEIN 3g; CARBOHYDRATE 17.8g; FIBER 1.9g; CHOLESTEROL 15mg; IRON 0.9mg; SODIUM 182mg; CALCIUM 23mg

(pictured on page 75)

▶ carbo rating: 17
Whole-Grain Cornsticks

These cornsticks are higher in fiber than traditional cornsticks because the all-purpose flour is replaced with whole wheat flour.

 ¾   cup whole wheat flour
 ¾   cup yellow cornmeal
 3   tablespoons grated fresh Parmesan cheese
 2   teaspoons baking powder
 1½   teaspoons chili powder
 1   teaspoon salt
 ¾   cup plus 2 tablespoons fat-free milk
 2   tablespoons olive oil
 2   tablespoons honey
 1   large egg, lightly beaten
 ¾   cup frozen whole-kernel corn, thawed
 ⅓   cup minced red onion
 2   tablespoons minced jalapeño pepper
Cooking spray

1. Preheat oven to 425°.
2. Lightly spoon flour into dry measuring cups; level with a knife. Combine flour and next 5 ingredients in a large bowl. Make a well in center of mixture. Combine milk, oil, honey, and egg. Add to flour mixture, stirring just until moist. Fold in corn, onion, and jalapeño.
3. Place a cast iron cornstick pan in a 425° oven for 5 minutes. Remove from oven; coat immediately with cooking spray. Spoon batter into pan. Bake at 425° for 18 minutes or until lightly browned. Remove from pan immediately; serve warm. Yield: 12 servings (serving size: 1 cornstick).

Note: You can prepare these cornsticks in muffin cups, but the cast iron cornstick pan makes a crisper crust.

CALORIES 120; FAT 3.6g (sat 0.8g); PROTEIN 4g; CARBOHYDRATE 19g; FIBER 2g; CHOLESTEROL 19mg; IRON 0.7mg; SODIUM 325mg; CALCIUM 96mg

▶ carbo rating: 20
Savory Herb Bread

This lightly herbed whole wheat loaf received our Test Kitchens' highest rating.

2	cups whole wheat flour
1¾	cups all-purpose flour
2	tablespoons nonfat dry milk
2	tablespoons minced fresh parsley
1	tablespoon minced fresh dill
1	teaspoon salt
¾	teaspoon minced fresh rosemary
¼	teaspoon ground white pepper
1	package dry yeast (about 2¼ teaspoons)
1¼	cups fat-free milk
½	cup minced onion
¼	cup butter
2	tablespoons honey
	Cooking spray

1. Lightly spoon flours into dry measuring cups; level with a knife. Combine whole wheat flour, dry milk, and next 6 ingredients in a large bowl; stir well. Set aside.
2. Combine milk, onion, butter, and honey in a small saucepan. Cook over medium heat until butter melts. Cool to 120° to 130°. Add milk mixture to whole wheat flour mixture. Beat with a mixer at low speed just until blended; beat at high speed 3 minutes. Gradually stir in 1¾ cups all-purpose flour to make a soft dough.
3. Turn dough out onto a lightly floured surface, and knead until smooth and elastic (8 to 10 minutes). Place in a large bowl coated with cooking spray, turning to coat top. Cover and let rise in a warm place (85°), free from drafts, 1 hour or until doubled in size. (Gently press two fingers into dough. If indentation remains, dough has risen enough.)
4. Punch dough down; turn out onto a lightly floured surface. Roll dough into a 14 x 7-inch rectangle. Roll up rectangle tightly, starting with a short edge, pressing firmly to eliminate air pockets. Pinch seam and ends to seal. Place roll, seam side down, in a 9 x 5-inch loaf pan coated with cooking spray. Cover and let rise in a warm place, free from drafts, 40 minutes or until dough is doubled in size.
5. Preheat oven to 350°.

6. Bake at 350° for 45 to 50 minutes or until loaf sounds hollow when tapped. (Cover with aluminum foil the last 15 minutes of baking to prevent excess browning, if necessary.) Remove from pan; cool on a wire rack. Yield: 18 servings (serving size: 1 [½-inch] slice).

CALORIES 130; FAT 3g (sat 1.7g); PROTEIN 4.1g; CARBOHYDRATE 22.6g; FIBER 2.1g; CHOLESTEROL 7mg; IRON 1.2mg; SODIUM 169mg; CALCIUM 36mg

▶ carbo rating: 21
Banana-Bran Soy Muffins

These hearty, filling muffins offer a double dose of soy in both the milk and the flour. Soy may help prevent heart disease and some forms of cancer.

1	cup wheat bran
1	cup mashed ripe banana (about 1 large)
⅔	cup soy milk
¼	cup packed brown sugar
2	tablespoons prune baby food or prune butter
1	large egg, lightly beaten
1¼	cups all-purpose flour
¼	cup soy flour
¼	cup finely chopped pecans
2	teaspoons baking powder
1	teaspoon ground cinnamon
½	teaspoon salt
	Cooking spray

1. Preheat oven to 375°.
2. Combine first 3 ingredients; let stand 5 minutes. Add sugar, baby food, and egg; mix well. Lightly spoon flours into dry measuring cups; level with a knife. Combine flours and next 4 ingredients in a bowl; make a well in center of mixture. Add bran mixture to flour mixture, stirring just until moist.
3. Spoon batter into 12 muffin cups coated with cooking spray. Bake at 375° for 20 minutes or until muffins spring back when touched lightly in center.
4. Remove muffins from pans immediately; cool muffins completely on a wire rack. Yield: 12 servings (serving size: 1 muffin).

CALORIES 134; FAT 3.2g (sat 0.5g); PROTEIN 4.3g; CARBOHYDRATE 24.7g; FIBER 3.5g; CHOLESTEROL 18mg; IRON 1.9mg; SODIUM 193mg; CALCIUM 76mg

▶ **carbo rating: 25**

Flaxseed Bread

Flaxseed can be found in health-food stores and some supermarkets. Because it's rich in fat, store ground flaxseed in the refrigerator or freezer. It will stay fresh for up to 90 days. Whole flaxseed can be stored at room temperature for up to one year.

1¼	cups whole wheat flour
1	cup bread flour
1	cup warm water (100° to 110°)
1	package dry yeast (about 2¼ teaspoons)
½	cup plus 2 tablespoons flaxseed, divided
3	tablespoons nonfat dry milk
2	tablespoons shreds of wheat bran cereal (such as All-Bran)
3	tablespoons honey
1	tablespoon molasses
1	teaspoon salt
3	tablespoons bread flour

Cooking spray

2	teaspoons cornmeal
1	large egg white, lightly beaten
1	teaspoon flaxseed

1. Lightly spoon whole wheat flour and 1 cup bread flour into dry measuring cups; level with a knife. Combine 1 cup bread flour, water, and yeast in a large bowl; stir well with a whisk. Cover yeast mixture, and let stand at room temperature 1 hour.

2. Place ½ cup flaxseed in a spice or coffee grinder; process until finely ground to measure ¾ cup. Add ground flaxseed, whole wheat flour, 2 tablespoons whole flaxseed, and next 5 ingredients to yeast mixture, and stir until a soft dough forms (dough will feel tacky).

3. Turn dough out onto a lightly floured surface. Knead until smooth and elastic (about 5 minutes); add enough of 3 tablespoons bread flour, 1 tablespoon at a time, to prevent dough from sticking to hands. Shape dough into a 5-inch round loaf; place on a baking sheet coated with cooking spray and sprinkled with cornmeal. Brush loaf with egg white; sprinkle with 1 teaspoon flaxseed. Make 3 diagonal cuts ¼ inch deep across top of loaf using a sharp knife. Cover and let rise in a warm place (85°), free from drafts, 1 hour or until doubled in size. (Press two fingers into dough. If indention remains, dough has risen enough.)

4. Preheat oven to 375°.

5. Bake at 375° for 30 minutes or until bread sounds hollow when tapped. Remove from pan; cool on a wire rack. Yield: 12 servings (serving slice: 1 slice).

CALORIES 165; FAT 4.7g (sat 0.4g); PROTEIN 6.4g; CARBOHYDRATE 28.8g; FIBER 4.1g; CHOLESTEROL 0mg; IRON 2.3mg; SODIUM 224mg; CALCIUM 60mg

► carbo rating: 26
Wheat Berry-Walnut Bread

This dense, round loaf is great for sandwiches or as an accompaniment to soup or stew. Wheat berries, which can be cooked and eaten as a cereal or softened and added to baked goods, are whole, unprocessed kernels of wheat. Look for them in health-food stores and some supermarkets.

2½	cups whole wheat flour, divided
½	cup rye flour
¼	cup all-purpose flour
1½	cups warm 1% low-fat milk (100° to 110°)
2	tablespoons shreds of wheat bran cereal (such as All-Bran)
1	package dry yeast (about 2¼ teaspoons)
½	cup water
2	tablespoons uncooked wheat berries
6	tablespoons chopped walnuts, divided
2	tablespoons honey
1	teaspoon salt
	Cooking spray
1	teaspoon vegetable oil

1. Lightly spoon flours into dry measuring cups; level with a knife.

2. Combine ½ cup whole wheat flour, warm milk, cereal, and yeast in a large bowl; stir well with a whisk. Cover and let stand at room temperature 1 hour.

3. Combine ½ cup water and wheat berries in a small microwave-safe bowl. Microwave at HIGH 1 minute or until mixture boils. Cover and let stand 1 hour. Drain.

4. Add wheat berries, 2 cups whole wheat flour, rye flour, ¼ cup chopped walnuts, honey, and salt to yeast mixture; stir until a soft dough forms (dough will feel tacky). Turn dough out onto a lightly floured surface. Knead dough until smooth and elastic (about 5 minutes); add enough of all-purpose flour, 1 tablespoon at a time, to prevent dough from sticking to hands. Place dough on a baking sheet coated with cooking spray. Shape dough into an 8-inch round loaf. Make a ¼-inch-deep "X" design in top of dough using a sharp knife. Brush dough with oil, and sprinkle with 2 tablespoons chopped walnuts. Cover and let rise in a warm place (85°), free from drafts, 30 minutes or until doubled in size. (Press two fingers into dough. If indentation remains, dough has risen enough.)

5. Preheat oven to 375°.

6. Uncover dough. Bake at 375° for 25 minutes or until loaf sounds hollow when tapped. Remove from baking sheet; cool on a wire rack. Yield: 12 servings (serving size: 1 slice).

CALORIES 172; FAT 3.6g (sat 0.5g); PROTEIN 6.7g; CARBOHYDRATE 30.5g; FIBER 4.6g; CHOLESTEROL 1mg; IRON 1.6mg; SODIUM 220mg; CALCIUM 53mg

wheat berries

Wheat berries are the whole, unprocessed kernels of wheat grain. (Wheat bran, the exterior layer of the grain, is rich in fiber.) They are big, chewy, and take about an hour to cook. Once cooked, they can go into salads, soups, and mixed-grain dishes. They are also great kneaded into bread, providing welcome texture.

Cracked wheat is wheat berries that have been broken into fragments, either fine, medium, or coarse.

▶ carbo rating: 27
Cinnamon-Scented Sweet Potato Chapati

Chapati *is an unleavened bread from India. It looks like a pancake and is usually made with a simple mixture of whole wheat flour and water. This one has added flavor from barley flour and sweet potato. The traditional way to serve chapatis is to let people tear off pieces of the bread and use it as a scoop or pusher.*

1½   cups whole wheat flour
½   cup barley flour
1   cup mashed cooked sweet potato
1   tablespoon butter, melted
1   teaspoon salt
½   teaspoon ground cinnamon
¼   cup water

1. Lightly spoon flours into dry measuring cups; level with a knife. Combine flours, potato, butter, salt, and cinnamon in a large bowl; mix well. Add water; press mixture together with hands. Turn dough out onto a lightly floured surface; knead until smooth (about 2 minutes).

2. Divide dough into 16 equal portions, shaping each into a ball. Working with 1 ball at a time (cover remaining dough to prevent drying), roll into a 4-inch circle on a lightly floured surface (circles will be very thin).

3. Heat a medium cast iron skillet over medium-high heat until very hot. Place 1 dough circle in pan, and cook 2 minutes or until brown spots appear, turning after 1 minute. Place bread on a cooking rack over eye of a gas burner. Hold bread over flame with tongs, turning until both sides of bread are puffed and brown spots appear (some chapatis will puff more than others). Repeat procedure with remaining dough. Yield: 8 servings (serving size: 2 chapatis).

CALORIES 151; FAT 2.1g (sat 1g); PROTEIN 4.5g; CARBOHYDRATE 31.1g; FIBER 4.3g; CHOLESTEROL 4mg; IRON 1.3mg; SODIUM 312mg; CALCIUM 18mg

▶ carbo rating: 30
Hazelnut-Apple Bread

Fresh apple and a touch of cinnamon add sweetness to this hearty whole wheat bread, and hazelnuts add crunch.

⅓   cup hazelnuts (about 1¾ ounces)
1   cup coarsely shredded peeled cooking apple
¾   cup sugar
3   tablespoons vegetable oil
½   teaspoon grated lemon rind
½   teaspoon vanilla extract
1   large egg, lightly beaten
1   large egg white, lightly beaten
1½   cups all-purpose flour
½   cup whole wheat flour
1¼   teaspoons baking powder
¾   teaspoon ground cinnamon
½   teaspoon salt
½   teaspoon baking soda
Baking spray with flour

1. Preheat oven to 350°.

2. Place hazelnuts on a baking sheet. Bake at 350° for 15 minutes, stirring once. Turn nuts out onto a towel. Roll up towel, and rub off skins. Chop nuts, and set aside.

3. Combine apple and next 6 ingredients in a large bowl. Lightly spoon flours into dry measuring cups; level with a knife. Combine nuts, flours, and next 4 ingredients; add to apple mixture, stirring just until moist.

4. Spoon batter into an 8 x 4-inch loaf pan coated with baking spray. Bake at 350° for 1 hour and 5 minutes or until a wooden pick inserted in center comes out clean. Cool in pan for 10 minutes on a wire rack; remove from pan. Cool completely on wire rack. Yield: 12 servings (serving size: 1 slice).

CALORIES 197; FAT 6.6g (sat 1g); PROTEIN 3.6g; CARBOHYDRATE 32.1g; FIBER 1.9g; CHOLESTEROL 18mg; IRON 1.2mg; SODIUM 143mg; CALCIUM 37mg

(pictured on page 76)

► carbo rating: 31
Fruit-and-Nut Bread

When you choose to eat bread, why not maximize your nutrition benefits with one containing heart-healthy fruits and nuts?

⅔ cup hazelnuts
2½ cups all-purpose flour, divided
2 cups whole wheat flour
1½ cups warm water (100° to 110°)
1 package dry yeast (about 2¼ teaspoons)
1 cup coarsely chopped dried mixed fruit
⅓ cup packed brown sugar
2 tablespoons vegetable oil
1 teaspoon salt
1 large egg, lightly beaten
½ cup seedless red grapes
Cooking spray
2 teaspoons vegetable oil
1 tablespoon sunflower seed kernels

1. Preheat oven to 350°.
2. Place hazelnuts on a baking sheet. Bake nuts at 350° for 15 minutes, stirring once. Turn nuts out onto a towel. Roll up towel; rub off skins. Chop nuts.
3. Lightly spoon flours into dry measuring cups; level with a knife.
4. Combine 1 cup all-purpose flour, warm water, and yeast in a large bowl, and stir well with a whisk. Cover and let stand at room temperature 1 hour.
5. Add hazelnuts, 1 cup all-purpose flour, whole wheat flour, dried fruit, sugar, 2 tablespoons oil, salt, and egg to yeast mixture, and stir until a soft dough forms (dough will feel tacky). Turn dough out onto a lightly floured surface. Knead dough until smooth and elastic (about 5 minutes); add enough of remaining all-purpose flour, 1 tablespoon at a time, to prevent dough from sticking to hands. Arrange grapes over dough; gently knead on a lightly floured surface 4 to 5 times or just until grapes are incorporated into dough. Place dough on a baking sheet coated with cooking spray. Shape into an 8-inch round loaf. Brush dough with 2 teaspoons oil. Sprinkle surface of dough with sunflower kernels, gently pressing kernels into dough. Cover and let rise in a warm place (85°), free from drafts, 45 minutes or until doubled in size. (Press two fingers into dough. If indentation remains, the dough has risen enough.)
6. Preheat oven to 375°.
7. Uncover dough. Bake at 375° for 35 minutes or until loaf sounds hollow when tapped. Remove loaf from baking sheet; cool on a wire rack. Yield: 18 servings (serving size: 1 slice).

CALORIES 200; FAT 5.7g (sat 0.8g); PROTEIN 4.9g; CARBOHYDRATE 33.8g; FIBER 2.5g; CHOLESTEROL 12mg; IRON 1.9mg; SODIUM 138mg; CALCIUM 24mg

grape benefits

One cup of grapes has almost as much fiber as a slice of whole wheat toast, a good amount of potassium, just a trace of fat, and little more than 100 calories. But their most potent benefits lie in their phytonutrients, particularly in the compound resveratrol—found within the skin of grapes of all colors—that may help prevent several kinds of cancer and heart disease. Resveratrol may fight breast, skin, and colon cancers. Although scientists don't completely understand its protective effects, part of its magic lies in its anti-inflammatory properties. Resveratrol protects the grape from fungal infections, so similar mechanisms may be what protect us from cancer. Grapes are also packed with other flavenoids that may help prevent cancer and heart disease.

The best sources of resveratrol, besides unpeeled grapes themselves, are red wine and raisins—dried whole grapes.

▶ **carbo rating: 33**

Sturdy Multigrain Bread

With cereal and both whole wheat and rye flours, this bread is a good source of fiber.

1¾ cups water
1¼ cups uncooked multigrain hot cereal (such as Quaker)
1 package dry yeast (about 2¼ teaspoons)
1 tablespoon honey
1⅔ cups warm water (100° to 110°)
¼ cup plain low-fat yogurt
3 tablespoons vegetable oil
2½ cups bread flour, divided
2 cups whole wheat flour
1 cup rye flour
2 teaspoons salt
Cooking spray

1. Bring 1¾ cups water to a boil in a medium saucepan; stir in cereal. Cook 1 minute over medium-low heat or until liquid is nearly absorbed, stirring occasionally. Remove from heat; let stand, covered, 30 minutes or until cool.
2. Dissolve yeast and honey in warm water in a large bowl; let stand 5 minutes. Stir in yogurt and oil. Lightly spoon flours into dry measuring cups; level with a knife. Combine 1½ cups bread flour, whole wheat flour, rye flour, and salt; add to yeast mixture, stirring until well blended. Turn bread out onto a lightly floured surface; knead in cereal mixture. Knead until smooth and elastic (about 8 minutes); add enough of remaining flour, 1 tablespoon at a time, to prevent dough from sticking to hands.
3. Place dough in a large bowl coated with cooking spray, turning to coat top. Cover and let rise in a warm place (85°), free from drafts, 1 hour or until doubled in size. (Press two fingers into dough. If indentation remains, the dough has risen enough.) Punch dough down; roll into a 14 x 7-inch rectangle on a lightly floured surface. Roll up rectangle tightly, starting with a short edge, pressing firmly to eliminate air pockets; pinch seam and ends to seal. Place roll, seam side down, in a 9 x 5-inch loaf pan coated with cooking spray. Cover and let rise 1 hour or until doubled in size.

4. Preheat oven to 350°.
5. Uncover dough. Bake at 350° for 50 minutes or until loaf sounds hollow when tapped. Remove from pan; cool on a wire rack. Yield: 16 servings (serving size: 1 slice).

CALORIES 205; FAT 3.8g (sat 0.4g); PROTEIN 7g; CARBOHYDRATE 37.5g; FIBER 4.2g; CHOLESTEROL 0mg; IRON 2.2mg; SODIUM 298mg; CALCIUM 23mg

catching up with rye

Rye grain is most commonly seen as flour. Dark rye flour has more fiber than whole wheat flour; light rye flour has about half the fiber of whole wheat. Also available are whole rye berries, which are green and work nicely in salads. Rye berries are a lot like wheat berries, kamut berries, and other whole grains— chewy and neutral in flavor, they hold their shape when cooked. Like wheat berries, they can be added to breads.

Rye is often available rolled as well. Rolled rye cooks quickly and makes tasty breakfast cereals. Rye ferments easily, so it's not surprising that it's also used to make whiskey.

fish & shellfish

At last—something you can eat to your heart's content. Not only is fish low in carbs, nutrition research shows that eating fish at least 2 to 3 times a week may help prevent heart disease. Try *Grilled Pesto Salmon* (page 100) for dinner tonight.

► carbo rating: 0

Sesame Salmon

Salmon is naturally high in omega-3 fats (a heart-healthy type of fat) and has a strong, rich flavor. So it needs only a few simple seasonings such as soy sauce, sesame oil, and sesame seeds to dress it up. Sesame oil is strong-flavored, so you need only a small amount to make a flavor impact.

1	tablespoon low-sodium soy sauce
1	teaspoon sesame oil
4	(6-ounce) salmon fillets
1½	teaspoons sesame seeds

Cooking spray

1. Combine soy sauce and sesame oil. Brush mixture evenly over fillets. Sprinkle sesame seeds over 1 side of fillets.

2. Coat a large nonstick skillet with cooking spray, and place over medium-high heat. Add salmon; cook 4 minutes on each side or until fish flakes easily when tested with a fork. Yield: 4 servings (serving size: 1 fillet).

CALORIES 291; FAT 14.8g (sat 3.3g); PROTEIN 36.7g; CARBOHYDRATE 0.5g; FIBER 0g; CHOLESTEROL 87mg; IRON 0.8mg; SODIUM 214mg; CALCIUM 23mg

quick grill

When the weather's too cold to grill outside, you can get the same effect with a stovetop grill pan. This pan has ridges that elevate food so air can circulate underneath and fat can drip away. And a grill pan adds more than just pretty grill marks and smoky flavors. Your food doesn't sauté or steam as it does in a plain skillet; instead, flavor is seared into the food. Meat and fish turn out juicy, with no need for added fat. Vegetables stay crisp-tender, and their nutrients don't leach out into cooking water.

Here are some things to look for when selecting a grill pan.

• High ridges produce results similar to those of an outdoor grill. If the ridges are too low, you might as well be using a regular skillet.

• Low sides make flipping burgers and removing food with a spatula much easier.

• A pan with a square or oblong shape fits more food than a round pan.

• A lidless pan is a good choice, since there's no reason to lock in moisture when grilling.

► carbo rating: 1

Grilled Pesto Salmon

We prefer the flavor and texture of refrigerated pesto found in the produce section of the supermarket to the shelf-stable, jarred pesto. But either will work in this recipe.

	Cooking spray
4	(6-ounce) salmon fillets
¼	teaspoon salt
¼	teaspoon freshly ground black pepper
3	tablespoons commercial pesto
3	tablespoons dry white wine

1. Heat a large grill pan coated with cooking spray over medium heat.

2. Sprinkle fillets evenly with salt and pepper. Set aside.

3. Combine pesto and wine, stirring well.

4. Place fillets on grill pan, and grill 6 minutes on each side or until fish flakes easily when tested with a fork. Serve fish with pesto sauce. Yield: 4 servings (serving size: 1 fillet and 1½ tablespoons sauce).

CALORIES 280; FAT 11.7g (sat 2.5g); PROTEIN 38.9g; CARBOHYDRATE 1g; FIBER 0.4g; CHOLESTEROL 100mg; IRON 1.9mg; SODIUM 360mg; CALCIUM 108mg

▶ carbo rating: 1

Grilled Halibut with Olive Salsa

We prefer the briny flavor of kalamata olives in this salsa, but you can substitute a 2.25-ounce can of chopped ripe olives.

4	(6-ounce) skinless halibut fillets
½	teaspoon salt
¼	teaspoon black pepper
	Olive oil-flavored cooking spray
½	cup chopped ripe olives
2	tablespoons chopped fresh parsley
2	tablespoons chopped drained oil-packed sun-dried tomato halves
½	teaspoon bottled minced garlic

1. Heat a nonstick grill pan over medium-high heat until hot and a drop of water sizzles when dropped on the grill pan.
2. Sprinkle fish evenly with salt and pepper; coat with cooking spray. Grill 4 to 5 minutes on each side or until fish flakes easily when tested with a fork.
3. While fish cooks, combine olives and next 3 ingredients in a small bowl. Serve salsa over fish. Yield: 4 servings (serving size: 1 fillet and 3 tablespoons salsa).

CALORIES 221; FAT 6.8g (sat 0.9g); PROTEIN 35.9g; CARBOHYDRATE 2.5g; FIBER 1g; CHOLESTEROL 54mg; IRON 2.4mg; SODIUM 585mg; CALCIUM 105mg

watch for the sizzle

It's very important to let the grill pan get hot before cooking the fish. The quickest and safest way to check the temperature is with a drop of water. If the water sizzles, the pan is the correct temperature. You'll get the desired golden to dark brown grill marks without overcooking the fish. (See the previous page for more information on stovetop grill pans.)

"I don't eat red meat, so **it's important for me to have a big selection of seafood recipes** so that I can stick to my low-carb plan."

Pam Sutton

▶ carbo rating: 1

Blackened Catfish Fillets

If you don't have a cast iron skillet, use a nonstick skillet. Just reduce the starting temperature from high to medium-high.

1	tablespoon paprika
1½	teaspoons dried oregano
½	teaspoon salt
½	teaspoon black pepper
¼	teaspoon ground cumin
⅛	teaspoon garlic powder
4	(6-ounce) catfish fillets
1	tablespoon light butter
	Lemon slices (optional)

1. Combine first 6 ingredients in a small bowl, and stir well.
2. Rinse fillets, and pat dry with paper towels to remove excess moisture. Sprinkle paprika mixture evenly on both sides of fillets; gently rub in seasonings.
3. Place a 12-inch cast iron skillet over high heat until hot. Add 1½ teaspoons butter and tilt pan to coat bottom. Add 2 fillets, and cook 2 minutes. Reduce heat to medium; turn, and cook 4 minutes or until fish flakes easily when tested with a fork. Repeat procedure with remaining butter and fillets. Serve with lemon slices, if desired. Serve immediately. Yield: 4 servings (serving size: 1 fillet).

CALORIES 183; FAT 6.6g (sat 2.3g); PROTEIN 28.5g; CARBOHYDRATE 1.6g; FIBER 0.7g; CHOLESTEROL 104mg; IRON 1.3mg; SODIUM 383mg; CALCIUM 38mg

▶ carbo rating: 1

Flounder with Pimiento

A splash of lemon juice is a great way to perk up the flavor of foods, especially fish. A teaspoon of lemon juice has only 0.3 grams of carbohydrate.

1   small lemon
1   (2-ounce) jar diced pimiento, drained
4   (6-ounce) flounder fillets (or other white fish fillets such as orange roughy, cod, or perch)
Butter-flavored cooking spray
1   teaspoon extraspicy salt-free herb-and-spice blend (such as Mrs. Dash)
Oregano sprigs (optional)

1. Preheat oven to 425°.
2. Cut lemon in half. Squeeze juice from half of lemon (about 1 tablespoon) into a small bowl; set remaining lemon half aside. Add pimiento to juice, mixing well.
3. Place fillets in an 11 x 7-inch baking dish coated with cooking spray. Coat fish with cooking spray; sprinkle with herb-and-spice blend.
4. Spoon pimiento mixture evenly over fish. Bake, uncovered, at 425° for 12 minutes or until fish flakes easily when tested with a fork. While fish bakes, cut remaining lemon half into slices to serve with fish. Garnish with oregano sprigs, if desired. Yield: 4 servings (serving size: 1 fillet).

CALORIES 164; FAT 2.3g (sat 0.5g); PROTEIN 32.4g; CARBOHYDRATE 2.1g;
FIBER 0.7g; CHOLESTEROL 82mg; IRON 0.9mg; SODIUM 140mg; CALCIUM 35mg

(pictured on page 78)

▶ carbo rating: 1

Flounder Fillets with Béarnaise Sauce

To keep the fillets in one piece when turning them, place one spatula under the fillet and one spatula on top and gently flip.

4   (6-ounce) flounder fillets
¼   teaspoon pepper
Cooking spray
½   cup dry white wine
2   tablespoons minced fresh onion
1   garlic clove, minced
½   teaspoon dried tarragon
3   tablespoons light butter
1   tablespoon chopped fresh parsley
¼   teaspoon salt

1. Sprinkle fillets with pepper.
2. Heat a large nonstick skillet over medium-high heat. Coat fillets with cooking spray. Add 2 fillets to pan; cook 3 to 4 minutes on each side or until fish flakes easily when tested with a fork. Remove from pan, and keep warm. Repeat procedure with remaining fillets.
3. Add wine, onion, garlic, and tarragon to pan; bring to a boil. Reduce heat to medium-high, and cook 5 to 7 minutes or until liquid evaporates. Reduce heat to low; add butter, parsley, and salt. Cook 2 minutes or until butter melts.
4. Spoon sauce over fillets. Serve immediately. Yield: 4 servings (serving size: 1 fillet and about 1½ tablespoons sauce).

CALORIES 181; FAT 6.3g (sat 3.4g); PROTEIN 29.4g; CARBOHYDRATE 1.4g;
FIBER 0.2g; CHOLESTEROL 95mg; IRON 0.7mg; SODIUM 324mg; CALCIUM 30mg

fish substitutions

Fish divide easily into three categories: delicate, medium, and firm-fleshed. These categories reflect how fish respond to cooking methods and which substitutions work.

Category of fish	If a recipe calls for:	You can substitute:
Delicate Treat delicate fish with care when you cook them; they flake easily and have a soft texture when cooked. These fish are traditionally sold as fillets, and they are best prepared by poaching, braising, pan-frying, or baking.	sole/flounder	turbot, plaice, fluke, all varieties of sole/flounder
	cod	orange roughy (mild)
Medium These fish flake easily, but they have more resistance than delicate fish and are firmer when cooked. They are the most versatile fish to cook and can be used when your recipe specifies "or other flaky white fish." They are best prepared by baking, broiling, braising, pan-frying, or grilling.	arctic char	steelhead trout, salmon
	mahimahi	grouper, monkfish
	red snapper	halibut, walleye (sweet, delicate), all varieties of snapper
	tilapia	bass (fresh water), pike, tilefish
Firm These fish don't flake easily when cooked and have a meaty texture. They are best prepared over high heat—by grilling or sautéing, for example.	pompano	amberjack, catfish
	tuna	swordfish, trigger fish (mildly sweet)

▶ **carbo rating: 1**

Baked Grouper with Kalamata Mustard

Use mustard to transform foods from bland to big flavor. The possibilities are endless with the many flavors of mustards that are on the market. This topping has whole-grain Dijon, which has only 1 gram of carbohydrate per tablespoon.

 4 (6-ounce) grouper fillets (or other white fish fillets such as flounder, orange roughy, or perch)

Cooking spray

 ¼ teaspoon pepper

 ⅛ teaspoon paprika

 8 chopped pitted kalamata olives

 2 tablespoons light butter, softened

 1½ tablespoons whole-grain Dijon mustard

 ½ teaspoon dried basil

 2 tablespoons chopped fresh parsley

1. Preheat oven to 425°.

2. Arrange fillets on a baking sheet coated with cooking spray. Lightly coat tops of each fillet with cooking spray; sprinkle with pepper and paprika. Bake, uncovered, at 425° for 12 minutes or until fish flakes easily when tested with a fork.

3. Combine olives and next 3 ingredients in a bowl.

4. Remove fillets from baking sheet, and top evenly with olive mixture. Sprinkle with parsley. Serve immediately. Yield: 4 servings (serving size: 1 fillet and about 2 teaspoons mustard mixture).

CALORIES 210; FAT 6.7g (sat 2.6g); PROTEIN 33.8g; CARBOHYDRATE 1.1g; FIBER 0.2g; CHOLESTEROL 73mg; IRON 1.8mg; SODIUM 384mg; CALCIUM 55mg

▶ carbo rating: 1
Grouper Athenian

If you can't find basil-and tomato-flavored feta, regular feta adds plenty of flavor.

    4   (6-ounce) grouper fillets
    2   teaspoons salt-free Greek seasoning
Cooking spray
    1   (10-ounce) package frozen chopped spinach, thawed, drained, and squeezed dry
    1   plum tomato, coarsely chopped
    ¼   cup (1 ounce) crumbled feta cheese with basil and sun-dried tomatoes

1. Sprinkle both sides of fish with seasoning. Coat a large nonstick skillet with cooking spray; place over medium-high heat until hot. Add fish, and cook 3 minutes; remove pan from heat.
2. Turn fish; top with spinach, tomato, and cheese. Return pan to heat; cover and cook 3 to 4 minutes or until spinach is hot and fish flakes easily when tested with a fork. Serve immediately. Yield: 4 servings (serving size: 1 fillet and ¼ of spinach mixture).

CALORIES 197; FAT 3.8g (sat 1.6g); PROTEIN 36.4g; CARBOHYDRATE 3.6g; FIBER 2.3g; CHOLESTEROL 68mg; IRON 3mg; SODIUM 230mg; CALCIUM 146mg

(pictured on page 77)

is it done yet?

Timing is critical when cooking fish because it is so delicate. Perfectly cooked fish will be moist and tender; overcooked fish will be dry and tough. As fish cooks, its translucent flesh turns opaque (or solid) in appearance. If just a thin, translucent line remains when the fish is cut or flaked, remove it from the heat. Residual heat will finish cooking it on the way to the table.

mercury in fish

Certain fish contain high levels of a form of mercury that can cause chronic fatigue and memory loss in adults and harm an unborn child's developing nervous system. Eating them occasionally poses no real health risk. However, if you're pregnant, considering pregnancy, or nursing, it's best not to eat the following fish:

- Halibut
- King mackerel
- Large mouth bass
- Marlin
- Oysters (from the Gulf of Mexico)
- Sea bass
- Shark
- Swordfish
- Tilefish
- Tuna
- Walleye
- White croaker

▶ carbo rating: 1
Quick Seared Tuna Steaks

Transform fresh fish into a delicious entrée with a few simple low-carb ingredients.

    ¼   cup dry sherry
    2   tablespoons low-sodium soy sauce
    1   tablespoon fresh lime juice
    2   teaspoons olive oil
    4   (6-ounce) tuna steaks (about 1 inch thick)
    ½   teaspoon coarsely ground black pepper
    ¼   teaspoon salt

1. Combine first 3 ingredients in a small bowl, stirring well with a whisk. Set aside.
2. Heat oil in a large nonstick skillet over medium-high heat. Sprinkle steaks with pepper and salt; add steaks to pan. Cook 4 minutes on each side or until steaks are medium-rare or desired degree of doneness. Transfer to a serving dish, and keep warm. Pour sherry mixture into pan. Cook 1 to 1½ minutes or until reduced to 2 tablespoons, stirring to deglaze pan; pour over steaks. Yield: 4 servings (serving size: 1 steak and ½ tablespoon sauce).

CALORIES 203; FAT 4g (sat 0.9g); PROTEIN 38g; CARBOHYDRATE 1.2g; FIBER 0.1g; CHOLESTEROL 80mg; IRON 2.2mg; SODIUM 512mg; CALCIUM 52mg

► carbo rating: 1

Baked Snapper with Chipotle Butter

The chipotle butter is also good on broiled or grilled chicken.

½   teaspoon ground cumin
½   teaspoon paprika
¼   teaspoon salt
⅛   teaspoon pepper
4   (6-ounce) red snapper or other firm white fish fillets
Cooking spray
1   tablespoon butter, softened
1   canned chipotle chile in adobo sauce, finely minced
Lemon wedges

1. Preheat oven to 400°.
2. Combine first 4 ingredients, and sprinkle evenly over fish.
3. Place fish on a baking sheet coated with cooking spray; bake 15 minutes or until fish flakes easily when tested with a fork.
4. While fish bakes, combine butter and chile. Spread butter mixture evenly over fish. Serve with lemon wedges. Yield: 4 servings (serving size: 1 fillet).

CALORIES 203; FAT 5.4g (sat 2.3g); PROTEIN 35.2g; CARBOHYDRATE 1.6g; FIBER 0.4g; CHOLESTEROL 71mg; IRON 0.5mg; SODIUM 317mg; CALCIUM 63mg

► carbo rating: 1

Tarragon Snapper

This creamy low-carb topping is great on any broiled or grilled fish fillets.

2   tablespoons chopped fresh parsley
3   tablespoons light mayonnaise
1   tablespoon fresh lime juice
2   teaspoons olive oil
½   teaspoon dried tarragon
½   teaspoon Dijon mustard
¼   teaspoon salt
¼   teaspoon pepper
4   (6-ounce) red snapper fillets
Cooking spray

1. Preheat broiler.
2. Combine first 8 ingredients in a small bowl; set aside.
3. Place fish on a broiler pan coated with cooking spray; broil 5 minutes. Turn fish; spread mayonnaise mixture over fish. Broil 5 minutes or until fish flakes easily when tested with a fork. Yield: 4 servings (serving size: 1 fillet and 2 tablespoons sauce).

CALORIES 224; FAT 8.3g (sat 1.5g); PROTEIN 33.7g; CARBOHYDRATE 1.5g; FIBER 0.1g; CHOLESTEROL 64mg; IRON 0.5mg; SODIUM 325mg; CALCIUM 58mg

► carbo rating: 2

Easy Parmesan Flounder

For a shortcut, you can use frozen flounder instead of fresh. Thaw the fish according to package directions before proceeding with the recipe.

4   (6-ounce) flounder fillets
Cooking spray
1   tablespoon fresh lemon juice
¼   cup fat-free mayonnaise
3   tablespoons grated Parmesan cheese
1   tablespoon thinly sliced green onions
1   tablespoon reduced-calorie margarine, softened
⅛   teaspoon hot sauce

1. Preheat broiler.
2. Place fillets on a broiler pan coated with cooking spray; brush fillets with lemon juice. Broil 5 to 6 minutes or until fish flakes easily when tested with a fork.
3. Combine mayonnaise and next 4 ingredients, stirring well. Spread mayonnaise mixture evenly over 1 side of fillets. Broil 1 minute or until lightly browned and bubbly. Yield: 4 servings (serving size: 1 fillet).

CALORIES 197; FAT 5g (sat 1.6g); PROTEIN 33.7g; CARBOHYDRATE 2.6g; FIBER 0.4g; CHOLESTEROL 86mg; IRON 0.7mg; SODIUM 363mg; CALCIUM 85mg

how to buy and store fresh fish

What should I look for when buying fresh fish?

Look for fish that is free of blemishes, neither slick nor soggy, and springs back when touched. If it smells "fishy," it's not fresh. Avoid fish displayed directly on ice—the contact can cause quality to deteriorate. Buying fish that has been frozen at sea is your next best alternative.

Is it OK to buy frozen fish?

Yes. When possible, purchase vacuum-packed frozen fish, and look for "once frozen" on the label. Avoid any fish that has symptoms of freezer burn, such as brown or dry edges. Defrost frozen fish in the refrigerator overnight.

Is it better to buy fillets or the whole fish?

Buying fillets or steaks is the easiest and best way to buy fish, but buying it whole is the most economical way. If the fish market has whole fish, ask for it to be filleted and portioned. Cook what you need, and freeze the rest. Keep the bones so you can make fish stock for soups and stews—the bones will freeze, and the stock will, too.

What should I look for when buying a whole fresh fish?

Look for clear, glossy eyes; shiny, red gills; and a firm body, free of any dark blemishes. The tail should not be dried out or curled.

How should I store fresh fish?

Buy fish on your way out of the store, take it directly home, and cook (or freeze) it within 24 hours. Keep the fish as cold as possible until you are ready to cook it.

▶ carbo rating: 2

Grilled Halibut with Lemon Sauce

If you want to use all fresh herbs in this recipe, use ½ teaspoon each of chopped fresh oregano and rosemary.

- ¾ cup fat-free, less-sodium chicken broth
- ¼ cup fresh lemon juice (about 2 lemons)
- 1 tablespoon cornstarch
- 1 tablespoon minced fresh parsley
- ½ teaspoon salt
- ¼ teaspoon dried oregano
- ¼ teaspoon dried rosemary
- 8 (6-ounce) halibut fillets
- Cooking spray

1. Prepare grill.
2. Combine first 3 ingredients in a small saucepan. Bring to a boil. Cook 1 minute, stirring constantly. Remove from heat. Stir in parsley, salt, oregano, and rosemary; set mixture aside, and keep warm.
3. Place fillets on grill rack coated with cooking spray; cover and grill 6 minutes on each side or until fish flakes easily when tested with a fork. Serve with warm lemon sauce. Yield: 8 servings (serving size: 1 fillet and 2 tablespoons sauce).

CALORIES 197; FAT 4.2g (sat 0.6g); PROTEIN 35.6g; CARBOHYDRATE 1.7g; FIBER 0g; CHOLESTEROL 80mg; IRON 1.5mg; SODIUM 251mg; CALCIUM 82mg

citrus juices

Using citrus juices is a great low-carb way to add zesty flavor to fish. You need only a few tablespoons to add a burst of flavor, especially when the juice is combined with another ingredient such as soy sauce, broth, or vinegar. One tablespoon of fresh lemon or lime juice has 1.3 grams of carbohydrate; orange juice has 1.6 grams per tablespoon, and grapefruit juice has 1.4 grams.

▶ carbo rating: 2
Broiled Fish with Tapenade

*A **tapenade** (TA-puh-nahd) is a thick paste made from olives, olive oil, and a variety of seasonings. It's used as a spread or condiment for bread, vegetables, fish, or meat. This tapenade is a little different from the one in the Snacks and Beverages chapter on page 53—it has sun-dried tomatoes instead of onions and is stirred instead of processed in a food processor.*

¼	cup sliced sun-dried tomatoes, packed without oil
½	cup boiling water
8	kalamata olives, pitted and chopped
¼	cup chopped fresh parsley
1½	tablespoons chopped fresh basil
1	tablespoon red wine vinegar
1½	teaspoons olive oil
⅛	teaspoon salt
1	garlic clove, minced
	Cooking spray
4	(6-ounce) orange roughy fillets (about ½ inch thick)
2	teaspoons olive oil
¼	teaspoon paprika
¼	teaspoon freshly ground black pepper

1. Combine tomatoes and water; let stand 10 minutes. Drain.
2. Combine olives and next 6 ingredients. Chop tomatoes; add to olive mixture. Stir well; set aside.
3. Preheat broiler.
4. Place fish on a baking sheet coated with cooking spray. Drizzle with oil, and sprinkle with paprika and pepper. Broil 3 minutes. Top with olive mixture; broil 3 minutes or until fish flakes easily when tested with a fork. Yield: 4 servings (serving size: 1 fillet and 1½ tablespoons tapenade).

CALORIES 179; FAT 7.2g (sat 0.8g); PROTEIN 24.8g; CARBOHYDRATE 2.8g; FIBER 0.6g; CHOLESTEROL 33mg; IRON 0.9mg; SODIUM 350mg; CALCIUM 63mg

know your olives

Of the many olives available on the market, here are four distinct types along with a guide to their best uses. The carbohydrate value of an olive varies depending on the size and the variety, but the average carb value is 0.5 grams per olive.

Kalamata: One of the more popular varieties, these Greek black olives are plump and juicy with a powerful flavor, bright acidity, and high salt content. They are delicious with soy products like tofu and tempeh, and work wonders with leafy greens and cruciferous vegetables, such as broccoli and cauliflower, tempering bitterness with acidity.

Moroccan oil-cured: These black olives have a wrinkled, leathery surface, the result of a dry-salt curing process; later, a long, luxurious olive oil bath softens and enriches them. Because they retain more of their natural bitterness, oil-cured olives are best when cooked. These little olives go well with tangy tomatoes, celery, eggplant, citrus, and sweet root vegetables.

Picholine: A slender, full-flavored green olive from the south of France, the picholine is mildly bitter, faintly sweet, and tart with a nice, crunchy texture. Olives à la Picholine are steeped in a solution of lime and wood ashes before marinating in salty brine.

Niçoise: These are small, tart, red-brown olives with a light salty taste. They are interchangeable with Italian gaeta olives. (Gaetas are plump, brine-cured olives that are packed in oil.)

► carbo rating: 2

Tuna with Coriander Mayonnaise

A rule of thumb for cooking fish is to cook it about 8 to 10 minutes per inch thickness of fish. If you like fish such as tuna and salmon more on the rare side, decrease that time by a minute or two.

2 tablespoons light mayonnaise
4 teaspoons fat-free milk
1 tablespoon plain fat-free yogurt
⅛ teaspoon ground coriander
⅛ teaspoon freshly ground black pepper
¼ cup coriander seeds
½ teaspoon salt
¼ teaspoon freshly ground black pepper
4 (6-ounce) tuna steaks (about ¾ inch thick)
Cooking spray

1. Combine first 5 ingredients. Chill. Place seeds in a heavy-duty zip-top plastic bag; seal. Crush seeds with a rolling pin. Sprinkle salt and ¼ teaspoon pepper over steaks; press crushed coriander onto both sides of steaks.
2. Coat a large nonstick skillet with cooking spray; place over medium-high heat until hot. Add steaks; cook 4 minutes on each side until medium-rare or desired degree of doneness. Serve fish with mayonnaise mixture. Yield: 4 servings (serving size: 1 steak and about 1 tablespoon mayonnaise mixture).

CALORIES 286; FAT 11.4g (sat 2.2g); PROTEIN 40.8g; CARBOHYDRATE 3.9g; FIBER 1.5g; CHOLESTEROL 67mg; IRON 2.6mg; SODIUM 422mg; CALCIUM 50mg

► carbo rating: 2

Tuna with Tapenade

Tuna is one of the "fatty fishes" that contains omega-3 fats. This type of fat is believed to help prevent heart disease, so experts recommend that you eat fatty fish (such as tuna or salmon) at least twice a week.

1 (4-ounce) jar capers, drained
1 (4-ounce) jar diced pimiento, drained
1 tablespoon sun-dried tomato paste (such as Amore)
15 kalamata olives, pitted
3 garlic cloves, halved
6 (6-ounce) tuna steaks
¼ teaspoon salt
¼ teaspoon pepper
Cooking spray
Lemon wedges (optional)

1. Prepare grill.
2. Combine first 5 ingredients in a food processor. Pulse 5 times or until finely chopped, scraping down sides of bowl, if necessary. Transfer to a small bowl, and set aside.
3. Sprinkle steaks evenly with salt and pepper.
4. Place steaks on grill rack coated with cooking spray; grill, covered, 4 to 6 minutes on each side or until fish flakes easily when tested with a fork. Serve with tapenade. Garnish with lemon wedges, if desired. Yield: 6 servings (serving size: 1 steak and 2 tablespoons tapenade).

CALORIES 271; FAT 9.8g (sat 2.3g); PROTEIN 40.5g; CARBOHYDRATE 2.4g; FIBER 0.3g; CHOLESTEROL 65mg; IRON 2.5mg; SODIUM 1,062mg; CALCIUM 10mg

(pictured on page 80)

wild or farmed salmon?

As far as salmon fillets go, it's difficult to distinguish wild from farmed. Some farmed salmon, however, are fed carotene pigments to deepen their color, creating an orange hue. Wild-salmon flesh ranges from a light pink (pinks) to a deep red (sockeyes). A whole Atlantic salmon (the farmed choice) is easy to spot because of its sloping head and spots on its back resembling little "X"s. By contrast, wild king salmon has round spots on its skin, a somewhat squat head, and a black mouth. When sold whole, wild salmon is usually labeled as such.

Taste is also a good indicator of whether a salmon is wild or farmed. Wild salmon has a greater range of flavors, from rich, distinctive king salmon to delicately flavored pink. The flavor of farmed salmon will vary depending on the feed mixture each farm uses, but the end result is usually a midrange mild taste—a big improvement over the fish-oil aftertaste farmed salmon once had.

▶ carbo rating: 2

Orange-Glazed Salmon

For an Asian-style dinner, serve this succulent salmon with steamed fresh snow peas.

4	(6-ounce) salmon fillets (1 inch thick)
¼	teaspoon salt
¼	teaspoon pepper
	Cooking spray
3	tablespoons low-sodium soy sauce
3	tablespoons orange juice
½	teaspoon dark sesame oil

1. Sprinkle fish with salt and pepper. Coat a large non-stick skillet with cooking spray; place over high heat until hot. Add fish, and cook, uncovered, 3 minutes on each side. Cover and cook 3 minutes or until fish flakes easily when tested with a fork. Remove from pan; set aside, and keep warm.

2. Add soy sauce and orange juice to pan; cook over high heat 1 minute, stirring to deglaze pan. Add oil, and stir well. Pour sauce over fish; serve immediately. Yield: 4 servings (serving size: 1 fillet).

CALORIES 216; FAT 6.5g (sat 1g); PROTEIN 34.8g; CARBOHYDRATE 2.1g; FIBER 0.1g; CHOLESTEROL 88mg; IRON 1.3mg; SODIUM 713mg; CALCIUM 24mg

(pictured on page 145)

▶ carbo rating: 2

Herb-Baked Trout

The key to flavor in this recipe is using fresh lemon juice, fresh basil, and the freshest trout available.

¼	cup minced fresh basil
¼	cup fresh lemon juice (about 2 lemons)
2	teaspoons olive oil
4	(6-ounce) rainbow trout fillets
	Cooking spray
½	teaspoon freshly ground black pepper
¼	teaspoon salt
1	small lemon, thinly sliced

1. Preheat oven to 350°.

2. Combine first 3 ingredients in a liquid measuring cup.

3. Place fillets in a 13 x 9-inch baking dish coated with cooking spray. Sprinkle fillets with pepper and salt; top with lemon slices. Pour half of basil mixture over fillets.

4. Bake at 350° for 13 to 15 minutes or until fish flakes easily when tested with a fork. Spoon remaining basil mixture over fish before serving. Yield: 4 servings (serving size: 1 fillet).

CALORIES 264; FAT 11.6g (sat 3g); PROTEIN 35.8g; CARBOHYDRATE 2.6g; FIBER 0.5g; CHOLESTEROL 100mg; IRON 0.7mg; SODIUM 207mg; CALCIUM 123mg

▶ **carbo rating: 2**
Cajun Shrimp

Cook shrimp just until they appear opaque and turn pink. If you overcook shrimp, they'll be tough and rubbery.

1½ pounds large shrimp, peeled and deveined
1 teaspoon paprika
¾ teaspoon dried thyme
¾ teaspoon dried oregano
¼ teaspoon garlic powder
¼ teaspoon salt
¼ teaspoon pepper
¼ to ½ teaspoon ground red pepper
1 tablespoon vegetable oil

1. Combine first 8 ingredients in a large heavy-duty zip-top plastic bag; seal bag and shake to coat. Heat oil in a large nonstick skillet over medium-high heat until hot. Add shrimp; sauté 4 minutes or until shrimp are done. Yield: 4 servings (serving size: 5 ounces).

CALORIES 185; FAT 6g (sat 1.1g); PROTEIN 29g; CARBOHYDRATE 2.2g; FIBER 0.3g; CHOLESTEROL 215mg; IRON 4.1mg; SODIUM 357mg; CALCIUM 85mg

quick shrimp

To save time in recipes, we often call for peeled, deveined shrimp. You can buy peeled and deveined shrimp in the seafood department of the grocery store or in seafood markets.

The chart below shows how much unpeeled raw shrimp to buy when your recipe calls for peeled and deveined raw shrimp.

Unpeeled Raw Shrimp	Peeled and Deveined Raw Shrimp
⅔ pound	½ pound
1 pound	¾ pound
1⅓ pounds	1 pound
2 pounds	1½ pounds
2⅔ pounds	2 pounds
4 pounds	3 pounds

▶ **carbo rating: 3**
Herb-Marinated Shrimp

To prepare this recipe indoors, place a large grill pan over medium-high heat until hot; coat grill pan with cooking spray. Place skewers on grill pan, and cook 3 minutes on each side or until done.

⅓ cup basil leaves
¼ cup mint leaves
2 tablespoons oregano leaves
½ teaspoon salt
¼ teaspoon pepper
3 garlic cloves, halved
2½ teaspoons extravirgin olive oil
1¼ pounds peeled and deveined large shrimp
Cooking spray

1. Combine first 6 ingredients in a food processor, and pulse until mixture is coarsely chopped. Add olive oil, and process until well blended.
2. Combine herb mixture and shrimp in a large bowl; toss to coat. Cover and marinate shrimp in refrigerator 30 minutes.
3. Thread shrimp onto 6 (12-inch) skewers.
4. Prepare grill.
5. Place skewers on grill rack coated with cooking spray; grill 3 minutes on each side or until done. Yield: 3 servings (serving size: 2 skewers).

CALORIES 248; FAT 7.3g (sat 1.2g); PROTEIN 39.1g; CARBOHYDRATE 4.1g; FIBER 0.8g; CHOLESTEROL 287mg; IRON 5.7mg; SODIUM 670mg; CALCIUM 139mg

► carbo rating: 3

Cajun Barbecued Shrimp

For a shortcut, replace the first 8 ingredients with about 2 tablespoons of Cajun or Creole seasoning blend.

2	teaspoons garlic powder
2	teaspoons paprika
1	teaspoon onion powder
1	teaspoon dried thyme
½	teaspoon dried oregano
½	teaspoon ground red pepper
¼	teaspoon salt
¼	teaspoon freshly ground black pepper
1½	pounds peeled and deveined large shrimp
	Cooking spray

1. Prepare grill.

2. Combine first 8 ingredients in a large zip-top plastic bag. Add shrimp. Seal bag; shake to coat. Let stand 5 minutes.

3. Remove shrimp from bag; discard seasoning mixture. Thread shrimp onto 4 (12-inch) skewers. Place skewers on grill rack coated with cooking spray; grill over medium-hot coals (350° to 400°) 3 minutes on each side or until done. Yield: 4 servings (serving size: 1 skewer).

CALORIES 192; FAT 3.2g (sat 0.6g); PROTEIN 35.1g; CARBOHYDRATE 4.1g; FIBER 0.9g; CHOLESTEROL 237mg; IRON 4.7mg; SODIUM 379mg; CALCIUM 97mg

how much shrimp to buy?

When our recipes call for 1½ pounds peeled and deveined shrimp, that means you need to buy 1½ pounds of shrimp that has already been peeled and deveined. If the recipe calls for 1½ pounds shrimp, peeled and deveined, that means you need to buy 1½ pounds of unpeeled shrimp, then peel and devein the shrimp yourself.

don't skimp on shrimp

Although shrimp is a little higher in sodium and cholesterol than other types of seafood, it's still a terrific protein source and very low in fat. A 6-ounce portion of shrimp has 35 grams of protein and only 2.9 grams of fat. The carbohydrate content of shrimp is negligible, as long as you're not dipping it into a high-carb cocktail sauce.

► carbo rating: 3

Shrimp with Cilantro and Lime

Serve this spicy shrimp mixture over a bed of shredded lettuce or mixed greens.

1¾	pounds large shrimp, peeled and deveined
2	tablespoons fresh lime juice
½	teaspoon ground cumin
¼	teaspoon ground ginger
2	garlic cloves, minced
1	tablespoon olive oil
¼	cup chopped fresh cilantro
1	teaspoon grated lime rind
½	teaspoon salt
¼	teaspoon pepper

1. Combine first 5 ingredients in a large bowl; toss well. Heat oil in a large nonstick skillet over medium-high heat. Add shrimp mixture, and sauté 4 minutes or until shrimp are done. Remove from heat; stir in cilantro and remaining ingredients. Yield: 4 servings (serving size: about 1½ cups).

CALORIES 196; FAT 6.2g (sat 1g); PROTEIN 30.5g; CARBOHYDRATE 2.9g; FIBER 0.3g; CHOLESTEROL 226mg; IRON 3.8mg; SODIUM 512mg; CALCIUM 85mg

▶ carbo rating: 3

Shrimp Scampi

Shrimp scampi is often served over rice or pasta, but the flavors of the shrimp, garlic, and lemon juice are more pronounced when you serve the dish without the starch.

1½ tablespoons olive oil
1½ tablespoons bottled minced garlic
1½ pounds peeled and deveined large shrimp
¼ cup finely chopped fresh flat-leaf parsley
1½ tablespoons fresh lemon juice
½ teaspoon salt
⅛ teaspoon ground red pepper

1. Heat oil in a large nonstick skillet over medium-low heat; add garlic, and cook 1 minute. Add shrimp, and cook 5 minutes or until shrimp turn pink, stirring occasionally; remove from heat. Stir in parsley and remaining ingredients. Yield: 4 servings (serving size: 1 cup).

CALORIES 233; FAT 8g (sat 1.2g); PROTEIN 34.9g; CARBOHYDRATE 3.4g; FIBER 0.2g; CHOLESTEROL 258mg; IRON 4.4mg; SODIUM 549mg; CALCIUM 100mg

▶ carbo rating: 3

Tuna Steaks with Salsa

Made with fresh vegetables and lots of ripe tomatoes, salsa is a nutrition superstar, packed full of vitamin C and cancer-fighting antioxidants.

4 (6-ounce) tuna steaks (about ½ inch thick)
Olive oil-flavored cooking spray
½ teaspoon salt-free garlic-herb seasoning
1 cup chunky salsa

1. Lightly coat both sides of fish with cooking spray; sprinkle both sides with seasoning. Coat a large nonstick skillet with cooking spray. Place over medium-high heat until hot. Add fish; cook 2 minutes on each side or to desired degree of doneness. Serve immediately with salsa. Yield: 4 servings (serving size: 1 steak and ¼ cup salsa).

CALORIES 263; FAT 8.5g (sat 2.1g); PROTEIN 40.3g; CARBOHYDRATE 3.4g; FIBER 0.6g; CHOLESTEROL 64mg; IRON 1.8mg; SODIUM 430mg; CALCIUM 26mg

▶ carbo rating: 3

Grouper with Roasted Asparagus and Peppers

Roasting fresh vegetables brings out their natural sweetness, so you get a richer, more full-bodied flavor.

24 asparagus spears (about ½ pound)
1 cup red bell pepper strips (¼ inch thick), cut in half crosswise
1 tablespoon olive oil
Cooking spray
1 tablespoon fresh lemon juice
1 teaspoon dried dill, divided
½ teaspoon salt, divided
4 (6-ounce) grouper or other firm white fish fillets
⅛ teaspoon black pepper

1. Preheat oven to 425°.
2. Snap off tough ends of asparagus. Cut asparagus into 2-inch pieces. Toss asparagus and bell peppers with olive oil, and place on a jelly roll pan coated with cooking spray. Bake at 425° for 8 to 10 minutes or until crisp-tender, stirring occasionally. Remove from oven. Sprinkle with lemon juice, ¾ teaspoon dill, and ¼ teaspoon salt, tossing gently to coat. Set aside, and keep warm.
3. Arrange fillets on a jelly roll pan coated with cooking spray. Sprinkle fillets evenly with ¼ teaspoon dill, ¼ teaspoon salt, and black pepper. Bake at 425° for 10 to 12 minutes or until fish flakes easily when tested with a fork. Top with asparagus mixture. Serve immediately. Yield: 4 servings (serving size: 1 fillet and ½ cup asparagus mixture).

CALORIES 207; FAT 5.3g (sat 0.9g); PROTEIN 34.7g; CARBOHYDRATE 4.3g; FIBER 1.4g; CHOLESTEROL 63mg; IRON 2.2mg; SODIUM 388mg; CALCIUM 64mg

the fat in fish

The amount of fat in fish varies, but the fat is a heart-healthy type of fat that helps prevent heart disease.

Fish	*Serving Size (cooked)	Calories	Fat (grams)
Amberjack	4½ ounces	135	2.3
Arctic char	4½ ounces	234	10.1
Catfish	4½ ounces	194	10.2
Cod	4½ ounces	134	1.1
Halibut	4½ ounces	179	3.8
Mahimahi	4½ ounces	139	1.2
Pompano	4½ ounces	269	15.5
Red snapper	4½ ounces	163	2.2
Salmon	4½ ounces	224	10.5
Sole/Flounder	4½ ounces	149	2.0
Swordfish	4½ ounces	198	6.6
Tilapia	4½ ounces	106	1.0
Trout	4½ ounces	243	10.8
Tuna	4½ ounces	178	1.6

*Most of our fish recipes call for 6 ounces of uncooked fish per serving which, when cooked, is equal to 4½ ounces.

▶ carbo rating: 3

Moroccan-Roasted Salmon

If you cannot find the Moroccan spice blend, use equal parts of cinnamon, cloves, cumin, ground red pepper, and turmeric.

¼ cup plain low-fat yogurt
1½ teaspoons fresh lime juice
1 teaspoon chopped fresh mint
⅛ teaspoon salt
Olive oil-flavored cooking spray
2 (6-ounce) salmon fillets
2 lime wedges
1 teaspoon Moroccan rub (such as The Spice Hunter)
½ teaspoon salt

1. Preheat oven to 400°.

2. Combine yogurt, lime juice, mint, and ⅛ teaspoon salt; set aside.

3. Line broiler pan with foil; coat with cooking spray. Place fish on broiler pan. Squeeze lime juice from lime wedges over fish. Sprinkle fish with Moroccan seasoning and ½ teaspoon salt; coat with cooking spray. Bake at 400° for 15 minutes or until fish flakes easily when tested with a fork. Serve with yogurt sauce. Yield: 2 servings (serving size: 1 fillet and 2 tablespoons yogurt sauce).

CALORIES 220; FAT 6.4g (sat 1.3g); PROTEIN 35.6g; CARBOHYDRATE 3.4g; FIBER 0.3g; CHOLESTEROL 90mg; IRON 1.4mg; SODIUM 869mg; CALCIUM 80mg

▶ carbo rating: 3

Blackened Tuna with Orange-Zested Salsa

Letting the salsa mixture chill gives the ingredients time to blend, which enhances the flavor.

½ cup chopped yellow bell pepper
½ cup diced seeded tomato
¼ cup chopped green onions
2 tablespoons chopped fresh cilantro
1 tablespoon lime juice
1 teaspoon fresh grated orange rind
2 teaspoons cider vinegar
¼ teaspoon salt
1 finely chopped seeded jalapeño pepper
2 teaspoons blackening seasoning
4 (6-ounce) tuna steaks (about 1 inch thick)
1 teaspoon vegetable oil

1. Combine first 9 ingredients in a small bowl; toss gently. Cover and chill 1 hour.
2. Sprinkle blackening seasoning on both sides of fish, pressing down firmly to allow seasoning to adhere to fish.
3. Heat oil in a cast iron skillet over medium-high heat. Add fish, and cook 4 minutes on each side or until fish is medium-rare or desired degree of doneness. Yield: 4 servings (serving size: 1 steak and ⅓ cup salsa).

CALORIES 194; FAT 2.9g (sat 0.6g); PROTEIN 36.4g; CARBOHYDRATE 3.7g; FIBER 1.1g; CHOLESTEROL 77mg; IRON 2.3mg; SODIUM 399mg; CALCIUM 52mg

(pictured on page 79)

▶ carbo rating: 4

Grilled Tuna with Herbed Mayonnaise

Be creative and experiment with a variety of fresh herbs to make up your own herbed mayonnaise.

¼ cup fat-free mayonnaise
¼ cup plain fat-free yogurt
1 teaspoon chopped fresh oregano
1 teaspoon chopped fresh tarragon
1 teaspoon fresh lemon juice
¼ teaspoon salt
¼ teaspoon pepper
4 (6-ounce) tuna steaks (about 1 inch thick)
Cooking spray

1. Prepare grill.
2. Combine first 5 ingredients in a small bowl. Cover and chill.
3. Sprinkle salt and pepper over steaks. Place steaks on grill rack coated with cooking spray; grill 3 minutes on each side or until steaks are medium-rare or to desired degree of doneness. Top steaks with mayonnaise mixture before serving. Yield: 4 servings (serving size: 1 steak and 2 tablespoons mayonnaise mixture).

CALORIES 267; FAT 8.5g (sat 2.2g); PROTEIN 40.5g; CARBOHYDRATE 4.6g; FIBER 0.1g; CHOLESTEROL 65mg; IRON 8.6mg; SODIUM 414mg; CALCIUM 288mg

mayonnaise matters

Because tuna is a high-fat fish (but it's the heart-healthy type of fat), we used fat-free mayonnaise to keep the total fat from being too high. You can use light or regular mayonnaise if you prefer.

Here's a quick comparison of the carbohydrate content of three different types of mayo.

Mayonnaise	Carbohydrate (grams)
Fat-free, 1 tablespoon	2.0
Light, 1 tablespoon	1.3
Regular, 1 tablespoon	0.0

▶ carbo rating: 4

Cold Poached Salmon with Summer Tomato Dressing

Make this chilled fish dish in the steamy days of summer when the temperatures are high and tomatoes are at their peak.

1	cup water
1	cup dry white wine
6	(6-ounce) salmon fillets
¼	cup minced shallots
2	tablespoons white wine vinegar
1	tablespoon extravirgin olive oil
1	tablespoon Dijon mustard
2	garlic cloves, minced
½	teaspoon salt
¼	teaspoon freshly ground black pepper
1	large tomato, finely chopped
⅓	cup packed basil leaves, finely chopped

1. Combine water and wine in a large skillet. Bring to a boil. Add fillets, skin side up; cover, reduce heat, and simmer 5 minutes. Remove from heat, and let stand, covered, 20 minutes or until fish flakes easily when tested with a fork. Remove fillets from poaching liquid, reserving ½ cup liquid. Cover fillets, and chill.
2. Combine reserved ½ cup poaching liquid, shallots, and next 6 ingredients in a bowl; cover and chill.
3. Combine tomato and basil; cover and chill.
4. Remove and discard skin from fillets. Serve pink side up. Stir tomato and basil into shallot dressing just before serving. Spoon tomato dressing over fillets. Yield: 6 servings (serving size: 1 fillet and ⅓ cup dressing).

CALORIES 282; FAT 13.4g (sat 2g); PROTEIN 34.4g; CARBOHYDRATE 4.1g; FIBER 0.6g; CHOLESTEROL 94mg; IRON 1.9mg; SODIUM 353mg; CALCIUM 34mg

(pictured on page 80)

▶ carbo rating: 4

Cajun-Style Swordfish

The touch of sweetness from the pickle relish balances the spiciness of the blackening seasoning and the acidity of the lemon juice. A tablespoon of sweet relish has 5 grams of carbohydrate, or about 1 gram per serving in this recipe.

4	(6-ounce) swordfish fillets (1 inch thick)
	Olive oil-flavored cooking spray
1½	teaspoons blackening seasoning, divided
⅓	cup fat-free mayonnaise
1	tablespoon sweet pickle relish
1	teaspoon fresh lemon juice
	Lemon wedges (optional)

1. Preheat broiler.
2. Coat both sides of fish with cooking spray; sprinkle evenly with 1¼ teaspoons blackening seasoning. Place fish on broiler pan coated with cooking spray. Broil 6 minutes on each side or until fish flakes easily when tested with a fork.
3. While fish broils, combine mayonnaise, ¼ teaspoon seasoning, relish, and lemon juice, stirring well. Serve fish immediately with mayonnaise mixture and, if desired, lemon wedges. Yield: 4 servings (serving size: 1 fillet and 1½ tablespoons mayonnaise mixture).

CALORIES 226; FAT 7.4g (sat 2g); PROTEIN 33.7g; CARBOHYDRATE 4.1g; FIBER 0.5g; CHOLESTEROL 68mg; IRON 1.4mg; SODIUM 487mg; CALCIUM 8.3mg

▶ carbo rating: 4

Catfish Baked with Tomato-Kalamata Topping

When you use flavor-packed ingredients such as cilantro and kalamata olives, you don't need to add much of anything else to give the fish "pizzazz."

2¼   cups seeded chopped plum tomato
½   cup pitted chopped kalamata olives
⅓   cup chopped fresh cilantro
Cooking spray
4   (6-ounce) farm-raised catfish fillets

1. Preheat oven to 375°.
2. Combine first 3 ingredients in a bowl; stir well.
3. Place fillets in a 13 x 9-inch baking dish coated with cooking spray; top with tomato mixture. Bake fillets at 375° for 25 minutes or until fish flakes easily when tested with a fork. Yield: 4 servings (serving size: 1 fillet and about ¾ cup tomato topping).

CALORIES 232; FAT 9.3g (sat 2g); PROTEIN 31.2g; CARBOHYDRATE 5.3g; FIBER 1.6g; CHOLESTEROL 97mg; IRON 2.7mg; SODIUM 268mg; CALCIUM 89mg

▶ carbo rating: 4

Sautéed Scallops with White Wine Reduction

As it evaporates and reduces, the wine combines with the flavorful browned bits in the pan to create a rich sauce.

⅓   cup dry white wine
3   tablespoons water
2   tablespoons minced fresh onion
1   garlic clove, minced
1   teaspoon Dijon mustard
½   teaspoon dried oregano
1   pound sea scallops
½   teaspoon salt
¼   teaspoon freshly ground black pepper
2   teaspoons olive oil
2   tablespoons light butter
2   tablespoons chopped fresh parsley

1. Combine first 6 ingredients; set aside.
2. Sprinkle scallops with salt and pepper. Heat oil in a large nonstick skillet over medium-high heat until hot. Add scallops; cook 2 minutes on each side or until done. Remove scallops from pan; keep warm.
3. Pour wine mixture into pan; cook over medium-high heat, scraping pan to loosen browned bits. Bring to a boil, and cook 1 minute or until reduced to ⅓ cup. Remove from heat; stir in butter. Spoon sauce over scallops; sprinkle scallops with parsley. Yield: 4 servings (serving size: 3 ounces scallops and 2 tablespoons sauce).

CALORIES 152; FAT 6.3g (sat 2.4g); PROTEIN 19.8g; CARBOHYDRATE 4.1g; FIBER 0.3g; CHOLESTEROL 47mg; IRON 0.7mg; SODIUM 543mg; CALCIUM 39mg

► **carbo rating: 4**

Lobster Tails with Chunky Tomato Salsa

If you don't want to use fresh lobster tails, the frozen ones are fine.

1½   cups finely chopped seeded tomato (about 2 medium)
2   tablespoons minced green onions
2   tablespoons finely chopped fresh parsley
1   tablespoon balsamic vinegar
1   teaspoon water
1   teaspoon olive oil
½   teaspoon dried whole tarragon
⅛   teaspoon salt
⅛   teaspoon pepper
4   (6- or 7-ounce) lobster tails
1   tablespoon balsamic vinegar
1   tablespoon water
½   teaspoon olive oil
¼   teaspoon dried tarragon

1. Combine first 9 ingredients in a bowl. Cover and chill 1 hour.
2. Preheat broiler.
3. Gently loosen lobster meat from top inside of shells. Cut lengthwise through top of shells using kitchen shears; press shells open. Starting at cut end of tails, carefully loosen meat from bottom of shells; keep meat attached at end of tails. Lift meat through top shell opening; place on top of shells.
4. Place lobster tails on a rack in a shallow roasting pan. Combine vinegar, water, oil, and tarragon; brush lobster with half of vinegar mixture. Broil 10 minutes or until lobster flesh turns opaque; baste with remaining vinegar mixture after 5 minutes. Serve with salsa. Yield: 4 servings (serving size: 1 lobster tail and ½ cup salsa).

CALORIES 126; FAT 2.5g (sat 0.4g); PROTEIN 20.5g; CARBOHYDRATE 5g; FIBER 0.9g; CHOLESTEROL 69mg; IRON 1mg; SODIUM 447mg; CALCIUM 69mg

► **carbo rating: 5**

Grouper with Tomato, Olive, and Wine Sauce

Use a dry white wine such as an American Sauvignon Blanc, which will be very dry and will offer an herbal flavor that enhances the dish.

Cooking spray
½   cup chopped onion
2   teaspoons bottled minced garlic
½   cup dry white wine
⅓   cup fat-free, less-sodium chicken broth
1   cup quartered cherry tomatoes
¼   cup pitted ripe olives, halved
1   tablespoon chopped fresh herbs, such as basil, parsley, or oregano
1   tablespoon olive oil
4   (6-ounce) grouper fillets (about ½ inch thick)
¼   teaspoon salt
¼   teaspoon pepper

1. Heat a medium saucepan coated with cooking spray over medium-high heat. Add onion and garlic; sauté 3 minutes. Add wine and broth; reduce heat, cover, and simmer 3 minutes. Stir in tomatoes, olives, and herbs; cover and cook 3 minutes. Remove from heat; keep warm.
2. Heat oil in a large nonstick skillet over medium-high heat. Sprinkle both sides of fish with salt and pepper. Add fish to pan; cook 4 minutes on each side or until fish flakes easily when tested with a fork. Top with tomato mixture. Yield: 4 servings (serving size: 1 fillet and ¼ cup tomato mixture).

CALORIES 268; FAT 9.3g (sat 1.9g); PROTEIN 28.9g; CARBOHYDRATE 6.9g; FIBER 1.9g; CHOLESTEROL 82mg; IRON 1.6mg; SODIUM 717mg; CALCIUM 63mg

▶ carbo rating: 5

Flounder Florentine

Popeye will probably never need glasses, since spinach contains lutein, a substance that may help prevent macular degeneration—the most common cause of blindness in the elderly.

Cooking spray
- ½ cup minced onion
- 2 garlic cloves, minced
- 1 (10-ounce) package frozen chopped spinach, thawed, drained, and squeezed dry
- ½ cup (4 ounces) tub-style light cream cheese
- 3 tablespoons grated fresh Parmesan cheese
- 2 tablespoons 1% low-fat milk
- ¼ teaspoon salt
- ¼ teaspoon black pepper
- ⅛ teaspoon ground red pepper
- 4 (6-ounce) flounder fillets

1. Preheat oven to 350°.
2. Heat a large nonstick skillet coated with cooking spray over medium heat. Add onion and garlic; sauté 3 minutes or until tender. Add spinach, and cook 1 minute.
3. Turn heat to low; add cream cheese and next 5 ingredients. Stir well; remove from heat.
4. Divide spinach mixture among fillets, spreading evenly over each and leaving a ¼-inch margin around edges.
5. Roll up each fillet, jelly roll fashion, starting with tail end, and secure with wooden picks.
6. Place fish in a 13 x 9-inch baking dish coated with cooking spray. Bake at 350° for 20 to 22 minutes or until fish flakes easily when tested with a fork. Serve immediately. Yield: 4 servings (serving size: 1 fillet).

CALORIES 271; FAT 8.7g (sat 5g); PROTEIN 38.4g; CARBOHYDRATE 7.7g; FIBER 2.6g; CHOLESTEROL 106mg; IRON 2mg; SODIUM 574mg; CALCIUM 223mg

▶ carbo rating: 5

Caesar Mahimahi

*Mahimahi (dolphinfish) is a moderately fat fish with firm, flavorful flesh. Although it's called dolphinfish, it is not the same as the mammal dolphin. To avoid this confusion, dolphinfish is usually referred to by its Hawaiian name—**mahimahi**.*

- ¼ cup plain fat-free yogurt
- 2 tablespoons grated Parmesan cheese
- 2 tablespoons fresh lemon juice
- 2 tablespoons low-fat buttermilk
- 1 tablespoon Dijon mustard
- 2 teaspoons Worcestershire sauce
- 2 teaspoons anchovy paste
- ¼ teaspoon pepper
- 6 garlic cloves, crushed
- 4 (6-ounce) mahimahi or other firm white fish fillets

Cooking spray

1. Combine first 9 ingredients, and stir well with a whisk. Pour yogurt mixture into a large zip-top plastic bag; add fish to bag. Seal and marinate in refrigerator 20 minutes.
2. Prepare grill or broiler.
3. Remove fish from bag, reserving marinade. Place fish on grill rack or broiler pan coated with cooking spray. Cook 3 minutes on each side or until fish flakes easily when tested with a fork, basting frequently with reserved marinade. Yield: 4 servings (serving size: 1 fillet).

CALORIES 193; FAT 3g (sat 0.8g); PROTEIN 34.7g; CARBOHYDRATE 4.7g; FIBER 0.1g; CHOLESTEROL 127mg; IRON 2.1mg; SODIUM 728mg; CALCIUM 84mg

► carbo rating: 5

Greek-Style Orange Roughy

The black-purple, almond-shaped kalamata olive is also known as a Greek-style olive.

    1   tablespoon olive oil
    1   onion, halved and thinly sliced (about 2 cups)
    1   green bell pepper, thinly sliced (about 1½ cups)
    1   red bell pepper, thinly sliced (about 1½ cups)
    5   garlic cloves, coarsely chopped
    1   medium tomato, chopped (about 1¼ cups)
    ¾   teaspoon salt
    6   (6-ounce) orange roughy fillets
  Cooking spray
    ¼   cup chopped pitted kalamata olives

1. Preheat oven to 425°.

2. Place oil in a large nonstick skillet over medium-high heat until hot. Add onion and next 3 ingredients; cook 10 minutes or until vegetables are crisp-tender, stirring frequently. Add tomato and salt; cook 2 minutes, stirring frequently.

3. Place fillets in a 13 x 9-inch baking dish coated with cooking spray. Place onion mixture on top of fillets. Sprinkle with olives. Bake, uncovered, at 425° for 20 minutes or until fish flakes easily when tested with a fork. Yield: 6 servings (serving size: 1 fillet and about ⅔ cup onion mixture).

CALORIES 180; FAT 4.9g (sat 0.4g); PROTEIN 26.1g; CARBOHYDRATE 7g; FIBER 1.5g; CHOLESTEROL 34mg; IRON 0.9mg; SODIUM 445mg; CALCIUM 67mg

(pictured on page 146)

► carbo rating: 5

Creole Baked Snapper

To decrease the spiciness of this dish, use a mild hot sauce such as Crystal Hot Sauce in place of regular hot sauce.

    1   tablespoon olive oil
    ½   cup chopped green bell pepper
    ½   cup chopped celery
    ½   cup chopped onion
    ½   teaspoon dried thyme
  1¼   cups coarsely chopped tomato
    ¼   teaspoon salt
    ¼   teaspoon black pepper
    2   garlic cloves, minced
    2   teaspoons hot sauce
  Cooking spray
    4   (6-ounce) red snapper fillets
    ½   teaspoon Creole seasoning
    ¼   cup finely chopped fresh parsley

1. Preheat oven to 400°.

2. Heat oil in a large nonstick skillet over medium-high heat. Sauté bell pepper, celery, onion, and thyme 5 minutes or until onion just begins to brown. Stir in tomato and next 3 ingredients. Bring to a boil; cover, reduce heat, and simmer 2 minutes. Remove from heat. Stir in hot sauce.

3. Arrange fish in a single layer in a 13 x 9-inch baking dish coated with cooking spray. Sprinkle with Creole seasoning, and top with vegetables. Bake at 400° for 15 minutes or until fish flakes easily when tested with a fork. Sprinkle with parsley. Yield: 4 servings (serving size: 1 fillet).

CALORIES 224; FAT 5.9g (sat 1g); PROTEIN 34.8g; CARBOHYDRATE 7g; FIBER 1.9g; CHOLESTEROL 60mg; IRON 1.2mg; SODIUM 329mg; CALCIUM 76mg

► carbo rating: 5
Scallops with Basil and Tomato

The delicate flavor of sweet scallops comes alive when they're tossed with fresh tomatoes and olive oil.

1	cup chopped seeded tomato (about 1 large)
2	tablespoons chopped fresh parsley
½	teaspoon dried basil leaves
1	garlic clove, minced
½	teaspoon salt
¼	teaspoon freshly ground black pepper
1	tablespoon olive oil
1	tablespoon light butter
1	pound sea scallops

Lemon wedges (optional)

1. Combine first 6 ingredients in a small bowl. Set aside.
2. Heat oil and butter in a large nonstick skillet over medium-high heat. Add scallops, and cook 2 minutes on each side.
3. Add tomato mixture to pan, and cook 1 minute, stirring gently, until thoroughly heated. Serve immediately with lemon wedges, if desired. Yield: 4 servings (serving size: ½ cup).

CALORIES 154; FAT 5.9g (sat 1.6g); PROTEIN 19.8g; CARBOHYDRATE 5.3g; FIBER 0.7g; CHOLESTEROL 42mg; IRON 0.7mg; SODIUM 496mg; CALCIUM 37mg

► carbo rating: 5
Pan-Seared Scallops with Cilantro

Two things are important when searing any food: Use a very hot skillet, and cook the food in small batches. The high heat seals in the juices so that the food browns quickly.

1	pound sea scallops
1	teaspoon chili powder
½	teaspoon salt
¼	teaspoon black pepper
1	tablespoon light butter, divided

Cooking spray

¼	cup water
½	jalapeño pepper, seeded and minced
2	tablespoons fresh lime juice
2	tablespoons minced fresh cilantro

1. Sprinkle both sides of scallops with chili powder, salt, and black pepper.
2. Melt 1½ teaspoons butter in a large nonstick skillet coated with cooking spray over medium-high heat. Add half of scallops; cook 3 minutes on each side or until done. Remove scallops from pan; keep warm. Repeat procedure with remaining butter and scallops.
3. Add water, jalapeño pepper, and lime juice to pan; cook 1 minute, scraping bottom and sides of pan to loosen browned bits. Spoon sauce over scallops; sprinkle with cilantro. Yield: 4 servings (serving size: 3 ounces scallops and about 2 tablespoons sauce).

CALORIES 118; FAT 2.5g (sat 1.1g); PROTEIN 19.5g; CARBOHYDRATE 4.1g; FIBER 0.3g; CHOLESTEROL 42mg; IRON 0.4mg; SODIUM 497mg; CALCIUM 31mg

▶ carbo rating: 6

Grilled Tuna Steaks with Horseradish Sauce

If you eat a 6-ounce tuna steak instead of the same size filet mignon, you'll save about 250 calories and 33 grams of fat.

¼	cup Worcestershire sauce
2	tablespoons low-sodium soy sauce
1	tablespoon olive oil
1	teaspoon dried oregano
½	teaspoon freshly ground black pepper
2	garlic cloves, minced
4	(6-ounce) tuna steaks (about 1 inch thick)
½	cup reduced-fat sour cream
1½	teaspoons prepared horseradish
½	teaspoon salt
½	teaspoon Dijon mustard
¼	teaspoon Worcestershire sauce

Cooking spray

1. Combine first 6 ingredients in a large zip-top plastic bag. Add fish to bag; seal and marinate in refrigerator 1 hour, turning once.
2. Combine sour cream and next 4 ingredients in a small bowl; set aside.
3. Prepare grill.
4. Remove fish from marinade, reserving marinade. Place fish on grill rack coated with cooking spray; grill 6 minutes on each side or until fish is medium-rare or desired degree of doneness, basting frequently with reserved marinade. Serve with sour cream mixture. Yield: 4 servings (serving size: 1 steak and 2 tablespoons sour cream mixture).

CALORIES 268; FAT 8.8g (sat 3.4g); PROTEIN 38.1g; CARBOHYDRATE 6.6g; FIBER 0.4g; CHOLESTEROL 92mg; IRON 3.3mg; SODIUM 864mg; CALCIUM 127mg

fire up the coals

Grilling seafood is easy if you know which kinds work best. You want fish that has a thick, firm, meaty texture so that it won't fall apart while cooking. The seafood listed below is particularly suitable for the grill.

Grouper: This white-meat fish is sold in fillets and steaks. If you can't find grouper, use sea bass, orange roughy, or mahimahi.

Halibut: The meat of halibut is white and mild-flavored, and comes in steaks and fillets. Although it's a firm fish, it's a tad more delicate than others—so be gentle when turning it on the grill.

Salmon: With a range of flavor from rich to mild, salmon can take on a char and still keep its distinctive taste. Salmon comes in steaks and fillets.

Scallops: This bivalve is usually classified into two groups: bay scallops and sea scallops. The larger sea scallops are best for grilling because, like shrimp, they have a meatier texture and can be easily skewered. They cook fast, though, so keep a close eye on them.

Shrimp: Large shrimp are best for grilling. They can be easily skewered, and they cook quickly.

Swordfish: This mild fish has a firm, meaty texture. Its natural oil content keeps it moist while grilling. You can usually find it sold as steaks.

Tuna: If you're new to grilling fish, fresh tuna is a good place to start. It cooks like a beef steak, and its deep-red meat almost never sticks to the grill.

▶ carbo rating: 6
Tilapia en Papillote

En papillote *refers to food baked inside a wrapping of parchment paper. It's a great way to cook fish because the fish stays moist and tender. If you don't have parchment paper, you can use a sheet of foil.*

  2   (6-ounce) tilapia fillets
  6   grape tomatoes, halved lengthwise
  ¼   cup thinly sliced yellow squash (about 1 small)
  ¼   cup thinly sliced zucchini (about ½ small)
  ¼   cup (1 ounce) crumbled feta cheese with garlic and herbs
  2   tablespoons sliced green onions (about 1 onion)
  ¼   teaspoon salt
  ¼   teaspoon freshly ground black pepper
  3   tablespoons reduced-calorie olive oil vinaigrette

1. Preheat oven to 400°.
2. Cut 2 (15 x 13-inch) rectangles of parchment paper; fold each rectangle in half lengthwise. Place parchment sheets on an ungreased baking sheet, and open out flat.
3. Place 1 fillet on half of each parchment sheet near the crease. Place 6 tomato halves, cut sides down, on 1 side of each fillet; place squash and zucchini slices alternately on other side of each fillet. Sprinkle fish with cheese, green onions, salt, and pepper. Drizzle vinaigrette over fish.
4. Fold paper edges over to seal securely; cut off open corners to make a half-moon. Starting with rounded edge of fold, pleat and crimp edges of parchment to make an airtight seal. Bake at 400° for 15 minutes or until packets are puffed.
5. Place packets on individual serving plates. Cut an opening in the top of each packet, and fold paper back. Serve immediately. Yield: 2 servings (serving size: 1 fillet and ½ of vegetable mixture).

CALORIES 256; FAT 9.8g (sat 2.8g); PROTEIN 34.9g; CARBOHYDRATE 7g; FIBER 1.3g; CHOLESTEROL 94mg; IRON 1.2mg; SODIUM 776mg; CALCIUM 114mg

(pictured on page 147)

▶ carbo rating: 7
Corfu-Style Cod

When you simmer a mixture with wine, most of the alcohol evaporates, leaving only the flavor of the wine in this Greek-style dish.

  1   tablespoon olive oil
  2   cups chopped leek
  2   garlic cloves, minced
  1½   teaspoons paprika
  ¼   teaspoon ground red pepper
  1   cup dry red wine
  1   tablespoon tomato paste
  1   teaspoon salt
  4   (6-ounce) cod fillets

1. Heat oil in a large nonstick skillet over medium-high heat until hot. Add leek and garlic; sauté 3 minutes. Add paprika and red pepper; sauté 1 minute. Add wine and tomato paste; reduce heat, and simmer 4 minutes.
2. Sprinkle salt evenly over both sides of fillets. Add to pan, nestling fillets in leek mixture. Cover, reduce heat, and simmer 15 minutes or until fish flakes easily when tested with a fork. Yield: 4 servings (serving size: 1 fillet and ⅓ cup sauce).

CALORIES 204; FAT 4.8g (sat 0.7g); PROTEIN 31.3g; CARBOHYDRATE 7.8g; FIBER 0.9g; CHOLESTEROL 73mg; IRON 1.9mg; SODIUM 689mg; CALCIUM 59mg

leek lessons

Although leeks resemble large green onions, they're milder and sweeter, and they don't cause any tears when they're chopped. Unlike other alliums such as onions, leeks are almost always enjoyed cooked since they're very fibrous when raw. The tougher, green part usually has a coarser flavor than the white part. Use the green part to flavor soups and stocks; add the white part (which is tender and needs only brief cooking) to soups and stews toward the end of cooking. Leeks are often paired with ingredients such as coriander, bay, and oregano to create a Greek-style flavor.

▶ carbo rating: 7

Halibut Provençale

Serve this Mediterranean dish in a big shallow bowl to hold all the delicious juices.

1	tablespoon olive oil
2	garlic cloves, sliced
2½	cups slivered onion
½	teaspoon salt, divided
2	cups chopped peeled plum tomato (about 4 tomatoes)
1¾	cups thinly sliced fennel bulb (about 1 small bulb)
1	cup dry white wine
⅓	cup chopped fresh basil
¼	cup chopped pitted kalamata olives
1	tablespoon tomato paste
2	teaspoons capers
⅛	teaspoon crushed red pepper
1	bay leaf
½	cup water
⅛	teaspoon black pepper
6	(6-ounce) halibut or cod fillets

1. Preheat oven to 450°.
2. Heat oil in a large ovenproof skillet over medium-high heat, and add garlic. Sauté 30 seconds; add onion and ¼ teaspoon salt. Cook 2 minutes, stirring occasionally. Add tomato and next 8 ingredients; cook 10 minutes. Stir in water.
3. Sprinkle ¼ teaspoon salt and black pepper over fish; place fish on top of onion mixture. Cover and bake at 450° for 10 minutes or until fish flakes easily when tested with a fork. Discard bay leaf. Yield: 6 servings (serving size: 1 fillet and ⅔ cup onion mixture).

CALORIES 279; FAT 7g (sat 0.9g); PROTEIN 37g; CARBOHYDRATE 10g; FIBER 2.6g; CHOLESTEROL 54mg; IRON 2.4mg; SODIUM 392mg; CALCIUM 119mg

▶ carbo rating: 7

Trout with Almonds

Although this recipe is higher in fat than most of the fish entrées in this chapter, the fats are mostly monounsaturated and polyunsaturated, the heart-healthy types of fat. Compare the 15.6 grams of fat in one serving of this dish to the 54 grams of fat found in a serving of traditional trout amandine.

¼	cup all-purpose flour
¼	teaspoon salt
¼	teaspoon pepper
4	(6-ounce) rainbow trout fillets
3	tablespoons yogurt-based spread (such as Brummel & Brown), divided
2	tablespoons fresh lemon juice
2	tablespoons chopped fresh parsley
¼	cup slivered almonds, toasted

1. Combine first 3 ingredients in a large heavy-duty zip-top plastic bag. Add fish; seal bag, and turn gently to coat.
2. Heat 1 tablespoon spread in a large nonstick skillet over medium-high heat. Add fish to pan; cook, turning once, 5 to 6 minutes, or until fish flakes easily when tested with a fork. Set fish aside, and keep warm.
3. Add 2 tablespoons spread, lemon juice, and parsley to pan. Bring to a simmer. Spoon sauce over fish; sprinkle with almonds. Yield: 4 servings (serving size: 1 fillet, 1 tablespoon sauce, and 1 tablespoon almonds).

CALORIES 339; FAT 16.5g (sat 3.7g); PROTEIN 37.8g; CARBOHYDRATE 8.2g; FIBER 1.1g; CHOLESTEROL 100mg; IRON 1.3mg; SODIUM 275mg; CALCIUM 136mg

▶ carbo rating: 7

Broiled Salmon with Cucumber-Dill Sauce

The crisp coolness of cucumber and the bite of fresh dill make a refreshing summer sauce for salmon.

¾   cup reduced-fat sour cream
1   small cucumber, peeled, seeded, and chopped (about ¾ cup)
1   small shallot, peeled and finely chopped
2   tablespoons chopped fresh dill
½   teaspoon salt, divided
½   teaspoon freshly ground black pepper, divided
4   (6-ounce) salmon fillets
Cooking spray
Lemon wedges (optional)

1. Preheat broiler.
2. Combine first 4 ingredients in a small serving bowl; stir in ¼ teaspoon each of salt and pepper. Cover and chill until ready to serve.
3. Sprinkle fillets with ¼ teaspoon each of salt and pepper. Place fillets, skin side up, on broiler rack coated with cooking spray. Broil 7 minutes; turn fillets, and broil 5 to 7 minutes or until fish flakes easily when tested with a fork. Remove skin from fillets. Serve fillets with sauce and lemon wedges, if desired. Yield: 4 servings (serving size: 1 fillet and ⅓ cup sauce).

CALORIES 262; FAT 9.3g (sat 3.8g); PROTEIN 35.8g; CARBOHYDRATE 7.9g; FIBER 0.4g; CHOLESTEROL 95mg; IRON 1mg; SODIUM 421mg; CALCIUM 134mg

▶ carbo rating: 7

Shrimp with Feta

The sprinkle of calorie-free sweetener helps round out the flavors in this dish by balancing the acidity of the tomatoes and the saltiness of the cheese. It's the same reason Italian grandmothers add a pinch of sugar to their tomato sauces.

1   teaspoon olive oil
1½   pounds large shrimp, peeled and deveined
1   cup sliced green onions
4   garlic cloves, minced
1   (14.5-ounce) can diced tomatoes, undrained
1   teaspoon dried oregano
1   teaspoon dried basil
¼   teaspoon "measures-like-sugar" calorie-free sweetener
¼   teaspoon ground red pepper
¾   cup (3 ounces) crumbled feta cheese

1. Preheat broiler.
2. Heat oil in a large nonstick skillet over medium-high heat until hot. Add shrimp; cook, stirring constantly, 3 minutes or until done. Divide shrimp evenly among 4 individual gratin dishes; set aside.
3. Return pan to medium-high heat. Add green onions and garlic; cook, stirring constantly, 1 minute. Add tomatoes, oregano, basil, sweetener, and red pepper; cook 3 minutes or until liquid almost evaporates. Spoon tomato mixture evenly over shrimp, and sprinkle with cheese.
4. Broil 5 minutes or until cheese softens (cheese will not melt). Yield: 4 servings (serving size: 1 gratin dish).

CALORIES 237; FAT 8g (sat 3.8g); PROTEIN 30.5g; CARBOHYDRATE 10.3g; FIBER 2.7g; CHOLESTEROL 213mg; IRON 4.3mg; SODIUM 561mg; CALCIUM 224mg

(pictured on page 148)

▶ **carbo rating: 7**

Baked Shrimp in Lemony Garlic Sauce

This low-fat buttery sauce is good over any type of fish. (See page 111 for the note on buying peeled and deveined shrimp.)

1   pound peeled and deveined large shrimp
Cooking spray
¼   cup fresh lemon juice (about 2 lemons)
2   tablespoons light butter, melted
3   garlic cloves, minced
1   teaspoon Worcestershire sauce
¾   teaspoon lemon pepper seasoning
¼   teaspoon ground red pepper
2   tablespoons chopped fresh parsley

1. Preheat oven to 425°.
2. Arrange shrimp in a single layer in a 13 x 9-inch baking dish coated with cooking spray. Combine lemon juice and next 5 ingredients; pour over shrimp.
3. Bake at 425° for 8 to 10 minutes or until shrimp are done. Sprinkle parsley over shrimp; serve immediately. Yield: 2 servings (serving size: 8 ounces shrimp and ¼ cup sauce).

CALORIES 310; FAT 10g (sat 4.8g); PROTEIN 47.6g; CARBOHYDRATE 7.3g; FIBER 0.4g; CHOLESTEROL 365mg; IRON 6mg; SODIUM 609mg; CALCIUM 138mg

▶ **carbo rating: 7**

Curried Sea Scallops

Scallops are a low-fat source of high-quality protein, with about 1 gram of fat and 24 grams of protein per 5-ounce serving.

⅔   cup fat-free, less-sodium chicken broth
¼   cup fat-free half-and-half
1½ teaspoons fresh lemon juice
¾   teaspoon curry powder
½   teaspoon salt
¼   teaspoon pepper
1¼ pounds sea scallops
4   teaspoons all-purpose flour
Cooking spray
2   teaspoons olive oil, divided
2   tablespoons chopped fresh parsley
2   tablespoons thinly sliced green onions

1. Combine first 6 ingredients in a bowl; stir well, and set aside.
2. Pat scallops dry with paper towels to remove excess moisture; lightly coat with flour. Coat a large nonstick skillet with cooking spray; add 1 teaspoon oil. Place pan over medium-high heat until hot. Add half of scallops; cook 2 minutes on each side. Remove scallops from pan; set aside, and keep warm. Repeat procedure with remaining oil and scallops.
3. Return scallops to pan. Add broth mixture; bring to a boil. Cook 3 minutes or until sauce is slightly thickened. Sprinkle with parsley and green onions. Yield: 4 servings (serving size: 5 ounces scallops and 2 tablespoons sauce).

CALORIES 171; FAT 3.4g (sat 0.4g); PROTEIN 24.7g; CARBOHYDRATE 7.9g; FIBER 0.4g; CHOLESTEROL 47mg; IRON 0.8mg; SODIUM 639mg; CALCIUM 50mg

▶ carbo rating: 8
Lemon-Dill Scallops and Snow Peas

If fresh snow peas aren't available, use frozen sugar snap peas instead.

Cooking spray
- 2 teaspoons reduced-calorie margarine
- ¾ pound bay scallops
- 6 ounces fresh snow pea pods, trimmed at stem end
- 2 teaspoons fresh lemon juice
- ¼ teaspoon salt
- ¼ teaspoon dried dill or ¾ teaspoon chopped fresh dill

1. Lightly coat a nonstick skillet with cooking spray; add margarine, and place over high heat until margarine melts. Add scallops; cook 2 minutes, stirring often. Add snow peas and remaining ingredients; cook 2 minutes, stirring often. Yield: 2 servings (serving size: 6 ounces scallops and 3 ounces peas).

CALORIES 203; FAT 3.4g (sat 0.5g); PROTEIN 31.3g; CARBOHYDRATE 10.4g; FIBER 2.4g; CHOLESTEROL 56mg; IRON 2.1mg; SODIUM 616mg; CALCIUM 80mg

(pictured on page 149)

▶ carbo rating: 8
Shrimp Rémoulade

Rémoulade *is a classic French sauce made with mayonnaise, mustard, capers, chopped gherkins, herbs, and anchovies. This low-carb, reduced-fat version is made with yogurt and light mayonnaise, and has green onions instead of sweet pickles.*

- 3 quarts water
- 2 tablespoons liquid shrimp and crab boil
- 1½ pounds unpeeled medium shrimp
- ⅓ cup minced green onions
- ¼ cup plain fat-free yogurt
- 3 tablespoons Creole mustard
- 3 tablespoons light mayonnaise
- 1 tablespoon olive oil
- ¼ teaspoon dried tarragon
- ⅛ teaspoon salt

1. Combine water and crab boil in a Dutch oven; bring to a boil. Add shrimp; return to a boil, and cook 2 minutes. Remove from heat, and let stand 5 minutes. Drain and rinse with cold water. Peel and chill shrimp.
2. Combine onions and next 6 ingredients in a small bowl, stirring well. Serve sauce with shrimp. Yield: 3 servings (serving size: 6 ounces shrimp and 3 tablespoons sauce).

CALORIES 303; FAT 12.6g (sat 2g); PROTEIN 39g; CARBOHYDRATE 8.3g; FIBER 0.3g; CHOLESTEROL 264mg; IRON 4.4mg; SODIUM 846mg; CALCIUM 140mg

Steamed Mussels with Garlic, Wine, and Cilantro

This simply seasoned dish brings out the fresh-from-the-sea flavor of the mussels.

1½   teaspoons olive oil
8   garlic cloves, thinly sliced
1½   cups water
¾   cup dry white wine
4   pounds small mussels, scrubbed and debearded
¼   teaspoon freshly ground black pepper
½   cup chopped fresh cilantro

1. Heat oil in a large stockpot over medium-high heat. Add garlic; sauté 3 minutes. Add water and wine; bring to a boil. Add mussels; cover and cook over medium-high heat 6 minutes or until shells open, stirring well after 3 minutes. Remove from heat; discard any unopened shells. Sprinkle with pepper and cilantro.
2. Remove mussels with a slotted spoon, and arrange in each of 8 shallow bowls. Yield: 8 servings (serving size: about 12 mussels).

CALORIES 156; FAT 4.8g (sat 0.8g); PROTEIN 17.8g; CARBOHYDRATE 10.2g; FIBER 0.8g; CHOLESTEROL 38mg; IRON 6.6mg; SODIUM 398mg; CALCIUM 70mg

buying, storing, and cleaning clams, oysters, and mussels

Here are some things to keep in mind when you buy fresh oysters, clams, or mussels.
• Bivalves must be alive when you buy them, so it's important that shells are not chipped, cracked, or open. To determine if bivalves that gape are still alive, tap them a few times on a counter. If they close, they're alive. Ask for the shipper's tag that must accompany all mollusks.
• Most fish markets will shuck oysters and clams if you call a few hours ahead.
• Ask for bivalves to be packed on ice on warm days; they prefer cool, damp conditions. Store them between 32° and 40° F (keep mussels at the low end and clams at the high end). Put them in net bags, on trays, or in large bowls draped with wet cloths—this keeps them moist and allows them to breathe. If kept in closed containers, bivalves suffocate.
• It's no longer necessary to place clams in a sink or bowl full of water with cornmeal to get rid of sand and grit before cooking them. Most bivalves now are farm-raised and aren't as sandy.
• Mussels contain beards, or wisps of fibrous material that protrude from the shell; snip or pull these just prior to cooking.

▶ carbo rating: 9

Greek-Style Scampi

The addition of flavorful feta cheese transforms a traditional shrimp scampi recipe into a specialty worthy of the Greek Isles. (See the note on page 111 about buying shrimp.)

1	teaspoon olive oil
5	garlic cloves, minced
2	(28-ounce) cans whole tomatoes, drained and coarsely chopped
½	cup chopped fresh parsley, divided
1½	pounds large shrimp, peeled and deveined
1	cup (4 ounces) crumbled feta cheese
2	tablespoons fresh lemon juice
¼	teaspoon freshly ground pepper

1. Preheat oven to 400°.
2. Heat oil in a large Dutch oven over medium heat. Add garlic; sauté 30 seconds. Add tomatoes and ¼ cup parsley; reduce heat, and simmer 10 minutes. Add shrimp, and cook 5 minutes. Pour mixture into a 13 x 9-inch baking dish; sprinkle with cheese. Bake at 400° for 10 minutes. Sprinkle with remaining parsley, juice, and pepper. Yield: 6 servings (serving size: 2 cups).

CALORIES 203; FAT 8.1g (sat 4.5g); PROTEIN 22.6g; CARBOHYDRATE 10g; FIBER 1.2g; CHOLESTEROL 154mg; IRON 3mg; SODIUM 975mg; CALCIUM 236mg

▶ carbo rating: 9

Vegetable-Steamed Orange Roughy

Steaming fish over a bed of vegetables keeps the fish tender, moist, and infused with flavor.

1	tablespoon olive oil
1	cup green bell pepper strips (about 1 large)
1	cup red bell pepper strips (about 1 large)
1	cup chopped onion (about 1 large)
3	garlic cloves, minced
2	cups yellow squash, cut in half lengthwise and sliced (about 1 large)
⅓	cup water
2	tablespoons fresh lemon juice
1	tablespoon chopped fresh thyme, divided
¾	teaspoon salt, divided
¼	teaspoon hot sauce
4	(6-ounce) orange roughy fillets
¼	teaspoon black pepper

1. Heat olive oil in a 2-inch-deep, straight-sided non-stick skillet or Dutch oven over medium-high heat. Add bell pepper strips, onion, and garlic; sauté 2 minutes. Add squash; sauté 2 minutes.
2. Reduce heat to medium; add water, lemon juice, 2 teaspoons thyme, ½ teaspoon salt, and hot sauce. Arrange fillets in a single layer over vegetable mixture; sprinkle fillets with 1 teaspoon thyme, ¼ teaspoon salt, and black pepper. Cover, reduce heat, and simmer 12 minutes or until fish flakes easily when tested with a fork. Yield: 4 servings (serving size: 1 fillet and 1 cup vegetables).

CALORIES 161; FAT 4.7g (sat 0.6g); PROTEIN 18.7g; CARBOHYDRATE 11.9g; FIBER 3.1g; CHOLESTEROL 23mg; IRON 2.2mg; SODIUM 518mg; CALCIUM 40mg

► carbo rating: 9

Pan-Roasted Grouper with Provençale Vegetables

Use a broiler pan for both the vegetables and the fish in this recipe. The fennel-tomato mixture cooks in the bottom of the pan, helping to steam the fish on the rack above.

2 cups thinly sliced fennel bulb (about 1 medium bulb)
2 tablespoons fresh orange juice
16 picholine olives, pitted and chopped
1 (28-ounce) can whole tomatoes, drained and coarsely chopped
½ teaspoon salt, divided
½ teaspoon black pepper, divided
Cooking spray
2 teaspoons olive oil
1 garlic clove, minced
4 (6-ounce) grouper fillets (about 1 inch thick)

1. Preheat oven to 450°.
2. Combine first 4 ingredients. Add ¼ teaspoon salt and ¼ teaspoon pepper; toss well. Spoon mixture into bottom of a broiler pan coated with cooking spray. Bake at 450° for 10 minutes; stir once.
3. Combine ¼ teaspoon salt, ¼ teaspoon pepper, oil, and garlic; brush evenly over fish. Remove pan from oven. Place fish on rack of pan coated with cooking spray; place rack over fennel mixture.
4. Bake at 450° for 10 minutes or until fish flakes easily when tested with a fork. Yield: 4 servings (serving size: 1 fillet and ¾ cup fennel mixture).

CALORIES 247; FAT 6.9g (sat 0.7g); PROTEIN 33.6g; CARBOHYDRATE 11.5g; FIBER 2.8g; CHOLESTEROL 60mg; IRON 2.6mg; SODIUM 898mg; CALCIUM 91mg

► carbo rating: 9

Tuscan Cod

Look for capers in the condiment section of the grocery store. Capers have an assertive, briny flavor, so you only need to use a few to make a difference in a recipe. A bottle of capers will last for up to a year in the refrigerator.

1 teaspoon olive oil
½ cup thinly sliced onion, separated into rings
½ cup diced red bell pepper
1 garlic clove, minced
1 cup chopped tomato
1 tablespoon capers
¼ teaspoon ground cumin
⅛ teaspoon crushed red pepper
2 (6-ounce) cod fillets

1. Heat oil in a large nonstick skillet over medium-high heat. Add onion, bell pepper, and garlic; sauté 2 minutes. Add tomato and next 3 ingredients; cook over medium heat 5 minutes, stirring occasionally. Add fish to pan, spooning sauce over fish. Cover and cook 10 minutes or until fish flakes easily when tested with a fork. Yield: 2 servings (serving size: 1 fillet and ½ cup sauce).

CALORIES 214; FAT 4.1g (sat 0.6g); PROTEIN 32.4g; CARBOHYDRATE 11.8g; FIBER 2.7g; CHOLESTEROL 73mg; IRON 1.9mg; SODIUM 439mg; CALCIUM 49mg

▶ carbo rating: 9
Catfish with Dill Sauce

The small amount of honey in this sauce provides a sweet contrast to the dill.

¾	cup fat-free sour cream
½	cup fresh parsley leaves
½	cup fresh dill
½	cup chopped green onions
3	tablespoons rice vinegar
1	tablespoon honey
1	garlic clove, chopped
¾	teaspoon salt, divided
1	tablespoon vegetable oil, divided
6	(6-ounce) catfish fillets
¼	teaspoon freshly ground black pepper

1. Combine first 7 ingredients in a food processor; add ½ teaspoon salt. Process until pureed.
2. Heat 1½ teaspoons oil in a large nonstick skillet over medium-high heat. Sprinkle fish with ¼ teaspoon salt and pepper. Add 3 fillets to pan; cook 3 minutes per side or until fish flakes easily when tested with a fork.
3. Remove from pan, and keep warm. Repeat procedure with remaining oil and fillets; serve with sauce. Yield: 6 servings (serving size: 1 fillet and about 2 tablespoons sauce).

CALORIES 231; FAT 7.5g (sat 1.8g); PROTEIN 29.7g; CARBOHYDRATE 9.2g; FIBER 0.4g; CHOLESTEROL 102mg; IRON 1.1mg; SODIUM 395mg; CALCIUM 85mg

▶ carbo rating: 10
Pan-Seared Mahimahi with Tropical Salsa

The peppery seeds of the papaya are edible. Reserve about a tablespoon to give the salsa additional flavor.

1	cup diced peeled papaya (about ½ medium papaya)
⅔	cup chopped fresh pineapple
1	kiwifruit, peeled and chopped
1	jalapeño pepper, seeded and minced
3	tablespoons finely chopped red onion
2	tablespoons chopped fresh cilantro
2	tablespoons fresh pineapple juice
4	(6-ounce) mahimahi or other firm white fish fillets
¼	teaspoon salt
¼	teaspoon pepper

Cooking spray

1. Combine first 7 ingredients in a medium bowl; toss gently. Cover and chill.
2. Sprinkle fillets with salt and pepper. Heat a large nonstick skillet over high heat until hot. Coat fillets with cooking spray; add fillets to pan. Cook fillets 1 minute on each side or just until lightly browned. Reduce heat to medium, and cook, uncovered, 7 minutes or until fish flakes easily when tested with a fork.
3. Place fillets on individual serving plates; spoon salsa over fillets. Yield: 4 servings (serving size: 1 fillet and ½ cup salsa).

CALORIES 194; FAT 1.6g (sat 0.4g); PROTEIN 32.3g; CARBOHYDRATE 12.1g; FIBER 1.7g; CHOLESTEROL 124mg; IRON 2.2mg; SODIUM 299mg; CALCIUM 48mg

(pictured on page 150)

▶ **carbo rating: 10**

Red Snapper Veracruz

While the fish bakes, prepare the vegetable topping and toss a salad to go with your meal.

4	(6-ounce) red snapper fillets

Olive oil-flavored cooking spray

½	cup fresh orange juice, divided
2	teaspoons olive oil, divided
½	teaspoon salt
1	(10-ounce) can diced tomatoes and green chiles (such as Rotel), undrained
1	large green bell pepper, cut into thin strips
1	small red onion, cut into thin strips
2	teaspoons bottled minced garlic
¼	cup sliced pitted green olives
1	tablespoon minced fresh cilantro
1	tablespoon capers
1	tablespoon caper juice

1. Preheat oven to 350°.

2. Place fillets in a 13 x 9-inch baking dish coated with cooking spray. Combine 2 tablespoons orange juice and 1 teaspoon olive oil; pour over fillets, and sprinkle with salt. Bake at 350° for 20 minutes or until fish flakes easily when tested with a fork.

3. Drain tomatoes, reserving ¼ cup juice; set both aside. Coat a large nonstick skillet with cooking spray; add 1 teaspoon oil, and place over medium-high heat until hot. Add bell pepper, onion, and garlic; sauté 7 minutes. Add 6 tablespoons orange juice, tomatoes, reserved ¼ cup tomato juice, olives, and next 3 ingredients; cook until thoroughly heated. Spoon vegetable mixture over fillets. Yield: 4 servings (serving size: 1 fillet and ½ cup vegetable mixture).

CALORIES 247; FAT 5.5g (sat 0.9g); PROTEIN 35g; CARBOHYDRATE 12.6g; FIBER 2.4g; CHOLESTEROL 60mg; IRON 1.7mg; SODIUM 994mg; CALCIUM 125mg

▶ **carbo rating: 10**

Cod Poached in Spicy Tomato Broth

This quick and easy recipe is made with ingredients you probably already have on hand, aside from the fish. You can use flounder instead of cod, if you prefer.

1	tablespoon olive oil
1½	teaspoons bottled minced garlic
1	cup water
¾	cup dry white wine
2	tablespoons capers
¾	teaspoon crushed red pepper
1	(14.5-ounce) can diced tomatoes with basil, garlic, and oregano
4	(6-ounce) cod fillets
10	kalamata olives, pitted and chopped

1. Heat oil in a large nonstick skillet over medium-high heat. Add garlic; sauté 1 minute or until lightly browned. Add water and next 4 ingredients; bring to a boil. Reduce heat, and simmer 2 minutes. Add fillets; cover and simmer 5 minutes or until fish flakes easily when tested with a fork. Top with olives. Yield: 4 servings (serving size: 1 fillet and about ⅔ cup sauce).

CALORIES 272; FAT 7.1g (sat 1g); PROTEIN 32.4g; CARBOHYDRATE 11.4g; FIBER 1.3g; CHOLESTEROL 73mg; IRON 2.5mg; SODIUM 907mg; CALCIUM 104mg

▶ carbo rating: 10

Pan-Seared Scallops with Ginger-Orange Spinach

When you cook the vodka and vermouth, almost all of the alcohol evaporates, leaving just the flavor. One-half cup of vodka contains 0 grams of carbohydrate; vermouth has about 0.5 grams.

  1   tablespoon julienne-cut peeled fresh ginger
  1   tablespoon sliced green onions
  4   garlic cloves, minced
 20   sea scallops (about 1½ pounds)
  ½   cup vodka
  ¼   cup dry vermouth
  1   teaspoon margarine or butter
  1   teaspoon grated orange rind
  ⅓   cup fresh orange juice
 1½   pounds chopped fresh spinach
  ½   teaspoon salt
  ⅛   teaspoon pepper
Cooking spray

1. Combine first 3 ingredients in a bowl.
2. Place scallops in a shallow dish. Add vodka, vermouth, and half of ginger mixture; toss gently. Cover and marinate in refrigerator 30 minutes.
3. Melt margarine in a large skillet over high heat. Add remaining ginger mixture, and sauté 30 seconds. Add orange rind and juice, and bring to a boil. Stir in spinach, salt, and pepper; cook 2 minutes or until spinach wilts. Remove from pan, and keep warm.
4. Remove scallops from marinade, reserving marinade. Place pan, coated with cooking spray, over high heat until hot. Add scallops; cook 1½ minutes on each side or until golden brown. Remove from pan; keep warm. Add reserved marinade to pan. Bring to a boil; cook until sauce is reduced to ¼ cup (about 5 minutes).
5. Arrange scallops over spinach mixture; drizzle with sauce. Yield: 4 servings (serving size: 5 scallops, ¾ cup spinach mixture, and 1 tablespoon sauce).

CALORIES 247; FAT 5.3g (sat 1.9g); PROTEIN 34.2g; CARBOHYDRATE 16.7g; FIBER 6.9g; CHOLESTEROL 56mg; IRON 5.2mg; SODIUM 727mg; CALCIUM 221mg

▶ carbo rating: 11

Mediterranean Orange Roughy

Make sure that all the fillets you buy are approximately the same thickness so that they'll bake evenly and all be done at the same time.

  2   teaspoons olive oil
 1⅔   cups vertically sliced onion
  1   cup chopped orange sections (about 3 oranges)
 1½   teaspoons chopped fresh or ½ teaspoon dried oregano
  ¼   teaspoon salt
  ¼   teaspoon pepper
  8   pitted ripe olives, halved
  1   garlic clove, minced
Cooking spray
  4   (6-ounce) orange roughy or other white fish fillets
  ⅓   cup fat-free, less-sodium chicken broth
  1   teaspoon grated orange rind

1. Preheat oven to 450°.
2. Heat oil in a large nonstick skillet over medium-high heat. Add onion; cook 7 minutes or until lightly browned, stirring occasionally. Remove from heat. Stir in orange sections and next 5 ingredients.
3. Arrange fillets in a single layer in a 13 x 9-inch baking dish coated with cooking spray. Combine broth and rind; pour over fish. Spoon onion mixture over fish. Bake at 450° for 15 minutes or until fish flakes easily when tested with a fork. Yield: 4 servings (serving size: 5 ounces fish and ⅓ cup onion topping).

CALORIES 210; FAT 4.6g (sat 0.5g); PROTEIN 26.6g; CARBOHYDRATE 15.5g; FIBER 4.9g; CHOLESTEROL 34mg; IRON 0.9mg; SODIUM 318mg; CALCIUM 56mg

▶ carbo rating: 12

Oven-Fried Catfish

In most breaded fish dishes, the fish is coated with a flour or cornmeal mixture and fried, making the fish high in both carbs and fat. In this recipe, the coating is whole wheat cereal crumbs, and the fish is oven-fried.

Butter-flavored cooking spray
⅔   cup whole wheat flake cereal crumbs
¼   teaspoon salt
¼   teaspoon ground red pepper
4   (6-ounce) farm-raised catfish fillets
2   large egg whites, lightly beaten
Lemon wedges

1. Preheat oven to 450°.
2. Line a baking sheet with foil. Coat with cooking spray.
3. Combine crumbs, salt, and red pepper in a small bowl; stir well. Dip fillets in beaten egg white; dredge in crumb mixture. Place fillets on pan. Bake at 450° for 8 to 10 minutes or until fish flakes easily when tested with a fork. Serve immediately with lemon wedges. Yield: 4 servings (serving size: 1 fillet).

CALORIES 298; FAT 13.6g (sat 3.2g); PROTEIN 29.7g; CARBOHYDRATE 14g; FIBER 1.6g; CHOLESTEROL 80mg; IRON 11.4mg; SODIUM 376mg; CALCIUM 602mg

(pictured on page 151)

▶ carbo rating: 12

Salmon with Moroccan Tomato Relish

Often, a relish topping or chutney will be sweet and high in carbohydrate. But this savory tomato relish gets its flavor from spices such as cinnamon and ginger, and a splash of orange juice.

½   teaspoon salt, divided
4   (6-ounce) skinless salmon fillets
2   teaspoons olive oil, divided
1¾   cups chopped red onion
1   tablespoon minced peeled fresh ginger
4½   cups coarsely chopped tomato
1   teaspoon grated orange rind
2   tablespoons fresh orange juice
1   tablespoon capers
1   tablespoon fresh lemon juice
1   teaspoon grated lemon rind
¼   teaspoon ground cinnamon
¼   cup chopped fresh mint
3   tablespoons chopped fresh cilantro
Mint sprigs (optional)

1. Sprinkle ¼ teaspoon salt evenly over fillets. Heat 1 teaspoon oil in a large nonstick skillet over medium-high heat until hot. Add fillets; cook 3 minutes on each side or until lightly browned. Remove from pan; set aside, and keep warm.
2. Add 1 teaspoon oil to pan; place over medium-high heat until hot. Add onion and ginger; sauté 2 minutes. Add ¼ teaspoon salt, tomato, and next 6 ingredients; cook 5 minutes, stirring occasionally.
3. Return fillets to pan, nestling fillets in tomato mixture; cook 3 minutes until fish is medium-rare or desired degree of doneness. Remove from heat; place fillets on individual plates. Stir chopped mint and cilantro into tomato mixture; spoon mixture around each fillet. Garnish with mint sprigs, if desired. Yield: 4 servings (serving size: 1 fillet and ¾ cup tomato relish).

CALORIES 334; FAT 13.1g (sat 2.3g); PROTEIN 39.3g; CARBOHYDRATE 14.9g; FIBER 3.1g; CHOLESTEROL 66mg; IRON 2.4mg; SODIUM 559mg; CALCIUM 28mg

► carbo rating: 12

Grouper à la Mango

There's no sugar in the salsa—the sweetness is from the vitamin C-packed mango.

1½   cups finely chopped peeled mango (about 2 mangoes)
½   cup finely chopped red bell pepper
⅓   cup finely chopped red onion
¼   cup chopped fresh cilantro
2   tablespoons fresh lime juice
½   teaspoon salt, divided
4   (6-ounce) grouper fillets
¼   teaspoon ground red pepper
Cooking spray
Cilantro sprigs (optional)

1. Preheat oven to 425°.
2. Combine mango, red bell pepper, onion, cilantro, lime juice, and ¼ teaspoon salt in a small bowl; toss well to combine. Set aside or chill, if desired.
3. Sprinkle fillets evenly with ¼ teaspoon salt and ground red pepper; arrange in an 11 x 7-inch baking dish coated with cooking spray. Bake at 425° for 20 minutes or until fish flakes easily when tested with a fork. Serve with mango salsa. Garnish with cilantro sprigs, if desired. Yield: 4 servings (serving size: 1 fillet and ½ cup salsa).

CALORIES 210; FAT 2g (sat 0.5g); PROTEIN 33.7g; CARBOHYDRATE 13.7g; FIBER 1.8g; CHOLESTEROL 63mg; IRON 1.8mg; SODIUM 387mg; CALCIUM 59mg

(pictured on page 152)

► carbo rating: 12

Basil Shrimp Kebabs

In terms of taste, efficiency, and appearance, there is no difference between metal and wooden skewers. But if you use wooden skewers, remember to soak them in water 10 minutes before using so they don't burn on the grill. (See the note on page 111 about buying peeled and deveined shrimp.)

¼   cup white wine vinegar
2   tablespoons olive oil
2   teaspoons Dijon mustard
1   garlic clove, cut in half
12   basil leaves
¾   pound peeled and deveined large shrimp
1   small red onion, quartered and separated
1   green bell pepper, cut into 1-inch pieces
½   (8-ounce) package mushrooms
6   cherry tomatoes
Cooking spray

1. Prepare grill.
2. Combine first 5 ingredients in a blender; process until smooth. Transfer to a small bowl.
3. Thread shrimp, onion, bell pepper, and mushrooms alternately onto 4 (15-inch) skewers; brush with basil sauce. Thread cherry tomatoes onto 1 (15-inch) skewer; brush with basil sauce.
4. Place shrimp kebabs on grill rack coated with cooking spray; grill, covered, 10 minutes or until shrimp are done and vegetables are crisp-tender, turning and basting occasionally with basil sauce. Place tomato kebab on rack; grill, covered, 3 to 4 minutes, basting occasionally with basil sauce. Serve immediately. Yield: 2 servings (serving size: 2 skewers and 3 tomatoes).

CALORIES 375; FAT 17.9g (sat 2.6g); PROTEIN 38.1g; CARBOHYDRATE 15.2g; FIBER 3g; CHOLESTEROL 259mg; IRON 5.2mg; SODIUM 388mg; CALCIUM 98mg

► carbo rating: 14

Tandoori-Marinated Red Snapper

A tandoori paste is a mixture of yogurt and spices that is traditional in Indian cooking and gives foods a reddish-orange tint.

1½   cups plain low-fat yogurt
¼   cup fresh lemon juice
2   tablespoons garam masala (such as McCormick)
2   tablespoons Hungarian sweet paprika
1   tablespoon minced peeled fresh ginger
1   tablespoon minced garlic
1½   teaspoons salt
1½   to 2 teaspoons ground red pepper
1   teaspoon ground turmeric
½   teaspoon freshly ground black pepper
6   (6-ounce) red snapper or other firm white fish fillets
½   cup vertically sliced red onion
2   tablespoons fresh lemon juice
½   teaspoon salt
⅛   teaspoon garam masala
2   cups plain low-fat yogurt
1   cup finely chopped English cucumber
½   cup chopped fresh cilantro
⅛   teaspoon freshly ground black pepper
Cooking spray

1. Combine first 10 ingredients in a 13 x 9-inch baking dish, stirring with a whisk. Add fish, turning to coat.
2. Cover and marinate in refrigerator 2 hours.
3. Combine onion, 2 tablespoons juice, ½ teaspoon salt, and ⅛ teaspoon garam masala in a medium bowl; let stand 1 hour. Add 2 cups yogurt, cucumber, cilantro, and ⅛ teaspoon black pepper, tossing gently to combine.
4. Preheat broiler.
5. Remove fish from dish; discard marinade. Place fish on a broiler pan coated with cooking spray. Broil 10 minutes or until fish is firm to the touch with a fork, turning once. Serve salad with fish. Yield: 6 servings (serving size: 1 fillet and ½ cup salad).

CALORIES 279; FAT 4.7g (sat 1.9g); PROTEIN 43.2g; CARBOHYDRATE 15g; FIBER 1.3g; CHOLESTEROL 77mg; IRON 1.2mg; SODIUM 606mg; CALCIUM 351mg

► carbo rating: 14

Oven-Poached Halibut Provençale

*The term **provençale** refers to foods that are prepared in the style of Provence, a region in southern France. The trademark flavors of this type of cooking are all low-carb ingredients: garlic, tomato, olive oil, onions, olives, and eggplant.*

Cooking spray
1   cup dry white wine
6   (6-ounce) halibut steaks
6   cups diced tomato
2   cups finely chopped onion
¼   cup chopped fresh or 4 teaspoons dried basil
¼   cup chopped fresh parsley or 4 teaspoons dried parsley flakes
2   tablespoons minced kalamata olives
1   tablespoon olive oil
½   teaspoon salt
½   teaspoon anchovy paste
⅛   teaspoon pepper
2   garlic cloves, minced
¼   cup dry breadcrumbs
1   tablespoon grated Parmesan cheese
1   teaspoon olive oil

1. Preheat oven to 350°.
2. Coat a 13 x 9-inch baking dish with cooking spray. Pour wine into dish, and arrange halibut steaks in dish.
3. Combine tomato and next 9 ingredients in a bowl; stir well, and spoon over steaks. Bake at 350° for 35 minutes or until fish flakes easily when tested with a fork.
4. Combine breadcrumbs, cheese, and 1 teaspoon oil in a bowl; stir well. Sprinkle over tomato mixture, and broil until crumbs are golden. Serve immediately. Yield: 6 servings (serving size: 5 ounces fish and 1 cup tomato mixture).

CALORIES 300; FAT 8.6g (sat 1.3g); PROTEIN 38.8g; CARBOHYDRATE 16.9g; FIBER 3.2g; CHOLESTEROL 81mg; IRON 3mg; SODIUM 437mg; CALCIUM 131mg

► carbo rating: 14

Halibut Fillets with Teriyaki Sauce

Teriyaki sauce recipes often have a lot of brown sugar; this one gets its sweetness from pineapple juice and a touch of honey.

½   cup pineapple juice
3   tablespoons low-sodium teriyaki sauce
1   tablespoon honey
¾   teaspoon cornstarch
¼   teaspoon garlic powder
⅛   teaspoon ground red pepper
2   tablespoons seasoned breadcrumbs
4   (6-ounce) halibut fillets, skinned (1 inch thick)
1   tablespoon vegetable oil

1. Combine first 6 ingredients in a small bowl; stir well with a whisk. Set aside.
2. Combine breadcrumbs and halibut in a large zip-top plastic bag. Seal and shake to coat; set aside.
3. Heat oil in a large nonstick skillet over medium heat. Add fillets; cook 4 minutes on each side or until fish flakes easily when tested with a fork. Remove fish from pan; set aside, and keep warm.
4. Add teriyaki mixture to pan. Bring to a boil; cook 1 minute, stirring constantly. Pour over fish. Yield: 4 servings (serving size: 1 fillet and 2 tablespoons sauce).

CALORIES 280; FAT 7.4g (sat 1.2g); PROTEIN 36.9g; CARBOHYDRATE 14.1g; FIBER 0.1g; CHOLESTEROL 80mg; IRON 1.9mg; SODIUM 304mg; CALCIUM 96mg

► carbo rating: 19

Teriyaki Tuna with Fresh Pineapple

Tuna is less forgiving than other fish, so be sure not to overcook it or it will be dry and tough.

1   small pineapple, peeled and cored
¼   cup low-sodium soy sauce
3   tablespoons honey
3   tablespoons mirin (sweet rice wine)
2   teaspoons minced peeled fresh ginger
½   teaspoon hot sauce
1   garlic clove, minced
6   (6-ounce) tuna steaks (about ¾ inch thick)
Cooking spray
Green onions (optional)

1. Cut pineapple lengthwise into 6 spears. Combine soy sauce and next 5 ingredients in a large zip-top plastic bag. Add pineapple and fish to bag; seal and marinate in refrigerator 30 minutes, turning bag once. Remove fish and pineapple from bag, reserving marinade.
2. Prepare grill.
3. Place fish and pineapple on grill rack coated with cooking spray; cover and grill 4 minutes on each side or until fish is medium-rare or desired degree of doneness, basting frequently with reserved marinade. Garnish with green onions, if desired. Yield: 6 servings (serving size: 1 steak and 1 pineapple spear).

CALORIES 326; FAT 9.1g (sat 2.2g); PROTEIN 40.3g; CARBOHYDRATE 20.7g; FIBER 1.8g; CHOLESTEROL 65mg; IRON 2.4mg; SODIUM 149mg; CALCIUM 11mg

▶ carbo rating: 22

Brook Trout Grilled with Wild Rice

Wild rice is not really rice—it's actually the seed of water grass. Wild rice has about the same amount of fiber as brown rice, but 5 fewer grams of carbohydrate per ½-cup serving.

1	tablespoon olive oil
2	cups thinly sliced leek, divided
1½	cups sliced mushrooms
1	garlic clove, crushed
4	cups water
½	cup uncooked wild rice
¼	teaspoon salt, divided
¼	teaspoon pepper, divided
4	thyme sprigs
4	(8-ounce) cleaned brook trout
1	tablespoon butter
1	tablespoon chopped fresh parsley

Thyme sprigs (optional)

1. Heat oil in a medium saucepan over medium-high heat. Add ¼ cup leek, mushrooms, and garlic; sauté 3 minutes. Add water, rice, ⅛ teaspoon salt, ⅛ teaspoon pepper; bring to a boil. Cover, reduce heat, and simmer 50 minutes or until rice is tender. Drain rice, reserving 1 cup cooking liquid; set rice aside. Return cooking liquid to pan. Bring to a boil, and cook 8 minutes or until reduced to ½ cup. Remove from heat; set broth aside, and keep warm.

2. Place 1 thyme sprig in the center of each of 4 (10-inch) squares of aluminum foil. Place 1 fish on top of each thyme sprig. Sprinkle remaining salt and pepper over inside cavities of fish. Stuff ½ cup rice mixture into cavity of each fish. Wrap fish in foil, twisting ends to seal.

3. Prepare grill.

4. Place foil-wrapped fish on grill rack; grill 10 minutes on each side or until fish flakes easily when tested with a fork. Unwrap fish; remove and discard skin. Set fish aside, and keep warm.

5. Melt butter in a small saucepan over medium-high heat. Add remaining leek, and sauté 2 minutes or until tender. Divide leek evenly among 4 individual plates, and top with fish. Drizzle 2 tablespoons broth over each fish, and sprinkle with parsley. Garnish with thyme sprigs, if desired. Yield: 4 servings (serving size: 1 fish).

CALORIES 397; FAT 17.3g (sat 4.1g); PROTEIN 36.1g; CARBOHYDRATE 24.3g; FIBER 2.2g; CHOLESTEROL 96mg; IRON 4.3mg; SODIUM 268mg; CALCIUM 105mg

meatless main dishes

Meats are not your only low-carb options for entrées. You can get your protein from eggs, cheese, beans, soy products, and whole grains. Try *Crustless Green Chile Quiche* (page 140), *Spinach and Barley-Stuffed Portobellos* (page 144), and *Cheesy Bean Casserole* (page 164) for meat-free main dishes without all the carbohydrate.

▶ carbo rating: 4

Crustless Spinach Quiche

When you're cutting back on carbs, a quiche minus the pastry crust is the way to go. You'd get about 23 grams of carbohydrate in a slice of spinach quiche with a crust. With this cheesy, veggie-packed filling, you won't miss the crust.

  3   ounces ⅓-less-fat cream cheese, softened
  1   cup fat-free milk
  1   cup egg substitute
  ¼   teaspoon pepper
  3   cups (12 ounces) shredded reduced-fat Cheddar cheese
Cooking spray
  1   (10-ounce) package frozen chopped spinach, thawed, drained, and squeezed dry
  1   (10-ounce) package frozen chopped broccoli, thawed, drained, and squeezed dry
  1   small onion, finely chopped
  5   whole mushrooms, sliced
Salsa (optional)

1. Preheat oven to 350°.
2. Beat cream cheese in a large bowl with a mixer at medium speed until creamy. Add milk, egg substitute, and pepper; beat until smooth. Stir in cheese.
3. Coat a large nonstick skillet with cooking spray; place over medium heat until hot. Cook spinach and next 3 ingredients just until tender and liquid evaporates. Cool slightly.
4. Combine egg mixture and spinach mixture, stirring well. Pour into a 10-inch quiche dish coated with cooking spray. Bake, uncovered, at 350° for 45 to 50 minutes or until center is set. Remove from oven and cool on a wire rack 10 minutes.
5. Cut into 8 wedges, and serve with salsa, if desired (salsa not included in analysis). Yield: 8 servings (serving size: 1 wedge).

CALORIES 198; FAT 10.4g (sat 6.7g); PROTEIN 19.6g; CARBOHYDRATE 5.4g; FIBER 1.5g; CHOLESTEROL 29mg; IRON 1.2mg; SODIUM 412mg; CALCIUM 486mg

making sense of salsa

There are a wide variety of jarred salsas available on the market today. Most of the tomato salsas are fairly low in carbohydrate, ranging from 2 to 6 grams per ¼-cup serving, although some may be higher if they contain sugar or other sweeteners. Generally, the thick and chunky-style salsas will have a little more fiber than the regular ones. Check the label for the carbohydrate and fiber content of your favorite salsas.

▶ carbo rating: 5

Crustless Green Chile Quiche

Look for jars of roasted red bell peppers in either the produce section of the supermarket or on the shelves near the olives, pickles, and other condiments.

  1   cup egg substitute
  2   tablespoons all-purpose flour
  2   tablespoons reduced-calorie margarine, melted
  1   tablespoon Dijon mustard
  ⅛   teaspoon hot sauce
  1   cup fat-free cottage cheese
  6   tablespoons (1½ ounces) shredded reduced-fat Monterey Jack cheese
  ¼   cup canned chopped green chiles
  ¼   cup chopped drained roasted red bell pepper
Cooking spray
  1   tablespoon grated fresh Parmesan cheese

1. Preheat oven to 350°.
2. Combine first 5 ingredients in a bowl, stirring well with a wire whisk. Stir in cottage cheese, Monterey Jack cheese, green chiles, and roasted red bell pepper. Pour mixture into a 9-inch pie plate coated with cooking spray; sprinkle with Parmesan cheese.
3. Bake at 350° for 30 to 32 minutes or until set. Let stand 10 minutes before cutting into wedges. Yield: 6 servings (serving size: 1 wedge).

CALORIES 107; FAT 3.8g (sat 1.5g); PROTEIN 11.9g; CARBOHYDRATE 6.2g; FIBER 0.5g; CHOLESTEROL 7mg; IRON 1.1mg; SODIUM 444mg; CALCIUM 112mg

▶ carbo rating: 9

Mediterranean Eggplant Provolone

The inspiration for this dish is a traditional eggplant Parmesan in which the eggplant slices are coated with breadcrumbs and fried. The carbo rating for one serving of the traditional version is 24. In our recipe, we simply bake the eggplant and top the slices with fresh tomatoes instead of a tomato sauce. And for a slightly different flavor, we've used provolone cheese instead of Parmesan.

2 cups finely chopped plum tomatoes (about 4)
⅔ cup chopped fresh parsley
1½ tablespoons chopped fresh basil, divided
2 tablespoons capers, drained
1 tablespoon balsamic vinegar
⅛ teaspoon salt
8 eggplant slices, cut diagonally into ½-inch slices (about 2 medium)
Cooking spray
4 (1.5-ounce) slices provolone cheese

1. Preheat oven to 450°.
2. Combine tomato, parsley, 1 tablespoon basil, capers, vinegar, and salt in a bowl; set aside.
3. Place eggplant slices on a baking sheet coated with cooking spray; lightly coat eggplant with cooking spray. Bake at 450° for 10 minutes; turn. Bake an additional 2 minutes or until almost tender. Sprinkle with 1½ teaspoons basil.
4. Cut each cheese slice in half; place 1 cheese slice half on each eggplant slice. Bake 1 minute or until cheese melts. Remove from baking dish with a wide spatula. Place on individual plates; spoon ¾ cup tomato mixture over each serving. Yield: 4 servings (serving size: 2 eggplant slices and ¾ cup tomato mixture).

CALORIES 207; FAT 12.1g (sat 7.4g); PROTEIN 13.3g; CARBOHYDRATE 13.7g; FIBER 4.5g; CHOLESTEROL 29mg; IRON 1.6mg; SODIUM 795mg; CALCIUM 355mg

▶ carbo rating: 12

Italian Eggplant

If frozen meatless sausage crumbles are available, use them instead of the patties; you'll need about 1¾ cups.

4 (1.3-ounce) frozen meatless sausage patties (such as Morningstar Farms)
1 (1½-pound) eggplant
Cooking spray
¼ teaspoon salt
¾ cup tomato-and-basil pasta sauce (such as Classico)
1 teaspoon dried basil
⅛ teaspoon crushed red pepper
1 cup (4 ounces) shredded part-skim mozzarella cheese

1. Preheat broiler.
2. Partially thaw breakfast patties in microwave at HIGH 10 to 15 seconds; crumble into small pieces.
3. Remove stem end of eggplant; slice eggplant lengthwise into 4 (½-inch) slices. Arrange slices on a baking sheet coated with cooking spray. Lightly coat slices with cooking spray; broil 4 minutes. Turn slices, coat with cooking spray, and broil 2 minutes.
4. Sprinkle salt over eggplant; top evenly with crumbled breakfast patties, and broil 1 minute.
5. Combine pasta sauce, basil, and red pepper. Spoon sauce over eggplant; top with cheese. Broil 1 minute. Yield: 4 servings (serving size: 1 eggplant slice, about 1 ounce sausage, and 3 tablespoons sauce).

CALORIES 219; FAT 8g (sat 3.4g); PROTEIN 19.3g; CARBOHYDRATE 19.5g; FIBER 7.3g; CHOLESTEROL 17mg; IRON 2.9mg; SODIUM 730mg; CALCIUM 260mg

not just the pasta, but the sauce

It's not just the pasta that contains a lot of carbohydrate—some jarred pasta sauces contain as much as 12 grams per ½-cup serving because of added sugar. Check the labels to find the brands and flavors with the lowest amount of carbohydrate. The lowest we've found among the regular brands is about 9 grams per serving, although some of the new low-carb sauces on the market have as little as 7 grams.

soy store

Soy products contain isoflavones—plant chemicals—that have impressive disease-fighting properties. Soy has been shown to reduce the risk of certain cancers and heart disease, strengthen bones, reduce the risk of osteoporosis, and decrease hot flashes associated with menopause. If you want to increase the soy in your diet, you've got plenty of options. Here's a quick guide to soy products.

Edamame: fresh soybeans. These beans are available in Asian markets from late spring to early fall. Frozen soybeans are available year-round in the pods or shelled in most supermarkets.

Tofu: soybean curd; a soft, cheeselike food that's made from curdled soy milk. Tofu is available in firm, extrafirm, soft, silken, and low-fat varieties.

• Soft or silken tofu can be used as a substitute for sour cream, yogurt, cream cheese, or cottage cheese in beverages, dips, puddings, soups, and salad dressings.

• Firm tofu can be cubed, crumbled, or sliced, and used in salads, stir-frys, and pasta dishes.

• Low-fat firm silken tofu has 1 gram of fat per 3 ounces; regular firm silken tofu has 2.3 grams.

Soy milk: the milk of the soybean. It's lactose-free and comes in regular and low-fat versions. Soy milk isn't naturally high in calcium, but many brands are fortified with calcium, as well as vitamins D and B12.

Tempeh: a fermented soybean cake with a yeasty flavor and a texture similar to that of tofu. Tempeh is often used in stir-fry recipes.

Miso: fermented soybean paste with the consistency of peanut butter. It comes in a variety of flavors and colors; the flavor can vary based on the length of time the paste is aged.

Veggie Sausage: made from textured soy protein with a variety of flavors. Veggie sausage is available in patties, links, and crumbles.

Veggie Burgers and Burger Crumbles: made with textured soy protein with a flavor and texture similar to that of ground beef. Use the patties and the crumbles just as you would ground beef, but reduce the cooking time slightly.

▶ carbo rating: 16

Tempeh Vegetable Stir-Fry

Tempeh *is a fermented soybean cake that has a texture similar to soft tofu. Look for tempeh in the refrigerated produce section of the supermarket, or wherever tofu and other soy products are sold.*

⅓   cup low-sodium soy sauce
4   teaspoons dry sherry
2   teaspoons sugar
½   teaspoon cornstarch
2   teaspoons dark sesame oil
1   (8-ounce) package tempeh, cut into ½-inch cubes
1½ cups broccoli florets
1   cup (⅛-inch-thick) diagonally sliced carrot
½   cup diced red bell pepper
1   cup thinly sliced shiitake mushroom caps (about 3 ounces)
1   teaspoon minced peeled fresh ginger
2   garlic cloves, minced
2   cups fresh bean sprouts
½   cup (1-inch) sliced green onions

1. Combine first 4 ingredients in a small bowl; set aside.

2. Heat oil in a large nonstick skillet or wok over medium-high heat until hot. Add tempeh; stir-fry 3 minutes or until light brown. Add broccoli, carrot, and bell pepper; stir-fry 2 minutes. Add mushrooms, ginger, and garlic; stir-fry 1 minute.

3. Stir soy sauce mixture into tempeh mixture; bring to a boil. Stir in sprouts and green onions. Yield: 4 servings (serving size: 1¼ cups).

CALORIES 207; FAT 7.2g (sat 1.2g); PROTEIN 16.3g; CARBOHYDRATE 23.6g; FIBER 7.9g; CHOLESTEROL 0mg; IRON 2.1mg; SODIUM 664mg; CALCIUM 59mg

► carbo rating: 16

Grilled Portobello Pizzas

Pizza? On a low-carb diet? Sure, when you put the toppings on a portobello cap instead of a bread crust.

½	cup finely chopped fresh basil
2	teaspoons olive oil
1	teaspoon bottled minced roasted garlic
12	plum tomatoes, seeded and chopped
1½	tablespoons minced fresh thyme
1	tablespoon bottled minced roasted garlic
1	teaspoon olive oil
4	(4-inch) portobello mushroom caps

Cooking spray

¼	teaspoon salt
¼	teaspoon pepper
½	cup (2 ounces) shredded part-skim mozzarella cheese

1. Prepare grill.
2. Combine first 3 ingredients in a small bowl; stir well, and set aside. Combine tomato and next 3 ingredients in a medium bowl; stir well, and set aside.
3. Remove brown gills from undersides of mushrooms using a spoon; discard gills. Coat top and bottom of mushroom caps evenly with cooking spray; sprinkle with salt and pepper.
4. Place mushrooms, top sides up, on grill rack coated with cooking spray; grill, covered, 4 minutes. Turn mushrooms over; spoon tomato mixture evenly into caps. Top each mushroom with 1 tablespoon basil mixture and 2 tablespoons cheese. Grill, covered, 4 minutes or until mushrooms are tender and cheese melts. Yield: 2 servings (serving size: 2 mushroom pizzas).

CALORIES 250; FAT 12.6g (sat 4.1g); PROTEIN 17.6g; CARBOHYDRATE 22.8g; FIBER 6.7g; CHOLESTEROL 15mg; IRON 3.2mg; SODIUM 470mg; CALCIUM 264mg

types of mushrooms

More than 2,500 varieties of mushrooms grow around the world. The most readily available varieties are cultivated. Some cultivated mushrooms are so flavorful and unique that consumers tend to think of them as wild. These farm-grown mushrooms have been termed "exotics" by the United States Department of Agriculture (USDA) to distinguish them from the true wild ones that pop up in forests, fields, and even deserts. Portobello, shiitake, cremini, and oyster mushrooms account for most of the exotic mushroom sales in the United States. Here's a guide to some of the most popular mushrooms.

Button: Also called a white mushroom, this cultivated variety is the all-purpose mushroom that is seen often in grocery stores, either whole or sliced.

Chanterelle: This mushroom is golden yellow and shaped like a trumpet. It ranges in size from the size of a fingernail to about 4 inches.

Cremini: These mushrooms are common brown mushrooms and are closely related to the button mushroom. They can be used in place of button (or white) mushrooms, although they have a firmer texture and fuller flavor.

Oyster: Although they used to be wild only, these mushrooms are now cultivated. They are cream-colored to pale gray with a fan shape.

Porcini: These mushrooms are plump, with a firm texture, sweet fragrance, and earthy flavor. They are not cultivated and have caps similar in shape and color to cremini, but their stems are thick. These mushrooms are often hard to find in the United States.

Portobello: This cultivated mushroom is a mature version of a cremino mushroom and has a cap about 6 inches in diameter. It is dark brown and has a rich, meaty flavor and texture. When using portobellos, remove the thick, tough stems and save them for flavoring stocks or sauces.

Shiitake: Available both fresh and dried, this mushroom is buff-colored to dark brown and has a smooth, plump white cap. Remove the stems before using in recipes.

▶ carbo rating: 19

Spinach and Barley-Stuffed Portobellos

Spoon this creamy grain mixture, packed with vegetables, onto broiled portobello caps for a whole meal on a mushroom. (See pages 143 and 328 for more information on portobello mushrooms.)

6	medium portobello mushroom caps (about 1½ pounds)
⅔	cup 2% reduced-fat milk
2	tablespoons all-purpose flour

Cooking spray

½	cup coarsely chopped carrot
½	cup coarsely chopped onion
5	garlic cloves, minced
¾	teaspoon salt
1	(10-ounce) bag fresh spinach (about 10 cups)
1	cup cooked quick-cooking pearl barley
1	cup (4 ounces) grated Gruyère cheese, divided
½	teaspoon freshly ground black pepper
⅛	teaspoon ground nutmeg
½	cup fresh whole wheat breadcrumbs

1. Preheat broiler.
2. Remove brown gills from undersides of mushrooms using a spoon; discard gills.
3. Combine milk and flour, stirring with a whisk until blended.
4. Place a large nonstick skillet coated with cooking spray over medium-high heat until hot. Add carrot and next 3 ingredients; sauté 5 minutes. Add spinach; sauté 4 minutes or until spinach wilts.
5. Stir in flour mixture; bring to a boil. Reduce heat; simmer 1 to 2 minutes or until thick. Stir in cooked barley, ½ cup cheese, pepper, and nutmeg; cook 1 minute or until cheese melts.
6. Coat reserved mushroom caps with cooking spray; place on a broiler pan. Broil 5 minutes or until tender. Fill each cap with about ½ cup spinach-barley mixture, pressing firmly to pack. Broil 3½ minutes.
7. Combine breadcrumbs and ½ cup cheese; sprinkle evenly on top of each mushroom. Broil 1½ minutes or until cheese melts. Yield: 6 servings (serving size: 1 mushroom and ½ cup spinach-barley mixture).

CALORIES 209; FAT 8.1g (sat 4.2g); PROTEIN 12.2g; CARBOHYDRATE 24.4g; FIBER 5.4g; CHOLESTEROL 23mg; IRON 3.6mg; SODIUM 461mg; CALCIUM 299mg

barley benefits

Barley is a hearty grain that dates back to the Stone Age but provides some very modern health benefits.
Hulled or whole-grain barley has only the outer husk removed and is the most nutritious form of the grain.
Pearl barley has the outer husk removed and has been steamed and polished. Pearl barley is the form you'll see most often in the grocery store. Pearl barley is an excellent source of soluble fiber—that's the kind of fiber that helps lower cholesterol. With 6 grams of fiber per ½-cup serving, it's one of the top five cereal sources of fiber. Plus, it's practically fat- and sodium-free.
The new quick-cooking barley provides the same nutritional benefits as regular barley, but cooks in 10 minutes.

Orange-Glazed Salmon
▶ carbo rating: 2
page 109

**Greek-Style
Orange Roughy**
▶ carbo rating: 5
page 119

Tilapia en Papillote
▶ carbo rating: 6
page 122

Shrimp with Feta
▶ carbo rating: 7
page 124

Lemon-Dill Scallops and Snow Peas
▶ carbo rating: 8
page 126

Pan-Seared Mahimahi with
Tropical Salsa
▶ carbo rating: 10
page 130

Oven-Fried Catfish
▶ carbo rating: 12
page 133

Grouper à la Mango
▶ carbo rating: 12
page 134

152

Four-Cheese Eggplant
Casserole
▶ carbo rating: 19
page 161

Vegetable-Bean Hot Pot
▶ carbo rating: 20
page 162

Italian Stuffed Eggplant
▶ carbo rating: 26
page 169

Garlic-Studded Pork Loin Roast
▶ carbo rating: 0
page 184

Southwestern
Grilled Flank Steak
▶ carbo rating: 1
page 188

Sirloin Steak with
Garlic Sauce
▶ carbo rating: 2
page 197

Greek Stuffed Steak
▶ carbo rating: 3
page 201

Veal Piccata
▶ carbo rating: 3
page 203

Greek-Style Lamb
▶ carbo rating: 4
page 208

Seared Steaks with Creamy
Horseradish Sauce
▶ carbo rating: 5
page 208

▶ carbo rating: 19
Four-Cheese Eggplant Casserole

Instead of topping a casserole with crushed saltine crackers, switch to whole wheat crackers. This will increase the fiber and decrease the carbo rating.

4¾ pounds eggplant (about 4 large)
⅔ cup grated Parmesan cheese, divided
1½ cups (6 ounces) crumbled feta cheese
1 cup part-skim ricotta cheese
½ cup fat-free cottage cheese
¼ cup egg substitute
1 teaspoon freshly ground black pepper
⅛ teaspoon salt
8 woven whole wheat crackers (such as Triscuits), finely crushed
Cooking spray

1. Preheat oven to 350°.
2. Pierce eggplant several times with a fork; place on a microwave-safe plate. Microwave at HIGH 8 minutes or until very tender but not mushy. Cool slightly.
3. Cut each eggplant in half lengthwise; scoop out pulp, and chop pulp. Drain pulp well in colander. Combine eggplant pulp, ⅓ cup Parmesan cheese, feta cheese, and next 6 ingredients in a large bowl. Spoon mixture into an 11 x 7- inch baking dish coated with cooking spray. Sprinkle remaining Parmesan cheese evenly over casserole. Bake at 350° for 1 hour or until top is golden brown. Let stand 15 minutes before serving. Yield: 8 servings (serving size: about 1 cup).

CALORIES 298; FAT 13.7g (sat 8.3g); PROTEIN 19.5g; CARBOHYDRATE 26.7g; FIBER 7.9g; CHOLESTEROL 46mg; IRON 1.8mg; SODIUM 866mg; CALCIUM 416mg

(pictured on page 153)

▶ carbo rating: 20
Seasoned Cannellini Beans

Pair this simple bean dish with a tossed green salad for a light supper, or decrease the portion size to about ⅔ cup and serve it as a side dish.

1 teaspoon olive oil
1 cup finely chopped celery
2 teaspoons bottled minced garlic
1 cup vegetable broth
2 (15.5-ounce) cans cannellini beans or other white beans, rinsed and drained
1 tablespoon finely chopped fresh sage or 1 teaspoon dried rubbed sage
¼ teaspoon salt
¼ teaspoon pepper
¼ cup coarsely chopped fresh flat-leaf parsley
¼ cup (1 ounce) grated fresh Parmesan cheese

1. Heat oil in a large saucepan over medium-high heat. Add celery and garlic; sauté 3 minutes or until tender. Add broth and next 4 ingredients; bring to a boil. Reduce heat; simmer, uncovered, 10 minutes.
2. Spoon beans into bowls; sprinkle evenly with parsley and cheese. Yield: 3 servings (serving size: 1⅓ cups).

CALORIES 203; FAT 5.3g (sat 1.9g); PROTEIN 11.4g; CARBOHYDRATE 27.5g; FIBER 7.5g; CHOLESTEROL 7mg; IRON 3mg; SODIUM 939mg; CALCIUM 202mg

better beans

Beans are high in fiber and protein, low in fat, and good sources of B vitamins and iron. Because they have so many nutrients, specifically soluble and insoluble fiber, beans can help reduce the risk of diabetes, heart disease, and some types of cancer.

If canned beans have been off-limits for you because of their sodium content, take heart. Most types of beans are now available in low-sodium canned versions. You can substitute the low-sodium beans for regular in any recipe that calls for canned beans. And, when you rinse regular canned beans in a strainer under cool running water, you reduce the sodium content by about 40 percent.

▶ **carbo rating: 20**

Vegetable-Bean Hot Pot

A traditional English hot pot is a hearty stew of potatoes and meat, either beef, lamb, or even rabbit. Our updated, vegetable-rich version is higher in fiber and lower in fat, but just as flavorful and filling.

Cooking spray
1   cup chopped carrot
½   cup chopped onion
1   cup chopped red bell pepper
1   (14½-ounce) can no-salt-added stewed tomatoes, undrained
1   cup water
2   tablespoons tomato paste
1   teaspoon onion powder
1   teaspoon garlic powder
½   teaspoon salt
½   teaspoon ground cumin
1   (16-ounce) can red kidney beans, rinsed and drained
½   cup sliced mushrooms
½   cup (2 ounces) grated fresh Parmesan cheese
¼   cup chopped fresh parsley

1. Coat a large saucepan with cooking spray; place over medium-high heat until hot. Add carrot and onion; sauté 3 minutes or until onion is soft. Add red bell pepper; sauté 1 minute.
2. Stir in tomatoes and next 6 ingredients; bring to a boil. Cover, reduce heat, and simmer 30 minutes or until carrot is tender. Stir in kidney beans and mushrooms; cook, uncovered, 5 minutes. Ladle into individual serving bowls; sprinkle each serving with 2 tablespoons Parmesan cheese and 1 tablespoon parsley. Yield: 4 servings (serving size: about 1¾ cups).

CALORIES 175; FAT 3.3g (sat 1.8g); PROTEIN 10g; CARBOHYDRATE 28.9g; FIBER 8.8g; CHOLESTEROL 7mg; IRON 2.2mg; SODIUM 722mg; CALCIUM 187mg

(pictured on page 154)

▶ **carbo rating: 21**

White Bean and Asparagus Tabbouleh

Tabbouleh *is a Middle Eastern dish made primarily of bulgur wheat. Using a commercial mix allows you to capture the flavors of traditional tabbouleh with fewer ingredients.*

1   (5.25-ounce) package tabbouleh mix
1   cup boiling water
1   (10-ounce) package frozen asparagus spears
1   (16-ounce) can navy beans, rinsed and drained
1½ tablespoons fresh lemon juice
1   tablespoon extravirgin olive oil
¼   teaspoon salt
⅛   teaspoon coarsely ground black pepper

1. Combine tabbouleh mix (bulgur wheat and spice packet) and boiling water in a large bowl. Cover and let stand at room temperature 15 minutes or until water is absorbed.
2. Cook asparagus according to package directions; drain in a colander, and cool under running water. Drain well; cut into bite-sized pieces.
3. Combine tabbouleh mix, asparagus, beans, and remaining ingredients in a large bowl. Yield: 3 servings (serving size: 1⅓ cups).

CALORIES 233; FAT 9.8g (sat 1.4g); PROTEIN 11g; CARBOHYDRATE 28.9g; FIBER 7.8g; CHOLESTEROL 0mg; IRON 2.9mg; SODIUM 877mg; CALCIUM 80mg

▶ carbo rating: 21

Spinach, Rice, and Feta Pie

Serve this crustless main dish pie with the Mediterranean Tossed Salad, page 281, for a light lunch or dinner.

2 teaspoons butter
¾ cup chopped onion
2 teaspoons all-purpose flour
½ teaspoon salt
¼ teaspoon pepper
1½ cups 1% low-fat milk
2 cups cooked brown rice
¾ cup (3 ounces) crumbled feta cheese
1 (10-ounce) package frozen chopped spinach, thawed, drained, and squeezed dry
1 large egg, lightly beaten
2 large egg whites, lightly beaten
Olive oil-flavored cooking spray
2 tablespoons grated Parmesan cheese

1. Preheat oven to 400°.
2. Melt butter in a large saucepan over medium heat. Add onion, and sauté 3 minutes. Stir in flour, salt, and pepper. Gradually add milk, stirring with a whisk until well blended. Bring mixture to a simmer; cook 1 minute or until slightly thick, stirring constantly. Remove saucepan from heat; stir in rice, feta cheese, and spinach. Add egg and egg white, stirring until blended.
3. Pour spinach mixture into a 9-inch pie plate coated with cooking spray. Sprinkle Parmesan cheese over pie. Bake at 400° for 35 minutes or until golden. Yield: 6 servings (serving size: 1 wedge).

CALORIES 199; FAT 7.2g (sat 4g); PROTEIN 10.6g; CARBOHYDRATE 23.8g; FIBER 3g; CHOLESTEROL 55mg; IRON 1.7mg; SODIUM 487mg; CALCIUM 254mg

▶ carbo rating: 22

Spicy Beans and Greens

*Instead of the usual Tex-Mex fare, try this unique Mexican meal. It's a version of a dish called **quelites**, which features beans, wild greens, and pine nuts.*

1 (16-ounce) package fresh turnip greens
2 cups fat-free, less-sodium chicken broth, divided
2 teaspoons ground cumin
1 teaspoon ground coriander
¾ teaspoon hot chili powder
¾ teaspoon dried oregano
1 cup finely chopped onion
2 garlic cloves, minced
2 (16-ounce) cans pinto beans, rinsed and drained
¼ cup pine nuts, toasted

1. Combine greens and ½ cup chicken broth in a large microwave-safe bowl; cover with plastic wrap, and vent. Microwave at HIGH 8 to 10 minutes or until tender; drain well.
2. Combine cumin, coriander, and chili powder in a large nonstick skillet; place over medium-low heat. Cook, stirring constantly, 2 minutes or until fragrant. Add 1½ cups broth, oregano, onion, and garlic; bring to a simmer and cook 5 minutes. Stir in beans; cook 2 minutes. Stir in greens. Spoon onto plates; top each serving with 1 tablespoon pine nuts. Serve immediately. Yield: 4 servings (serving size: 1½ cups).

CALORIES 228; FAT 6.3g (sat 1g); PROTEIN 12.7g; CARBOHYDRATE 33.8g; FIBER 11.9g; CHOLESTEROL 0mg; IRON 4.7mg; SODIUM 760mg; CALCIUM 304mg

▶ **carbo rating: 22**
Stuffed Portobello Mushrooms

Bake the mushrooms on a rack over a pan to catch breadcrumbs that may fall.

4	(4-inch) portobello mushrooms

Cooking spray

2	teaspoons olive oil
4	cups finely chopped Vidalia or other sweet onion
½	cup dry red wine
1	tablespoon balsamic vinegar
2	teaspoons finely chopped fresh thyme, divided
½	teaspoon sea salt
¾	cup chopped pitted kalamata olives
1	teaspoon grated lemon rind
¼	teaspoon black pepper
3	(1-ounce) slices whole wheat bread
⅓	cup (about 1½ ounces) grated fresh Parmesan cheese
¼	cup finely chopped fresh flat-leaf parsley

1. Preheat oven to 350°.
2. Remove stem and brown gills from undersides of mushrooms using a spoon; discard gills. Place mushrooms, stem sides down, on a baking sheet coated with cooking spray. Bake at 350° for 10 minutes; cool mushrooms on a wire rack.
3. Heat oil in a large nonstick skillet over medium-high heat. Add onion; sauté 12 minutes. Stir in wine, vinegar, 1 teaspoon thyme, and salt; bring to a boil. Cover, reduce heat, and simmer 25 minutes.
4. Uncover mixture, and increase heat to medium-high; cook 5 minutes or until liquid evaporates. Stir in olives, rind, and pepper.
5. Place bread in a food processor; pulse 10 times or until coarse crumbs form to measure 1½ cups. Combine 1 teaspoon thyme, crumbs, cheese, and parsley. Place mushrooms on a wire rack over a baking sheet. Spoon ½ cup olive mixture into each mushroom; top with ¾ cup cheese mixture. Bake at 350° for 25 minutes. Yield: 4 servings (serving size: 1 stuffed mushroom).

CALORIES 246; FAT 8.1g (sat 2.2g); PROTEIN 7.6g; CARBOHYDRATE 27.6g; FIBER 5.4g; CHOLESTEROL 7mg; IRON 1.3mg; SODIUM 700mg; CALCIUM 134mg

▶ **carbo rating: 23**
Cheesy Bean Casserole

Beans and cheese pack this casserole full of good-for-you fiber and calcium.

Cooking spray

1	cup chopped onion
2	(16-ounce) cans chili hot beans, drained
2	(14½-ounce) cans no-salt-added whole tomatoes, drained and chopped
½	teaspoon garlic powder
¼	teaspoon pepper
1	cup (4 ounces) shredded reduced-fat sharp Cheddar cheese

1. Preheat oven to 400°.
2. Coat a nonstick skillet with cooking spray; place over medium-high heat until hot. Add onion; sauté until tender. Stir in beans and next 3 ingredients. Cook 3 minutes or until thoroughly heated, stirring well.
3. Spoon mixture into 4 individual baking dishes or 1 (8-inch) square baking dish; sprinkle with cheese. Bake, uncovered, at 400° for 5 minutes or until cheese melts. Let stand 5 minutes. Yield: 4 servings (serving size: about 2 cups).

CALORIES 274; FAT 6.9g (sat 4.1g); PROTEIN 17.6g; CARBOHYDRATE 35.4g; FIBER 12.8g; CHOLESTEROL 20mg; IRON 0.8mg; SODIUM 257mg; CALCIUM 250mg

▶ **carbo rating: 23**

Mediterranean-Style Stuffed Eggplant

Couscous is tiny beadlike pasta that's traditional in Mediterranean cuisine. It soaks up the fresh flavors of ingredients like tomatoes, balsamic vinegar, and herbs. Because it has a slightly higher fiber content, we recommend using whole wheat instead of plain couscous. You'll find whole wheat couscous on the grocery shelves with other types of couscous, or look for it at health-food stores.

2	small eggplants
1	(14½-ounce) can Italian-style stewed tomatoes, undrained
1	cup water
1	tablespoon balsamic vinegar
½	teaspoon dried marjoram
¼	teaspoon ground allspice
1½	cups uncooked whole wheat couscous
	Cooking spray
5	ounces (about 1 cup) crumbled feta cheese with black peppercorns

1. Preheat oven to 350°.
2. Prick each eggplant several times with a fork. Place eggplant on a baking sheet, and bake at 350° for 20 minutes. Cool. Cut each eggplant in half lengthwise; scoop out pulp, leaving ¼-inch-thick shells. Chop pulp; set shells and pulp aside.
3. Combine tomato and next 4 ingredients in a medium saucepan; bring to a boil, and stir in couscous. Cover, remove from heat, and let stand 5 minutes. Fluff with a fork; stir in eggplant pulp.
4. Spoon couscous mixture evenly into eggplant shells; place in a 13 x 9-inch baking dish coated with cooking spray. Top evenly with cheese. Cover and bake at 350° for 25 minutes or until thoroughly heated. Yield: 4 servings (serving size: 1 stuffed eggplant half).

CALORIES 233; FAT 8.1g (sat 5.3g); PROTEIN 10.4g; CARBOHYDRATE 31.3g; FIBER 7.9g; CHOLESTEROL 32mg; IRON 1.5mg; SODIUM 681mg; CALCIUM 226mg

▶ **carbo rating: 24**

Broccoli-Tofu Stir-Fry with Cashews

If you prefer to serve this spicy stir-fry over ½-cup portions of brown rice instead of whole wheat noodles, the carbo rating will be 29 instead of 24.

6	ounces uncooked whole wheat spaghetti
3	tablespoons soy sauce
2	tablespoons seasoned rice vinegar
2	teaspoons chopped peeled fresh or bottled ginger
1½	teaspoons bottled minced garlic
1	(1-pound) package firm tofu, drained and cut into ½-inch cubes
1	tablespoon dark sesame oil, divided
5	cups broccoli florets
½	cup chopped green onions
2	tablespoons minced seeded jalapeño pepper
⅓	cup cashews

1. Cook whole wheat spaghetti according to package directions; drain.
2. Combine soy sauce and next 3 ingredients in a shallow dish; stir well. Add tofu cubes, stirring gently to coat. Let stand 15 minutes.
3. Remove tofu from dish, reserving marinade. Heat 2 teaspoons oil in a wok or nonstick skillet over medium-high heat. Add tofu; cook 2 minutes or until browned. Remove tofu; set aside, and keep warm.
4. Add 1 teaspoon oil, broccoli, green onions, and jalapeño pepper to pan; sauté 2 minutes. Stir in reserved marinade, tofu, and cashews; serve over spaghetti. Yield: 5 servings (serving size: about 1½ cups stir-fry and ½ cup spaghetti).

CALORIES 268; FAT 11.3g (sat 2g); PROTEIN 15.5g; CARBOHYDRATE 30.1g; FIBER 6.6g; CHOLESTEROL 0mg; IRON 3.2mg; SODIUM 917mg; CALCIUM 93mg

► carbo rating: 24

Brown Rice with Vegetable Sauté

Cooking brown rice in vegetable broth instead of water adds flavor but not carbs.

1	cup quick-cooking brown rice
1¼	cups vegetable broth
2	teaspoons butter or margarine
1	cup chopped onion (about 1 large)
2	cups small broccoli florets
1	(8-ounce) package sliced mushrooms
1	teaspoon dried thyme
½	teaspoon salt
½	teaspoon minced garlic
¼	teaspoon pepper
½	cup (2 ounces) shredded part-skim mozzarella cheese
3	tablespoons chopped walnuts, toasted

1. Cook rice according to package directions, using vegetable broth instead of water and omitting salt and fat.
2. Melt butter in a large nonstick skillet over medium-high heat. Add onion; sauté 5 minutes. Add broccoli; cover and cook over low heat 3 minutes. Uncover; add mushrooms and next 4 ingredients. Sauté 5 minutes or until mushrooms are tender.
3. Spoon vegetable mixture over rice. Sprinkle evenly with cheese and walnuts. Yield: 4 servings (serving size: ½ cup rice and ¾ cup vegetable mixture).

CALORIES 216; FAT 8.9g (sat 3g); PROTEIN 10g; CARBOHYDRATE 27.5g; FIBER 3.7g; CHOLESTEROL 8mg; IRON 1.9mg; SODIUM 619mg; CALCIUM 136mg

► carbo rating: 24

Meatless Chili

Meatless burger crumbles are made with textured soy protein and have a flavor and texture similar to that of ground beef. Use the crumbles just as you would ground beef, but reduce the cooking time slightly.

	Cooking spray
2	teaspoons bottled minced garlic
1	large onion, chopped
1	(16-ounce) can chili hot beans, undrained
1	(14.5-ounce) can no-salt-added diced tomatoes, undrained
1	teaspoon chili powder
1	teaspoon ground cumin
12	ounces frozen meatless burger crumbles (about 3 cups)

1. Coat a 4-quart saucepan with cooking spray. Place pan over medium-high heat until hot. Add garlic and onion; sauté 3 minutes. Add beans and next 3 ingredients. Bring to a boil, stirring occasionally; reduce heat, and simmer 5 minutes. Add protein crumbles, and cook 3 minutes or until thoroughly heated. Yield: 4 servings (serving size: 1½ cups).

CALORIES 241; FAT 1.9g (sat 0.6g); PROTEIN 22.4g; CARBOHYDRATE 33.2g; FIBER 9.3g; CHOLESTEROL 0mg; IRON 2.9mg; SODIUM 874mg; CALCIUM 82mg

▶ **carbo rating: 25**

Tuscan Skillet Supper

Beans, greens, and pasta are all hallmarks of Tuscan-style recipes. Instead of pasta, this one-dish meal features additional fresh vegetables.

2	teaspoons olive oil
1¼	cups chopped zucchini
½	cup sliced onion
½	cup sliced celery
½	cup diced red bell pepper
1	teaspoon dried oregano
2	garlic cloves, minced
1	cup diced tomato
1	(15-ounce) can cannellini beans or other white beans, rinsed and drained
2	rosemary sprigs
1	cup chopped spinach
¼	teaspoon salt
⅛	teaspoon black pepper
½	cup (2 ounces) shredded part-skim mozzarella cheese

1. Heat oil in a large nonstick skillet over medium-high heat. Add zucchini and next 5 ingredients; sauté 10 minutes. Stir in tomato, beans, and rosemary; cook 5 minutes, stirring frequently.
2. Add chopped spinach, salt, and pepper to zucchini mixture; cook 1 minute or until spinach wilts. Sprinkle with cheese; cover and let stand 1 to 2 minutes or until cheese begins to melt. Remove from heat, and discard rosemary. Yield: 2 servings (serving size: 1¾ cups).

CALORIES 318; FAT 10.4g (sat 3.6g); PROTEIN 18.3g; CARBOHYDRATE 38.2g; FIBER 12.9g; CHOLESTEROL 16mg; IRON 4.8mg; SODIUM 766mg; CALCIUM 280mg

▶ **carbo rating: 25**

Saucy Cannellini Beans

When you rinse and drain canned beans, you reduce the sodium by about 40 percent. Place a colander in the bottom of the sink. Pour in the beans and rinse well under cold running water. Leave the colander in the sink to allow the beans to drain well. Or place the colander on a plate on the counter to catch any liquid that drains from the beans.

2	teaspoons olive oil
2	medium zucchini, halved lengthwise and sliced (about 2 cups)
2	(14.5-ounce) cans diced tomatoes with balsamic vinegar and basil
1	(15.5-ounce) can cannellini beans, rinsed and drained
¼	teaspoon dried or ½ teaspoon fresh oregano
¼	teaspoon coarsely ground black pepper
¼	cup (1 ounce) shredded fresh Parmesan cheese
4	teaspoons chopped fresh flat-leaf parsley

1. Heat olive oil in a large saucepan over medium-high heat. Add zucchini; sauté 3 minutes or until tender.
2. Add tomatoes and next 3 ingredients. Simmer, uncovered, 10 to 12 minutes or to desired consistency. Ladle into bowls; sprinkle evenly with Parmesan cheese and parsley just before serving. Yield: 4 servings (serving size: 1¼ cups).

CALORIES 186; FAT 4g (sat 1.2g); PROTEIN 8.8g; CARBOHYDRATE 30g; FIBER 5.3g; CHOLESTEROL 4mg; IRON 4.4mg; SODIUM 1,285mg; CALCIUM 230mg

▶ carbo rating: 25

Layered Vegetable Lasagna

This lasagna has 4 more grams of fiber than a meat and cheese lasagna with regular noodles. The carbo rating for a similar-sized serving of traditional lasagna is 38.

1   (10-ounce) package frozen chopped spinach, thawed, drained, and squeezed dry
1   (12-ounce) carton 1% low-fat cottage cheese
¼   cup egg substitute
2   teaspoons olive oil
¾   cup minced onion
1   cup sliced mushrooms
2   garlic cloves, minced
2   (14½-ounce) cans no-salt-added whole tomatoes, drained and chopped
¼   cup minced fresh parsley
¼   cup dry red wine
¼   cup no-salt-added tomato paste
2   teaspoons dried basil
1½ teaspoons dried oregano
½   teaspoon pepper
¼   teaspoon salt
Cooking spray
6   uncooked whole wheat lasagna noodles
5   cups thinly sliced zucchini (about 1¼ pounds)
1½ cups (6 ounces) finely shredded part-skim mozzarella cheese
¼   cup (1 ounce) grated fresh Parmesan cheese

1. Combine spinach, cottage cheese, and egg substitute in a medium bowl; stir well, and set aside.
2. Heat oil in a large saucepan over medium-high heat. Add onion; sauté 3 minutes or until tender. Add mushrooms and garlic; sauté 2 minutes or until mushrooms are tender. Add tomatoes and next 7 ingredients; stir well. Reduce heat, and simmer, uncovered, 20 minutes. Remove tomato mixture from heat; set aside.
3. Coat a 13 x 9-inch baking dish with cooking spray. Spoon one-third of tomato mixture into baking dish. Arrange 3 uncooked noodles lengthwise in a single layer over tomato mixture; top with 1¼ cups spinach mixture. Layer 2½ cups zucchini over spinach; sprinkle with ½ cup mozzarella cheese. Repeat layers; top with remaining tomato mixture. Cover and chill 8 hours.
4. Preheat oven to 350°.
5. Remove lasagna from refrigerator; bake, covered, at 350° for 1 hour and 30 minutes. Uncover; sprinkle with ½ cup mozzarella cheese and Parmesan cheese. Cover; let stand 5 minutes before serving. Yield: 6 servings (serving size: about 2 cups).

CALORIES 289; FAT 8.8g (sat 4.4g); PROTEIN 24.8g; CARBOHYDRATE 31.7g; FIBER 6.6g; CHOLESTEROL 20mg; IRON 3.9mg; SODIUM 617mg; CALCIUM 420mg

whole wheat vs. plain pasta

See the comparisons below for plain and whole wheat pastas.

Type of pasta (½ cup, cooked)	Carbohydrate (grams)	Fiber (grams)	Carbo Rating
spaghetti	19.8	1.2	**19**
whole wheat spaghetti	18.6	3.2	**15**
lasagna noodles	19.8	0.9	**19**
whole wheat lasagna noodles	18.6	2.0	**17**
reduced-carb lasagna noodles	16.0	6.0	**10**
macaroni	18.2	0.0	**18**
whole wheat macaroni	18.6	2.0	**17**

▶ **carbo rating: 26**

Italian Stuffed Eggplant

You can assemble the stuffed eggplant shells a few hours ahead and keep them covered in the refrigerator. Before baking, let the dish come to room temperature or your baking time will be longer.

2 medium eggplants
Garlic-flavored cooking spray
1¼ cups chopped onion
1¼ cups chopped zucchini
1 cup sliced mushrooms
¾ cup chopped green bell pepper
¾ cup chopped tomato
1 (8-ounce) can no-salt-added tomato sauce
1 cup cooked brown rice
¼ cup (1 ounce) grated fresh Parmesan cheese
1 tablespoon unsalted sunflower kernels, toasted
1 teaspoon dried Italian seasoning
1 cup (4 ounces) shredded part-skim mozzarella cheese

1. Preheat oven to 350°.
2. Wash eggplants; cut each in half lengthwise. Remove pulp, leaving ¼-inch-thick shells. Chop pulp; set aside 2 cups. (Reserve remaining pulp for another use.)
3. Coat a large nonstick skillet with cooking spray; place over medium heat. Add onion and next 3 ingredients; sauté until tender. Stir in 2 cups pulp, tomato, and tomato sauce. Cook, uncovered, 15 minutes. Remove from heat; stir in rice and next 3 ingredients.
4. Arrange shells in a baking dish coated with cooking spray; spoon vegetable mixture evenly into shells. Bake, uncovered, at 350° for 10 minutes. Sprinkle with mozzarella cheese; bake 5 minutes. Yield: 4 servings (serving size: 1 stuffed eggplant half).

CALORIES 249; FAT 8.7g (sat 4.4g); PROTEIN 14.8g; CARBOHYDRATE 30g; FIBER 4.3g; CHOLESTEROL 22mg; SODIUM 272mg; CALCIUM 322mg

(pictured on page 155)

▶ **carbo rating: 27**

Rice Gratin with Spinach and Leeks

*A **gratin** is any dish topped with cheese or breadcrumbs mixed with bits of butter and baked until the top is brown and crispy. This gratin has more fiber than most because of the whole wheat breadcrumbs, brown rice, spinach, and leeks.*

1 cup uncooked instant brown rice
1 cup water
½ (1-ounce) slice whole wheat bread
1 tablespoon light butter
1¼ cups thinly sliced leeks (about 2)
2 teaspoons all-purpose flour
1⅔ cups 1% low-fat milk
¾ cup (3 ounces) shredded reduced-fat Swiss cheese, divided
1 (10-ounce) package frozen chopped spinach, thawed, drained, and squeezed dry
2 large eggs, lightly beaten
½ teaspoon dried basil
½ teaspoon salt
¼ teaspoon pepper
Cooking spray

1. Cook rice in 1 cup water according to package directions to yield 2 cups cooked rice.
2. Preheat oven to 375°.
3. Place bread in a food processor; pulse 10 times or until coarse crumbs measure ¼ cup. Set aside.
4. Melt butter in a large nonstick skillet over medium heat. Add leek; sauté 6 minutes. Sprinkle with flour; stir well. Add milk; increase heat to medium-high, and cook, stirring constantly, until mixture comes to a simmer. Reduce heat; simmer 1 minute, stirring constantly. Remove from heat; add rice, ½ cup cheese, and next 5 ingredients. Stir. Spoon into a 10-inch quiche dish or 9-inch pie plate coated with cooking spray. Combine remaining cheese and breadcrumbs; sprinkle over gratin. Bake at 375° for 30 minutes or until set. Cool in dish 5 minutes on a wire rack. Yield: 8 servings (serving size: 1 wedge).

CALORIES 251; FAT 8.3g (sat 4.4g); PROTEIN 15.3g; CARBOHYDRATE 29.8g; FIBER 3.2g; CHOLESTEROL 91mg; IRON 2.1mg; SODIUM 382mg; CALCIUM 408mg

▶ **carbo rating: 28**

Barley with Pinto Beans, Tomatoes, and Mushrooms

When you use barley as a base instead of white rice, you can get at least 10 times more fiber per ½-cup serving. (See page 144 for more information on barley.)

Cooking spray
2   teaspoons olive oil
½   cup finely chopped onion
1   (6-ounce) package sliced portobello mushrooms, coarsely chopped
1   (15.5-ounce) can pinto beans, rinsed and drained
1   (14.5-ounce) can diced tomatoes with mild green chiles
1   cup vegetable broth
2   garlic cloves, minced
1   tablespoon tomato paste
¾   teaspoon dried oregano
¼   teaspoon salt
⅛   teaspoon pepper
2   cups hot cooked pearl barley
¼   cup (1 ounce) shredded Monterey Jack cheese
4   teaspoons minced fresh cilantro

1. Heat oil in a large nonstick skillet coated with cooking spray over medium heat. Add onion and mushrooms; sauté 6 minutes. Add beans, tomatoes, and next 6 ingredients; stir well. Bring to a boil. Cover, reduce heat, and simmer 10 minutes, stirring occasionally. Serve tomato mixture over barley, and sprinkle evenly with cheese and cilantro. Yield: 4 servings (serving size: 1 cup tomato mixture and ½ cup barley).

CALORIES 235; FAT 5.9g (sat 1.9g); PROTEIN 10.3g; CARBOHYDRATE 36.5g; FIBER 8.1g; CHOLESTEROL 6mg; IRON 2.3mg; SODIUM 837mg; CALCIUM 128mg

▶ **carbo rating: 28**

Spinach Pie with Rice Crust

Before you start assembling this pie, you'll need to cook the brown rice and the spinach first. You'll need about 1 pound of washed and trimmed spinach to get 2 cups of cooked. Cook 1 cup rice in 1 cup water according to package directions to get 2 cups cooked rice.

2   cups cooked instant brown rice
¾   cup egg substitute, divided
½   cup finely chopped onion
1   tablespoon margarine, melted
Cooking spray
⅓   cup evaporated fat-free milk
⅛   teaspoon salt
⅛   teaspoon white pepper
2   cups drained cooked spinach
⅔   cup (2.6 ounces) shredded Swiss cheese
1   tomato, sliced

1. Preheat oven to 350°.
2. Combine rice, ¼ cup egg substitute, onion, and margarine; press mixture into bottom and up sides of a 9-inch pie plate coated with cooking spray. Set aside.
3. Combine ½ cup egg substitute, milk, salt, and pepper; stir in spinach and cheese.
4. Pour spinach mixture into prepared rice crust; arrange tomato slices around edge of pie. Bake at 350° for 30 minutes or until set. Let stand 10 minutes before cutting into 4 wedges. Yield: 4 servings (serving size: 1 wedge).

CALORIES 279; FAT 9.3g (sat 4.1g); PROTEIN 17.1g; CARBOHYDRATE 32.8g; FIBER 4.9g; CHOLESTEROL 18mg; IRON 4.7mg; SODIUM 315mg; CALCIUM 392mg

▶ **carbo rating: 28**

Spaghetti Squash with Tomatoes and Beans

Instead of spooning tomato sauce over spaghetti noodles, try it over strands of spaghetti squash. In addition to being very low in carbohydrate, spaghetti squash has more flavor than plain noodles.

1   (2½-pound) spaghetti squash
Cooking spray
1   (15-ounce) can salsa-style chunky tomatoes, undrained
1   (15-ounce) can black beans, rinsed and drained
¾   cup (3 ounces) shredded reduced-fat Monterey Jack cheese, divided
¼   cup minced fresh cilantro
1   teaspoon ground cumin
¼   teaspoon freshly ground black pepper

1. Preheat oven to 375°.
2. Wash squash; cut in half lengthwise. Remove and discard seeds. Place squash halves, cut sides down, in a 13 x 9-inch baking dish coated with cooking spray. Add water to depth of ½ inch. Bake at 375° for 25 minutes or until squash is tender; cool slightly. Using a fork, remove spaghetti-like strands; discard shells. Reduce oven temperature to 350°.
3. Combine squash strands, tomato, beans, ½ cup cheese, ¼ cup cilantro, cumin, and pepper in a large bowl, stirring well. Spoon into a 1½-quart casserole coated with cooking spray. Sprinkle with ¼ cup cheese.
4. Bake, uncovered, at 350° for 35 minutes or until thoroughly heated. Serve immediately. Yield: 4 servings (serving size: 1½ cups).

Microwave Tip: You can save time by cooking spaghetti squash in the microwave. Place seeded squash halves, cut sides down, in a baking dish. Prick the skin with a fork, and add ¼ cup water to dish. Cover with plastic wrap; microwave at HIGH 7 to 10 minutes or until tender.

CALORIES 232; FAT 5.4g (sat 2.5g); PROTEIN 14.4g; CARBOHYDRATE 32.4g; FIBER 4.7g; CHOLESTEROL 11mg; IRON 3.1mg; SODIUM 902mg; CALCIUM 223mg

▶ **carbo rating: 28**

Asian Vegetable Stir-Fry

Look for 16-ounce bags of cut assorted fresh vegetables in the produce section of your local supermarket.

1   cup uncooked instant brown rice
1   cup water
¼   cup plus 1 tablespoon low-sodium soy sauce, divided
1   (10.5-ounce) package firm tofu, drained and cut into 1-inch cubes
1   tablespoon cornstarch
1   tablespoon water
1   tablespoon rice vinegar
1   teaspoon dark sesame oil
2   garlic cloves, minced
2   teaspoons minced peeled fresh ginger
4½   cups cut assorted fresh stir-fry vegetables

1. Cook rice in 1 cup water according to package directions to yield 2 cups cooked rice.
2. Sprinkle 1 tablespoon soy sauce over tofu; set aside.
3. Combine cornstarch and water in a small bowl; stir until smooth. Add ¼ cup soy sauce and vinegar.
4. Heat sesame oil in a large nonstick skillet over medium-high heat. Add garlic and ginger; sauté 30 seconds. Add vegetables; stir-fry 3 minutes. Stir cornstarch mixture, and add to pan. Stir-fry 3 minutes or until vegetables are crisp-tender and sauce is thick. Add tofu mixture; cook until thoroughly heated. Serve over rice. Yield: 4 servings (serving size: 1½ cups vegetables and ½ cup rice).

CALORIES 198; FAT 4.1g (sat 0.6g); PROTEIN 9.6g; CARBOHYDRATE 30.6g; FIBER 2.8g; CHOLESTEROL 0mg; IRON 1.8mg; SODIUM 724mg; CALCIUM 85mg

▶ **carbo rating: 30**

Sesame Vegetable Tofu Stir-Fry

When tofu is pressed to extract excess liquid, it absorbs even more of the soy sauce, ginger, and garlic seasonings. Start cooking the rice while the tofu cubes are standing in the soy sauce mixture.

1	(10½-ounce) package extrafirm tofu
¼	cup low-sodium soy sauce
1	tablespoon minced peeled fresh ginger
2	teaspoons "measures-like-sugar" calorie-free sweetener
2	teaspoons dark sesame oil
2	garlic cloves, minced
2	teaspoons vegetable oil
2	cups broccoli florets
1	cup thinly sliced red bell pepper
2	cups thinly sliced napa (Chinese) cabbage
1	cup fresh bean sprouts
2	teaspoons sesame seeds, toasted
2	cups hot cooked brown rice

1. Place tofu between 2 flat plates or cutting boards. Weight the top with a heavy can (sides of tofu should be bulging slightly, but not cracking). Let stand 40 to 45 minutes; pour off and discard liquid. Cut tofu into ½-inch cubes, and set aside.
2. Combine soy sauce and next 4 ingredients in a medium bowl, stirring well. Add tofu, and toss to coat. Let stand 10 minutes. Remove tofu from marinade, reserving marinade.
3. Drizzle vegetable oil around top of a wok, coating sides. Heat at medium-high (375°) until hot. Add tofu; stir-fry 4 minutes. Add broccoli and bell pepper; stir-fry 2 minutes. Add cabbage and bean sprouts; stir-fry 2 minutes or until vegetables are crisp-tender. Add reserved marinade; toss gently, and cook 30 seconds or until thoroughly heated. Stir in sesame seeds.
4. Spoon ½ cup rice onto 4 serving plates. Top evenly with vegetable mixture. Yield: 4 servings (serving size: about 2 cups vegetable mixture and ½ cup rice).

CALORIES 283; FAT 10.7g (sat 1.6g); PROTEIN 13g; CARBOHYDRATE 34.1g; FIBER 4.4g; CHOLESTEROL 0mg; IRON 4.6mg; SODIUM 551mg; CALCIUM 110mg

▶ **carbo rating: 31**

Spicy Asparagus-Tempeh Stir-Fry

Brown rice is the only whole-grain rice; it still has the bran intact, so it's higher in fiber and other nutrients than white rice.

¾	pound asparagus spears
¾	cup vegetable broth
¼	cup low-sodium soy sauce
2	teaspoons cornstarch
2	tablespoons sesame oil, divided
1	(8-ounce) package multigrain tempeh (such as White Wave Five-Grain), thinly sliced
4	garlic cloves, minced
½	teaspoon crushed red pepper
1	(6-ounce) package sliced shiitake mushrooms
2	cups hot cooked instant brown rice

1. Snap off tough ends of asparagus. Cut spears diagonally into 2-inch pieces.
2. Combine vegetable broth, soy sauce, and cornstarch in a small bowl; stir with a whisk until smooth.
3. Heat 1 tablespoon sesame oil in a large nonstick skillet over medium-high heat. Add tempeh; stir-fry 4 to 5 minutes or until golden. Remove tempeh from pan; set aside.
4. Heat 1 tablespoon sesame oil in same pan. Add garlic, red pepper, asparagus, and mushrooms to pan; stir-fry 3 minutes or until asparagus is crisp-tender. Add broth mixture; bring to a boil, and cook 2 to 3 minutes or until thick. Add tempeh; cook 1 minute or until thoroughly heated. Serve over brown rice. Yield: 4 servings (serving size: 1 cup stir-fry and ½ cup brown rice).

CALORIES 336; FAT 14.2g (sat 2.5g); PROTEIN 17.3g; CARBOHYDRATE 38.2g; FIBER 7.3g; CHOLESTEROL 0mg; IRON 3.8mg; SODIUM 743mg; CALCIUM 99mg

▶ **carbo rating: 31**

Portobello Tetrazzini

There's no slicing, dicing, or chopping required in this recipe. Because the chopped onion, bell pepper, and celery blend has been frozen, it tends to lose water as it thaws. Drain well, and lightly press between two paper towels before adding to the skillet.

4   ounces uncooked whole wheat spaghetti
Cooking spray
2   (6-ounce) packages sliced portobello mushrooms, coarsely chopped
1   cup frozen chopped onion, bell pepper, and celery blend (such as McKenzie's), thawed and drained
1   (10¾-ounce) can condensed reduced-fat, reduced-sodium cream of mushroom soup, undiluted
½   cup fat-free milk
3   tablespoons sherry
½   teaspoon salt
¼   teaspoon freshly ground black pepper
¼   cup (1 ounce) shredded fresh Parmesan cheese

1. Cook spaghetti according to package directions, omitting salt and fat; drain.
2. Heat a large nonstick skillet coated with cooking spray over high heat. Add mushrooms; sauté 4 minutes or until tender. Add vegetable blend; cook 1 minute. Add soup and next 4 ingredients; reduce heat to medium, and simmer 5 minutes or until thick. Add spaghetti; toss well. Spoon pasta mixture onto 4 plates; top each serving with Parmesan cheese. Serve immediately. Yield: 4 servings (serving size: 1¼ cups pasta mixture and 1 tablespoon Parmesan cheese).

Note: The sherry (fortified wine) really makes a difference in the flavor of this dish. Cooking sherry will not add the same great flavor, but if you choose to use it, leave out the salt in the recipe because cooking sherry contains salt.

CALORIES 227; FAT 4.6g (sat 2.3g); PROTEIN 10.5g; CARBOHYDRATE 35.9g; FIBER 4.9g; CHOLESTEROL 11mg; IRON 1mg; SODIUM 650mg; CALCIUM 179mg

▶ **carbo rating: 33**

Asparagus-Parmesan Pita Rounds

Instead of a thick, high-carb pizza crust dough, this veggie pizza base is a crispy whole wheat pita round. A 6-inch Boboli® pizza crust has a carbo rating of 48; a 6-inch whole wheat pita has a carbo rating of 30.

2   cups (2-inch) sliced asparagus (about 1 pound)
2   teaspoons extravirgin olive oil
2   garlic cloves, minced
4   (6-inch) whole wheat pitas
3   plum tomatoes, thinly sliced (about ½ pound)
1   teaspoon dried basil
¼   teaspoon salt
¼   teaspoon crushed red pepper (optional)
6   tablespoons (1.5 ounces) shredded fresh Parmesan cheese

1. Preheat oven to 450°.
2. Steam asparagus, covered, 2 to 3 minutes or until crisp-tender. Rinse with cold water; drain.
3. Combine oil and garlic. Brush over pitas. Arrange tomato slices and asparagus on pitas. Sprinkle with basil, salt, and pepper, if desired. Top evenly with Parmesan cheese. Bake at 450° for 7 to 8 minutes or until edges are golden. Yield: 4 servings (serving size: 1 pita).

CALORIES 245; FAT 5.4g (sat 1.8g); PROTEIN 10.5g; CARBOHYDRATE 40g; FIBER 6.9g; CHOLESTEROL 5mg; IRON 2.7mg; SODIUM 601mg; CALCIUM 177mg

"Whole wheat pitas are now a staple in my kitchen. Use them as pizza crusts, for sandwiches, and for snacks." (See Quick Pita Chips, page 63.)

Laurl Self

▶ carbo rating: 33

Whole Wheat Spaghetti with Arugula

If you don't care for the pungent flavor of arugula, you can substitute baby spinach leaves without a significant change in the amount of carbohydrate.

8	ounces uncooked whole wheat spaghetti
2	tablespoons olive oil, divided
¼	teaspoon crushed red pepper
2	garlic cloves, minced
1	cup chopped tomato
1	pound arugula, trimmed and torn (about 16 cups)
1½	tablespoons red wine vinegar
¾	teaspoon salt
½	teaspoon freshly ground black pepper
½	cup (2 ounces) grated fresh Parmesan cheese

1. Cook pasta according to package directions; drain.
2. Heat 1 tablespoon oil over medium-high heat in a Dutch oven. Add red pepper and garlic; sauté 20 seconds. Add tomato and arugula; sauté 2 minutes or until arugula wilts. Spoon into a large bowl. Add 1 tablespoon oil, spaghetti, vinegar, salt, and black pepper; toss well. Sprinkle with cheese. Yield: 4 servings (serving size: 1½ cups pasta and 2 tablespoons cheese).

CALORIES 347; FAT 11.6g (sat 4.3g); PROTEIN 17.5g; CARBOHYDRATE 41.6g; FIBER 8.2g; CHOLESTEROL 10mg; IRON 4.4mg; SODIUM 705mg; CALCIUM 322mg

arugula

Also known as rocket, roquette, rugula, and rucola, this peppery, pungent, leafy green is a staple of Italian fare and often found in mesclun salad mixes, where it behaves like a cross between a lettuce and an herb.

Most arugula bought from a grocery store has short, tender stems. If you buy yours in bulk or from a farmers' market, however, you may encounter longer, thicker stems. Trim these away by cutting them off at the base of the leaf. To measure arugula, lightly pack clean, stem-free leaves in your measuring cup.

▶ carbo rating: 34

Spinach-Spaghetti Bake

This casserole boasts more fiber than the usual pasta dish because it has whole wheat spaghetti and is topped with fresh spinach.

7	ounces uncooked whole wheat spaghetti
1	cup shredded carrot
Cooking spray	
1	(26-ounce) jar fire-roasted tomato and garlic pasta sauce (such as Classico)
1	cup part-skim ricotta cheese
1	large egg, lightly beaten
¾	teaspoon salt, divided
1	teaspoon olive oil
4	garlic cloves, minced
1	(10-ounce) package fresh spinach
1	cup (4 ounces) shredded part-skim mozzarella cheese

1. Preheat oven to 350°.
2. Cook spaghetti in a Dutch oven according to package directions, omitting salt and fat. Add carrot to spaghetti during last 2 minutes of cooking time. Drain. Place pasta mixture in an 11 x 7-inch baking dish coated with cooking spray; stir in pasta sauce.
3. Combine ricotta cheese, egg, and ½ teaspoon salt in a small bowl; stir until smooth. Spread ricotta mixture over pasta mixture.
4. Heat olive oil in Dutch oven over medium-high heat until hot; add garlic, spinach, and remaining ¼ teaspoon salt. Cover and cook 2 minutes or until spinach begins to wilt; cook, uncovered, stirring constantly, 3 minutes or until liquid evaporates. Arrange spinach over ricotta mixture. Sprinkle mozzarella cheese over top of spinach.
5. Cover and bake at 350° for 20 minutes. Uncover and bake an additional 5 minutes or until thoroughly heated and mozzarella cheese melts. Yield: 6 servings (serving size: about 1⅓ cups).

CALORIES 337; FAT 10.4g (sat 5g); PROTEIN 18.5g; CARBOHYDRATE 41.6g; FIBER 8g; CHOLESTEROL 61mg; IRON 2.6mg; SODIUM 919mg; CALCIUM 388mg

▶ carbo rating: 35

Lentils with Eggplant and Garam Masala

Bring the taste of exotic India to your table with this spiced lentil and vegetable dinner. Cook the brown rice while the lentil mixture is simmering.

2	teaspoons olive oil
1	cup chopped onion
1½	teaspoons Garam Masala (recipe at right)
1	(1-pound) eggplant, peeled and chopped
1	cup chopped tomato
1	teaspoon ground turmeric
1	teaspoon grated peeled fresh ginger
2	garlic cloves, minced
4	cups water
1	cup dried lentils
1½	teaspoons salt
2	bay leaves
2	cups chopped zucchini
3	cups hot cooked brown rice

1. Heat oil in a Dutch oven over medium-high heat. Add onion and Garam Masala; sauté 3 minutes or until onion is tender. Stir in eggplant and next 4 ingredients; sauté 7 minutes or until eggplant is tender.

2. Add water, lentils, salt, and bay leaves to pan; bring to a boil. Cover, reduce heat, and simmer 15 minutes. Stir in zucchini; bring to a boil. Reduce heat; simmer 10 minutes or until zucchini is tender. Discard bay leaves. Serve over rice. Yield: 6 servings (serving size: 1¼ cups lentil mixture and ½ cup rice).

CALORIES 274; FAT 3.2g (sat 0.5g); PROTEIN 13.3g; CARBOHYDRATE 50.2g; FIBER 14.7g; CHOLESTEROL 0mg; IRON 4.1mg; SODIUM 602mg; CALCIUM 51mg

Garam Masala:

2	tablespoons coriander seeds
2	tablespoons cumin seeds
2	tablespoons black peppercorns
1½	teaspoons whole cloves
¾	teaspoon cardamom seeds
1	(1-inch) cinnamon stick

1. Heat a medium skillet over medium heat; add all ingredients. Cook 2 minutes or until toasted, stirring frequently. Place spice mixture in a spice or coffee grinder; process until finely ground. Store in an airtight container in the freezer for up to 6 months. Use to season tofu, couscous, and steamed vegetables. Yield: about ⅓ cup.

CALORIES 27; FAT 1g (sat 0.6g); PROTEIN 0.9g; CARBOHYDRATE 4.4g; FIBER 1.7g; CHOLESTEROL 0mg; IRON 2.2mg; SODIUM 6mg; CALCIUM 58mg

► **carbo rating: 35**

Farrotto with Greens and Parmesan

This spin on Italian risotto uses spelt, or farro, instead of rice. Spelt is an ancient grain with a mellow, nutty flavor. It's higher in protein than wheat and is easily digestible, so it can usually be tolerated by people with wheat allergies.

1	tablespoon olive oil
2¼	cups chopped red onion
4	garlic cloves, minced
1	cup uncooked spelt (farro), rinsed and drained
1	cup Chardonnay or other dry white wine
1	(14½-ounce) can vegetable broth
2	cups water
¼	teaspoon freshly ground black pepper
4	cups chopped gourmet salad greens
½	cup (2 ounces) grated Parmigiano-Reggiano cheese

1. Heat oil in a large saucepan over medium-high heat. Add onion and garlic; sauté 7 minutes or until golden brown. Add spelt; sauté 2 minutes. Stir in wine; cook 3 minutes. Add broth; cook 12 minutes or until liquid is nearly absorbed, stirring frequently. Stir in water and pepper; cook 12 minutes or until liquid is nearly absorbed, stirring frequently. Remove mixture from heat. Stir in greens and cheese. Yield: 4 servings (serving size: 1 cup).

CALORIES 283; FAT 9g (sat 2.9g); PROTEIN 12.1g; CARBOHYDRATE 44.8g; FIBER 10.2g; CHOLESTEROL 15mg; IRON 3.1mg; SODIUM 605mg; CALCIUM 220mg

► **carbo rating: 36**

Spaghetti Squash with White Beans Provençale

If you've given up pasta, replace spaghetti noodles with strands of spaghetti squash. The squash does not really taste like pasta—it's better!

1	(2½-pound) spaghetti squash
	Cooking spray
1	teaspoon vegetable oil
2	cups thinly sliced leek (about 1 leek)
2	(16-ounce) cans navy beans, drained
1	(14½-ounce) can no-salt-added stewed tomatoes, undrained
2	tablespoons chopped ripe olives
1	tablespoon balsamic vinegar
¼	teaspoon salt
¼	teaspoon pepper

1. Preheat oven to 350°.
2. Wash squash; cut in half lengthwise. Remove and discard seeds. Place squash, cut sides down, in a 13 x 9-inch baking dish coated with cooking spray. Add water to depth of ½ inch. Bake at 350° for 45 minutes or until tender when pierced with a fork; cool slightly. Using a fork, scrape spaghetti-like strands onto a platter; set aside, and keep warm.
3. Coat a saucepan with cooking spray; add oil. Place over medium-high heat until hot. Add leek; sauté 3 minutes or until tender. Add beans and tomatoes; cook over medium heat 5 minutes. Stir in olives and next 3 ingredients; cook until thoroughly heated. Spoon bean mixture over squash. Yield: 4 servings (serving size: ¾ cup squash and 1¾ cups bean mixture).

CALORIES 226; FAT 2.9g (sat 0.6g); PROTEIN 10.5g; CARBOHYDRATE 43g; FIBER 6.8g; CHOLESTEROL 0mg; IRON 4.3mg; SODIUM 508mg; CALCIUM 157mg

▶ carbo rating: 37
Tabbouleh

Tabbouleh *is a traditional Middle Eastern-style grain salad that usually features bulgur wheat, tomatoes, parsley, and mint. This version is especially high in fiber because it has lentils in addition to the bulgur.*

½	cup dried lentils
2	cups water
1	cup uncooked bulgur
2	cups boiling water
½	cup fresh lemon juice
1	cup coarsely chopped fresh parsley
1	cup coarsely chopped fresh mint
1	cup cherry tomato halves
1	cup sliced canned artichoke hearts, drained
1	cup diced seeded peeled cucumber
½	cup minced red onion
½	teaspoon pepper
1½	tablespoons olive oil
2	garlic cloves, minced

1. Combine lentils and 2 cups water in a medium saucepan. Bring to a boil; cover, reduce heat, and simmer 40 minutes or until lentils are tender. Drain, rinse under cold water, and drain again. Transfer to a large bowl.
2. Combine bulgur, boiling water, and lemon juice in a medium bowl; cover and let stand 30 minutes. Add bulgur mixture, parsley, and next 8 ingredients to lentils; toss well. Cover and chill at least 30 minutes. Yield: 4 servings (serving size: 2 cups).

CALORIES 274; FAT 6.1g (sat 0.9g); PROTEIN 10.4g; CARBOHYDRATE 50.3g; FIBER 13.2g; CHOLESTEROL 0mg; IRON 6.9mg; SODIUM 163mg; CALCIUM 115mg

▶ carbo rating: 38
Lentils and Brown Rice Pilaf

The combination of lentils, brown rice, and fresh vegetables contributes to the high fiber content of this dish—it's about half of the recommended 20 to 35 grams of fiber per day.

2½	cups water
½	cup dried lentils
½	cup uncooked brown rice
	Cooking spray
2	tablespoons olive oil
2	cups chopped yellow onion
¾	cup chopped red bell pepper
¾	cup chopped green bell pepper
1	(8-ounce) package mushrooms, quartered
4	garlic cloves, minced
½	cup chopped fresh parsley
1½	tablespoons low-sodium soy sauce
1½	tablespoons fresh lime juice
1	tablespoon Worcestershire sauce
¾	teaspoon salt
¼	teaspoon black pepper

1. Bring water to a boil in a saucepan. Add lentils and rice; return to a boil. Cover, reduce heat, and simmer 25 minutes or until rice is tender and liquid is almost absorbed. Remove from heat; let stand 5 minutes or until liquid is absorbed.
2. Coat a large nonstick skillet with cooking spray; add oil, and place over medium-high heat. Add onion and bell peppers; sauté 2 minutes or until lightly browned. Add mushrooms and garlic; sauté 4 minutes or until tender.
3. Add vegetables and remaining ingredients to lentils and rice. Let stand 15 minutes for flavors to blend. Yield: 4 servings (serving size: 1¼ cups).

CALORIES 301; FAT 8.2g (sat 1.2g); PROTEIN 11.9g; CARBOHYDRATE 48g; FIBER 10.2g; CHOLESTEROL 0mg; IRON 4.3mg; SODIUM 683mg; CALCIUM 68mg

► carbo rating: 39

Mediterranean Bulgur Pilaf

Since this is a meat-free pilaf, we call for vegetable broth. But use chicken broth if you wish; the carbo rating will be the same.

- 1 teaspoon olive oil
- 1 cup sliced green onions
- ½ cup sliced celery
- 2 garlic cloves, minced
- 1¼ cups water
- 1¼ cups vegetable broth
- 1½ teaspoons curry powder
- 1 teaspoon ground cumin
- ½ teaspoon salt
- ¼ teaspoon ground red pepper
- 1⅓ cups uncooked bulgur
- ¼ cup dried currants
- ¼ cup pine nuts, toasted
- 1 tablespoon chopped fresh parsley
- 1 (15.5-ounce) can chickpeas (garbanzo beans), rinsed and drained

1. Heat oil in a large saucepan over medium-high heat until hot. Add green onions, celery, and garlic; cook, stirring constantly, 3 minutes. Add water and next 5 ingredients; bring to a boil. Stir in bulgur; remove from heat. Cover and let stand 30 minutes or until liquid is absorbed.
2. Add currants and remaining ingredients to bulgur mixture; toss well. Serve at room temperature. Yield: 6 servings (serving size: 1 cup).

CALORIES 254; FAT 7g (sat 0.8g); PROTEIN 12g; CARBOHYDRATE 42g; FIBER 3.5g; CHOLESTEROL 0mg; IRON 4.2mg; SODIUM 551mg; CALCIUM 62mg

► carbo rating: 39

Tempeh Fajitas

Use a wire grilling basket for the onion and bell pepper so they don't fall into the grill. You can also heat the tortillas as the onion mixture and tempeh cook. Wrap in heavy-duty foil, and grill about 5 minutes.

- 1 (8-ounce) package five-grain tempeh
- 1 cup pineapple juice
- ¼ cup low-sodium soy sauce
- 2 tablespoons fresh lime juice
- 2 teaspoons ground cumin
- 2 teaspoons canola oil
- ½ teaspoon freshly ground black pepper, divided
- 1 garlic clove, minced
- 2 cups (½-inch) vertically sliced onion
- 1½ cups (½-inch-thick) slices green bell pepper
- Cooking spray
- ¼ teaspoon salt
- 4 (8-inch) whole wheat tortillas
- ¼ cup chipotle salsa

1. Cut tempeh in half horizontally; cut each half lengthwise into 6 strips. Place tempeh in a shallow dish. Combine pineapple juice, soy sauce, lime juice, cumin, oil, ¼ teaspoon black pepper, and garlic in a small saucepan; bring to a boil. Pour juice mixture over tempeh. Marinate at room temperature 30 minutes or up to 2 hours.
2. Prepare grill.
3. Coat onion and bell pepper with cooking spray; sprinkle with salt and ¼ teaspoon black pepper. Arrange vegetables in a grilling basket coated with cooking spray. Place basket on grill rack, and grill 5 minutes or until lightly browned, turning occasionally. Remove tempeh from dish, reserving marinade. Place tempeh on grill rack coated with cooking spray; grill 2 minutes on each side, basting with reserved marinade.
4. Warm tortillas according to package directions. Arrange 3 tempeh pieces, ½ cup onion mixture, and 1 tablespoon salsa down center of each tortilla; roll up. Yield: 4 servings (serving size: 1 fajita).

CALORIES 259; FAT 5.1g (sat 0.7g); PROTEIN 14.6g; CARBOHYDRATE 47.3g; FIBER 8g; CHOLESTEROL 0mg; IRON 3.1mg; SODIUM 712mg; CALCIUM 64mg

▶ **carbo rating: 39**

Ratatouille with Chickpeas

Ratatouille, *a popular side dish from the Provence region of France, combines eggplant, tomatoes, onions, peppers, and herbs simmered in olive oil. The vegetables can vary, and the mixture is served either warm, cold, or at room temperature. This main-dish version has plenty of protein because of the chickpeas. Cook the couscous while the ratatouille is simmering.*

1	tablespoon olive oil
1½	cups thinly sliced onion (about 1 large)
5	garlic cloves, minced
4	cups cubed eggplant (about ¾ pound)
2	cups cubed yellow squash (about 3 large)
1¾	cups chopped green bell pepper
1	pound mushrooms, halved
1	(28-ounce) can diced tomatoes, undrained
1	(15.5-ounce) can chickpeas (garbanzo beans), rinsed and drained
1½	teaspoons salt
½	teaspoon black pepper
¼	cup chopped fresh or 1 tablespoon dried basil
3	cups hot cooked whole wheat couscous

1. Heat oil in a Dutch oven over medium-high heat. Add onion and garlic; sauté 4 to 5 minutes or until onion is golden. Add eggplant, squash, bell pepper, and mushrooms; sauté 5 minutes. Add tomatoes and next 3 ingredients; bring to a boil. Cover, reduce heat, and simmer 20 minutes or until vegetables are tender.
2. Stir in basil and cook, uncovered, 10 minutes or until some of the liquid evaporates. Serve over couscous. Yield: 6 servings (serving size: 1½ cups ratatouille and ½ cup couscous).

CALORIES 265; FAT 4.4g (sat 0.4g); PROTEIN 11g; CARBOHYDRATE 50.5g; FIBER 12g; CHOLESTEROL 0mg; IRON 3.5mg; SODIUM 864mg; CALCIUM 81mg

▶ **carbo rating: 40**

Baked Lentils with Mushrooms

If your low-carb plan restricts carrots, you can leave them out and add 1½ cups diced celery.

1	cup uncooked brown basmati rice
8¼	cups water, divided
1	cup lentils
	Cooking spray
2	teaspoons olive oil
1½	cups diagonally sliced carrot
1	(8-ounce) package sliced mushrooms
1	(14.5-ounce) can diced tomatoes, undrained
1	tablespoon balsamic vinegar
½	teaspoon dried thyme
1	bay leaf
½	teaspoon salt
¼	teaspoon pepper
⅓	cup (1.3 ounces) crumbled feta cheese

1. Combine rice and 2¼ cups water in a saucepan, and bring to a boil. Cover, reduce heat, and simmer 45 minutes or until liquid is absorbed. Let rice stand 10 minutes.
2. Combine 6 cups water and lentils in a large saucepan; bring to a boil. Cover, reduce heat, and simmer 20 minutes or until tender. Drain, reserving 1 cup cooking liquid.
3. Preheat oven to 400°.
4. Heat oil in a nonstick skillet coated with cooking spray over medium-high heat. Add carrot and mushrooms; sauté 6 minutes or until mushrooms are lightly browned.
5. Combine lentils, reserved cooking liquid, mushroom mixture, tomatoes, and next 5 ingredients. Spoon mixture into a 2-quart baking dish coated with cooking spray. Cover and bake at 400° for 30 minutes or until bubbly. Remove and discard bay leaf. Spoon lentil mixture over rice; sprinkle with cheese. Yield: 6 servings (serving size: 1 cup lentil mixture, ½ cup rice, and 1 tablespoon feta cheese).

CALORIES 285; FAT 5.2g (sat 2g); PROTEIN 12.9g; CARBOHYDRATE 50.2g; FIBER 10.5g; CHOLESTEROL 8mg; IRON 3.9mg; SODIUM 402mg; CALCIUM 88mg

▶ carbo rating: 42
Vegetable Fried Rice

The best way to make fried rice is with leftover rice. If you don't have any, cook ¾ cup instant rice in ⅔ cup water, and chill it in the freezer for 10 minutes.

½	cup egg substitute
1¼	teaspoons dark sesame oil, divided
1⅓	cups sliced green onions
1½	cups chilled cooked instant brown rice
2	tablespoons low-sodium soy sauce
¼	teaspoon pepper
¼	teaspoon ground ginger
1	cup frozen baby green peas, thawed and drained

1. Cook egg substitute in ¼ teaspoon sesame oil in a large nonstick skillet or wok until set on bottom (do not stir). Turn and cook 1 minute. Cut cooked egg into thin strips; set aside.
2. Cook green onions in 1 teaspoon sesame oil in pan 1 minute. Add rice and next 3 ingredients; cook 2 minutes or until thoroughly heated, stirring often. Gently stir in reserved egg strips and green peas. Serve immediately. Yield: 2 servings (serving size: 1¾ cups).

CALORIES 301; FAT 4.6g (sat 0.7g); PROTEIN 15.3g; CARBOHYDRATE 50.7g; FIBER 8.3g; CHOLESTEROL 0mg; IRON 4.2mg; SODIUM 735mg; CALCIUM 103mg

▶ carbo rating: 44
Baked Barley with Shiitake Mushrooms and Caramelized Onions

Slow baking allows the barley to absorb the woodsy flavor of the mushrooms and the sweetness of the caramelized onion.

2	tablespoons butter
4½	cups chopped onion (about 3 medium)
1	teaspoon sugar
3	cups sliced button mushrooms (about 9 ounces)
3	cups sliced shiitake mushroom caps (about 8 ounces)
1½	cups uncooked pearl barley
1	tablespoon low-sodium soy sauce
¼	teaspoon salt
¼	teaspoon black pepper
⅛	teaspoon dried thyme
4	cups vegetable broth

1. Melt butter in a Dutch oven over medium heat. Add onion and sugar; cover and cook 25 minutes or until golden brown, stirring frequently. Add mushrooms; cook 10 minutes or until browned, stirring frequently. Add barley, and cook 2 minutes, stirring frequently. Remove from heat. Stir in soy sauce, salt, pepper, and dried thyme.
2. Preheat oven to 350°.
3. Bring broth to a boil in a medium saucepan. Pour broth over barley mixture; cover and bake at 350° for 1 hour or until barley is tender. Let stand 10 minutes. Yield: 6 servings (serving size: about 1⅔ cups).

CALORIES 292; FAT 5.4g (sat 2.6g); PROTEIN 9.5g; CARBOHYDRATE 55.1g; FIBER 10.7g; CHOLESTEROL 10mg; IRON 2.4mg; SODIUM 908mg; CALCIUM 42mg

▶ carbo rating: 45

Peas and Quinoa Hoppin' John

Eaten on New Year's Day in the South, Hoppin' John (black-eyed peas and rice) is said to bring good luck in the year ahead. This version uses pink-eyed peas in place of black-eyed peas and quinoa instead of white rice.

1	tablespoon olive oil
2¾	cups chopped onion
4	bacon slices, cut into ¼-inch pieces
3	cups fresh pink-eyed peas
2	cups water
1	cup dry white wine
2	garlic cloves, minced
1	bay leaf
1¼	cups fat-free, less-sodium chicken broth
1	cup uncooked quinoa, rinsed
1	teaspoon salt
½	teaspoon pepper
2	tablespoons thinly sliced green onions
1	tablespoon chopped fresh parsley

1. Heat oil in a Dutch oven over medium-high heat. Add chopped onion; sauté 2 minutes. Add bacon; sauté 5 minutes. Add peas and next 4 ingredients; bring to a boil. Reduce heat; simmer, partially covered, 30 minutes or until tender. Discard bay leaf.

2. Combine broth, quinoa, salt, and pepper in a saucepan; bring to a boil over medium-high heat. Cover, reduce heat, and simmer 30 minutes. Add quinoa mixture to pea mixture; stir. Sprinkle with green onions and parsley. Yield: 5 servings (serving size: about 1¼ cups).

CALORIES 339; FAT 10.2g (sat 2.4g); PROTEIN 10.2g; CARBOHYDRATE 48.9g; FIBER 3.8g; CHOLESTEROL 8mg; IRON 4.6mg; SODIUM 667mg; CALCIUM 156mg

quinoa

Quinoa is an ancient grain that's still around today. It's higher in protein than any other grain, and is a good alternative to rice because of its lightness. The beige-colored seeds are about the size of couscous pellets and cook in about 20 minutes. The only special handling required with quinoa is to put it in a sieve or strainer with a fine mesh and give it a good rinse before cooking; otherwise, the grains can be bitter. A good source of protein and fiber, ½ cup of uncooked quinoa has 14 grams of protein, 62 grams of carbohydrate, and 6 grams of fiber.

meats

Since meats are one of the preferred food groups on a low-carb diet, make meat the star of your meal with these high-flavor, low-fat recipes. **Give your taste buds a treat** with these entrées: *Three-Pepper Pork Cutlets* (page 194), *Balsamic Pan-Seared Steaks* (page 209), or *Picante Meat Loaf* (page 214).

▶ carbo rating: 0
Garlic-Studded Pork Loin Roast

Here's an easy way to infuse pork with garlic: Thinly slice the garlic horizontally. Use a thin boning knife to make 1-inch-deep slits in the roast. Stuff with garlic slices.

1   (2¼-pound) boned pork loin roast
1   tablespoon white vinegar
2   large garlic cloves, thinly sliced
½   teaspoon salt
½   teaspoon cracked black pepper
Cooking spray
Sage, oregano, and rosemary sprigs (optional)

1. Preheat oven to 350°.
2. Trim fat from roast. Rub surface of roast with vinegar. Make several 1-inch-deep slits in roast, and stuff with garlic slices. Sprinkle ½ teaspoon salt and ½ teaspoon pepper over roast.
3. Place roast on a broiler pan coated with cooking spray. Bake at 350° for 1 hour and 40 minutes or until a meat thermometer registers 155°. Remove from pan; cover and let stand 10 minutes or until thermometer registers 160°. Garnish roast with herb sprigs, if desired. Yield: 8 servings (serving size: 3 ounces).

CALORIES 185; FAT 10.6g (sat 3.7g); PROTEIN 20.4g; CARBOHYDRATE 0.4g; FIBER 0g; CHOLESTEROL 69mg; IRON 0.9mg; SODIUM 199mg; CALCIUM 9mg

(pictured on page 155)

▶ carbo rating: 0
Eye-of-Round with Horseradish Cream

Yes, the 20-minute cook time is correct for this recipe. By baking at a high temperature and keeping the oven door closed 2 hours, this roast cooks up extra tender and flavorful. Be sure not to open the oven door at any time during the 2 hours or you will lose heat and the roast will not get to the proper temperature. If the meat has not reached 145° when you check it, put it back in the oven and bake at 325° until it reaches at least 145°.

1   (8-ounce) package ⅓-less-fat cream cheese, softened
1½   tablespoons prepared horseradish
2   teaspoons Dijon mustard
1   cup dry red wine
½   cup light butter, melted
1   (4-pound) eye-of-round roast
1   tablespoon salt
1   teaspoon pepper

1. Combine cream cheese, horseradish, and mustard, stirring until smooth. Cover and chill.
2. Combine wine and butter in a large heavy-duty zip-top plastic bag; add roast. Seal and chill at least 8 hours or up to 24 hours, turning occasionally.
3. Preheat oven to 500°.
4. Remove roast from marinade, discarding marinade. Place roast in a 13 x 9-inch pan lined with heavy-duty foil. Combine salt and pepper, and rub over surface of roast.
5. Bake, uncovered, at 500° for 20 to 30 minutes. Turn oven off. Do not open oven door for 2 hours. Meat thermometer should register 145° (medium-rare) to 160° (medium). Thinly slice meat, reserving pan juices. Serve meat with pan juices and horseradish cream. Yield: 16 servings (serving size: about 3 ounces meat and 1 tablespoon cream).

CALORIES 243; FAT 14.3g (sat 4.7g); PROTEIN 25.5g; CARBOHYDRATE 1g; FIBER 0.1g; CHOLESTEROL 80mg; IRON 1.7mg; SODIUM 536mg; CALCIUM 18mg

► carbo rating: 0
Marinated Tenderloin of Venison

The meat from wild game such as venison can be tougher than the meat from domestic animals, but the meat is also very lean. Marinating the venison in this flavorful herb and spice mixture adds both flavor and tenderness.

¾	cup dry red wine
2	tablespoons freshly ground black pepper
2	tablespoons chopped fresh rosemary
2	tablespoons chopped fresh thyme
3	tablespoons olive oil
2	tablespoons red wine vinegar
2	tablespoons Dijon mustard
1	teaspoon crushed juniper berries
1	teaspoon ground coriander seeds
½	teaspoon salt
½	teaspoon ground cardamom
4	garlic cloves, minced
½	teaspoon ground star anise (about 1 pod)
1	bay leaf
1	pound venison tenderloin

Cooking spray

1. Combine first 14 ingredients in a large heavy-duty zip-top plastic bag. Add tenderloin to bag; seal. Marinate tenderloin in refrigerator 24 hours, turning bag occasionally.

2. Preheat broiler.

3. Remove venison from bag; discard marinade. Place venison on a broiler pan coated with cooking spray; broil 10 minutes on each side or until done. Cut venison crosswise into thin slices. Yield: 8 servings (serving size: 3 ounces).

CALORIES 154; FAT 4.2g (sat 1.2g); PROTEIN 25.8g; CARBOHYDRATE 0.7g; FIBER 0.2g; CHOLESTEROL 95mg; IRON 4mg; SODIUM 78mg; CALCIUM 12mg

► carbo rating: 0
Lemon-Herb Lamb Chops

This simple lemon-herb mixture adds great flavor to the grilled chops.

4	(5-ounce) lean lamb loin chops
1	teaspoon dried rosemary
1	teaspoon dried rubbed sage
1	teaspoon grated lemon rind
¼	teaspoon salt
¼	teaspoon pepper

Cooking spray

1. Prepare grill.

2. Trim fat from chops. Combine rosemary and next 4 ingredients in a small bowl. Rub herb mixture on both sides of chops. Place chops on grill rack coated with cooking spray; cover and grill 8 to 10 minutes on each side or until desired degree of doneness. Yield: 4 servings (serving size: 1 chop).

CALORIES 187; FAT 8.5g (sat 3g); PROTEIN 25.6g; CARBOHYDRATE 0.4g; FIBER 0.2g; CHOLESTEROL 81mg; IRON 1.9mg; SODIUM 218mg; CALCIUM 24mg

how hot?

The best way to measure the temperature of an open fire is the time-honored hand test. Simply hold your hand (a cook's tool employed universally since antiquity) about 3 inches above the grate, then time how long you can keep your hand there before you're forced to withdraw it.

1 to 2 seconds—signifies a hot fire that's perfect for searing a steak or grilling shrimp

3 seconds—indicates medium-high heat, which is great for most fish

4 to 5 seconds—signifies a medium range, ideal for most chicken and vegetables

7 to 8 seconds—indicates the temperature is low and perfect for grilling delicate vegetables and fruit

grilling guide

Grilling may be the ultimate high-flavor, low-carb cooking method. It intensifies the flavor of all sorts of foods without relying on sugary sauces or excess fat.

Grilling Basics

Charcoal or Gas? Some people claim to detect a taste advantage with charcoal, but we really haven't found that to be the case as long as the two fuels provide a similar temperature range. We've cooked on several good gas grills, and the results are always just as tasty as those from charcoal.

Firepower Advantage The main advantage of charcoal over other fuels is that it generates high heat, even with the lid open. This isn't normally true of the gas burners in grills; you have to shop carefully to find a gas grill with the same heat range as any inexpensive charcoal model.

Covered or Uncovered?

As a rule, cover the grill when doing slow, indirect grilling with large pieces of food. **Resist the temptation to peek; you lose all the built-up heat and add 5 to 10 minutes to your cook time for each peek.** Leave the grill uncovered when doing fast or direct grilling with smaller items that cook quickly.

The Two-Level Fire

Many foods reach their peak when you grill them at two different temperatures, usually starting at a high level and then finishing at a lower level.

On charcoal grills that have an adjustable grate or firebox, lower the heat by increasing the distance between the coals and the food. If you don't have that feature, build two similarly sized cooking areas on opposite sides of the grill by stacking and spreading the charcoal differently. For the hot section, pile coals between two and three deep; for the medium area, scatter them in a single layer so that they're just touching one another. Doing this may seem a bit of a bother, but with many foods, building a two-level fire often improves results.

On gas grills you can make temperature adjustments with nothing more than the turn of a knob. With smaller models that have one or two burners, simply turn down the heat at the appropriate time, and move food temporarily to a cooler edge of the grate to speed the temperature transition. With gas grills that have three or more burners, you can usually keep a hot fire and a medium fire going simultaneously from the beginning.

Grilling: Direct and Indirect Heat

There are two ways to grill: with direct heat or with indirect heat.

Direct Direct grilling involves putting food on a grill rack directly over hot coals. **The best candidates for direct grilling are firm-fleshed fish and shellfish such as salmon, tuna, swordfish, halibut, mahimahi,**

and shrimp; chicken breasts and thighs; chops; burgers; and steaks. Vegetables can also be grilled directly—just be sure to cut them large enough so that they don't fall through the rack (or use a grill basket). **Indirect** This method is similar to oven roasting. Both sides of the grill are fired up, then one side is turned off. If using a charcoal grill, push the hot coals to one side. A disposable aluminum foil pan (also called a drip pan) containing water (or wine, broth, or other liquid) is placed directly over the coals on the side of a gas or electric grill where the heat has been turned off. On a charcoal grill, the pan is placed on the side where the charcoal has been moved. The food is then placed on the rack over the pan. The pan serves two purposes: It creates a steamy environment in which the food can cook, and it catches drippings from the food, minimizing flare-ups. **Good candidates for this type of grilling include whole chickens, roasts, turkey breasts, and other large foods.**

Marinades and Rubs

You can use two methods—both low in carbs—to perk up the flavors of meat, poultry, or seafood before you grill—one wet, one dry.

Marinade The wet way—called marinating—relies on a seasoned liquid in which the food is soaked to absorb flavor. Generally speaking, the longer you marinate a food, the stronger it will taste. Remember, however, that some foods, such as delicate fish, should not marinate longer than 2 to 4 hours. As a rule, ⅔ to 1 cup of marinade will flavor 1 to 1½ pounds of food. Mix the marinade in a zip-top plastic bag, toss your food inside, seal the bag, and chill. Marinated foods lend themselves well to grilling because you can baste the food with the remaining marinade.

Rub The alternative to marinating—a dry rub—is a blend of dry herbs and spices. Many rub recipes call for whole spices to be crushed; to do this, a mortar and pestle are the tools of choice. Or you can place whole spices in a plastic bag, and pound with a rolling pin. Store dry rubs indefinitely in an airtight container in a cool, dry place.

When using rubs, apply them to a food that is completely dry. The most effective way to apply the rub is

the right fire for the food

To get the best results when you're grilling, be sure to use the right level of heat for the food. Here's what we've found works best.

Medium Heat
- Bell peppers, corn on the cob (shucked), eggplant, and most other vegetables
- Chicken breasts and halves
- Duck breasts
- Pork chops and most other pork cuts
- Pork ribs (after baking in an oven or cooking on a covered grill until tender)
- Turkey fillets
- Veal chops (can also cook on medium-low)

Medium-High Heat
- Most fish and shellfish

High Heat
- Calamari
- Salmon fillets and steaks
- Scallops
- Shrimp (peeled)

Sear on high heat; finish on medium heat
- Beef and pork tenderloin
- Chicken thighs and drumsticks
- Hamburgers (switch to medium after searing each side 1 minute)
- Hot dogs (switch to medium when deeply browned all over)
- Lamb chops and butterflied leg of lamb
- Steak
- Tuna steaks
- Uncooked sausage
- Venison steaks

to place the mixture in a zip-top plastic bag, put the food inside, and shake. Although the amount of rub you use is up to your taste buds, a general rule is 3 tablespoons per 1 pound of food.

grilling tips

Here are some tips for getting the best results every time you grill.

1. **Be organized.** Have the food, marinade, sauces, and utensils grillside and ready to go before you start cooking. Make sure you have enough gas or charcoal before you start.

2. **Take the chill off.** If you take marinated meats out of the refrigerator and let them stand at room temperature for 10 to 15 minutes before grilling, you won't end up with a cold center.

3. **Keep it clean.** We recommend cleaning your grill twice: once after preheating the grill, and again when you've finished grilling. Use both a metal spatula and a wire brush to scrape the grates clean.

4. **Oil the grate or coat it with cooking spray before placing food on it.** Quickly run a paper towel that is moist with oil over the grates. This seasons the grill, helps clean it, and helps prevent food from sticking.

5. **Know when to baste.** Too many people ruin great food by basting it too early with sugar-based sauces, which results in charring. If you use yogurt-, citrus-, or oil and vinegar-based sauces, you can baste throughout cooking. If you use the marinade to baste, stop just before the last 3 minutes of cooking.

6. **Go light on the sugar in homemade sauces,** and avoid those bottled sauces that are mostly sugar and salt. Sometimes all you need is a little salt and pepper.

7. **Give it a rest.** Meat will taste better and be juicier if given a chance to rest a few minutes after you take it off the grill.

8. **Turn; don't stab.** Use tongs or a spatula to turn the meat. Don't use a carving fork because it pierces the food and lets valuable juices out.

9. **Don't overcook.** Know in advance how long you expect to grill the food, and set a timer to alert you to check it. For large cuts of meat and poultry, use an instant-read meat thermometer to gauge doneness.

10. **Control flare-ups, and don't let food burn.** When dripping fat produces a flame in one spot, move food to a different area on the grill. Keep a spray bottle of water by the grill to put out accidental flare-ups.

▶ carbo rating: 1

Southwestern Grilled Flank Steak

A homemade spice mix takes just a minute or two to assemble and gives flank steak a real flavor boost.

1	(1½-pound) lean flank steak (about ¾ inch thick)
2	tablespoons Hungarian sweet paprika
1	tablespoon chili powder
2	teaspoons ground cumin
1	teaspoon ground cinnamon
½	teaspoon salt

Cooking spray

1. Trim excess fat from steak. Combine paprika and next 4 ingredients; rub over both sides of steak. Place steak in a dish; cover and marinate in refrigerator at least 4 hours or overnight.

2. Prepare grill.

3. Place steak on grill rack coated with cooking spray; cover and grill 4 minutes on each side or until desired degree of doneness. Remove steak from grill; let stand 5 minutes before slicing. Cut steak diagonally across grain into thin slices. Yield: 6 servings (serving size: 3 ounces).

CALORIES 271; FAT 16.5g (sat 6.9g); PROTEIN 27.5g; CARBOHYDRATE 2.6g; FIBER 1.1g; CHOLESTEROL 74mg; IRON 4mg; SODIUM 298mg; CALCIUM 25mg

(pictured on page 156)

paprika pointers

Paprika is an orange-red powder made by grinding sweet red pepper pods. Its flavor can range from mild to pungent to hot. Hungarian paprika is generally considered to be superior in flavor to other paprikas, some of which don't have much flavor at all, but are used to add color.

Hungarian paprika is lighter in color than regular paprika, but it's more pungent. You'll find it labeled either sweet (meaning mild) or hot. Look for it in the spice aisle of your supermarket or in specialty food stores.

► carbo rating: 1

Savory Sirloin Steak

The Dijon mustard and Worcestershire sauce add a punch to the creamy yogurt sauce that you spoon over the steak.

    1   (1-pound) lean boneless sirloin steak
        (¾ inch thick)
    ¾   teaspoon minced fresh rosemary
    ¼   teaspoon pepper
Cooking spray
    1   teaspoon reduced-calorie margarine
    1   tablespoon plain fat-free yogurt
    1   tablespoon Dijon mustard
    1   tablespoon low-sodium Worcestershire sauce
    1   tablespoon chopped fresh parsley
Rosemary sprigs (optional)
Lemon wedges (optional)

1. Trim fat from steak. Combine rosemary and pepper; sprinkle over steak.
2. Coat a large nonstick skillet with cooking spray; add margarine, and place over medium heat until margarine melts. Add steak, and cook 6 minutes on each side or until desired degree of doneness. Remove steak from pan; transfer to a serving platter, and keep warm.
3. Combine yogurt, mustard, and Worcestershire sauce in a small saucepan. Cook over low heat, stirring constantly, until thoroughly heated (do not boil). Spoon sauce over steak. Sprinkle with parsley. If desired, garnish with rosemary sprigs and lemon wedges. Yield: 4 servings (serving size: 3 ounces steak and about 1 tablespoon sauce).

CALORIES 235; FAT 13.9g (sat 5.2g); PROTEIN 24.9g; CARBOHYDRATE 1.2g; FIBER 0.1g; CHOLESTEROL 67mg; IRON 2.3mg; SODIUM 203mg; CALCIUM 20mg

► carbo rating: 1

Filet Mignon with Béarnaise Sauce

A traditional béarnaise sauce is not particularly high in carbs, but is extremely high in fat. In this lightened version, we've cut the fat but have not increased the carbohydrate. This dish is very rich, so a small portion should be plenty.

    3   tablespoons dry white wine
    2   tablespoons tarragon vinegar
    1   tablespoon minced shallots
    ½   teaspoon dried tarragon
    ¼   teaspoon freshly ground black pepper
    ¼   cup egg substitute
    3   tablespoons reduced-calorie margarine
    1   tablespoon fat-free sour cream
    4   (4-ounce) beef tenderloin steaks
Cooking spray
    ½   teaspoon salt-free lemon pepper seasoning

1. Preheat broiler.
2. Combine first 5 ingredients in a small nonstick skillet. Bring mixture to a boil. Reduce heat, and simmer, uncovered, until mixture is reduced to 2 tablespoons.
3. Pour mixture through a wire-mesh strainer into the top of a double boiler, discarding shallots. Add egg substitute, and stir well. Bring water in bottom of double boiler to a boil, stirring constantly. Reduce heat to low. Add margarine, 1 tablespoon at a time, stirring constantly with a wire whisk until blended. Cook, stirring constantly, until sauce thickens slightly. Remove from heat; stir in sour cream. Set aside, and keep warm.
4. Place steaks on a broiler pan coated with cooking spray. Sprinkle steaks with lemon pepper seasoning. Broil 8 minutes on each side or until desired degree of doneness. Serve with sauce. Yield: 4 servings (serving size: 1 steak and about 2 tablespoons sauce).

CALORIES 232; FAT 13.5g (sat 3.1g); PROTEIN 25.9g; CARBOHYDRATE 1g; FIBER 0.1g; CHOLESTEROL 71mg; IRON 3.5mg; SODIUM 162mg; CALCIUM 14mg

▶ carbo rating: 1
Grilled Sirloin Steak with Stilton Sauce

Stilton cheese stars in this delectable sauce, which provides the perfect topping for grilled steak.

1½   cups (6 ounces) Stilton cheese, crumbled
⅓   cup light butter, melted
¼   cup low-sodium Worcestershire sauce
1   garlic clove, crushed
2   pounds lean boneless sirloin steak (3 inches thick)
¼   teaspoon salt
¼   teaspoon pepper
Cooking spray

1. Prepare grill.
2. Combine first 4 ingredients in a medium saucepan. Cook over low heat until cheese melts, stirring constantly. Set aside ½ cup sauce; keep remaining sauce warm.
3. Sprinkle steak with salt and pepper. Place steak on grill rack coated with cooking spray; cover and grill 18 minutes on each side or until desired degree of doneness, basting often with ½ cup sauce.
4. Cut steak diagonally across grain into thin slices. Serve with remaining sauce. Yield: 8 servings (serving size: 3 ounces steak and 1 tablespoon sauce).

CALORIES 301; FAT 19.7g (sat 10.4g); PROTEIN 29.4g; CARBOHYDRATE 1g; FIBER 0g; CHOLESTEROL 103mg; IRON 2.8mg; SODIUM 480mg; CALCIUM 124mg

▶ carbo rating: 1
Stuffed Tenderloin

This is a great low-carb dish to serve when you're entertaining.

1   (3-pound) beef tenderloin
2   tablespoons light butter
1   (8-ounce) package sliced mushrooms
4   green onions, chopped
2   tablespoons chopped fresh parsley
1   garlic clove, minced
3   tablespoons crumbled blue cheese
1   tablespoon light butter, melted
Cooking spray

1. Prepare grill by piling charcoal on one side of grill, leaving other side empty. (For gas grills, light only one side.)
2. Slice tenderloin lengthwise to, but not through, the center, leaving 1 long side connected; set aside.
3. Melt 2 tablespoons butter in a large nonstick skillet over medium-high heat. Add mushrooms and next 3 ingredients; cook 5 minutes or until tender, stirring often. Spoon mixture into opening of tenderloin, leaving a ½-inch border on all sides. Sprinkle cheese over mushroom mixture. Close tenderloin, and tie securely with heavy string at 2-inch intervals. Brush with melted butter.
4. Place tenderloin on unlit side of grill rack coated with cooking spray; cover and grill 45 minutes or until a meat thermometer registers 145° (medium-rare) to 160° (medium). Let stand 10 minutes before slicing. Yield: 12 servings (serving size: about 3 ounces).

CALORIES 171; FAT 9g (sat 4g); PROTEIN 20.6g; CARBOHYDRATE 1.3g; FIBER 0.4g; CHOLESTEROL 64mg; IRON 2.8mg; SODIUM 92mg; CALCIUM 22mg

holiday menu

Tangy Cranberry Coolers (page 83)

Salmon Pâté (page 54)

mixed green salad

Mushroom-Stuffed Beef Tenderloin

Garlic-Roasted Green Beans (page 327)

Cauliflower with Chives and Lemon (page 321)

Chocolate Mousse (page 378)

▶ carbo rating: 31

▶ carbo rating: 1
Mushroom-Stuffed Beef Tenderloin

Let this entrée be the star at your next holiday celebration. You can assemble it the day before and keep it covered in the refrigerator until you're ready to bake.

Cooking spray
1   (8-ounce) package sliced mushrooms
4   ounces coarsely chopped shiitake
    mushrooms
½   cup chopped fresh parsley
3   tablespoons minced green onions
2   garlic cloves, minced
¼   cup (1 ounce) grated fresh Parmesan cheese
¼   cup egg substitute
2   tablespoons bourbon
½   teaspoon salt
1   (4½-pound) beef tenderloin

1. Preheat oven to 500°.
2. Coat a large nonstick skillet with cooking spray; place over medium-high heat until hot. Add mushrooms, parsley, onions, and garlic; sauté until tender. Remove from heat; stir in cheese, egg substitute, bourbon, and salt.
3. Trim fat from tenderloin. Slice tenderloin lengthwise to, but not through, the center, leaving 1 long side connected. Spoon mushroom mixture into opening of tenderloin. Fold top side over mushroom mixture, and

tie securely with heavy string at 2-inch intervals. Place tenderloin, seam side down, on a broiler rack in a roasting pan coated with cooking spray.
4. Place tenderloin in oven. Reduce heat to 350°, and bake for 55 minutes or until a meat thermometer registers 145° (medium-rare) to 160° (medium). Remove from oven; let stand 10 minutes. Cut diagonally across grain into ¼-inch-thick slices, and arrange on a serving platter. Yield: 18 servings (serving size: about 3 ounces).

CALORIES 158; FAT 7.2g (sat 2.8g); PROTEIN 20.6g; CARBOHYDRATE 1.2g; FIBER 0.3g; CHOLESTEROL 58mg; IRON 2.8mg; SODIUM 136mg; CALCIUM 24mg

▶ carbo rating: 1
Beef Tenderloin au Poivre

Peppercorns and mustard coat this entrée with savory goodness. Sometimes, a few simple ingredients can bake into incredible results.

1   (4-pound) beef tenderloin, trimmed
⅓   cup Dijon mustard
1½   tablespoons white peppercorns, crushed
1½   tablespoons black peppercorns, crushed
Cooking spray

1. Preheat oven to 425°.
2. Evenly shape tenderloin by tucking small end underneath; tie with string. Rub tenderloin with mustard.
3. Combine crushed peppercorns, and press evenly over surface of tenderloin. Place on a broiler pan coated with cooking spray; bake, uncovered, at 425° for 45 minutes or until a meat thermometer registers 145° (medium-rare) to 160° (medium). Let stand 10 minutes before slicing. Yield: 16 servings (serving size: about 3 ounces).

CALORIES 184; FAT 8.5g (sat 3g); PROTEIN 24.3g; CARBOHYDRATE 1.4g; FIBER 0.4g; CHOLESTEROL 71mg; IRON 3.3mg; SODIUM 180mg; CALCIUM 17mg

crushing peppercorns

Crush peppercorns easily in a clean coffee grinder or by using a mortar and pestle.

▶ carbo rating: 1
Rosemary-Mustard Lamb Chops

The chops only need to marinate in the mustard-herb rub for about 30 minutes in order for the great flavor to permeate the lamb. If you want to go longer than 30 minutes, or even overnight, that's fine, too.

2   tablespoons chopped fresh rosemary
2   tablespoons Dijon mustard
¼   teaspoon salt
¼   teaspoon pepper
2   garlic cloves, minced
8   (4-ounce) lean lamb loin chops (about 1¼ inches thick)
Cooking spray

1. Combine first 5 ingredients in a small bowl; stir well. Rub mixture evenly over both sides of lamb chops. Place chops on a baking sheet or platter; cover and marinate in refrigerator at least 30 minutes.
2. Prepare grill.
3. Place chops on grill rack coated with cooking spray; cover and grill 8 minutes on each side or until desired degree of doneness. Yield: 4 servings (serving size: 2 chops).

Note: To prepare indoors, place a grill pan over high heat until hot; coat with cooking spray. Add lamb, and cook 8 minutes on each side or until desired degree of doneness.

CALORIES 203; FAT 8.5g (sat 2.9g); PROTEIN 27.3g; CARBOHYDRATE 2.1g; FIBER 0.8g; CHOLESTEROL 86mg; IRON 3mg; SODIUM 459mg; CALCIUM 40mg

start with the best

Start with quality ingredients. Because it's a dry, high-heat cooking method, grilling accentuates the natural flavor of food. No amount of seasoning will change the essential quality of the ingredients you use, so start with the best cuts of meat.

▶ carbo rating: 1
Grilled Leg of Lamb

Welcome springtime with a meal of grilled lamb and crisp, tender asparagus. (See the recipe for Roasted Asparagus on page 323.)

1   (3½-pound) lean boneless leg of lamb
¼   cup low-sodium soy sauce
3   tablespoons water
3   tablespoons Dijon mustard
2   tablespoons vegetable or olive oil
2   teaspoons dried rosemary
2   teaspoons finely chopped garlic
1   teaspoon ground ginger
Cooking spray

1. Trim fat from lamb. Combine soy sauce and next 6 ingredients in a large heavy-duty zip-top plastic bag. Add lamb; seal bag, and shake until lamb is well coated. Marinate in refrigerator 8 hours, turning bag occasionally.
2. Prepare grill.
3. Remove lamb from marinade, reserving marinade.
4. Place reserved marinade in a small saucepan; bring to a boil. Boil 1 minute.
5. Place lamb on grill rack coated with cooking spray; grill, covered, 15 minutes on each side or until a meat thermometer registers 145° (medium-rare) to 160° (medium), turning and basting occasionally with reserved marinade. Let stand 10 minutes before slicing. Yield: 14 servings (serving size: 3 ounces).

CALORIES 188; FAT 8.8g (sat 2.8g); PROTEIN 24.2g; CARBOHYDRATE 0.7g; FIBER 0.1g; CHOLESTEROL 76mg; IRON 1.9mg; SODIUM 265mg; CALCIUM 11mg

▶ carbo rating: 1

Mediterranean Grilled Lamb

The marinade of red wine, olive oil, rosemary, and garlic gives the lamb its Mediterranean flavor.

1½   pounds boneless leg of lamb, trimmed
¼   cup dry red wine
2   tablespoons chopped fresh rosemary
2   teaspoons olive oil
½   teaspoon salt
¼   teaspoon pepper
4   large garlic cloves, minced
Cooking spray

1. Slice lamb lengthwise, cutting to, but not through, other side. Open the halves, laying lamb flat. Slice each half lengthwise, cutting to, but not through, other side; open flat.
2. Combine wine and next 5 ingredients in a large heavy-duty zip-top plastic bag. Add lamb to bag; seal. Marinate in refrigerator 8 hours, turning bag occasionally.
3. Prepare grill.
4. Remove lamb from bag, reserving marinade. Place reserved marinade in a small saucepan; bring to a boil. Boil 1 minute.
5. Place lamb on grill rack coated with cooking spray; cover and grill 20 minutes or until a meat thermometer registers 145° (medium-rare) or desired degree of doneness, turning and basting lamb once with reserved marinade. Let stand 10 minutes before slicing. Yield: 6 servings (serving size: 3 ounces).

CALORIES 121; FAT 5.4g (sat 1.6g); PROTEIN 16.2g; CARBOHYDRATE 1g;
FIBER 0.1g; CHOLESTEROL 50mg; IRON 1.3mg; SODIUM 233mg; CALCIUM 11mg

▶ carbo rating: 1

Southwestern Pork Chops

Use your favorite tomato-based salsa as a quick and easy way to get spicy Southwestern flavor without a lot of chopping.

Cooking spray
4   (4-ounce) lean boneless pork loin chops, trimmed
⅓   cup salsa
2   tablespoons fresh lime juice
¼   cup chopped fresh cilantro or parsley (optional)

1. Coat a large skillet with cooking spray; place over high heat until hot. Press chops with palm of hand to flatten slightly; add to pan and cook 1 minute on each side or until browned. Reduce heat to medium-low.
2. Combine salsa and lime juice; pour over chops. Simmer, uncovered, 8 minutes or until chops are done. If desired, sprinkle chops with cilantro. Yield: 4 servings (serving size: 1 chop and about 1½ tablespoons salsa).

CALORIES 190; FAI 8.3g (sat 2.8g); PROTEIN 25.3g; CARBOHYDRATE 2g;
FIBER 0.6g; CHOLESTEROL 71mg; IRON 1.3mg; SODIUM 132mg; CALCIUM 21mg

cilantro substitution

The strong lemonlike flavor of cilantro is traditional in Southwestern cuisine, but you can always substitute parsley if cilantro is unavailable. Generally, cilantro and parsley are shelved together in the produce section of the supermarket. Unfortunately, they're so similar in appearance that they're frequently mislabeled. A quick check to make sure that you've selected the correct herb is to press a leaf between your fingers. Cilantro has a very strong and distinct lemonlike aroma while parsley has a milder, fresher smell. If cilantro isn't available, the milder parsley is a good substitute.

▶ carbo rating: 1

Three-Pepper Pork Cutlets

Not just one but three types of ground pepper add a huge flavor kick to this pork tenderloin. (Technically, paprika is also a ground pepper, but it adds a subtle sweetness rather than heat.)

1   (1-pound) pork tenderloin
2   teaspoons Hungarian sweet paprika
1   teaspoon dried thyme
1   teaspoon olive oil
½   teaspoon dried oregano
½   teaspoon dried rosemary, crushed
½   teaspoon salt
¼   teaspoon white pepper
¼   teaspoon freshly ground black pepper
⅛   teaspoon ground red pepper
2   large garlic cloves, minced
Cooking spray

1. Trim fat from pork; cut pork crosswise into 8 slices. Place between 2 sheets of heavy-duty plastic wrap, and flatten each slice to ¼-inch thickness, using a meat mallet or rolling pin.
2. Preheat broiler.
3. Combine paprika and next 9 ingredients; rub pork with paprika mixture. Place pork on a broiler pan coated with cooking spray. Broil 5 minutes on each side or until pork is done. Yield: 4 servings (serving size: 2 cutlets).

CALORIES 160; FAT 5.5g (sat 1.6g); PROTEIN 24.8g; CARBOHYDRATE 1.8g; FIBER 0.5g; CHOLESTEROL 79mg; IRON 2.2mg; SODIUM 351mg; CALCIUM 25mg

pounding pointer

Pork tenderloin is a very tender cut of meat. Rather than getting out the meat mallet or rolling pin, use the heel of your hand to press the slices of pork into ¼-inch-thick cutlets. Just make sure you get it to the right thickness so the cooking time will be correct.

standing time

Because heat draws moisture to the surface of a roast during cooking, cover the roast and let it stand for 10 minutes before slicing. This will help the roast reabsorb the juices. Also, it continues to cook—this is when the roast actually reaches its proper end-point temperature.

▶ carbo rating: 1

Roast Pork with Lemon-Pepper Crust

Coarse-ground sea salt tastes saltier than regular table salt, so you can use less and still get the desired flavor.

1   tablespoon grated lemon rind
1   teaspoon dried oregano
¾   teaspoon coarse-ground sea salt
½   teaspoon freshly ground black pepper
½   teaspoon olive oil
3   garlic cloves, minced
1   (1-pound) pork tenderloin, trimmed
Cooking spray

1. Preheat oven to 450°.
2. Combine first 6 ingredients. Spread mixture evenly over pork.
3. Place pork on a broiler pan coated with cooking spray. Bake, uncovered, at 450° for 25 minutes or until a meat thermometer registers 155°. Remove pork from oven; cover and let stand 10 minutes or until thermometer registers 160°. Yield: 4 servings (serving size: 3 ounces).

CALORIES 151; FAT 4.7g (sat 1.5g); PROTEIN 24.2g; CARBOHYDRATE 1.4g; FIBER 0.4g; CHOLESTEROL 67mg; IRON 1.5mg; SODIUM 480mg; CALCIUM 18mg

► carbo rating: 1

Pork Tenderloin with Rosemary and Garlic

Rosemary is one of the stronger-flavored herbs, so just wrapping the sprigs in foil with the meat allows the flavor to permeate the pork.

2   (¾-pound) pork tenderloins
3   garlic cloves, sliced
1   tablespoon water
1   teaspoon olive oil
¼   teaspoon salt
¼   teaspoon pepper
4   rosemary sprigs
Rosemary sprigs (optional)

1. Preheat oven to 400°.
2. Trim fat from tenderloins; make ½-inch-deep slits on outside of tenderloins, and stuff with garlic slices. Combine water, oil, salt, and pepper in a small bowl. Rub surface of tenderloins evenly with oil mixture.
3. Place tenderloins lengthwise on a double thickness of foil, 15 inches long. Top with 4 rosemary sprigs, and wrap securely. Place tenderloins on a baking sheet or roasting pan. Insert meat thermometer through foil into center of 1 tenderloin.
4. Bake at 400° for 20 minutes or until a meat thermometer registers 155°. Remove from oven; let stand until thermometer registers 160°. Discard cooked rosemary sprigs. Garnish with additional rosemary sprigs, if desired. Yield: 6 servings (serving size: 3 ounces).

CALORIES 150; FAT 4.8g (sat 1.5g); PROTEIN 24.6g; CARBOHYDRATE 0.6g; FIBER 0g; CHOLESTEROL 79mg; IRON 1.4mg; SODIUM 155mg; CALCIUM 11mg

► carbo rating: 1

Spicy Pork Roast

The brown sugar is necessary in the rub to balance out the pungency of the spices. It's only 1 tablespoon, so it contributes only 0.7 gram of carbohydrate per serving.

1   tablespoon cumin seeds
1   tablespoon coriander seeds
1½   teaspoons black peppercorns
1½   teaspoons mustard seeds
1   tablespoon dark brown sugar
2¼   teaspoons chili powder
1½   teaspoons paprika
½   teaspoon salt
¼   teaspoon ground red pepper
¼   teaspoon ground cinnamon
1   (3-pound) lean boneless pork loin roast
4   (3-inch) chunks mesquite wood
6   (12-ounce) cans beer or 9 cups hot water

1. Place a nonstick skillet over medium heat until hot. Add first 4 ingredients; sauté 2 minutes or until fragrant. Remove from heat; cool completely. Place mixture in a spice or coffee grinder; process until ground.
2. Combine ground spices, brown sugar, and next 5 ingredients. Trim fat from roast; rub spice mixture evenly over roast. Place roast in a large heavy-duty zip-top plastic bag; seal bag, and marinate in refrigerator 8 hours, turning bag occasionally.
3. Soak mesquite chunks in water 30 minutes to 1 hour. Drain well.
4. Prepare charcoal fire in meat smoker; let burn 15 to 20 minutes or until center coals are covered with gray ash. Place soaked mesquite wood chunks on top of coals. Place water pan in smoker; add beer or hot water to pan to within 1 inch of rim.
5. Place roast on rack in smoker. Cover with smoker lid; cook 4 hours or until a meat thermometer registers 155°. Refill water pan with water and add charcoal to fire as needed. Remove roast from smoker; cover and let stand 10 minutes or until thermometer registers 160°. Yield: 12 servings (serving size: 3 ounces).

CALORIES 211; FAT 11.9g (sat 4.1g); PROTEIN 22.9g; CARBOHYDRATE 1.4g; FIBER 0.3g; CHOLESTEROL 77mg; IRON 1.3mg; SODIUM 162mg; CALCIUM 14mg

▶ **carbo rating: 2**

Shiitake Steak

Let this entrée be the star of a simple steak dinner with a bit of Asian flair. Serve it with steamed sugar snap peas.

1	teaspoon cracked black pepper
1	(1-pound) flank steak (½ inch thick)

Cooking spray

½	pound fresh shiitake mushrooms
½	teaspoon olive oil
⅓	cup chopped green onions
1	tablespoon diced pimiento
3	tablespoons balsamic vinegar
¼	teaspoon salt
1	garlic clove, minced

1. Preheat broiler.
2. Press pepper onto both sides of steak. Place steak on a broiler pan coated with cooking spray. Broil 8 minutes on each side or until steak is done.
3. Remove and discard stems from mushrooms. Heat oil in a large nonstick skillet over medium heat. Add mushroom caps and green onions; sauté 3 minutes. Add pimiento, vinegar, salt, and garlic; sauté 1 minute.
4. Cut steak diagonally across grain into thin slices. Spoon mushroom mixture over steak. Yield: 4 servings (serving size: 3 ounces steak and ¼ of mushroom mixture).

CALORIES 228; FAT 13.7g (sat 5.5g); PROTEIN 22.7g; CARBOHYDRATE 3.2g; FIBER 0.8g; CHOLESTEROL 60mg; IRON 3.6mg; SODIUM 221mg; CALCIUM 17mg

---

▶ **carbo rating: 2**

Dijon Sirloin

Add fresh lime juice and garlic to Dijon mustard for an easy little sauce with a big flavor punch.

3	tablespoons whole-grain Dijon mustard
1	tablespoon fresh lime juice (about ½ lime)
¼	teaspoon salt
2	garlic cloves, minced, or 2 teaspoons bottled minced garlic
1	pound boneless sirloin steak (¾ inch thick)

Cooking spray

2	tablespoons chopped fresh parsley
½	teaspoon coarsely ground black pepper

1. Preheat broiler.
2. Combine first 4 ingredients in a small bowl; stir well.
3. Place steak on a broiler pan coated with cooking spray. Spoon half of mustard mixture evenly over steak, and broil 4 minutes. Turn steak; spread remaining mustard mixture over steak. Broil 3 minutes or until desired degree of doneness. Place steak on a serving platter; sprinkle with parsley and pepper. Yield: 4 servings (serving size: 3 ounces).

CALORIES 193; FAT 8g (sat 2.7g); PROTEIN 27.1g; CARBOHYDRATE 2.3g; FIBER 0.3g; CHOLESTEROL 77mg; IRON 3.4mg; SODIUM 490mg; CALCIUM 32mg

---

sautéing shiitakes

This Asian mushroom's soft, brown, open cap lends itself to several cooking styles. Sautéing brings out the shiitake's strong smoky flavor, softens the texture to velvety smoothness, and provides an easy mingling with other ingredients. For maximum flavor, use dried shiitakes—they are chewier and have a more intense flavor than fresh. Discard the thin, tough stalks, or use them to flavor stock.

▶ carbo rating: 2

Sirloin Steak with Garlic Sauce

If you want to roast extra garlic cloves, add some more to the pan and freeze them for later use.

1	pound boneless top sirloin steak (1 inch thick)
1	teaspoon dried thyme
¼	teaspoon salt
¼	teaspoon freshly ground black pepper
	Cooking spray
8	large garlic cloves, unpeeled
⅓	cup low-salt beef broth
	Fresh thyme (optional)

1. Preheat broiler.

2. Sprinkle both sides of steak with thyme, salt, and pepper. Place steak on a broiler pan coated with cooking spray; arrange garlic cloves around steak. Broil steak and garlic 5 to 6 minutes on each side or until desired degree of doneness. Transfer steak to a cutting board; cover loosely with foil to keep warm.

3. Cut off bottom of each garlic clove. Squeeze out soft garlic into a food processor; process until smooth. Add broth; process until combined. Transfer garlic sauce to a microwave-safe dish. Microwave at HIGH 40 seconds.

4. Cut steak diagonally across grain into thin slices; spoon garlic sauce over steak. Garnish with fresh thyme, if desired. Yield: 4 servings (serving size: 3 ounces steak and about 2 tablespoons sauce).

CALORIES 188; FAT 6.6g (sat 2.5g); PROTEIN 27.7g; CARBOHYDRATE 2.5g; FIBER 0.2g; CHOLESTEROL 80mg; IRON 3.6mg; SODIUM 208mg; CALCIUM 28mg

(pictured on page 157)

---

crushing whole spices

Try this quick way to crush whole spices such as juniper berries or whole peppercorns: Place the whole spices in a heavy-duty zip-top plastic bag and crush with a rolling pin or meat mallet.

▶ carbo rating: 2

Tenderloin Steaks with Garlic Sauce

Look for dried juniper berries in the spice section of the grocery store. Crush them before adding them to the recipe to release their pungent, ginlike flavor.

¼	cup fat-free beef broth
2	tablespoons dry red wine
1	tablespoon balsamic vinegar
⅛	teaspoon salt
1	large garlic clove, minced
1	teaspoon crushed juniper berries (optional)
¼	teaspoon salt
¼	teaspoon coarsely ground black pepper
2	(4-ounce) beef tenderloin steaks (¾ to 1 inch thick)

1. Combine first 5 ingredients and juniper berries, if desired. Set aside.

2. Press ¼ teaspoon salt and pepper evenly onto steaks. Heat a heavy skillet over high heat until hot. Place steaks in pan; cook 3 minutes on each side or to desired degree of doneness. Transfer steaks to a plate; keep warm.

3. Reduce heat to medium; add broth mixture. Cook 2 minutes or until sauce is slightly reduced, scraping pan to loosen browned bits. Serve sauce over steaks. Yield: 2 servings (serving size: 1 steak and about 2 tablespoons sauce).

CALORIES 190; FAT 8.4g (sat 3.1g); PROTEIN 24.5g; CARBOHYDRATE 2.3g; FIBER 0.1g; CHOLESTEROL 70mg; IRON 3.1mg; SODIUM 512mg; CALCIUM 13mg

▶ carbo rating: 2
Beef Tenderloins in Wine Sauce

You can use an additional ¼ cup beef broth in place of the wine; the carbo rating stays essentially the same.

¼ cup low-salt beef broth
¼ cup ruby port or other sweet red wine
¾ teaspoon all-purpose flour
½ teaspoon Worcestershire sauce
½ teaspoon Dijon mustard
¼ teaspoon salt
¼ teaspoon coarsely ground black pepper
Cooking spray
½ teaspoon butter
2 (4-ounce) beef tenderloin steaks, trimmed
  (1 to 1¼ inch thick)

1. Combine first 7 ingredients, whisking to dissolve flour.
2. Coat a medium nonstick skillet with cooking spray; add butter. Place over medium-high heat until hot. Add steaks, and cook 4 minutes on each side or to desired degree of doneness. Transfer steaks to a plate; keep warm.
3. Whisk broth mixture; add to pan. Bring to a boil; cook 1 minute or until reduced to ¼ cup, scraping pan to loosen browned bits. Serve sauce over steaks. Yield: 2 servings (serving size: 1 steak and 2 tablespoons sauce).

CALORIES 195; FAT 9.5g (sat 3.8g); PROTEIN 24.2g; CARBOHYDRATE 1.7g; FIBER 0.1g; CHOLESTEROL 73mg; IRON 3.4mg; SODIUM 459mg; CALCIUM 13mg

▶ carbo rating: 2
Savory Beef Roast

When you cook a lean cut of meat such as a rump roast for several hours, it becomes fork-tender.

1 (4-pound) lean boneless rump roast
Cooking spray
½ teaspoon garlic powder
¼ teaspoon salt
1 cup hot water
2 tablespoons low-sodium Worcestershire sauce
1 teaspoon beef-flavored bouillon granules
2 tablespoons all-purpose flour
1 teaspoon salt-free lemon pepper seasoning
¾ cup fat-free milk
¼ cup plain fat-free yogurt
1 teaspoon Dijon mustard
½ teaspoon anchovy paste
¼ cup minced fresh parsley
1 tablespoon shredded fresh Parmesan cheese

1. Trim fat from roast. Coat a Dutch oven with cooking spray; place over medium-high heat until hot. Add roast, and cook until browned on all sides.
2. Sprinkle roast with garlic powder and salt. Combine water, Worcestershire sauce, and bouillon granules, stirring well. Pour Worcestershire sauce mixture over roast. Bring to a boil; cover, reduce heat, and simmer 2 to 2½ hours or until roast is tender. Transfer roast to a serving platter; set aside, and keep warm.
3. Skim fat from juices in pan; reserve ¼ cup pan juices. Discard remaining juices. Return ¼ cup juices to pan.
4. Combine flour and seasoning; add to juices in pan, stirring until smooth. Gradually add milk, stirring constantly. Cook over medium heat, stirring constantly, until thickened. Combine yogurt, mustard, and anchovy paste; add to milk mixture, stirring just until blended.
5. Cut roast diagonally across grain into ¼-inch-thick slices. Top with gravy, and sprinkle with parsley and cheese. Yield: 16 servings (serving size: 3 ounces roast and 1 tablespoon gravy).

CALORIES 157; FAT 4.9g (sat 1.7g); PROTEIN 24.7g; CARBOHYDRATE 2g; FIBER 0.1g; CHOLESTEROL 64mg; IRON 2.3mg; SODIUM 138mg; CALCIUM 32mg

► **carbo rating: 2**

Veal Roast with Mustard Cream Sauce

Adding sugar-free syrup to the creamy mustard sauce creates a pleasing combination of sweet and tangy flavors that's perfect with the mild-flavored veal roast.

1	(3½ pound) boneless veal roast
2	tablespoons minced fresh basil
¼	teaspoon garlic powder
¼	teaspoon pepper

Cooking spray

¾	cup dry white wine
½	teaspoon beef-flavored bouillon granules
1	cup fat-free sour cream
¼	cup Dijon mustard
2	tablespoons sugar-free maple syrup
1	teaspoon minced peeled fresh ginger

1. Preheat oven to 325°.
2. Trim fat from roast. Combine minced basil, garlic powder, and pepper; sprinkle basil mixture over entire surface of roast.
3. Place a large ovenproof Dutch oven coated with cooking spray over medium-high heat until hot. Add roast; cook until browned on all sides, turning occasionally.
4. Combine white wine and bouillon granules. Pour wine mixture over roast. Cover and bake at 325° for 1 hour and 30 minutes or until roast is tender, basting frequently with pan juices. Transfer roast to a serving platter; set aside, and keep warm.
5. Skim fat from pan juices. Reserve ¼ cup pan juices; discard remaining pan juices. Combine ¼ cup pan juices, sour cream, Dijon mustard, maple syrup, and ginger in pan; cook over medium heat, stirring constantly, until sour cream mixture is thoroughly heated (do not boil). Cut roast diagonally across grain into thin slices; serve with mustard sauce. Yield: 14 servings (serving size: 3 ounces roast and 1½ tablespoons cream sauce).

CALORIES 187; FAT 6g (sat 1.6g); PROTEIN 28.3g; CARBOHYDRATE 2g; FIBER 0g; CHOLESTEROL 100mg; IRON 1.1mg; SODIUM 251mg; CALCIUM 31mg

► **carbo rating: 2**

Spicy Pork au Jus

Because of the juiciness of the meat and the zesty flavor of the seasonings, this 12-minute pork recipe just might become a regular at your dinner table. It's important to cook the meat just until done. Overcooking may cause the meat to be tough.

4	(4-ounce) boneless pork loin chops
1	teaspoon blackening seasoning
1	teaspoon vegetable oil
¼	cup water
1½	tablespoons low-sodium Worcestershire sauce
1½	tablespoons balsamic vinegar
1½	tablespoons low-sodium soy sauce
1½	teaspoons "measures-like-sugar" calorie-free sweetener

1. Sprinkle both sides of pork chops with seasoning. Place a large skillet over high heat until hot; add oil. Add pork chops, and cook 4 minutes on each side or just until done. Remove pork from pan; set aside, and keep warm.
2. Combine water and next 4 ingredients. Add soy sauce mixture to pan, and cook over medium-high heat 45 seconds or until mixture reduces to ¼ cup, scraping sides and bottom of pan to loosen browned bits. Serve over pork. Yield: 4 servings (serving size: 1 chop and 1 tablespoon sauce).

CALORIES 182; FAT 7.6g (sat 2.3g); PROTEIN 24.6g; CARBOHYDRATE 1.9g; FIBER 0.1g; CHOLESTEROL 67mg; IRON 1.2mg; SODIUM 363mg; CALCIUM 24mg

► carbo rating: 2

Pork Satay with Peanut Sauce

The peanut sauce is better and creamier if you use regular peanut butter instead of a natural-style peanut butter. You can use one of the creamy low-carb peanut butters, but the carbo rating will be the same.

2　pounds lean boneless pork loin
½　cup chopped onion
½　cup rice wine vinegar
1　tablespoon chopped fresh cilantro
2　tablespoons water
1　teaspoon minced garlic
1　teaspoon minced peeled fresh ginger
1　teaspoon hot Oriental chili sauce
1　teaspoon vegetable oil
6　tablespoons water
3　tablespoons creamy peanut butter
2　tablespoons low-sodium soy sauce
1½　tablespoons prepared mustard
1　teaspoon ground turmeric
1　teaspoon hot Oriental chili sauce
Cooking spray

1. Trim fat from pork; cut pork into ¾-inch cubes. Combine onion and next 7 ingredients in a large heavy-duty zip-top plastic bag. Add pork; seal bag, and shake until pork is well coated. Marinate pork in re-frigerator 8 hours, turning bag occasionally.
2. Soak 8 (10-inch) wooden skewers in water for at least 30 minutes.
3. Prepare grill.
4. Combine 6 tablespoons water and next 5 ingredients in a small bowl, stirring well with a whisk. Set aside.
5. Remove pork from marinade; discard marinade. Thread pork onto skewers. Place skewers on grill rack coated with cooking spray; cover and grill 10 to 12 minutes or until pork is done, turning occasionally. Serve warm with peanut sauce. Yield: 8 servings (serv-ing size: 3 ounces pork and 1½ tablespoons sauce).

CALORIES 209; FAT 9.9g (sat 2.9g); PROTEIN 26.2g; CARBOHYDRATE 2.7g;
FIBER 0.6g; CHOLESTEROL 67mg; IRON 1.3mg; SODIUM 283mg; CALCIUM 26mg

► carbo rating: 2

Pork Medallions with Mustard Sauce

You can change the flavor of the pork by substituting different flavors of mustard. Except for honey mustard, most mustards contain a negligible amount of carbohydrate.

1　(1-pound) pork tenderloin
Cooking spray
1　teaspoon vegetable oil
½　cup fat-free milk
2　tablespoons Dijon mustard
3　green onions, sliced

1. Trim fat from pork. Cut pork into 1-inch-thick slices. Place slices between 2 sheets of heavy-duty plastic wrap, and flatten to ½-inch thickness, using a meat mallet or rolling pin.
2. Coat a large nonstick skillet with cooking spray; add oil, and place pan over medium-high heat until hot. Add half of pork, and cook 3 minutes on each side or until browned. Remove from pan; set aside, and keep warm. Repeat procedure with remaining half of pork.
3. Reduce heat to low; add milk to pan, stirring con-stantly, scraping pan to loosen browned bits. Stir in mustard and green onions. Return pork to pan; cover and cook 2 minutes, turning to coat with sauce. Yield: 4 servings (serving size: 3 ounces).

CALORIES 160; FAT 4.7g (sat 1.2g); PROTEIN 24.9g; CARBOHYDRATE 2.4g;
FIBER 0.2g; CHOLESTEROL 74mg; IRON 1.6mg; SODIUM 295mg; CALCIUM 50mg

▶ carbo rating: 3

Peppery Mushroom Burgers

Be sure to make the patties ¼ inch thick—if they're thicker, they'll take longer to cook. The chopped mushrooms added to the ground round keep the burger juicy and moist, and add depth of flavor to the sauce.

1   (8-ounce) package sliced mushrooms, divided
1   pound ground round
2   teaspoons instant minced onion
2   teaspoons low-sodium Worcestershire sauce
1   teaspoon freshly ground black pepper
¼   cup dry red wine or low-salt beef broth
¼   cup water

1. Coarsely chop 1½ cups sliced mushrooms. Combine beef, chopped mushrooms, onion, and Worcestershire sauce in a bowl; shape into 4 equal patties, ¼ inch thick. Sprinkle pepper evenly on both sides of patties.
2. Place a large nonstick skillet over medium-high heat until hot. Add patties, and cook 5 to 6 minutes on each side or until done. Transfer to a serving platter, and keep warm.
3. Add wine, water, and remaining mushrooms to pan; cook over medium heat, stirring constantly, scraping pan to loosen browned bits about 3 minutes or until mushrooms are tender. Pour mushroom mixture over patties. Yield: 4 servings (serving size: 3 ounces meat and about ⅓ cup mushroom mixture).

CALORIES 181; FAT 6g (sat 2.1g); PROTEIN 26.3g; CARBOHYDRATE 4.4g;
FIBER 0.9g; CHOLESTEROL 66mg; IRON 3.4mg; SODIUM 78mg; CALCIUM 13mg

▶ carbo rating: 3

Greek Stuffed Steak

It's important to drain the spinach well on paper towels and squeeze it dry, or your stuffing mixture will be wet and gummy.

1   (10-ounce) package frozen chopped spinach, thawed, drained, and squeezed dry
⅓   cup finely chopped red onion
⅓   cup chopped pickled pepperoncini peppers
2   tablespoons dry breadcrumbs
¼   teaspoon garlic powder
¼   teaspoon salt
1   (1½-pound) flank steak
Cooking spray
1   (14½-ounce) can beef broth
½   cup dry red wine
½   cup water
½   teaspoon dried oregano

1. Combine first 6 ingredients in a bowl; set aside.
2. Trim fat from steak. Cut horizontally through center of steak, cutting to, but not through, other side; open flat as you would a book. Place steak between 2 sheets of heavy-duty plastic wrap; flatten to an even thickness, using a meat mallet or rolling pin.
3. Spread spinach mixture over steak, leaving a 1-inch margin around outside edges. Roll up steak, jelly roll fashion, starting with short side. Secure roll at 2-inch intervals with heavy string.
4. Coat a large Dutch oven with cooking spray, and place over medium-high heat until hot. Add steak, browning well on all sides. Add broth, wine, water, and oregano to pan; bring to a boil. Cover, reduce heat, and simmer 1 hour and 30 minutes or until tender, turning meat once. Add additional water during cooking, if necessary. Remove string, and cut steak into 8 slices. Serve with cooking liquid. Yield: 8 servings (serving size: 1 steak slice and about 2 tablespoons cooking liquid).

CALORIES 177; FAT 8.3g (sat 3.5g); PROTEIN 20.6g; CARBOHYDRATE 4.4g;
FIBER 1.3g; CHOLESTEROL 43mg; IRON 3mg; SODIUM 528mg; CALCIUM 56mg

(pictured on page 158)

▶ **carbo rating: 3**

Sirloin Steak with Sherry-Soy Sauce

If you don't have sherry on hand, use ⅓ cup of low-salt beef broth.

⅓ cup sherry
1 tablespoon "measures-like-sugar" calorie-free sweetener
2 tablespoons low-sodium soy sauce
2 tablespoons red wine vinegar
2 garlic cloves, minced
¼ teaspoon crushed red pepper
1 pound boneless sirloin steak (about ½ inch thick)
¼ teaspoon salt
¼ teaspoon black pepper

1. Combine sherry and next 5 ingredients in a small bowl; set aside.
2. Sprinkle both sides of steak with salt and black pepper.
3. Place a large nonstick skillet over high heat; add steak, and cook 3 minutes. Reduce heat to medium-high; turn steak, and cook 3 minutes or until desired degree of doneness. Remove steak, and set aside.
4. Add sherry mixture, scraping bottom and sides of pan to loosen browned bits; cook over medium heat 1 minute, stirring constantly. Slice steak, and serve with sauce. Yield: 4 servings (serving size: 3 ounces meat and 2 tablespoons sauce).

CALORIES 227; FAT 12.2g (sat 4.9g); PROTEIN 25g; CARBOHYDRATE 2.8g; FIBER 0.2g; CHOLESTEROL 67mg; IRON 2.4mg; SODIUM 483mg; CALCIUM 13mg

▶ **carbo rating: 3**

Steak au Poivre

Poivre *is the French word for "pepper." Simple and elegant, this classic steak dish is a great choice for a special dinner for two.*

1 tablespoon cracked black pepper
2 (4-ounce) beef tenderloin steaks (1 inch thick)
Cooking spray
¼ cup brandy
½ cup beef broth
¼ teaspoon salt
¼ teaspoon "measures-like-sugar" calorie-free sweetener
3 tablespoons reduced-fat sour cream

1. Press cracked black pepper evenly onto both sides of steaks.
2. Coat a large nonstick skillet with cooking spray; place pan over medium-high heat until hot. Add steaks, and cook 5 minutes on each side or until desired degree of doneness. Transfer to a serving platter; set aside, and keep warm.
3. Add brandy to pan; let simmer 30 seconds or until liquid is reduced to a glaze. Add beef broth, salt, and sweetener. Simmer, uncovered, 4 to 5 minutes or until liquid is reduced by half.
4. Remove pan from heat; stir in sour cream. Serve with steak. Yield: 2 servings (serving size: 1 steak and 2 tablespoons sauce).

CALORIES 222; FAT 9.8g (sat 4.4g); PROTEIN 20.8g; CARBOHYDRATE 3.5g; FIBER 0.8g; CHOLESTEROL 66mg; IRON 2.8mg; SODIUM 551mg; CALCIUM 41mg

> "I'm always looking for some familiar dishes that can be part of a low-carb diet. **Veal Piccata has always been one of my favorite special entrées.**"
>
> *Brad Sims*

▶ **carbo rating: 3**
Veal Piccata

You can substitute pork medallions or boneless chicken breasts for the veal cutlets, though you may have to cook them a little longer. Be sure to flatten or pound both pork and chicken to about ¼-inch thickness. Pounding makes the meat more tender and helps it to cook quickly.

 ⅓ cup dry vermouth
 2 tablespoons fresh lemon juice (about 1 lemon)
 ¼ teaspoon garlic powder
 ⅛ teaspoon salt
Butter-flavored cooking spray
 ½ pound (¼-inch-thick) veal cutlets
 6 tablespoons chopped fresh parsley

1. Combine first 4 ingredients, stirring well.
2. Coat a medium nonstick skillet with cooking spray; place over medium-high heat until hot. Add half of veal cutlets to pan; cook 1 minute on each side. Transfer veal to a serving platter, and keep warm. Recoat pan with cooking spray, and repeat procedure with remaining veal cutlets.
3. Add vermouth mixture to pan. Cook over high heat 1 minute, stirring constantly, scraping pan to loosen browned bits. Pour sauce over veal; sprinkle with parsley, and serve immediately. Yield: 2 servings (serving size: 3 ounces meat and about 3 tablespoons sauce).

CALORIES 143; FAT 3.6g (sat 1g); PROTEIN 23.1g; CARBOHYDRATE 3.2g; FIBER 0.1g; CHOLESTEROL 94mg; IRON 1.2mg; SODIUM 243mg; CALCIUM 23mg

(pictured on page 159)

▶ **carbo rating: 3**
Tarragon-Mustard Lamb

For the best browning and most desirable degree of doneness, place the broiler pan on the middle rack of the oven.

 6 (4-ounce) lamb loin chops, trimmed
 3 garlic cloves, halved
Cooking spray
 3 tablespoons Dijon mustard
 ¾ teaspoon dried tarragon
 ½ teaspoon salt
 ¼ teaspoon coarsely ground black pepper
 ¼ teaspoon paprika

1. Preheat broiler.
2. Rub both sides of each lamb chop with garlic. Place chops on a broiler pan coated with cooking spray.
3. Combine mustard, tarragon, salt, and pepper in a small bowl; spoon half of mustard mixture evenly over lamb. Broil 9 minutes. Turn; spoon remaining mustard mixture over lamb. Sprinkle with paprika; broil 9 minutes. Yield: 3 servings (serving size: 2 chops).

CALORIES 201; FAT 8.7g (sat 2.7g); PROTEIN 26.9g; CARBOHYDRATE 3.1g; FIBER 0.4g; CHOLESTEROL 81mg; IRON 3mg; SODIUM 854mg; CALCIUM 47mg

▶ carbo rating: 3

Thai Pork Rolls

You can use 12 smaller cabbage leaves instead of 6 large napa cabbage leaves. Place 2 leaves side by side, fill, and roll.

8	cups water
1	pound lean ground pork
2	large garlic cloves, minced
1	cup fresh bean sprouts
¼	cup chopped fresh cilantro
3	tablespoons oyster sauce
2	teaspoons salt-free Thai seasoning (such as The Spice Hunter)
6	large napa (Chinese) cabbage leaves

Cilantro sprigs (optional)

1. Bring 8 cups water to a boil in a large Dutch oven.
2. Cook pork and garlic in a large nonstick skillet over medium heat until pork is browned, stirring to crumble. Drain and return pork to pan. Add bean sprouts and next 3 ingredients to pork mixture; cook until thoroughly heated.
3. Add cabbage leaves to boiling water; cook 30 seconds. Drain.
4. Spoon about ½ cup pork mixture onto 1 end of each cabbage leaf; roll up, leaving ends open. Garnish with cilantro, if desired, and serve immediately. Yield: 6 servings (serving size: 1 roll).

CALORIES 163; FAT 8.8g (sat 3g); PROTEIN 17g; CARBOHYDRATE 3.8g; FIBER 0.7g; CHOLESTEROL 54mg; IRON 0.9mg; SODIUM 206mg; CALCIUM 57mg

oyster sauce

Oyster sauce is high in sodium, but not in carbohydrate. One tablespoon has only 0.4 grams of carbohydrate, but 109 milligrams of sodium. Oyster sauce is a common ingredient in many Asian-style dishes and stir-fries.

▶ carbo rating: 3

Hot Peppered Pork

Ginger, garlic, and dried crushed red pepper give pork strips a sweet-hot bite. When you serve the tender pork over a bed of cool, crunchy napa cabbage, you get a refreshing flavor contrast.

1	pound lean boneless pork loin
1	tablespoon low-sodium soy sauce

Cooking spray

1	red bell pepper, seeded and sliced into thin strips
1	teaspoon vegetable oil
2	teaspoons minced peeled fresh ginger
½	teaspoon crushed red pepper
2	garlic cloves, minced
¼	cup low-salt beef broth
4	cups shredded napa (Chinese) cabbage

1. Partially freeze pork; trim fat. Slice pork into ¼-inch-thick strips; cut strips into 2-inch pieces. Combine pork and soy sauce in a large heavy-duty zip-top plastic bag; seal bag, and turn to coat pork. Let stand 5 minutes.
2. Coat a large nonstick skillet with cooking spray; place over medium-high heat until hot. Add red bell pepper; cook 3 minutes or until crisp-tender, stirring often. Remove from pan, and set aside.
3. Add oil to pan; place over medium-high heat until hot. Add ginger, crushed red pepper, and garlic; sauté 30 seconds. Add pork to pan; cook 5 minutes or until pork is done, stirring often. Add red bell pepper and broth to pan; bring to a boil. Reduce heat, and simmer 2 to 3 minutes or until most of liquid evaporates.
4. Top shredded cabbage with pork mixture. Serve immediately. Yield: 4 servings (serving size: 1 cup cabbage and about 1 cup pork mixture).

CALORIES 212; FAT 10.2g (sat 3.2g); PROTEIN 24.8g; CARBOHYDRATE 4.3g; FIBER 1.3g; CHOLESTEROL 68mg; IRON 2mg; SODIUM 210mg; CALCIUM 73mg

> ### "I love to eat barbecue, but a lot of the store-bought sauces have way too much sugar."
> *Wade Lowery*

▶ carbo rating: 3
Three-Alarm Barbecue

Instead of a sugary, tomato-based sauce, this fiery barbecue has a vinegar-based one with a splash of hot sauce and a sprinkle of pepper.

1   (2½-pound) boned pork loin roast
1   cup cider vinegar
1   tablespoon hot sauce
1   teaspoon cracked black pepper
1   teaspoon low-sodium Worcestershire sauce
¾   teaspoon ground red pepper
½   teaspoon salt
4   (3-inch) chunks hickory wood
Cooking spray

1. Trim fat from roast. Combine pork and next 6 ingredients in a large zip-top plastic bag. Seal; marinate in refrigerator 8 hours, turning bag occasionally. Remove roast from bag, reserving marinade.
2. Soak hickory wood chunks in water 1 to 24 hours. Drain well. Prepare charcoal fire in meat smoker; let burn 15 to 20 minutes. Place hickory chunks on top of coals. Place water pan in smoker; fill with hot tap water.
3. Coat grill rack with cooking spray; place roast on rack in smoker. Cover with smoker lid; cook 3 to 4 hours or until a meat thermometer registers 155°. Refill water pan with water and add additional charcoal to fire as needed.
4. Remove roast from smoker; cover and let stand 10 minutes or until thermometer registers 160°. Separate roast into bite-sized pieces, using 2 forks. Place roast pieces in a medium bowl.
5. Place reserved marinade in a small saucepan over medium heat; bring marinade to a boil. Remove from heat. Pour over pork, and toss well. Yield: 6 servings (serving size: 3 ounces).

CALORIES 280; FAT 15.8g (sat 5.4g); PROTEIN 30.3g; CARBOHYDRATE 2.9g; FIBER 0.2g; CHOLESTEROL 102mg; IRON 1.7mg; SODIUM 294mg; CALCIUM 15mg

smoking to perfection

The appearance of smoked foods is unique, particularly in light-colored meats such as pork and poultry. The outside is a pinkish-red, while the inside is often pink, so color is not always a good measure of doneness.

After setting up the smoker, leave it covered until the suggested minimum time. For example, if the recipe says to cook for 3 to 4 hours, check the internal temperature for the first time at 3 hours. Each time a smoker is opened, heat, and more importantly, moisture escape, adding 15 minutes to the cooking time.

Manufacturer's directions and our recipes assume the use of a charcoal smoker under ideal conditions. The outside air temperature, humidity, wind, quality of the charcoal, and internal temperature of the smoker are variables, so you may need to adjust your cooking time.

Onion-Smothered Pork Tenderloin

The sautéed onions add a rich sweetness to the savory pork tenderloin.

2	(¾-pound) pork tenderloins
	Cooking spray
2	teaspoons butter
2	cups sliced onion
½	teaspoon dried thyme
½	teaspoon salt
¼	teaspoon pepper

1. Preheat oven to 400°.

2. Trim fat from pork; cut a lengthwise slit down center of each tenderloin, cutting about two-thirds of the way through meat. Place on a broiler pan coated with cooking spray.

3. Melt butter in a large nonstick skillet over medium-high heat. Add onion, and sauté 5 to 6 minutes or until tender. Add thyme, salt, and pepper. Spread onion mixture evenly over tenderloins. Bake at 400° for 45 minutes or until a meat thermometer registers 160° (slightly pink). Yield: 6 servings (serving size: 3 ounces).

CALORIES 168; FAT 5.5g (sat 2.2g); PROTEIN 25g; CARBOHYDRATE 3.4g; FIBER 0.7g; CHOLESTEROL 83mg; IRON 1.6mg; SODIUM 267mg; CALCIUM 18mg

Flank Steak with Mushrooms

Marinating this cut of beef in an acidic mixture of lemon juice and soy sauce both tenderizes and flavors the meat.

1	(1-pound) lean flank steak
¼	cup low-sodium soy sauce
2	tablespoons lemon juice
1	teaspoon freeze-dried chives
¼	teaspoon dried marjoram
2	garlic cloves, minced
	Cooking spray
1	teaspoon olive oil
3	cups sliced mushrooms
2	tablespoons minced fresh parsley

1. Trim fat from steak. Combine soy sauce and next 4 ingredients in a large heavy-duty zip-top plastic bag. Add steak; seal bag, and shake until steak is well coated. Marinate in refrigerator 8 hours, turning bag occasionally.

2. Remove steak from marinade, reserving marinade. Cut steak diagonally across grain into ¼-inch-thick strips.

3. Heat oil in a large nonstick skillet coated with cooking spray over medium-high heat. Add steak; cook 5 to 6 minutes or until browned on all sides, stirring frequently. Remove steak from pan. Drain and pat dry with paper towels. Wipe drippings from pan with a paper towel.

4. Coat pan with cooking spray; place over medium-high heat until hot. Add mushrooms; sauté 3 minutes. Stir in reserved marinade and parsley. Cover, reduce heat to medium, and cook 5 minutes. Return steak to pan; cook until thoroughly heated. Yield: 4 servings (serving size: 3 ounces meat and ½ cup mushroom mixture).

CALORIES 248; FAT 14.5g (sat 5.6g); PROTEIN 23.3g; CARBOHYDRATE 4.6g; FIBER 1g; CHOLESTEROL 60mg; IRON 3.2mg; SODIUM 464mg; CALCIUM 15mg

▶ carbo rating: 4

All-American Grilled Steak

There's no need to use one of the low-carb ketchups in this marinade. One-fourth cup of regular ketchup has 14 grams of carbohydrate, which means that ketchup contributes about 2 grams of carbohydrate per serving in this recipe. The sweetness of the ketchup is balanced by the dry wine, vinegar, and mustard.

1	cup dry red wine
¼	cup ketchup
3	tablespoons Dijon mustard
2	tablespoons red wine vinegar
½	teaspoon salt
½	teaspoon dried thyme
½	teaspoon pepper
2	garlic cloves, minced
1	bay leaf
1	(1½-pound) lean boneless top round steak (about 1½ inches thick)

Cooking spray

1. Combine first 9 ingredients in a large heavy-duty zip-top plastic bag; add steak, and seal bag. Marinate in refrigerator 8 hours or overnight, turning bag occasionally.

2. Prepare grill.

3. Remove steak from bag, reserving marinade; discard bay leaf. Place marinade in a saucepan. Bring to a boil; remove from heat.

4. Place steak on grill rack coated with cooking spray; cover and grill 5 minutes on each side or until desired degree of doneness, basting with reserved marinade. Cut steak diagonally across grain into thin slices. Yield: 6 servings (serving size: 3 ounces).

CALORIES 177; FAT 5.2g (sat 1.7g); PROTEIN 26.2g; CARBOHYDRATE 4.5g; FIBER 0.2g; CHOLESTEROL 65mg; IRON 2.8mg; SODIUM 599mg; CALCIUM 13mg

▶ carbo rating: 4

Beef Tenderloin with Horseradish-Mustard Crust

We replaced the plain white breadcrumbs with whole wheat breadcrumbs in this recipe to take advantage of the extra fiber. It takes about 1½ slices of bread to make 1 cup of breadcrumbs.

1¾	pounds beef tenderloin, trimmed
¼	teaspoon freshly ground black pepper

Cooking spray

1½	tablespoons Dijon mustard
1½	tablespoons prepared horseradish
1	cup whole wheat breadcrumbs
1	tablespoon chopped fresh parsley
2	teaspoons olive oil
⅛	teaspoon salt
⅛	teaspoon freshly ground black pepper
2	garlic cloves, minced

1. Preheat oven to 400°.

2. Sprinkle tenderloin with pepper. Coat a large nonstick skillet with cooking spray; place over medium-high heat until hot. Add beef, and cook 10 minutes or until browned.

3. Combine mustard and horseradish; spread onto beef. Combine breadcrumbs and next 5 ingredients; pat onto beef, pressing firmly. Coat beef with cooking spray. Bake at 400° for 35 to 40 minutes or until a meat thermometer registers 145° (medium-rare) to 160° (medium).

4. Place beef on a platter; cover with foil. Let stand 10 minutes before slicing. Yield: 7 servings (serving size: 3 ounces).

CALORIES 183; FAT 9g (sat 2.9g); PROTEIN 20.3g; CARBOHYDRATE 4.5g; FIBER 0.7g; CHOLESTEROL 57mg; IRON 2.9mg; SODIUM 236mg; CALCIUM 21mg

▶ carbo rating: 4

Greek-Style Lamb

Rather than take the time to thread the meat and vegetables on skewers, we took the quick and easy route and used a grill basket.

1   pound boneless leg of lamb, cut into 1-inch pieces
1   yellow bell pepper, seeded and cut into large pieces
1   small zucchini, cut into ½-inch-thick slices
½   red onion, cut into wedges
3   garlic cloves, minced
1   tablespoon dried oregano
2   tablespoons fresh lemon juice (about 1 lemon)
2   tablespoons olive oil
½   teaspoon salt
½   teaspoon pepper
Cooking spray

1. Prepare grill.
2. Combine first 4 ingredients in a large bowl. Add garlic and next 5 ingredients; toss gently to coat.
3. Arrange lamb mixture in a grilling basket coated with cooking spray on grill rack. Cover and grill 14 minutes, turning once, until lamb is done and vegetables are tender. Yield: 4 servings (serving size: 1¾ cups).

CALORIES 232; FAT 12g (sat 2.8g); PROTEIN 24.5g; CARBOHYDRATE 6.1g; FIBER 2g; CHOLESTEROL 73mg; IRON 3.1mg; SODIUM 368mg; CALCIUM 44mg

(pictured on page 159)

▶ carbo rating: 5

Seared Steaks with Creamy Horseradish Sauce

Searing steaks in a skillet or grill pan is a great way to maximize the meat's flavor without having to go to the grill. The trick to searing meat is a hot skillet or grill pan. Drop a small amount of water on the hot skillet. If the water balls up, sizzles, and dances along the surface of the skillet before evaporating, the skillet is hot enough to sear the meat. Serve the steaks with Roasted Onions and Peppers (page 328), if desired.

1   pound boneless sirloin steak, trimmed (about 1 inch thick)
3   garlic cloves, divided
Cooking spray
½   teaspoon salt, divided
⅛   teaspoon coarsely ground black pepper
⅓   cup fat-free sour cream
1½   tablespoons light mayonnaise
1   tablespoon prepared horseradish
¼   teaspoon coarsely ground black pepper

1. Cut steak into 4 equal pieces. Cut 2 garlic cloves in half, and rub both sides of each steak with garlic. Place a large nonstick skillet or grill pan coated with cooking spray over high heat. Add steaks; cook 4 minutes. Turn steaks, and cook 3 minutes. Reduce heat to medium; sprinkle steaks with ¼ teaspoon salt and ⅛ teaspoon black pepper. Cook 2 minutes or until desired degree of doneness.
2. Mince 1 garlic clove. Combine garlic, sour cream, mayonnaise, horseradish, ¼ teaspoon pepper, and ¼ teaspoon salt. Serve steaks with horseradish sauce. Yield: 4 servings (serving size: 3 ounces steak and 2 tablespoons sauce).

CALORIES 218; FAT 9.1g (sat 3.1g); PROTEIN 27.4g; CARBOHYDRATE 5g; FIBER 0.2g; CHOLESTEROL 81mg; IRON 3mg; SODIUM 423mg; CALCIUM 47mg

(pictured on page 160)

► carbo rating: 5
Sirloin Tips with Vegetables

If you can't find precut sirloin tips, have the butcher cut a trimmed sirloin steak into 1½-inch pieces.

    2   teaspoons olive oil
    1   pound sirloin tips
    ½   teaspoon salt, divided
    ¼   teaspoon freshly ground black pepper
    1   large Vidalia or other sweet onion, cut into
        1½-inch pieces
    1   green bell pepper, seeded and cut into 1½-inch
        pieces
    1   red bell pepper, seeded and cut into 1½-inch
        pieces
    6   tablespoons water, divided
    2   teaspoons tomato, basil, and garlic seasoning
        blend (such as Mrs. Dash)

1. Heat oil in a large nonstick skillet over high heat. Sprinkle beef with ¼ teaspoon salt and pepper. Add beef to pan; cook, stirring frequently, 3 to 5 minutes or until desired degree of doneness. Remove beef from pan; set aside, and keep warm.
2. Reduce heat to medium-high. Add onion and bell pepper to pan; sauté 3 minutes. Add 2 tablespoons water; cook 1 minute.
3. Add beef to onion mixture; sprinkle with seasoning blend and ¼ teaspoon salt. Add ¼ cup water to pan; bring to a boil, scraping pan to loosen browned bits. Cook, stirring constantly, 1 minute. Yield: 4 servings (serving size: 1½ cups).

CALORIES 240; FAT 8.4g (sat 2.4g); PROTEIN 33.4g; CARBOHYDRATE 6.3g; FIBER 1.7g; CHOLESTEROL 92mg; IRON 3.7mg; SODIUM 370mg; CALCIUM 18mg

► carbo rating: 5
Balsamic Pan-Seared Steaks

You don't need to do much to beef tenderloin to get great flavor. These are seared in the skillet and served with a simple sauce of olive oil, balsamic vinegar, and beef broth—all ingredients you probably have on hand.

    4   (4-ounce) lean boneless beef tenderloin steaks
        (1 inch thick)
    1   teaspoon garlic-pepper seasoning
    ¼   teaspoon salt
    1   teaspoon olive oil
    ½   cup balsamic vinegar
    ⅓   cup beef broth

1. Sprinkle both sides of steaks with garlic-pepper seasoning and salt. Heat oil in a large nonstick skillet over medium-high heat. Add steaks, and cook 3 minutes on each side or until done. Remove steaks from pan; keep warm.
2. Combine vinegar and broth in pan. Bring to a boil over high heat; reduce heat to medium-high, and cook 5 minutes or until sauce is reduced to ¼ cup, stirring occasionally. Spoon sauce over steaks. Yield: 4 servings (serving size: 1 steak and 1 tablespoon sauce).

CALORIES 213; FAT 9.8g (sat 3.3g); PROTEIN 24.5g; CARBOHYDRATE 5.1g; FIBER 0g; CHOLESTEROL 71mg; IRON 3.3mg; SODIUM 367mg; CALCIUM 16mg

"I like to use low-carb recipes that have great flavor and are easy to prepare in less than 30 minutes."
Laurl Self

► carbo rating: 5

Flank Steak with Tomato-Avocado Salsa

The habanero pepper is extremely hot and is used in many Caribbean-style dishes. Note that the carbo rating for this recipe includes the salsa.

½ cup minced green onions
2 tablespoons cider vinegar
1 tablespoon minced peeled fresh ginger
4 teaspoons Jamaican jerk seasoning
2 garlic cloves, minced
1 habanero pepper, seeded and minced
1 (1¾-pound) flank steak, trimmed
Cooking spray
Tomato-Avocado Salsa (recipe at right)
Cilantro sprigs (optional)

1. Combine first 6 ingredients in a small bowl. Score a diamond pattern on steak. Place steak in a shallow dish. Spread green onion mixture on steak. Cover and marinate in refrigerator at least 8 hours.
2. Prepare grill.
3. Place steak on grill rack coated with cooking spray; grill 6 minutes on each side or until desired degree of doneness. Let stand 5 minutes. Cut steak diagonally across grain into thin slices. Serve with Tomato-Avocado Salsa. Garnish with cilantro sprigs, if desired. Yield: 6 servings (serving size: 3 ounces steak and ⅓ cup salsa).

CALORIES 246; FAT 12.9g (sat 4.4g); PROTEIN 24.9g; CARBOHYDRATE 7.6g; FIBER 2.3g; CHOLESTEROL 59mg; IRON 2.9mg; SODIUM 330mg; CALCIUM 19mg

scoring meat

Scoring meat before marinating helps tenderize the meat and allows it to absorb more flavors. To score a flank steak, use a sharp knife to make diagonal cuts across the grain of the meat about 1 inch apart and ⅛ inch deep on both sides of the meat. If time allows, place the steak in the freezer for about 10 to 15 minutes. The meat will freeze just enough to make scoring much easier.

Serve leftover salsa as a topping for fajitas, grilled fish, or chicken.

► carbo rating: 2

tomato-avocado salsa

1 teaspoon grated lime rind
2 tablespoons fresh lime juice
3 plum tomatoes, seeded and diced
1 ripe peeled avocado, seeded and diced
⅓ cup chopped onion
¼ cup chopped fresh cilantro
1 garlic clove, minced
⅛ teaspoon salt
⅛ teaspoon pepper

1. Combine all ingredients in a bowl; toss well, and chill. Yield: 2 cups (serving size: 1 tablespoon).

CALORIES 10; FAT 0.8g (sat 0.1g); PROTEIN 0.2g; CARBOHYDRATE 2g; FIBER 0.4g; CHOLESTEROL 0mg; IRON 0.1mg; SODIUM 11mg; CALCIUM 2mg

► carbo rating: 5

Peppered Fillets with Mushroom Sauce

To get maximum pepper flavor, use freshly ground. It's more pungent and flavorful than the ground pepper in cans or jars.

2   (4-ounce) beef tenderloin steaks (1 inch thick)
1   teaspoon freshly ground black pepper
Cooking spray
1   (8-ounce) package sliced mushrooms
2   green onions, sliced
¼   cup dry red wine or low-salt beef broth

1. Preheat broiler.
2. Sprinkle both sides of steaks evenly with pepper.
3. Place steaks on a broiler pan coated with cooking spray; broil 5 to 6 minutes on each side or until desired degree of doneness.
4. While steaks broil, coat a large nonstick skillet with cooking spray; place over medium-high heat until hot. Add mushrooms and onions; cook 5 minutes or until mushrooms are tender. Add wine; simmer 1 minute.
5. Place steaks on a serving platter; spoon mushroom mixture over steaks. Yield: 2 servings (serving size: 1 steak and ½ cup sauce).

CALORIES 211; FAT 8.7g (sat 3.2g); PROTEIN 26.7g; CARBOHYDRATE 6.8g; FIBER 1.9g; CHOLESTEROL 71mg; IRON 5mg; SODIUM 62mg; CALCIUM 23mg

(pictured on page 225)

► carbo rating: 5

Italian-Style Pork

When there's no time to simmer an all-day Italian sauce, try these speedy Italian-flavored pork chops.

4   (6-ounce) bone-in center-cut pork chops (about ½ inch thick)
2   garlic cloves, halved
1   teaspoon dried Italian seasoning
¼   teaspoon salt
Cooking spray
½   cup grape tomatoes, halved
½   cup chopped bottled roasted red bell peppers
¼   cup chopped fresh parsley
2   tablespoons capers, drained
2   tablespoons cider vinegar
⅛   teaspoon crushed red pepper

1. Rub both sides of pork chops with garlic halves; sprinkle with Italian seasoning and salt. Coat pork chops with cooking spray. Place a large nonstick skillet over medium heat until hot. Add pork chops, and cook 6 minutes on each side or until done. Transfer pork to a serving platter; keep warm.
2. Add tomatoes and next 5 ingredients to pan; cook 1 minute or until thoroughly heated. Spoon over pork. Yield: 4 servings (serving size: 1 pork chop and about ⅓ cup tomato mixture).

CALORIES 164; FAT 5.9g (sat 2.1g); PROTEIN 21.9g; CARBOHYDRATE 5.5g; FIBER 0.6g; CHOLESTEROL 58mg; IRON 1.2mg; SODIUM 376mg; CALCIUM 39mg

▶ carbo rating: 6

Favorite Meat Loaf

Meat loaf is sometimes higher in carbs than you might think because of the bread that is added, along with egg, as a binder. Our version has a small amount of breadcrumbs, and they're 100 percent whole wheat.

Cooking spray
½ cup chopped onion
¼ cup finely chopped celery
2 garlic cloves, minced
1½ pounds ground round
1 (14½-ounce) can diced tomatoes with Italian herbs, drained (such as Contadina)
3 (1-ounce) slices reduced-calorie whole wheat bread, torn into small pieces
1 tablespoon reduced-sodium Worcestershire sauce
1 large egg, lightly beaten
1 large egg white, lightly beaten
¼ teaspoon pepper
2 tablespoons chili sauce
1 tablespoon water

1. Preheat oven to 350°.
2. Coat a nonstick skillet with cooking spray; place over medium-high heat until hot. Add onion, celery, and garlic; sauté 3 minutes or until tender.
3. Combine onion mixture, ground round, and next 6 ingredients in a bowl; stir well. Shape meat mixture into a 9 x 5-inch loaf; place on a broiler pan coated with cooking spray. Combine chili sauce and water; brush over loaf. Bake, uncovered, at 350° for 1 hour or until a meat thermometer registers 160°. Let stand 10 minutes before slicing. Yield: 10 servings (serving size: 1 slice).

CALORIES 137; FAT 4.1g (sat 1.4g); PROTEIN 17.2g; CARBOHYDRATE 7.7g; FIBER 1.2g; CHOLESTEROL 62mg; IRON 2.2mg; SODIUM 213mg; CALCIUM 38mg

▶ carbo rating: 6

Beef Tenderloin with Marsala-Mushroom Sauce

The mushroom sauce is a great low-carb sauce because it's not thickened with flour or cornstarch. This is a wine- and broth-based sauce, and the flavors are concentrated as the mixture is reduced. See page 196 for information on shiitake mushrooms.

10 ounces shiitake mushrooms
4 (4-ounce) beef tenderloin steaks, trimmed
½ teaspoon pepper
¼ teaspoon salt
Cooking spray
1 teaspoon olive oil
¼ cup minced shallots
½ cup Marsala wine
¾ cups beef broth
½ teaspoon Dijon mustard
1 tablespoon light butter

1. Remove and discard stems from mushrooms; slice mushrooms.
2. Sprinkle steaks with pepper and salt; coat with cooking spray. Place a large nonstick skillet over high heat. Add steaks; cook 3 to 4 minutes on each side or until desired degree of doneness. Place steaks on a platter; keep warm.
3. Heat oil in pan over medium heat until hot; add shallots, and sauté 1 minute. Add sliced mushrooms; sauté 4 minutes or until tender. Add wine; bring to a boil, reduce heat, and simmer 2 minutes.
4. Add broth and Dijon mustard; boil 5 minutes or until liquid is reduced by half. Remove from heat. Add butter; stir until butter melts. Spoon sauce over steaks. Yield: 4 servings (serving size: 1 steak and ⅓ cup mushroom sauce).

CALORIES 231; FAT 10.2g (sat 4.2g); PROTEIN 26.3g; CARBOHYDRATE 6.4g; FIBER 0.9g; CHOLESTEROL 75mg; IRON 4.5mg; SODIUM 404mg; CALCIUM 14mg

> "I like to grill kebabs instead of steaks for company because they cook so fast that I'm not busy slaving over a hot grill while my guests are left to amuse themselves."
>
> *Wade Lowery*

▶ carbo rating: 6

Lamb Shish Kebabs

To be sure that the kebabs cook evenly, don't crowd the pieces of meat and vegetables on the skewers.

¼	cup dry red wine
1½	tablespoons dried oregano
1½	tablespoons dried mint flakes
2	tablespoons lemon juice
2	teaspoons olive oil
4	garlic cloves, minced
1½	pounds lean cubed boned leg of lamb
18	(1-inch) squares green bell pepper (about 3 large peppers)
18	cherry tomatoes
1	large onion, cut into 6 wedges

Cooking spray

1. Combine first 6 ingredients in a large heavy-duty zip-top plastic bag; add lamb, and seal bag. Marinate in refrigerator 12 to 24 hours, turning bag occasionally.
2. Prepare grill.
3. Remove lamb from bag, reserving marinade. Place marinade in a saucepan. Bring to a boil; remove from heat. Thread lamb, bell pepper, tomatoes, and onion alternately onto 12 (10-inch) skewers. Place skewers on grill rack coated with cooking spray. Grill, covered, 5 minutes on each side or until desired degree of doneness, turning and basting kebabs frequently with marinade. Yield: 6 servings (serving size: 2 kebabs).

CALORIES 195; FAT 7.1g (sat 2.1g); PROTEIN 24.6g; CARBOHYDRATE 8.3g; FIBER 1.8g; CHOLESTEROL 73mg; IRON 3.3mg; SODIUM 78mg; CALCIUM 39mg

(pictured on page 226)

how to grill kebabs

You may call them shish kebabs or skewers: They're the same thing. Kebabs are accommodating and easy to customize; they're a natural for mixing ingredients, flavors, and cooking styles.

And kebabs are as easy to serve as they are to prepare—with everything already cut into bite-sized pieces, your guests will be good to go with only a paper plate.

skewer savvy

Here are some tips for successful skewering.
• Soak wooden skewers in water for 15 to 30 minutes so they won't burn on the grill.
• When grilling meat kebabs, be sure the pieces are all the same size to ensure even cooking. Pounding chicken to an even thickness helps it cook quickly and evenly.
• Shrimp, scallops, and other wobbly bits benefit from the double-skewer technique: Thread the pieces on a skewer, then run another one through the pieces parallel to the first, about a half-inch away.
• Expecting vegetarians? Cook the meat and vegetables on separate skewers, so guests who don't want meat can pick up a stick of vegetables. If your guests will assemble their own skewers, place meat and vegetables in separate bowls.
• If you have to move the party inside, you can broil kebabs; it doesn't take any longer than grilling.

▶ carbo rating: 7
Picante Meat Loaf

Instead of spooning ketchup over a meat loaf, try using picante sauce. The picante sauce is lower in carbs than ketchup and adds a kick to the meat.

1	pound ground round
⅔	cup whole wheat breadcrumbs
½	cup chopped onion
¼	cup coarsely chopped carrot
2	large egg whites, lightly beaten
¼	teaspoon salt
¼	teaspoon dried rubbed sage
¼	teaspoon pepper

Cooking spray

½	cup picante sauce

1. Preheat oven to 400°.
2. Combine first 8 ingredients in a medium bowl. Shape mixture into a 6 x 4-inch loaf, and place on a rack in a broiler pan coated with cooking spray.
3. Bake at 400° for 35 minutes. Brush picante sauce over meat loaf. Return to oven, and bake an additional 5 minutes. Let stand 5 minutes before slicing. Yield: 6 servings (serving size: 1 slice).

CALORIES 224; FAT 8.2g (sat 3.1g); PROTEIN 27.6g; CARBOHYDRATE 8.1g; FIBER 1.1g; CHOLESTEROL 68mg; IRON 2.6mg; SODIUM 532mg; CALCIUM 17mg

ketchup comparison

Although ketchups, tomato salsas, and picante sauces have some similarities, their carbohydrate content varies slightly, with regular ketchup having the most carbs.

Product (1 Tbsp.)	Carbohydrate	Fiber	Carbo Rating
Salsa	1.0	0.3	1
Picante Sauce	1.0	0.0	1
Low-Carb Ketchup	0.5	0.0	1
Ketchup	3.6	0.2	3

▶ carbo rating: 7
Marjoram-Lemon Lamb Kebabs

You can also make these kebabs with boneless sirloin steak, cut into cubes.

1	cup dry red wine
¾	cup finely chopped onion
2	tablespoons olive oil
4	garlic cloves, minced
1½	pounds boneless leg of lamb, trimmed and cut into 1-inch cubes
12	small boiling onions, peeled
1½	tablespoons dried marjoram or oregano
1	tablespoon grated lemon rind
1	teaspoon sea or kosher salt
½	teaspoon ground cumin
½	teaspoon coarsely ground black pepper
1	green bell pepper, cut into 1-inch pieces
1	yellow bell pepper, cut into 1-inch pieces

Cooking spray

1. Combine first 4 ingredients in large zip-top plastic bag; add lamb to bag. Seal and marinate in refrigerator 2 to 12 hours, turning bag occasionally. Remove lamb from bag; discard marinade. Place lamb in a large bowl; set aside.
2. Cook boiling onions in boiling water 2 minutes or until tender. Drain and cool slightly.
3. Prepare grill, heating to medium-high heat.
4. Add marjoram, rind, salt, cumin, and black pepper to lamb; toss gently to coat.
5. Let stand at room temperature 10 minutes. Thread lamb, boiling onions, and bell pepper pieces alternately onto each of 6 (12-inch) skewers. Place kebabs on grill rack coated with cooking spray; grill 8 minutes or until desired degree of doneness, turning once. Yield: 6 servings (serving size: 1 kebab).

CALORIES 228; FAT 8.7g (sat 2.6g); PROTEIN 25.1g; CARBOHYDRATE 8.7g; FIBER 1.9g; CHOLESTEROL 77mg; IRON 2.9mg; SODIUM 453mg; CALCIUM 40mg

► carbo rating: 7

Marmalade Pork Chops

Low-sugar marmalades and jams make great low-carb sauces for meat. All you have to do is stir in a bit of vinegar to balance the sweetness, and heat in the skillet along with the meat.

1	teaspoon olive oil
Cooking spray	
4	(4-ounce) lean boneless pork loin chops, trimmed
2	teaspoons lemon pepper seasoning
2	tablespoons cider vinegar
¼	cup low-sugar orange marmalade

1. Heat oil in a large nonstick skillet coated with cooking spray over medium-high heat. Sprinkle chops on both sides with lemon pepper seasoning; add chops to pan, and cook 5 minutes on each side or until done. Remove from pan, and keep warm.

2. Add vinegar to pan; stir in marmalade. Return chops to pan, turning once to coat; cook 1 minute or until thoroughly heated. Serve immediately. Yield: 4 servings (serving size: 1 chop and about 1½ tablespoons sauce).

CALORIES 221; FAT 9.4g (sat 3g); PROTEIN 25.1g; CARBOHYDRATE 7.1g; FIBER 0g; CHOLESTEROL 71mg; IRON 1mg; SODIUM 245mg; CALCIUM 6mg

► carbo rating: 8

Jerk Meat Loaf

For a fiery version of this meat loaf, substitute two Scotch Bonnet peppers for the jalapeño peppers. We opted to use a low-carb ketchup in this recipe because there is enough carbohydrate coming from the whole wheat breadcrumbs.

1	pound ground round
1	cup whole wheat breadcrumbs
½	cup finely chopped green onions
¼	cup egg substitute
¼	cup fat-free milk
¼	cup low-carb or reduced-calorie ketchup
2	tablespoons white vinegar
1	teaspoon dried thyme
½	teaspoon salt
½	teaspoon ground allspice
½	teaspoon coarsely ground black pepper
⅛	teaspoon ground nutmeg
⅛	teaspoon ground cinnamon
2	jalapeño peppers, seeded and finely chopped
Cooking spray	

1. Preheat oven to 350°.

2. Combine all ingredients except cooking spray in a medium bowl. Shape mixture into an 8 x 4-inch loaf; place on a broiler pan coated with cooking spray. Bake at 350° for 1 hour. Cut into 6 slices. Yield: 6 servings (serving size: 1 slice).

CALORIES 151; FAT 3.6g (sat 1.2g); PROTEIN 19.8g; CARBOHYDRATE 8.3g; FIBER 0.8g; CHOLESTEROL 44mg; IRON 2.6mg; SODIUM 314mg; CALCIUM 41mg

Smothered Sirloin Patties with Veggies and Horseradish Sour Cream

To make this dish more kid-friendly, skip the horseradish sour cream.

½ cup fat-free sour cream
1 tablespoon prepared horseradish
½ teaspoon salt, divided
1 pound ground sirloin
1 teaspoon Cajun seasoning, divided
Cooking spray
¾ cup green bell pepper strips (about ½ medium, cut into ¼-inch strips)
2 yellow squash, quartered lengthwise
1 small onion, cut into eighths
¼ cup water

1. Combine sour cream, horseradish, and ¼ teaspoon salt; stir well with a whisk. Set aside.
2. Divide meat into 4 equal portions, shaping each into a ½-inch-thick patty.
3. Place patties in a nonstick skillet over medium-high heat. Sprinkle with ½ teaspoon Cajun seasoning. Cook 5 minutes; turn, sprinkle with ½ teaspoon Cajun seasoning, and cook 4 minutes. Remove patties from pan, and keep warm.
4. Coat pan with cooking spray, and place over medium-high heat. Add bell pepper, ¼ teaspoon salt, squash, and onion. Cover, reduce heat to medium-low, and cook 6 minutes or until squash is crisp-tender, stirring occasionally.
5. Return patties to pan; add water. Cover and cook over medium heat 3 minutes or until done. Serve with sour cream mixture. Yield: 4 servings (serving size: 1 patty, ¼ of vegetables, and 2 tablespoons sour cream mixture).

CALORIES 233; FAT 8.2g (sat 3.4g); PROTEIN 28.7g; CARBOHYDRATE 10g; FIBER 1.6g; CHOLESTEROL 81mg; IRON 3.3mg; SODIUM 496mg; CALCIUM 77mg

Flank Steak with Horseradish Cream

The tangy horseradish cream is great as a topping for any kind of beef.

¼ cup reduced-fat olive oil vinaigrette
1 teaspoon dried Italian seasoning
1 small onion, quartered
1 (1-pound) flank steak
Cooking spray
½ cup fat-free sour cream
2 tablespoons fat-free mayonnaise
1½ tablespoons prepared horseradish
Oregano sprigs (optional)

1. Combine first 3 ingredients in a food processor; process until onion is minced.
2. Place steak in a large heavy-duty zip-top plastic bag. Pour onion mixture over steak; seal bag, and shake until steak is well coated. Marinate in refrigerator 8 hours, turning bag occasionally.
3. Prepare grill.
4. Remove steak from marinade; discard marinade. Place steak on grill rack coated with cooking spray. Cover and grill 10 to 12 minutes or to desired degree of doneness. Let steak stand 5 minutes.
5. Combine sour cream, mayonnaise, and horseradish, stirring well. Cut steak diagonally across grain into thin slices. Garnish with oregano sprigs, if desired. Serve with horseradish mixture. Yield: 4 servings (serving size: 3 ounces steak and about 2½ tablespoons cream).

CALORIES 281; FAT 16.1g (sat 5.1g); PROTEIN 24.7g; CARBOHYDRATE 8.5g; FIBER 0.6g; CHOLESTEROL 65mg; IRON 2.4mg; SODIUM 316mg; CALCIUM 79mg

▶ **carbo rating: 8**

Beef Fillets with Vegetables

Beef broth provides the base for a quick, rich sauce to complement smoke-scented grilled steaks. Add a salad, and you have a low-carb meal.

Cooking spray
1   teaspoon olive oil
2   red bell peppers, seeded and cut into thin strips
2   zucchini, thinly sliced
1   small onion, thinly sliced
1   cup low-salt beef broth, divided
2   teaspoons minced fresh thyme or ½ teaspoon dried thyme
2   teaspoons all-purpose flour
4   (4-ounce) beef tenderloin steaks (about 1 inch thick)
2   large garlic cloves, halved
½   teaspoon freshly ground black pepper

1. Prepare grill.
2. Coat a large nonstick skillet with cooking spray; add oil. Place over medium-high heat until hot. Add bell pepper strips, zucchini, and onion; cook 5 minutes, stirring often. Add ½ cup broth and thyme. Cover, reduce heat, and simmer 5 minutes.
3. Combine ½ cup broth and flour, stirring well with a whisk. Add to vegetable mixture, stirring well. Cook, stirring constantly, until slightly thickened and bubbly.
4. Rub steaks with garlic halves; sprinkle with ½ teaspoon black pepper. Place steaks on grill rack coated with cooking spray; grill, covered, 4 minutes on each side or until desired degree of doneness. Spoon vegetables evenly onto individual serving plates; arrange steaks over vegetables. Yield: 4 servings (serving size: 1 steak and about 1 cup vegetables).

CALORIES 238; FAT 9.8g (sat 3.3g); PROTEIN 26.2g; CARBOHYDRATE 10.4g; FIBER 2.2g; CHOLESTEROL 71mg; IRON 4.7mg; SODIUM 61mg; CALCIUM 35mg

(pictured on page 227)

▶ **carbo rating: 9**

Peppered Beef Tenderloin

You can use 1 small, thinly sliced onion instead of shallots, but you'll get a stronger onion flavor.

2   (4-ounce) beef tenderloin steaks, trimmed (about 1 inch thick)
1   teaspoon freshly ground black pepper
⅛   teaspoon salt
Cooking spray
4   shallots, peeled and sliced
1   cup low-salt beef broth
2   teaspoons Dijon mustard
Thyme sprigs (optional)

1. Preheat broiler.
2. Sprinkle steaks with pepper and salt. Place steaks on a broiler pan coated with cooking spray; broil 5 minutes on each side or until desired degree of doneness.
3. Heat a nonstick skillet over medium-high heat. Coat shallots with cooking spray, and add to pan; sauté 2 minutes. Add broth; bring to a boil. Cook, stirring frequently, 5 minutes. Stir in mustard. Spoon sauce over steaks. Garnish with thyme, if desired. Yield: 2 servings (serving size: 1 steak and ¼ cup sauce).

CALORIES 232; FAT 8.9g (sat 3.2g); PROTEIN 26.6g; CARBOHYDRATE 10.8g; FIBER 1.5g; CHOLESTEROL 70mg; IRON 4.1mg; SODIUM 553mg; CALCIUM 39mg

(pictured on page 228)

Chestnut-Sage-Stuffed Pork Tenderloins

Fresh chestnuts are in season from September through February. Store unshelled nuts in a cool, dry place; store shelled nuts in a covered container in the refrigerator.

2   (½-pound) pork tenderloins
½   cup whole wheat breadcrumbs
⅓   cup coarsely chopped chestnuts
½   teaspoon dried rubbed sage
2   garlic cloves, minced
1   tablespoon thawed orange juice concentrate, undiluted
½   teaspoon coarsely ground black pepper
¼   teaspoon salt
¼   teaspoon poultry seasoning
¼   teaspoon dried rubbed sage
Cooking spray
Sage sprigs (optional)

1. Preheat oven to 400°.
2. Trim fat from pork. Cut each tenderloin lengthwise down center, cutting to, but not through, bottom. Place each tenderloin between 2 sheets of heavy-duty plastic wrap, and flatten to ¼-inch-thick rectangle, using a meat mallet or rolling pin.
3. Combine breadcrumbs and next 3 ingredients; stir well. Spoon one-half of mixture over 1 tenderloin; spread to within ½ inch of sides. Roll up tenderloin, jelly roll fashion, starting at narrow end. Tie with heavy string at 2-inch intervals. Repeat procedure with remaining tenderloin and breadcrumb mixture.
4. Combine orange juice concentrate and next 4 ingredients in a small bowl; rub mixture over entire surface of tenderloins.
5. Place tenderloins on a broiler pan coated with cooking spray. Bake, uncovered, at 400° for 45 minutes. Let stand 10 minutes; slice and arrange on a serving platter. Garnish with sage sprigs, if desired. Yield: 4 servings (serving size: 3 ounces stuffed pork).

CALORIES 189; FAT 4.4g (sat 1.5g); PROTEIN 24.9g; CARBOHYDRATE 11.2g; FIBER 1.2g; CHOLESTEROL 74mg; IRON 1.9mg; SODIUM 232mg; CALCIUM 21mg

Beef Curry with Toasted Spices

You can also prepare this recipe with cubed leg of lamb. Look for fenugreek seed at an ethnic grocery.

1   tablespoon curry powder
2   teaspoons freshly ground black pepper
1½   teaspoons salt
3½   pounds beef stew meat, trimmed and cut into bite-sized pieces
2   tablespoons coriander seeds
1   tablespoon cumin seeds
2   teaspoons fenugreek seeds
3   whole cloves
3   bay leaves
2   dried hot red chiles
1   (1-inch) cinnamon stick, broken
2   tablespoons sugar
½   teaspoon ground cardamom
¼   teaspoon salt
1   tablespoon olive oil, divided
3   cups vertically sliced onion
3   tablespoons minced peeled fresh ginger
¼   cup minced garlic
2   tablespoons Hungarian sweet paprika
2   cups plain low-fat yogurt
1½   cups low-salt beef broth
1   cup chopped red bell pepper
½   cup minced fresh cilantro stems
½   cup tomato puree

1. Combine first 3 ingredients; rub evenly over beef. Cover and chill 2 hours, tossing occasionally.
2. Heat a nonstick skillet over medium-high heat. Add coriander and next 6 ingredients; cook 1 minute or until fragrant, shaking pan constantly. Place coriander mixture, sugar, cardamom, and ¼ teaspoon salt in a spice or coffee grinder; process until finely ground.
3. Heat 1½ teaspoons oil in a Dutch oven over medium-high heat. Add half of beef mixture; sauté 5 minutes or until browned on all sides. Remove from pan with a slotted spoon. Repeat procedure with 1½ teaspoons oil and remaining beef mixture; remove from pan. Reduce heat to medium. Add onion and

ginger to pan; cook 6 minutes or until onion is tender, stirring occasionally. Add toasted spice mixture, garlic, and paprika; cook 1 minute, stirring constantly. Add beef, yogurt, and remaining ingredients; bring to a boil. Cover, reduce heat, and simmer 1½ hours or until beef is tender. Yield 12 servings (serving size: about 1 cup).

CALORIES 262; FAT 11g (sat 3.9g); PROTEIN 27.6g; CARBOHYDRATE 12.9g; FIBER 2.1g; CHOLESTEROL 79mg; IRON 4.1mg; SODIUM 440mg; CALCIUM 118mg

▶ carbo rating: 11
Grilled Pork Tenderloin with Black Bean Salad

The carbo rating for this grilled pork recipe includes the black bean salad.

- 2   (¾-pound) pork tenderloins, trimmed
- 2   tablespoons minced shallots
- 2   tablespoons fresh lime juice
- 1   tablespoon olive oil
- 2   teaspoons minced garlic
- ½   teaspoon salt
- ½   teaspoon freshly ground black pepper
- ½   teaspoon ground cumin

Cooking spray
Black Bean Salad (recipe at right)

1. Place pork in a large heavy-duty zip-top plastic bag. Combine shallots and next 6 ingredients, stirring well with a whisk; pour over pork. Seal bag; marinate in refrigerator 30 minutes. Remove pork from bag, reserving marinade.
2. Prepare grill.
3. Place pork on grill rack coated with cooking spray. Brush with reserved marinade. Cover and grill 20 minutes or until a meat thermometer registers 155°, turning pork occasionally. Remove pork from grill; cover and let stand 10 minutes or until thermometer registers 160°. Serve with Black Bean Salad. Yield: 6 servings (serving size: 3 ounces pork and ½ cup salad).

CALORIES 264; FAT 11.1g (sat 2.4g); PROTEIN 27.7g; CARBOHYDRATE 15.7g; FIBER 4.5g; CHOLESTEROL 67mg; IRON 2.9mg; SODIUM 861mg; CALCIUM 41mg

Make this salad ahead to allow the flavors to develop. You can also serve the black bean salad over grilled chicken or fish, or simply as a side dish.

▶ carbo rating: 10
black bean salad

- 1   (15-ounce) can black beans, rinsed and drained
- 1½   cups chopped seeded tomato (about 2 large)
- ⅓   cup chopped fresh cilantro
- ¼   cup fresh lime juice
- 2   tablespoons minced shallots
- 2   tablespoons olive oil
- 1   teaspoon minced garlic
- ½   teaspoon salt
- ½   teaspoon black pepper
- ¼   teaspoon crushed red pepper

1. Combine all ingredients, stirring well. Cover and let stand 1 hour. Yield: 6 servings (serving size: ½ cup).

CALORIES 96; FAT 4.8g (sat 0.8g); PROTEIN 4g; CARBOHYDRATE 13.6g; FIBER 4g; CHOLESTEROL 0mg; IRON 1.6mg; SODIUM 400mg; CALCIUM 32mg

"Love the pork. Love the salsa. Love them together. It's clean and complex at the same time."

Laurl Self

▶ carbo rating: 12

Osso Buco with Gremolata

Inexpensive veal shanks become a succulent meal in the slow cooker. Even if you aren't an anchovy lover, don't omit the anchovy paste—it adds immeasurably to the flavor.

⅔   cup all-purpose flour
¾   teaspoon freshly ground black pepper, divided
½   teaspoon kosher salt, divided
6   veal shanks, trimmed (about 5 pounds)
2   teaspoons butter, divided
2   teaspoons olive oil, divided
2   cups coarsely chopped red onion
1½ cups chopped celery
6   garlic cloves, minced
4   cups beef broth
2   cups dry white wine
1   tablespoon chopped fresh rosemary
1   tablespoon anchovy paste
½   cup chopped fresh flat-leaf parsley
1   tablespoon grated lemon rind
2   garlic cloves, minced

1. To prepare the osso buco, combine flour, ¼ teaspoon pepper, and ¼ teaspoon salt in a shallow dish. Dredge veal in flour mixture.
2. Heat 1 teaspoon butter and 1 teaspoon oil in a large skillet over medium heat. Add half of veal; cook 6 minutes, browning on both sides. Place browned veal in a large electric slow cooker. Repeat procedure with 1 teaspoon butter, 1 teaspoon oil, and remaining veal.
3. Add onion and celery to pan; sauté 5 minutes over medium-high heat or until tender. Add 6 garlic cloves to pan; sauté 1 minute. Stir in broth, wine, rosemary, and anchovy paste, scraping pan to loosen browned bits. Bring to a boil; cook 4 minutes. Pour over veal.
4. Cover and cook on low-heat setting 9 hours or until done. Sprinkle veal with ½ teaspoon pepper and ¼ teaspoon salt. Remove veal from cooker; cool slightly.
5. To prepare gremolata, combine chopped parsley, lemon rind, and 2 garlic cloves. Place ⅔ cup veal and ½ cup beef broth mixture into each of 8 shallow bowls. Reserve remaining beef broth mixture for another use. Sprinkle each serving with 1 tablespoon gremolata.

Yield: 8 servings (serving size: 3 ounces veal, ½ cup broth mixture, and 1 tablespoon gremolata).

CALORIES 263; FAT 8.5g (sat 2.8g); PROTEIN 32.4g; CARBOHYDRATE 12.6g; FIBER 0.9g; CHOLESTEROL 122mg; IRON 2.2mg; SODIUM 755mg; CALCIUM 72mg

▶ carbo rating: 12

Pork Medallions with Red Peppers and Artichokes

Two-ounce pork chops are wafer thin and are often referred to as "breakfast chops." If your chops are thicker, you'll need to cook them longer.

2   teaspoons olive oil
Cooking spray
8   (2-ounce) boneless center-cut loin pork chops
¼   teaspoon dried Italian seasoning
⅛   teaspoon salt
⅛   teaspoon coarsely ground black pepper
2   cups red bell pepper strips
1   cup fat-free, less-sodium chicken broth
2   tablespoons tomato paste
¼   teaspoon dried thyme
¼   teaspoon dried rubbed sage
1   (14-ounce) can artichoke hearts, drained

1. Heat oil in a large nonstick skillet coated with cooking spray over medium-high heat. Sprinkle pork with Italian seasoning, salt, and black pepper. Add pork to pan, and cook 1 minute on each side or until lightly browned. Remove from pan. Add bell pepper to pan; sauté 2 minutes.
2. Combine broth, tomato paste, thyme, and sage, stirring with a whisk. Return pork to pan, and add broth mixture and artichoke hearts. Cover, reduce heat, and simmer 8 minutes or until thoroughly heated. Remove pork from pan, and keep warm. Increase heat to medium-high; cook 2 minutes or until artichoke mixture is slightly thickened. Spoon artichoke mixture over pork. Yield: 4 servings (serving size: 2 pork chops and 1 cup artichoke mixture).

CALORIES 245; FAT 6.3g (sat 1.7g); PROTEIN 29.8g; CARBOHYDRATE 17.4g; FIBER 5.7g; CHOLESTEROL 74mg; IRON 2.5mg; SODIUM 782mg; CALCIUM 22mg

► carbo rating: 13

Lamb Shanks on Lentil-Spinach Ragoût

If you don't see lamb shanks out in the meat case of the grocery store, you may need to ask the butcher for them.

6	(1-pound) lamb shanks, trimmed
½	teaspoon pepper
¼	teaspoon salt
1	cup chopped onion
1	cup dry red wine
½	cup beef broth
4	carrots, scraped and sliced
2	celery stalks, sliced
1	(28-ounce) can no-salt-added diced tomatoes, undrained
1½	teaspoons dried rosemary leaves
2	bay leaves
3	center-cut bacon slices
2	(19-ounce) cans lentil soup (such as Progresso)
¾	cup tomato juice
1	tablespoon Dijon mustard
1	(10-ounce) package frozen chopped spinach, thawed, drained, and squeezed dry

1. Sprinkle lamb shanks with pepper and salt. Heat an extra-large Dutch oven over medium-high heat. Add half of lamb; cook 3 minutes on each side or until browned. Remove lamb shanks from pan; set aside. Repeat with remaining lamb. Reduce heat to medium; add chopped onion, red wine, beef broth, carrot, and celery. Cook mixture 5 minutes, scraping pan to loosen browned bits. Add diced tomatoes, rosemary, and bay leaves. Return lamb shanks to pan. Bring to a boil. Cover, reduce heat, and simmer 2 hours or until lamb is tender. Discard bay leaves and liquid.

2. Cook bacon in a large nonstick skillet over medium-high heat until crisp. Remove bacon from pan, and crumble. Discard pan drippings. Add bacon, soup, and next 3 ingredients to pan. Simmer, uncovered, 30 minutes, stirring occasionally.

3. Serve lamb shanks on a bed of lentil ragoût. Yield: 6 servings (serving size: 3 ounces cooked lamb and 1 cup ragoût).

Note: The discarded remaining braising liquid can be used to make a delicious soup; just skim the fat first.

CALORIES 277; FAT 8.1g (sat 2.3g); PROTEIN 31g; CARBOHYDRATE 19.9g; FIBER 6.8g; CHOLESTEROL 69mg; IRON 5.5mg; SODIUM 992mg; CALCIUM 96mg

carrot controversy

If you're on one of the low-carb diet plans that does not allow carrots, then you'll probably want to skip this recipe. One raw carrot has only 5.8 grams of carbohydrate and 1.8 grams of fiber, not to mention all of those great antioxidants founds in orange and yellow vegetables.

Cooked carrots do have a higher glycemic index than raw, but for the relatively small amount of carrot in this recipe, that value becomes negligible.

▶ carbo rating: 13

East Asian Pork Strips

The freshly ground pepper in the marinade releases an intense aroma when the pork chops are seared in a hot skillet.

½   cup chopped onion
2   tablespoons bourbon
½   teaspoon freshly ground black pepper
4   (4-ounce) boneless center-cut loin pork chops, trimmed and cut into ½-inch strips
¼   cup low-sodium soy sauce
1½ tablespoons white vinegar
4   teaspoons sugar
4   teaspoons chopped peeled fresh ginger
½   teaspoon cornstarch
½   teaspoon honey
3   tablespoons thinly sliced green onions
1½ teaspoons vegetable oil

1. Combine first 3 ingredients in a large zip-top plastic bag, and add pork to bag. Seal, and marinate in refrigerator 30 minutes.

2. Combine soy sauce and next 5 ingredients in a blender, and process until smooth. Pour soy mixture into a small saucepan, and bring to a boil. Cook for 1 minute, stirring constantly. Remove mixture from heat; stir in green onions.

3. Heat oil in a large nonstick skillet over medium-high heat. Add pork mixture to pan; cook, stirring frequently, 6 minutes or until pork loses its pink color. Serve pork with sauce. Yield: 4 servings (serving size: 3 ounces meat and about 1½ tablespoons sauce).

CALORIES 229; FAT 7.2g (sat 2.3g); PROTEIN 26g; CARBOHYDRATE 13.9g; FIBER 0.8g; CHOLESTEROL 63mg; IRON 1.4mg; SODIUM 675mg; CALCIUM 34mg

▶ carbo rating: 14

Cuban Pork Chops

When the best thing to balance the spiciness of meat is a sweet sauce, you can't go wrong if the sauce is sweetened with fruit. For this sauce, choose a banana that is firm, yet ripe, so that it will hold its shape when cooked.

2   teaspoons ground cumin
¼   teaspoon ground red pepper
¼   teaspoon ground cloves
¼   teaspoon salt
2   (4-ounce) boneless center-cut pork loin chops (about ½ inch thick)
Cooking spray
1   banana, diagonally cut into ¼-inch-thick slices
1   large garlic clove, minced
2   teaspoons grated lime rind
1   tablespoon fresh lime juice (about ½ lime)

1. Combine first 4 ingredients; rub spice mixture evenly over both sides of pork.

2. Heat a large nonstick skillet coated with cooking spray over medium-high heat. Add pork, and cook 3 minutes on each side or until done. Transfer pork to a plate, and keep warm.

3. Coat pan with cooking spray; add banana and garlic, and sauté 1 minute. Stir in lime rind and juice; cook 30 seconds.

4. Place pork chops on plates; spoon banana mixture over pork. Yield: 2 servings (serving size: 1 pork chop and about ¼ cup banana mixture).

CALORIES 244; FAT 8g (sat 2.8g); PROTEIN 26.9g; CARBOHYDRATE 16.4g; FIBER 2.6g; CHOLESTEROL 73mg; IRON 1.9mg; SODIUM 352mg; CALCIUM 48mg

▶ carbo rating: 14

Guinness-Braised Beef Brisket

Brisket is ideal for a slow cooker because it gets very tender when cooked over low heat for a long time. We recommend serving the brisket with grainy, coarse mustard.

2	cups water
1	cup chopped onion
1	cup chopped carrot
1	cup chopped celery
1	cup Guinness stout
⅔	cup packed brown sugar
¼	cup tomato paste
¼	cup chopped fresh or 1 tablespoon dried dill
1	(14-ounce) can low-salt beef broth
6	black peppercorns
2	whole cloves
1	(3-pound) cured corned beef brisket, trimmed

1. Combine first 11 ingredients in a large electric slow cooker, stirring until well blended; top with beef. Cover with lid; cook on high-heat setting 1 hour.
2. Reduce heat setting to low; cook 7 hours or until beef is tender.
3. Remove beef; cut diagonally across grain into ¼-inch slices. Discard broth mixture. Yield: 6 servings (serving size: 3 ounces).

CALORIES 226; FAT 9.7g (sat 3.2g); PROTEIN 17.9g; CARBOHYDRATE 15.2g; FIBER 0.9g; CHOLESTEROL 87mg; IRON 2.2mg; SODIUM 1,105mg; CALCIUM 28mg

▶ carbo rating: 18

Pork Tenderloin with Savory Cherry Port Sauce

Port is a sweet wine with intense flavor. Because it's fortified with a little more alcohol than table wine, it will last a little longer on the pantry shelf. If you don't have any port, you can use Madeira or sweet sherry.

⅔	cup port or other sweet red wine
¾	cup dried tart cherries
3	tablespoons all-purpose flour
½	teaspoon ground coriander
¼	teaspoon salt
¼	teaspoon black pepper
1½	pounds pork tenderloin, trimmed
1	tablespoon butter
2	tablespoons finely chopped shallots
1	cup fat-free, less-sodium chicken broth

1. Place port in a 1-cup glass measure. Microwave at HIGH 20 seconds or until very warm. Combine port and cherries; cover and let stand 10 minutes or until soft. Drain cherries in a colander over a bowl, reserving port.
2. Combine flour, coriander, salt, and pepper in a shallow dish. Dredge pork in flour mixture. Melt butter in a large heavy skillet over medium-high heat. Add pork; cook 3 minutes on each side or until browned. Remove pork; stir in reserved port, scraping pan to loosen browned bits. Add cherries and shallots. Reduce heat; cook 3 minutes, stirring frequently. Stir in broth; bring to a simmer.
3. Return pork to pan. Partially cover and cook 10 minutes. Uncover and cook 12 minutes or until a meat thermometer registers 155°, turning pork occasionally. Remove from oven; let stand until thermometer registers 160°. Cut into slices, and serve with sauce. Yield: 6 servings (serving size: 3 ounces meat and 2 tablespoons sauce).

CALORIES 220; FAT 4.9g (sat 2.2g); PROTEIN 25.5g; CARBOHYDRATE 18.5g; FIBER 0.9g; CHOLESTEROL 79mg; IRON 2.2mg; SODIUM 258mg; CALCIUM 22mg

▶ carbo rating: 18

Fruited Pork Tenderloin

Instead of a sugar-sweetened sauce, it's dried fruit that contributes sweetness to this pork dish, while Dijon mustard adds a touch of tanginess.

1   (1-pound) pork tenderloin, trimmed
½   teaspoon salt, divided
⅛   teaspoon pepper
2   teaspoons olive oil
Cooking spray
¼   cup chopped pitted dates
¼   cup golden raisins
¼   cup water
¼   cup apple juice
¼   cup tawny port or other sweet red wine
1   teaspoon Dijon mustard
2   whole cloves
Parsley sprigs (optional)

1. Cut pork crosswise into 8 slices; sprinkle with ¼ teaspoon salt and pepper. Heat oil in a large nonstick skillet coated with cooking spray over medium-high heat. Add pork; cook 2 minutes on each side or until browned.
2. Add ¼ teaspoon salt, dates, and next 6 ingredients. Cover; simmer 2 minutes or until pork is done. Remove pork from pan. Bring date mixture to a boil; cook until reduced to ⅔ cup (about 5 minutes). Remove cloves; discard. Garnish with parsley sprigs, if desired. Yield: 4 servings (serving size: 3 ounces pork and about 2½ tablespoons sauce).

CALORIES 265; FAT 8.6g (sat 2.5g); PROTEIN 23.9g; CARBOHYDRATE 19.7g; FIBER 1.6g; CHOLESTEROL 75mg; IRON 1.9mg; SODIUM 382mg; CALCIUM 16mg

▶ carbo rating: 22

Szechuan Pork

Dark sesame oil adds a more intense flavor to this stir-fry, but if you don't have dark, light sesame oil or vegetable oil will work fine.

2   teaspoons dark sesame oil
1   (1-pound) pork tenderloin, cut into 1-inch pieces
2   teaspoons minced peeled fresh ginger
3   garlic cloves, minced
1   red bell pepper, cut into strips
⅓   cup picante sauce
2   tablespoons natural peanut butter
     (such as Smucker's)
1   tablespoon low-sodium soy sauce
1½ cups hot cooked brown rice
¼   cup sliced green onions

1. Heat oil in a nonstick skillet over medium-high heat. Add pork, ginger, and garlic; stir-fry 1 minute. Add bell pepper; stir-fry 2 minutes. Add picante sauce, peanut butter, and soy sauce; stir-fry 3 minutes or until pork loses its pink color and sauce is thick.
2. Transfer pork and rice to individual plates and top with green onions. Yield: 4 servings (serving size: ½ cup meat mixture and about ⅓ cup rice).

CALORIES 307; FAT 10.9g (sat 2.4g); PROTEIN 28.3g; CARBOHYDRATE 24.1g; FIBER 2.2g; CHOLESTEROL 74mg; IRON 2.1mg; SODIUM 361mg; CALCIUM 24mg

Peppered Fillets with Mushroom Sauce

▶ carbo rating: 5

page 211

Lamb Shish Kebabs
▶ carbo rating: 6
page 213

Beef Fillets with
Vegetables
▶ carbo rating: 8
page 217

Peppered Beef Tenderloin
▶ carbo rating: 9
page 217

Lemon-Herb Roasted
Chicken
▶ carbo rating: 1
page 246

Grilled Spice-Rubbed
Cornish Hens
▶ carbo rating: 1
page 250

Seared Chicken with
Avocado
▶ carbo rating: 2
page 252

Jerk Smoked Chicken
▶ carbo rating: 4
page 260

Basil Chicken and Vegetables
▶ carbo rating: 5
page 262

Cajun Fire Chicken
▶ carbo rating: 8
page 268

Turkey Sausage with Peppers
▶ carbo rating: 12
page 272

Spinach Salad with
Strawberries and Pecans
▶ carbo rating: 4
page 282

Tossed Salad wth
Buttermilk Dressing
▶ carbo rating: 5
page 282

Greek Salad Bowl
▶ carbo rating: 8
page 288

Marinated Three-Tomato Salad
▶ carbo rating: 8
page 289

Chicken Salad
► carbo rating: 8
page 289

239

Mozzarella-Tomato Salad
▶ carbo rating: 10
page 290

► carbo rating: 23
Polynesian Beef Kebabs

This recipe is a complete and balanced one-dish meal, providing your meat, lots of vegetables, and even a little bit of fruit.

1½	pounds boneless sirloin steak
½	cup dry sherry
½	cup low-sodium soy sauce
2	tablespoons sugar
2	tablespoons white vinegar
½	teaspoon salt
½	teaspoon garlic powder
½	teaspoon black pepper
2	small red onions, each cut into 8 wedges
2	green bell peppers, cut into 1-inch pieces
1	(8-ounce) package mushrooms
1	small peeled and cored pineapple, cut into 1-inch pieces
2	cups cherry tomatoes
	Cooking spray

1. Trim fat from beef; cut beef into 1-inch cubes. Combine beef and next 7 ingredients in a large zip-top plastic bag; seal and marinate in refrigerator 2 to 24 hours, turning bag occasionally.
2. Remove beef from bag, reserving marinade. Place marinade in a small saucepan; bring to a boil over medium-high heat.
3. Prepare grill.
4. Thread beef, onion, pepper, mushrooms, and pineapple alternately onto 12 (12-inch) skewers. Thread tomatoes onto 6 (12-inch) skewers. Place beef-vegetable skewers on grill rack coated with cooking spray; cover and grill 10 minutes or until desired degree of doneness, turning and basting with reserved marinade. Grill tomato skewers 2 minutes or until thoroughly heated. Yield: 6 servings (serving size: 2 beef-vegetable skewers and 1 tomato skewer).

CALORIES 302; FAT 9.1g (sat 3.4g); PROTEIN 27.4g; CARBOHYDRATE 25.8g; FIBER 3.1g; CHOLESTEROL 65mg; IRON 3.4mg; SODIUM 979mg; CALCIUM 35mg

(pictured on cover, bottom right)

► carbo rating: 27
Bulgur and Lamb Meatballs in Tomato Sauce

High-fiber bulgur, rather than breadcrumbs or rice, is the binder in these meatballs. Refrigerating the meat mixture makes it easier to handle and helps the meatballs hold their shape. You can use fine or medium bulgur in this recipe. (See page 298 for more information on bulgur.)

1	cup uncooked bulgur
2	cups water
1	cup chopped fresh parsley
2	tablespoons chopped fresh dill
¾	teaspoon salt
½	teaspoon freshly ground black pepper
10	ounces lean ground lamb
2	large egg whites, lightly beaten
2	garlic cloves, minced
2	teaspoons olive oil
1	cup finely chopped onion
1	garlic clove, minced
½	cup dry red wine
½	cup water
⅛	teaspoon ground cinnamon
1	(28-ounce) can diced tomatoes, undrained

1. Soak bulgur in 2 cups water 2 minutes; drain through a fine sieve. Combine bulgur, parsley, and next 6 ingredients. Cover and chill 30 minutes. Shape lamb mixture into 18 (1-inch) meatballs; cover and chill 30 minutes.
2. Heat oil in a Dutch oven over medium heat. Add onion; cook 5 minutes, stirring occasionally. Add 1 minced garlic clove; cook 3 minutes, stirring frequently. Add wine; bring to a boil. Cook 2 minutes. Stir in ½ cup water, cinnamon, and tomatoes.
3. Add meatballs; bring to a boil. Cover, reduce heat, and simmer 10 minutes. Turn meatballs; cover and cook 10 minutes. Yield: 6 servings (serving size: 3 meatballs and about 1⅓ cups sauce).

CALORIES 309; FAT 13g (sat 5g); PROTEIN 14.2g; CARBOHYDRATE 32.4g; FIBER 5.7g; CHOLESTEROL 34mg; IRON 4.4mg; SODIUM 515mg; CALCIUM 55mg

poultry

If you're eating low-carb but your husband and kids live for fried chicken fingers, **make everyone happy** with *Pecan Chicken Fingers* (page 266).

▶ carbo rating: 0
Grilled Caribbean Chicken

Tart, fresh lime juice and Jamaican jerk seasoning add island flair to basic grilled chicken breasts. Look for jerk seasoning in the spice section of the supermarket.

4   (6-ounce) skinless, boneless chicken breast halves
2   teaspoons fresh lime juice
1   teaspoon vegetable oil
2   teaspoons Jamaican jerk seasoning
Cooking spray

1. Prepare grill.
2. Place chicken between 2 sheets of heavy-duty plastic wrap, and flatten to ¼-inch thickness, using a meat mallet or rolling pin.
3. Combine lime juice and oil; brush over both sides of chicken. Rub both sides of chicken with jerk seasoning.
4. Place chicken on grill rack coated with cooking spray; cover and grill 5 to 6 minutes on each side or until done. Yield: 4 servings (serving size: 1 chicken breast half).

CALORIES 198; FAT 3.3g (sat 1g); PROTEIN 39.3g; CARBOHYDRATE 0.2g; FIBER 0g; CHOLESTEROL 99mg; IRON 1.2mg; SODIUM 261mg; CALCIUM 19mg

skin or no skin?

Although the skin of poultry and turkey contains no carbohydrate, it is where most of the fat is in poultry. Because the fat in poultry skin is saturated, we recommend removing the skin before you eat chicken or turkey because a high intake of saturated fat increases your risk of developing heart disease.

▶ carbo rating: 0
Roasted Turkey Breast

If you're not having a huge crowd for Thanksgiving, you might want to roast a turkey breast instead of the whole bird.

1   (5½-pound) turkey breast
Cooking spray
1   teaspoon vegetable oil
Assorted fresh herbs (optional)

1. Preheat oven to 325°.
2. Trim fat from turkey. Rinse turkey under cold water, and pat dry.
3. Place turkey, skin side up, on a broiler pan coated with cooking spray. Brush turkey lightly with oil. Insert a meat thermometer into meaty part of breast, making sure not to touch bone. Bake at 325° for 2 to 2¼ hours or until thermometer registers 170°. Let turkey stand 15 minutes before slicing.
4. Place turkey on a platter, and garnish with fresh herbs, if desired. Remove and discard skin before eating, if desired (analysis does not include skin). Yield: 8 servings (serving size: 6 ounces).

CALORIES 288; FAT 6.4g (sat 1.9g); PROTEIN 53.8g; CARBOHYDRATE 0g; FIBER 0g; CHOLESTEROL 124mg; IRON 2.4mg; SODIUM 115mg; CALCIUM 34mg

The best thing about roasting chicken is the simplicity. Nothing is easier.

▶ **carbo rating: 0**

Grandma's Simple Roast Chicken

This roasted chicken boasts more flavor than the rotisserie chickens that you buy in the deli because of the vegetables that are placed in the cavity of the bird. The vegetables are not included in the carb count because they are discarded.

1	(4- to 5-pound) roasting chicken
½	teaspoon salt
½	teaspoon pepper
½	teaspoon paprika
1	onion, trimmed and quartered
1	celery stalk, cut into 3-inch pieces
1	carrot, cut into 3-inch pieces
1	garlic clove
1	bay leaf

Cooking spray

1. Preheat oven to 400°.

2. Remove and discard giblets and neck from chicken. Rinse chicken with cold water; pat dry. Trim excess fat.

3. Combine salt, pepper, and paprika. Sprinkle seasoning mixture over breast and drumsticks and into the body cavity. Place onion, celery, carrot, garlic, and bay leaf in body cavity. Lift wing tips up and over back; tuck under chicken.

4. Place chicken, breast side up, on a broiler pan coated with cooking spray. Insert meat thermometer into meaty part of thigh, making sure not to touch bone. Bake at 400° for 1 hour or until thermometer registers 180°. Cover chicken loosely with foil; let stand 10 minutes. Remove and discard vegetables, bay leaf, and, if desired, skin before eating (analysis does not include skin). Yield: 5 servings (serving size: about 6 ounces).

CALORIES 207; FAT 5g (sat 1g); PROTEIN 37.7g; CARBOHYDRATE 0.5g; FIBER 0.2g; CHOLESTEROL 120mg; IRON 2mg; SODIUM 375mg; CALCIUM 21mg

roasting tips

Here are some tips for getting great results every time you roast chicken.

• Always roast the chicken on a rack so that the fat can drip off and away from the bird.

• Don't worry that all of the flavor will be lost if you remove the skin. If seasonings are tucked under the skin, the flavors will permeate the meat as well as the pan drippings, creating flavorful juices for the gravy and sauce.

• Let roasted chicken stand for about 10 minutes after removing it from the oven. This standing time "sets" the juices and makes for a moister, more flavorful bird.

▶ carbo rating: 0

Roast Chicken with Lemon and Tarragon

The skin on this chicken locks in the natural juices of the chicken, keeping each bite moist and juicy.

1	(3-pound) roasting chicken
2	teaspoons dried tarragon, crushed
½	teaspoon salt
½	teaspoon pepper
1	lemon, cut in half

Cooking spray

1. Preheat oven to 350°.
2. Remove and discard giblets and neck from chicken. Rinse chicken with cold water; pat dry. Trim excess fat. Rub chicken with tarragon, salt, and pepper. Place lemon in body cavity. Secure lemon in cavity with skewers or wooden picks. Lift wing tips up and over back; tuck under chicken.
3. Place chicken, breast side up, on a broiler pan coated with cooking spray. Insert meat thermometer into meaty part of thigh, making sure not to touch bone. Bake at 350° for 75 to 90 minutes or until thermometer registers 180°. Remove chicken from oven; cover with foil, and let stand 10 minutes. Remove and discard lemon and, if desired, skin before eating (analysis does not include skin). Yield: 4 servings (serving size: about 6 ounces).

CALORIES 196; FAT 4.8g (sat 1.2g); PROTEIN 35.5g; CARBOHYDRATE 0.6g; FIBER 0.1g; CHOLESTEROL 113mg; IRON 2.2mg; SODIUM 426mg; CALCIUM 29mg

---

poultry temperatures

To prevent food-borne illness, poultry must be cooked to the proper temperature: 180° for thigh meat and 170° for breast meat. For whole birds, use an instant-read thermometer inserted in the thickest part of the thigh, making sure not to touch bone. For more food safety tips on poultry, call the USDA Meat and Poultry Hotline at 800-535-4555.

▶ carbo rating: 1

Lemon-Herb Roasted Chicken

Sometimes the simple things in life are the best—and you can't get any simpler or better than a flavorful roasted chicken. And with so few carbs, why not make it a regular on your dinner table?

1	teaspoon chopped fresh oregano
1	teaspoon chopped fresh rosemary
1	teaspoon chopped fresh thyme
½	teaspoon salt
½	teaspoon pepper
2	garlic cloves, minced
1	(3-pound) roasting chicken
1	lemon, thinly sliced

Cooking spray
Lemon slices (optional)
Herb sprigs (optional)

1. Preheat oven to 375°.
2. Combine first 6 ingredients; set aside.
3. Remove and discard giblets and neck from chicken. Rinse chicken under cold water; pat dry. Trim excess fat. Starting at neck cavity, loosen skin from breast and drumsticks by inserting fingers, gently pushing between skin and meat.
4. Rub herb mixture under loosened skin over breast; place lemon slices over herb mixture. Lift wing tips up and over back; tuck under chicken.
5. Place chicken, breast side up, on a broiler pan coated with cooking spray. Insert meat thermometer into meaty part of thigh, making sure not to touch bone. Bake, uncovered, at 375° for 1 hour or until thermometer registers 180°. Let stand 15 minutes before serving. If desired, garnish with lemon slices and fresh herbs. Remove and discard skin before eating, if desired (analysis does not include skin). Yield: 4 servings (serving size: about 6 ounces).

CALORIES 197; FAT 4.7g (sat 1.2g); PROTEIN 35.4g; CARBOHYDRATE 0.8g; FIBER 0.1g; CHOLESTEROL 113mg; IRON 2mg; SODIUM 426mg; CALCIUM 25mg

(pictured on page 229)

roasting guide

When you want to get a lot of flavor from chicken, roast it. Thanks to caramelization, roasting concentrates flavors and gives foods a crispy exterior, tender interior, and rich, dark color.

Roasting Poultry

As intense dry heat penetrates the chicken inside the oven, the juices bubble to the surface. The liquid evaporates, leaving proteins and sugars that caramelize the meat to create the characteristic roasted color, aroma, and flavor of a roasted bird.

Although a chicken or turkey needs to cook fully before you take it out of the oven, it needs to stand briefly so that the juices can settle and redistribute. That way, the juices will stay in the meat rather than escape to the cutting board. After you've taken the chicken or turkey from the oven and put it on a platter, you can deglaze the pan, which involves pouring liquid into the roasting pan and scraping up all the browned bits in the bottom. This broth can be served as is or used as the base for a sauce.

Equipment for Perfect Roasting

You need only a few essentials for roasting: an oven; a heavy, shallow roasting pan; and a thermometer to determine doneness. Here's how to make those essentials work optimally in the process.

Oven Position the rack in the center—usually the second level from the bottom—so hot air can evenly surround the chicken or turkey.

Pan Most roasting pans are at least 13 x 9 inches or larger and are designed for cooking large cuts of meat or a turkey. These heavy pans come in large rectangular or oval shapes with 2- to 4-inch vertical sides, which keep the pan juices from overflowing in the oven. **Ideally, the pan should extend 2 or 3 inches beyond the edges of the chicken or turkey. If the pan is too large, meat juices will** evaporate too quickly, and the drippings may burn instead of caramelizing.

Some pans come with racks; others are sold separately. If your pan doesn't have a rack, you can elevate the meat with vegetables (such as whole carrots and ribs of celery) or on a wire rack that fits the pan, unless the roast has to cook for several hours (in which case the drippings help the meat stay moist).

You don't need an expensive pan; your oven's broiler pan can work just as well. It sometimes comes with a rack that prevents the poultry from cooking in its drippings and allows adequate heat circulation.

Thermometer To make sure the chicken reaches the safe temperature of 180°, use a thermometer. There are three types of thermometers that you can use.
• A standard meat thermometer is inserted into the thickest part of the chicken or roast prior to cooking. It stays in the oven during the cooking process. These are inexpensive and, for the most part, accurate.
• An instant-read thermometer is inserted into the roast, read, then taken out. It does not stay in the oven. It's more accurate than a basic meat thermometer, but you have to check the temperature early and more frequently. If you wait too long into the cooking time, there is a possibility of overcooking your roast.
• There is also a digital thermometer that sits outside of the oven. You can keep track of the temperature without having to open the oven. You set the end temperature for the food (180° for roasted chicken, for example) and insert a probe, which continually monitors the heat, into the food. When the food reaches the temperature you've selected, an alarm sounds.

> You need only a few essentials for roasting: an oven; a heavy, shallow roasting pan; and a thermometer to determine doneness.

▶ **carbo rating: 1**
Grilled Herbed Chicken

If you have time to marinate the chicken in the herb mixture at least 15 minutes before grilling it, the herb flavor will be even stronger.

½   cup dry white wine
2   tablespoons fresh lemon juice
2½ teaspoons dried Italian seasoning
1   teaspoon olive oil
¼   teaspoon freshly ground black pepper
6   (6-ounce) skinless, boneless chicken breast halves
Cooking spray

1. Prepare grill.
2. Combine first 5 ingredients; set aside half of wine mixture for basting during grilling. Brush remaining half on chicken.
3. Place chicken on grill rack coated with cooking spray; cover and grill 5 minutes. Turn chicken; brush reserved wine mixture on chicken, and grill 5 minutes or until chicken is done. Yield: 6 servings (serving size: 1 chicken breast half).

CALORIES 198; FAT 2.9g (sat 0.7g); PROTEIN 39.4g; CARBOHYDRATE 1.1g; FIBER 0.3g; CHOLESTEROL 99mg; IRON 1.6mg; SODIUM 113mg; CALCIUM 32mg

▶ **carbo rating: 1**
Chicken Topped with Feta and Green Onions

Hot pepper sauce is made with green tabasco peppers and vinegar. Don't confuse this product with hot sauce, which is red and fiery hot.

½   cup (2 ounces) crumbled feta cheese with basil and sun-dried tomatoes
2   tablespoons minced green onions
1   teaspoon extravirgin olive oil
½   teaspoon dried basil
1   tablespoon country-style Dijon mustard
½   teaspoon hot pepper sauce
4   (6-ounce) skinless, boneless chicken breast halves
Cooking spray
⅛   teaspoon freshly ground black pepper

1. Preheat oven to 350°.
2. Combine first 4 ingredients in a small bowl; toss gently. Set aside.
3. Combine mustard and hot pepper sauce; stir well.
4. Place chicken on a broiler pan coated with cooking spray. Spread mustard mixture evenly over chicken. Bake at 350° for 20 minutes. Sprinkle evenly with cheese mixture. Bake 5 more minutes or until cheese melts slightly. Sprinkle with black pepper. Yield: 4 servings (serving size: 1 chicken breast half).

CALORIES 253; FAT 7.6g (sat 3.5g); PROTEIN 42.2g; CARBOHYDRATE 1.5g; FIBER 0.2g; CHOLESTEROL 115mg; IRON 1.6mg; SODIUM 431mg; CALCIUM 122mg

► carbo rating: 1

Greek Chicken with Lemon and Mint

When you tuck fresh herbs under the skin of the chicken breast, the chicken meat absorbs the flavor of the herbs, but not much of the fat in the skin.

3   tablespoons grated lemon rind
3   tablespoons chopped fresh mint
1   tablespoon chopped fresh oregano
1½   tablespoons olive oil
½   teaspoon salt
½   teaspoon coarsely ground black pepper
3   garlic cloves, minced
4   (8-ounce) bone-in chicken breast halves

1. Preheat oven to 375°.
2. Combine first 7 ingredients in a small bowl. Spread mixture under skin of each chicken breast.
3. Bake chicken at 375° for 1 hour or until done. Remove and discard skin before eating, if desired (analysis does not include skin). Yield: 4 servings (serving size: 1 chicken breast half).

CALORIES 253; FAT 7.4g (sat 1.3g); PROTEIN 42.2g; CARBOHYDRATE 2g; FIBER 0.7g; CHOLESTEROL 105mg; IRON 1.5mg; SODIUM 410mg; CALCIUM 39mg

► carbo rating: 1

Moroccan Chicken Thighs

Cinnamon and ginger add a hint of sweetness (without adding carbs) to the spice mixture coating.

8   (3-ounce) skinless, boneless chicken thighs
2   teaspoons grated lemon rind
1½   teaspoons ground cumin
½   teaspoon ground ginger
½   teaspoon salt
¼   teaspoon ground cinnamon
2   garlic cloves, minced
2   teaspoons olive oil
Cooking spray

1. Trim fat from chicken thighs, and set chicken aside.
2. Combine lemon rind and next 5 ingredients in a large bowl. Brush olive oil evenly over chicken. Add chicken to bowl, and toss well to coat chicken with spice mixture. Let stand 10 minutes.
3. Prepare grill.
4. Place chicken on grill rack coated with cooking spray. Cover and grill 6 minutes on each side or until done. Yield: 4 servings (serving size: 2 chicken thighs).

Note: To prepare indoors, place a grill pan over medium-high heat until hot; coat with cooking spray. Add chicken, and cook 7 minutes on each side or until done.

CALORIES 230; FAT 9.1g (sat 2g); PROTEIN 33.7g; CARBOHYDRATE 1.2g; FIBER 0.5g; CHOLESTEROL 141mg; IRON 2.2mg; SODIUM 441mg; CALCIUM 30mg

Grilled Spice-Rubbed Cornish Hens

Spice rubs are a great low-carb way to add flavor to grilled poultry and meats. In this recipe, you rub the spice mixture between the skin and the meat, so the flavor of the spice mixture permeates the meat.

2	teaspoons dried mint flakes
½	teaspoon ground cumin
¼	teaspoon salt
¼	teaspoon ground cinnamon
¼	teaspoon hot paprika
⅛	teaspoon ground nutmeg
3	garlic cloves, minced
2	(1½-pound) Cornish hens
¼	teaspoon salt
¼	teaspoon pepper

Cooking spray

1. Prepare grill.
2. Combine first 7 ingredients in a small bowl.
3. Remove and discard giblets and necks from hens. Rinse hens in cold water; pat dry. Split hens in halves lengthwise; trim excess fat. Starting at neck cavity, loosen skin from breasts and drumsticks by inserting fingers and gently pushing between skin and meat. Rub spice mixture under loosened skin. Sprinkle hens with ¼ teaspoon salt and pepper.
4. Place hens on grill rack coated with cooking spray; grill 10 minutes on each side or until a meat thermometer registers 180°. Remove and discard skin before eating, if desired (analysis does not include skin). Yield: 4 servings (serving size: about 4 ounces).

CALORIES 176; FAT 5g (sat 1.3g); PROTEIN 29.6g; CARBOHYDRATE 1.2g; FIBER 0.3g; CHOLESTEROL 133mg; IRON 1.5mg; SODIUM 395mg; CALCIUM 30mg

(pictured on page 230)

Rosemary Turkey Tenderloins

If you can't find turkey tenderloins, this recipe also works with pork tenderloins.

1½	tablespoons finely chopped fresh or 2 teaspoons dried rosemary
1	tablespoon olive oil
1	large garlic clove, minced
¼	teaspoon salt
¼	teaspoon coarsely ground black pepper

Cooking spray

3	(½-pound) turkey tenderloins
3	tablespoons dry vermouth or low-sodium chicken broth
2	tablespoons water
1	teaspoon cornstarch

Rosemary sprigs (optional)

1. Combine first 5 ingredients, stirring well. Rub mixture evenly over both sides of turkey.
2. Place turkey in a nonstick skillet coated with cooking spray. Cook over medium-high heat 7 to 8 minutes on each side or until done. Cut turkey diagonally across grain into thin slices. Arrange slices on a serving platter; keep warm.
3. Combine vermouth (or broth), water, and cornstarch, stirring well; add to pan. Bring to a boil; reduce heat, and simmer 1 minute or until thickened, stirring constantly.
4. Spoon sauce evenly over turkey, and garnish with rosemary sprigs, if desired. Yield: 4 servings (serving size: about 6 ounces).

CALORIES 218; FAT 4.5g (sat 0.8g); PROTEIN 40.6g; CARBOHYDRATE 1.4g; FIBER 0.3g; CHOLESTEROL 112mg; IRON 2.3mg; SODIUM 246mg; CALCIUM 26mg

▶ carbo rating: 2

Lemon Pepper Chicken

Lemon pepper and balsamic vinegar add big flavor to chicken, and they're ingredients that you can always keep on hand for a quick-fix recipe.

Cooking spray
1   teaspoon olive oil
4   (6-ounce) skinless, boneless chicken breast halves
1¼ teaspoons lemon pepper seasoning
¼   cup fat-free, less-sodium chicken broth
¼   cup balsamic vinegar

1. Heat oil in a large nonstick skillet coated with cooking spray over medium-high heat. Sprinkle both sides of chicken breasts evenly with lemon pepper seasoning. Add chicken to pan, and cook 4 to 5 minutes on each side or until chicken is done. Transfer chicken to a serving platter, and keep warm.
2. Add broth and vinegar to pan; cook, stirring constantly, 1 minute or until slightly thickened. Spoon sauce over chicken. Yield: 4 servings (serving size: 1 chicken breast half and about 2 tablespoons sauce).

CALORIES 209; FAT 3.3g (sat 0.7g); PROTEIN 39.5g; CARBOHYDRATE 2.5g; FIBER 0g; CHOLESTEROL 99mg; IRON 1.4mg; SODIUM 297mg; CALCIUM 24mg

▶ carbo rating: 2

Jalapeño Chicken

To crank up the heat in this dish, top each piece of chicken with sliced jalapeños.

1   tablespoon 40%-less-sodium taco seasoning
4   (6-ounce) skinless, boneless chicken breast halves
Cooking spray
½   cup (2 ounces) shredded Monterey Jack cheese with jalapeño peppers
2   tablespoons sliced jalapeño peppers (optional)

1. Sprinkle taco seasoning over both sides of chicken.
2. Place a large nonstick skillet over medium heat until hot. Coat chicken with cooking spray. Add chicken to pan, and cook 7 minutes on each side or until chicken is done.
3. Remove chicken from heat; sprinkle with cheese. Cover and let stand 3 to 4 minutes or until cheese melts. Garnish with jalapeño slices, if desired. Yield: 4 servings (serving size: 1 chicken breast half).

CALORIES 249; FAT 6.6g (sat 3.6g); PROTEIN 42.8g; CARBOHYDRATE 2.2g; FIBER 0.1g; CHOLESTEROL 114mg; IRON 1.2mg; SODIUM 329mg; CALCIUM 119mg

▶ carbo rating: 2
Seared Chicken with Avocado

If dried beans are allowed on your low-carb plan, serve this peppery chicken with black beans sprinkled with Monterey Jack cheese.

1½ teaspoons blackening seasoning
4 (6-ounce) skinless, boneless chicken breast halves
1 teaspoon olive oil
1 diced peeled avocado
2 tablespoons chopped fresh cilantro
2 tablespoons fresh lime juice (about 1 lime)
1 jalapeño pepper, seeded and finely chopped
¼ teaspoon salt
1 lime, cut into fourths

1. Sprinkle seasoning on both sides of chicken. Heat oil in a large nonstick skillet over high heat. Add chicken to pan, meaty side down; cook 1 minute or until seared. Reduce heat to medium; cook 3 minutes on each side or until lightly browned.
2. Combine avocado, cilantro, lime juice, pepper, and salt. Squeeze one-fourth lime over each piece of chicken before serving. Serve with avocado mixture. Yield: 4 servings (serving size: 1 chicken breast half and ¼ cup avocado mixture).

CALORIES 271; FAT 9.5g (sat 2g); PROTEIN 40.7g; CARBOHYDRATE 5.4g; FIBER 3.9g; CHOLESTEROL 99mg; IRON 1.3mg; SODIUM 400mg; CALCIUM 21mg

(pictured on page 231)

▶ carbo rating: 2
Grilled Lemon-Oregano Chicken

Because the lemon juice and olive oil mixture is so flavorful, you don't need to marinate the chicken— just brush the mixture on after chicken is grilled.

4 chicken drumsticks (about 1 pound), skinned
4 chicken thighs (about 1½ pounds), skinned
Cooking spray
⅓ cup fresh lemon juice
1 tablespoon extravirgin olive oil
2 teaspoons dried oregano
¾ teaspoon salt
¼ teaspoon garlic powder
¼ teaspoon pepper

1. Prepare grill.
2. Place chicken on grill rack coated with cooking spray; cover and grill 10 minutes on each side or until done.
3. Combine lemon juice and next 5 ingredients. Pour over grilled chicken; toss gently. Yield: 4 servings (serving size: 1 drumstick and 1 thigh).

CALORIES 231; FAT 9.5g (sat 2g); PROTEIN 32.3g; CARBOHYDRATE 2.4g; FIBER 0.4g; CHOLESTEROL 129mg; IRON 2.1mg; SODIUM 580mg; CALCIUM 31mg

▶ carbo rating: 2

Chicken Piccata with Capers

You can use this basic piccata recipe with pork or veal cutlets, too. Just make sure you pound the meat to ¼-inch thickness. The capers add an extra hit of flavor.

2	(6-ounce) skinless, boneless chicken breast halves
¼	teaspoon salt
2	teaspoons olive oil
¼	cup fat-free, less-sodium chicken broth
2	tablespoons fresh lemon juice (about 1 lemon)
1	tablespoon capers in white balsamic vinegar (such as Alessi) or regular capers
2	tablespoons chopped fresh parsley
¼	teaspoon freshly ground black pepper

1. Place chicken between 2 sheets of heavy-duty plastic wrap; pound to ¼-inch thickness. Sprinkle with salt.

2. Heat oil in a large nonstick skillet over medium-high heat. Add chicken; cook 3 to 4 minutes on each side or until golden brown.

3. Remove chicken from pan; keep warm. Add broth and lemon juice to pan, scraping pan to loosen browned bits. Cook, uncovered, over high heat 30 seconds or until slightly reduced. Stir in capers. Pour sauce over chicken. Sprinkle with parsley and pepper. Yield: 2 servings (serving size: 1 chicken breast half and 3 tablespoons sauce).

CALORIES 235; FAT 6.7g (sat 1.2g); PROTEIN 40.2g; CARBOHYDRATE 2g; FIBER 0.3g; CHOLESTEROL 99mg; IRON 1.6mg; SODIUM 642mg; CALCIUM 29mg

keeping capers on hand

Once you open a jar of capers, you can store it in the refrigerator for up to 1 year.

▶ carbo rating: 2

Turkey Cutlets with Tarragon

If you can't find turkey cutlets, you can use a turkey tenderloin instead. Just cut it into thin slices and pound to ¼-inch thickness.

1	(1½-pound) package turkey cutlets
2	garlic cloves, cut in half
¾	teaspoon dried tarragon
¼	teaspoon salt
¼	teaspoon pepper
	Cooking spray
1	tablespoon extravirgin olive oil
¼	cup lemon juice
¼	cup dry white wine
2	tablespoons chopped fresh parsley

1. Rub both sides of each turkey cutlet with garlic halves. Discard garlic halves.

2. Combine tarragon, salt, and pepper. Set aside.

3. Heat oil in a large nonstick skillet coated with cooking spray over medium-high heat. Add half of cutlets. Sprinkle half of tarragon mixture over cutlets. Cook 3 minutes on each side or until cutlets are done. Transfer cutlets to a serving platter; keep warm. Repeat procedure with remaining cutlets and tarragon mixture.

4. Add lemon juice and white wine to pan. Increase heat to high, and cook 1 minute, stirring constantly. Spoon wine mixture over turkey cutlets. Sprinkle with parsley. Yield: 4 servings (serving size: about 5 ounces).

CALORIES 238; FAT 4.7g (sat 0.9g); PROTEIN 42.2g; CARBOHYDRATE 2g; FIBER 0.2g; CHOLESTEROL 105mg; IRON 2.3mg; SODIUM 235mg; CALCIUM 30mg

► carbo rating: 3

Chicken with Creamy Tarragon-Mustard Sauce

Be sure to remove the skillet from the heat before making the sauce. There will be enough heat left in the pan to warm the sauce.

- 2 tablespoons Dijon mustard
- 2 tablespoons light mayonnaise
- 1½ teaspoons fresh lime juice
- ¼ teaspoon dried tarragon
- 2 teaspoons olive oil
- 4 (6-ounce) skinless, boneless chicken breast halves
- 2 tablespoons finely chopped green onions

1. Combine first 4 ingredients in a small bowl, stirring well with a whisk.

2. Heat oil in a large nonstick skillet over medium-high heat. Add chicken, and cook 3 minutes; turn and reduce heat to medium-low. Cover and cook 12 minutes or until chicken is done. Remove chicken from pan; keep warm.

3. Remove pan from heat. Add mustard mixture to drippings in pan; stir well. Spoon mustard sauce over chicken; top with green onions. Yield: 4 servings (serving size: 1 chicken breast half and about 1½ tablespoons sauce).

CALORIES 250; FAT 7.6g (sat 1.3g); PROTEIN 40.1g; CARBOHYDRATE 3.1g; FIBER 0.1g; CHOLESTEROL 101mg; IRON 1.7mg; SODIUM 360mg; CALCIUM 37mg

► carbo rating: 3

Chicken with Dijon Cream Sauce

Fat-free half-and-half is the key ingredient in this zesty and velvety sauce. If you can't find fat-free half-and-half, fat-free evaporated milk is a fine substitute. The carbo rating will be the same.

- 4 (6-ounce) skinless, boneless chicken breast halves
- Cooking spray
- 1½ teaspoons lemon pepper seasoning
- ⅓ cup fat-free, less-sodium chicken broth
- ⅓ cup fat-free half-and-half or fat-free evaporated milk
- 1½ tablespoons Dijon mustard

1. Coat chicken with cooking spray. Sprinkle both sides of chicken with seasoning. Place a large nonstick skillet over medium-high heat until hot. Add chicken to pan, and cook 4 to 5 minutes on each side or until browned. Remove chicken from pan; set aside, and keep warm.

2. Add broth to pan, scraping pan to loosen browned bits. Combine half-and-half and mustard; add to pan. Reduce heat; simmer 6 minutes or until sauce is slightly thick. Spoon sauce over chicken. Yield: 4 servings (serving size: 1 chicken breast half and about 2 tablespoons sauce).

CALORIES 210; FAT 2.6g (sat 0.6g); PROTEIN 39.9g; CARBOHYDRATE 2.9g; FIBER 0.1g; CHOLESTEROL 99mg; IRON 1.4mg; SODIUM 497mg; CALCIUM 41mg

cream and milk comparison

Because whole milk and regular cream are high in saturated fat, we choose to use the fat-free versions of these dairy products. The recipe will work fine if you prefer to use the full-fat products—it just won't be as heart-healthy.

Milk	Calories	Carbohydrate (grams)	Fat (grams)	Sat Fat (grams)
Fat-free half-and-half (⅓ cup)	53	8.0	0.0	0.0
Regular half-and-half (⅓ cup)	107	2.7	8.0	5.3
Fat-free evaporated milk (⅓ cup)	67	9.7	0.2	0.1
Evaporated whole milk (⅓ cup)	113	8.4	6.4	3.9

▶ **carbo rating: 3**

Fresh Salsa Chicken

Make this salsa ahead of time; its flavor develops as it chills.

6	ounces cherry tomatoes, quartered
½	cup finely chopped yellow bell pepper
2	tablespoons capers, drained
1	tablespoon cider vinegar
1½	teaspoons extravirgin olive oil
¾	teaspoon dried basil
⅛	teaspoon crushed red pepper
1	garlic clove, minced
4	(6-ounce) skinless, boneless chicken breast halves

Cooking spray

¼	teaspoon salt
¼	teaspoon black pepper

1. Preheat broiler.

2. Combine first 8 ingredients in a bowl; cover and chill until ready to serve.

3. Place chicken on a broiler pan coated with cooking spray; sprinkle with salt and black pepper. Broil 5 minutes on each side or until done. Serve tomato mixture over chicken. Yield: 4 servings (serving size: 1 chicken breast half and 1 cup salsa).

CALORIES 221; FAT 4.1g (sat 0.8g); PROTEIN 40g; CARBOHYDRATE 4.1g; FIBER 1.1g; CHOLESTEROL 99mg; IRON 1.7mg; SODIUM 389mg; CALCIUM 31mg

▶ **carbo rating: 3**

Poached Ginger Chicken

Poaching is a great way to cook chicken because the simmering liquid helps keep the chicken juicy and moist.

4	(6-ounce) skinless, boneless chicken breast halves
2	cups water

Cooking spray

1	teaspoon peanut oil
¾	cup chopped green onions
¼	cup grated peeled fresh ginger
2	tablespoons "measures-like-sugar" calorie-free sweetener
2	tablespoons dry sherry
2	tablespoons low-sodium soy sauce

Boston lettuce leaves (optional)

Green onions (optional)

1. Combine chicken and water in a large saucepan. Bring to a boil; cover, reduce heat, and simmer 20 minutes or until chicken is done.

2. Remove chicken from broth; discard broth. Cut chicken into thin slices; place slices in a shallow dish.

3. Heat oil over medium-high heat in a nonstick skillet coated with cooking spray. Add chopped green onions and ginger; sauté 30 seconds. Remove from heat, and spoon over chicken.

4. Add sweetener, sherry, and soy sauce to pan; bring to a boil. Boil 1 minute. Pour soy sauce mixture over chicken. Cover and chill thoroughly. If desired, spoon chicken mixture evenly onto individual lettuce-lined salad plates, and garnish with green onions. Yield: 4 servings (serving size: 5 ounces chicken and 1 tablespoon sauce).

CALORIES 214; FAT 3.3g (sat 0.8g); PROTEIN 40.2g; CARBOHYDRATE 3.6g; FIBER 0.7g; CHOLESTEROL 99mg; IRON 1.7mg; SODIUM 385mg; CALCIUM 41mg

► carbo rating: 3
Chicken and Mushroom Marsala

If you prefer a nonalcoholic version of this recipe, substitute 1 to 2 tablespoons balsamic vinegar and 2 tablespoons additional chicken broth for the Marsala.

- ¼ cup Marsala wine
- ⅓ cup fat-free, less-sodium chicken broth
- ¼ teaspoon salt
- ⅛ teaspoon freshly ground black pepper
- 2 (6-ounce) skinless, boneless chicken breast halves
- 1 teaspoon olive oil

Cooking spray
- 2 cups sliced mushrooms

1. Combine first 4 ingredients in a small bowl. Place each chicken breast half between 2 sheets of heavy-duty plastic wrap; flatten to ¼-inch thickness using a meat mallet or rolling pin. Heat oil in a nonstick skillet coated with cooking spray over medium-high heat. Add chicken, and cook 3 minutes on each side or until done. Remove from pan; keep warm.
2. Add mushrooms to pan; cook 6 minutes or until browned, stirring occasionally. Add Marsala mixture; simmer 4 minutes or until liquid is reduced to about ¼ cup, scraping pan to loosen browned bits. Spoon over chicken. Yield: 2 servings (serving size: 1 chicken breast half and 2 tablespoons sauce).

CALORIES 229; FAT 4.6g (sat 0.9g); PROTEIN 41.9g; CARBOHYDRATE 3.5g; FIBER 0.9g; CHOLESTEROL 99mg; IRON 2.1mg; SODIUM 512mg; CALCIUM 25mg

---

convenient cartons

Look for chicken broth in resealable cartons next to the canned broth in the grocery store. You can easily use what you need of the broth, reseal the container, and save in the refrigerator for later use.

► carbo rating: 3
Turkey Teriyaki

Although teriyaki sauce does have a small amount of sugar, it has only 2 grams of carbohydrate per tablespoon.

- ¼ cup low-sodium teriyaki sauce
- 1 tablespoon grated peeled fresh ginger
- 1 large garlic clove, minced
- 1½ pounds turkey tenderloin, cut into cubes
- 8 large green onions, cut into 1½-inch pieces

1. Combine first 3 ingredients in a large heavy-duty zip-top plastic bag. Add turkey; seal bag, and marinate in refrigerator 30 minutes. Remove turkey from marinade; reserve marinade. Place marinade in a saucepan; bring to a boil. Remove from heat.
2. Preheat broiler.
3. Thread turkey and onions alternately onto 4 (8-inch) skewers. Broil 3 minutes on each side or until turkey is done, basting with marinade. Yield: 4 servings (serving size: 5 ounces turkey and 2 green onions).

CALORIES 207; FAT 2.4g (sat 0.8g); PROTEIN 40.6g; CARBOHYDRATE 6.1g; FIBER 2.4g; CHOLESTEROL 83mg; IRON 1mg; SODIUM 359mg; CALCIUM 39mg

► carbo rating: 3

Hot Licks Chicken

The slightly sweet orange glaze tames some of the heat in the spicy rub. There is only 1 tablespoon of orange marmalade, so it doesn't contribute very much carbohydrate per serving.

2	teaspoons poultry seasoning
½	teaspoon salt
½	teaspoon ground cumin
½	teaspoon ground coriander
¼	teaspoon ground allspice
¼	teaspoon ground red pepper
¼	teaspoon black pepper
4	(6-ounce) skinless, boneless chicken breast halves
1	tablespoon olive oil

Cooking spray

¼	cup water
¼	cup dry white wine
1	tablespoon lemon juice
⅛	teaspoon salt
1	tablespoon low-sugar orange marmalade

1. Combine first 7 ingredients in a small bowl; rub chicken with spice mixture, and let stand 5 minutes.
2. Heat oil in a large nonstick skillet coated with cooking spray over medium-high heat. Add chicken; cook 1 minute on each side or until lightly browned. Add water and wine to pan; cover, reduce heat, and simmer 6 minutes or until chicken is done. Remove chicken from pan; keep warm. Add lemon juice and ⅛ teaspoon salt to pan. Bring to a boil; cook 4 minutes or until reduced to 3 tablespoons. Remove from heat; stir in marmalade. Spoon sauce over chicken. Yield: 4 servings (serving size: 1 chicken breast half and 1 tablespoon sauce).

CALORIES 195; FAT 5.4g (sat 1g); PROTEIN 31.7g; CARBOHYDRATE 3g; FIBER 0.5g; CHOLESTEROL 79mg; IRON 1.5mg; SODIUM 459mg; CALCIUM 29mg

► carbo rating: 4

Cumin Chicken with Spicy Tomato Relish

The tomato relish is similar to a salsa. It's great on fish as well as chicken.

¾	cup chopped tomato
½	cup chopped peeled cucumber
½	cup chopped green bell pepper
3	tablespoons chopped red onion
1	tablespoon fresh lime juice
1	teaspoon chopped fresh cilantro
2	teaspoons olive oil
¼	teaspoon salt
1	small jalapeño pepper, seeded and chopped
1	garlic clove, minced
1	tablespoon ground cumin
1	teaspoon black pepper
¼	teaspoon salt
4	(6-ounce) skinless, boneless chicken breast halves

1. Combine first 10 ingredients in a small bowl; set aside.
2. Combine cumin, black pepper, and ¼ teaspoon salt; rub chicken breast halves with cumin mixture.
3. Place a large cast iron skillet over medium-high heat until hot (about 2 minutes). Add chicken, and cook 7 minutes on each side or until done. Cut each chicken breast half diagonally across grain into thin slices, and arrange on individual serving plates. Serve with tomato relish. Yield: 4 servings (serving size: 1 chicken breast half and about ½ cup relish).

CALORIES 236; FAT 5g (sat 0.9g); PROTEIN 40.4g; CARBOHYDRATE 5.6g; FIBER 1.8g; CHOLESTEROL 99mg; IRON 2.2mg; SODIUM 411mg; CALCIUM 43mg

orange marmalade options

Here's a comparison of regular and low-sugar marmalades.

Marmalade (1 tablespoon)	Carbohydrate (grams)
Orange marmalade (Smucker's)	13
Orange marmalade, 100% fruit spread	10
Orange marmalade, low-sugar (Smucker's)	6

▶ carbo rating: 4
Chicken Piccata

Pounding the chicken into thin pieces helps tenderize the meat and keeps the cooking time to about 10 minutes or less.

3   tablespoons dry white wine
3   tablespoons fresh lemon juice
1   tablespoon butter
1   teaspoon chicken-flavored bouillon granules
4   (6-ounce) skinless, boneless chicken breast halves
2   tablespoons all-purpose flour
2   teaspoons paprika
¼   teaspoon ground red pepper
Cooking spray
2   tablespoons chopped fresh parsley
Lemon slices (optional)

1. Combine first 4 ingredients in a small saucepan; cook over medium heat until butter melts, stirring often. Set aside, and keep warm.
2. Place chicken between 2 sheets of heavy-duty plastic wrap; flatten to ¼-inch thickness using a meat mallet or rolling pin.
3. Combine flour, paprika, and red pepper in a shallow bowl; dredge chicken in flour mixture.
4. Coat a large nonstick skillet with cooking spray; place over medium heat. Add chicken, and cook 4 to 5 minutes on each side or until chicken is lightly browned.
5. Transfer chicken to a serving plate, and drizzle with wine mixture. Sprinkle with chopped parsley, and garnish with lemon slices, if desired. Yield: 4 servings (serving size: 1 chicken breast half).

CALORIES 235; FAT 5.2g (sat 2g); PROTEIN 40g; CARBOHYDRATE 5.2g; FIBER 0.6g; CHOLESTEROL 106mg; IRON 1.8mg; SODIUM 363mg; CALCIUM 26mg

"For me, the biggest challenge to eating low-carb is the time it takes to prepare meals. Healthy low-carb diets require prep time I don't always have. Both **Chicken Piccata** and **Szechuan Chicken and Vegetables** can be **prepared in less than 20 minutes.**"

Misty Chandler

▶ carbo rating: 4
Szechuan Chicken and Vegetables

Create your own combo of fresh stir-fry vegetables from the salad bar at the grocery store.

2   teaspoons dark or light sesame oil
1½   pounds chicken breast tenders
¼   teaspoon crushed red pepper
1   (10-ounce) package fresh stir-fry vegetables (about 2½ cups)
¼   cup low-sodium teriyaki sauce

1. Heat oil in a large nonstick skillet over medium-high heat. Add chicken, and sprinkle with crushed red pepper; stir-fry 3 minutes.
2. Add vegetables and teriyaki sauce; stir-fry 5 minutes or until vegetables are crisp-tender and chicken is thoroughly cooked. Yield: 4 servings (serving size: about 5 ounces chicken and ⅔ cup vegetables).

CALORIES 231; FAT 4.5g (sat 0.9g); PROTEIN 40.1g; CARBOHYDRATE 4.6g; FIBER 0.9g; CHOLESTEROL 99mg; IRON 1.5mg; SODIUM 398mg; CALCIUM 71mg

▶ carbo rating: 4

Artichoke-and-Goat Cheese-Stuffed Chicken Breasts

This company-worthy stuffed chicken is filled with a savory mixture of artichokes and goat cheese instead of a breadcrumb mixture.

1	(14-ounce) can artichoke bottoms
½	cup (2 ounces) crumbled goat cheese or feta cheese
¼	cup chopped chives, divided
1½	teaspoons chopped fresh thyme, divided
1½	teaspoons grated lemon rind, divided
8	(6-ounce) skinless, boneless chicken breast halves
¼	teaspoon freshly ground black pepper
2	teaspoons olive oil, divided
2	tablespoons fresh lemon juice
1	teaspoon cornstarch

1. Drain artichokes in a colander over a bowl, reserving liquid. Coarsely chop artichokes. Combine artichokes, cheese, 2 tablespoons chives, 1 teaspoon thyme, and 1 teaspoon lemon rind in a medium bowl.
2. Cut a horizontal slit through thickest portion of each chicken breast half to form a pocket. Stuff about ¼ cup artichoke mixture into pockets. Sprinkle chicken with pepper.
3. Heat 1 teaspoon oil in a large nonstick skillet over medium-high heat. Add 4 breast halves; cook 6 to 8 minutes on each side or until chicken is done. Remove chicken from pan; keep warm. Repeat with 1 teaspoon oil and 4 chicken breast halves. Add reserved artichoke liquid, ½ teaspoon thyme, and ½ teaspoon lemon rind to pan. Combine lemon juice and cornstarch; add to pan. Bring to a boil; cook 1 minute, stirring constantly. Return chicken to pan. Cover and simmer 2 minutes or until thoroughly heated. Spoon sauce over chicken. Top with 2 tablespoons chives. Yield: 8 servings (serving size: 1 stuffed chicken breast half).

CALORIES 251; FAT 5.8g (sat 2.5g); PROTEIN 42.7g; CARBOHYDRATE 4.6g; FIBER 0.7g; CHOLESTEROL 106mg; IRON 2.1mg; SODIUM 280mg; CALCIUM 85mg

▶ carbo rating: 4

Spinach-Stuffed Chicken Breasts

Spinach is one of the lowest-carb veggies out there— a 10-ounce bag of fresh spinach has only 10 grams of carbohydrate.

4	(6-ounce) skinless, boneless chicken breast halves
1	(10-ounce) bag fresh spinach
¼	cup water
½	teaspoon freshly ground black pepper
¼	teaspoon salt
2	garlic cloves, minced
2	tablespoons dried tomato bits
2	tablespoons pine nuts, toasted
½	teaspoon dried basil, divided
	Cooking spray
⅓	cup dry white wine

1. Place chicken breast halves between 2 sheets of plastic wrap, and flatten to ¼-inch thickness, using a meat mallet or rolling pin. Set aside.
2. Trim and chop spinach; place in a large nonstick skillet over medium-high heat. Add water and next 3 ingredients; bring to a boil. Cook 7 minutes or until spinach wilts, stirring occasionally. Remove from heat; stir in tomato bits, pine nuts, and ¼ teaspoon basil.
3. Divide spinach mixture evenly among chicken breast halves, spooning mixture onto center of each half. Roll chicken up lengthwise, tucking ends under; secure chicken with wooden picks.
4. Coat pan with cooking spray. Place over medium-high heat until hot. Add chicken, and cook 2 minutes on each side or until browned. Add wine and ¼ teaspoon basil; bring to a boil. Cover, reduce heat, and simmer 20 minutes or until chicken is done. Transfer chicken to a serving platter, and remove wooden picks. Spoon pan drippings over chicken. Yield: 4 servings (serving size: 1 stuffed chicken breast half).

CALORIES 237; FAT 4.6g (sat 0.9g); PROTEIN 42.7g; CARBOHYDRATE 5.3g; FIBER 1g; CHOLESTEROL 99mg; IRON 3.9mg; SODIUM 321mg; CALCIUM 100mg

▶ **carbo rating: 4**

Jerk Smoked Chicken

If habanero pepper sauce isn't available, substitute any red hot sauce.

2	limes
1	orange
⅔	cup sliced green onions
¼	cup habanero pepper sauce
1½	tablespoons dried thyme
1½	teaspoons ground allspice
1	teaspoon freshly ground black pepper
½	teaspoon salt
¼	teaspoon ground cloves
3	garlic cloves, peeled
2	(3-pound) broiler-fryers
4	(3-inch) chunks hickory wood

1. Squeeze juice from limes and orange; set citrus rinds aside. Combine citrus juice, onions, and next 7 ingredients in a blender or food processor; process until well blended.
2. Remove and discard giblets and neck from chickens. Rinse chickens under cold water, and pat dry. Trim excess fat from chickens. Starting at neck cavities, loosen skin from breasts and drumsticks by gently pushing fingers between skin and meat. Place citrus rinds in body cavities. Lift wing tips up and over backs; tuck under chickens.
3. Place chickens in a large zip-top plastic bag. Pour juice mixture under loosened skin of chickens. Seal bag, and marinate in refrigerator at least 2 hours, turning bag occasionally.
4. Soak hickory chunks in water 30 minutes to 1 hour. Drain well.

5. Prepare charcoal fire in meat smoker; let burn 15 to 20 minutes or until center coals are covered with gray ash. Place soaked hickory chunks on top of coals. Remove chickens from bag, reserving marinade. Place water pan in smoker; add reserved marinade and hot water to pan to within 1 inch of rim.
6. Place chickens, breast sides up, on rack in smoker, allowing enough room between chickens for air to circulate. Insert meat thermometer into meaty part of thigh, making sure not to touch bone. Cover with lid; cook 3 hours or until thermometer registers 180°. Refill water pan and add charcoal to fire as needed.
7. Remove chickens from smoker; let stand 10 minutes. Remove and discard skin before eating, if desired (analysis does not include skin). Yield: 6 servings (serving size: 5 ounces).

CALORIES 267; FAT 6.1g (sat 1.5g); PROTEIN 45g; CARBOHYDRATE 6g; FIBER 1.6g; CHOLESTEROL 142mg; IRON 3.4mg; SODIUM 611mg; CALCIUM 55mg

(pictured on page 232)

▶ **carbo rating: 4**

Citrus-Ginger Chicken

Fresh lime and ginger give this easy grilled chicken real zing.

2½	tablespoons low-sugar orange marmalade
⅛	teaspoon grated lime rind
1½	tablespoons fresh lime juice
1½	teaspoons grated peeled fresh ginger
	Cooking spray
4	(8-ounce) skinless, bone-in chicken breast halves

1. Prepare grill.
2. Combine first 4 ingredients in a small bowl.
3. Place chicken on grill rack coated with cooking spray; cover and grill 20 to 25 minutes or until chicken is done, turning and basting with marmalade mixture. Yield: 4 servings (serving size: 1 chicken breast half).

CALORIES 217; FAT 2.3g (sat 0.6g); PROTEIN 41.9g; CARBOHYDRATE 4.4g; FIBER 0g; CHOLESTEROL 105mg; IRON 1.3mg; SODIUM 118mg; CALCIUM 21mg

► **carbo rating: 4**

Stuffed Turkey Breast

If you don't eat carrots, just leave them out and add another ½ cup of chopped onion.

1   (3-pound) boneless turkey breast, skinned and trimmed of fat
Cooking spray
1   teaspoon butter
½   cup finely chopped onion
½   cup chopped mushrooms
½   cup shredded carrot
1   cup whole wheat breadcrumbs
¼   cup chopped fresh parsley
¼   cup fat-free, less-sodium chicken broth
½   teaspoon grated lemon rind
2   teaspoons lemon juice
½   teaspoon dried thyme
¼   teaspoon pepper
1   large egg, lightly beaten
2   tablespoons butter
1   tablespoon white wine Worcestershire sauce

1. Preheat oven to 325°.
2. Place turkey breast on plastic wrap. From center, slice horizontally through thickest part of each side, almost to outer edge; flip each cut piece. Flatten to ½-inch thickness, using a mallet or rolling pin.
3. Coat a large nonstick skillet with cooking spray; add 1 teaspoon butter. Place over medium-high heat until hot. Add onion, mushrooms, and carrot; sauté until crisp-tender. Stir in breadcrumbs and next 7 ingredients. Spoon over turkey, leaving a 2-inch border at sides; roll up, jelly roll fashion, starting at short side. Tie at 2-inch intervals with string. Place, seam side down, on a broiler pan coated with cooking spray.
4. Bake at 325° for 45 minutes. Combine 2 tablespoons butter and Worcestershire sauce; brush over turkey. Bake an additional 1½ hours or until a meat thermometer registers 180°, brushing with butter mixture after 1 hour. Remove string; let stand 10 minutes before slicing into 8 equal portions. Yield: 8 servings (serving size: 1 slice).

CALORIES 245; FAT 5.2g (sat 2.2g); PROTEIN 42.2g; CARBOHYDRATE 5.2g; FIBER 1g; CHOLESTEROL 147mg; IRON 2.7mg; SODIUM 177mg; CALCIUM 36mg

► **carbo rating: 4**

Teriyaki Roast Chicken

The roasting process itself results in great-flavored chicken, so you don't have to add a lot of other ingredients to enhance the chicken. An onion, a little sauce, and a sprinkle of seasoning does the trick.

1   (3-pound) broiler-fryer
1   small onion, quartered
⅓   cup low-sodium teriyaki sauce
1   teaspoon garlic pepper seasoning
Cooking spray

1. Preheat oven to 375°.
2. Remove and discard giblets and neck from chicken. Rinse chicken under cold water; pat dry. Trim excess fat from chicken.
3. Place onion in cavity of chicken. Brush chicken on all sides with about one-third of teriyaki sauce. Sprinkle with garlic pepper seasoning. Lift wing tips up and over back; tuck under chicken. Place chicken, breast side up, on a broiler pan coated with cooking spray. Insert meat thermometer into meaty part of thigh, making sure not to touch the bone. Pour remaining teriyaki sauce over chicken.
4. Bake, uncovered, at 375° for 1½ hours or until thermometer registers 180°. Remove and discard skin before eating, if desired (analysis does not include skin). Yield: 4 servings (serving size: about 6 ounces).

CALORIES 214; FAT 4.7g (sat 1.2g); PROTEIN 35.6g; CARBOHYDRATE 4.6g; FIBER 0.3g; CHOLESTEROL 113mg; IRON 2mg; SODIUM 477mg; CALCIUM 23mg

making breadcrumbs

To get 1 cup of whole wheat breadcrumbs, place 1½ slices whole wheat bread in a food processor; process until crumbly.

▶ carbo rating: 5

Lemon Turkey and Asparagus

Thaw the asparagus in the microwave while you combine the chicken broth mixture, chop the pepper, and cut the turkey. If you're using fresh asparagus, use about 1½ cups of chopped spears.

½   cup fat-free, less-sodium chicken broth
2   tablespoons fresh lemon juice
1   tablespoon low-sodium soy sauce
2   teaspoons cornstarch
¼   teaspoon black pepper
2   teaspoons vegetable oil, divided
Cooking spray
1   (9-ounce) package frozen asparagus cuts, thawed
1   small red bell pepper, chopped
1½   pounds turkey tenderloin, cut into 1-inch pieces

1. Combine first 5 ingredients, stirring well; set aside. Heat 1 teaspoon oil in a large nonstick skillet coated with cooking spray over medium-high heat. Add asparagus and red bell pepper; sauté 2 minutes or until tender. Transfer to a bowl; set aside, and keep warm.
2. Add 1 teaspoon oil and turkey to pan. Cook 3 minutes or until turkey is browned, stirring occasionally. Add broth mixture to pan; cook 2 minutes or until mixture is thickened and bubbly. Return asparagus mixture to pan. Stir just until coated. Yield: 4 servings (serving size: about 5 ounces turkey and about ⅔ cup vegetable mixture).

CALORIES 233; FAT 3.5g (sat 0.8g); PROTEIN 43.3g; CARBOHYDRATE 6.2g; FIBER 1.7g; CHOLESTEROL 112mg; IRON 2.7mg; SODIUM 286mg; CALCIUM 36mg

▶ carbo rating: 6

Basil Chicken and Vegetables

If carrots are not allowed on your low-carb plan, add another bell pepper, thinly sliced, in place of the sliced carrot.

Cooking spray
1½   pounds skinless, boneless chicken breast halves, cut into 1-inch strips
1   large bell pepper, thinly sliced
1   small zucchini, sliced
⅔   cup thinly sliced carrot
½   cup tightly packed shredded fresh basil
½   teaspoon freshly ground black pepper
4   teaspoons olive oil
¼   cup (1 ounce) grated fresh Parmesan cheese

1. Preheat oven to 375°.
2. Tear off 4 (12-inch) lengths of heavy-duty foil; fold each piece of foil in half, shiny sides together. Place on a baking sheet, and open out flat, shiny side up. Coat with cooking spray.
3. Arrange one-fourth of chicken strips on half of each foil square near the crease. Spoon vegetables evenly over chicken; sprinkle with basil and black pepper. Drizzle 1 teaspoon olive oil over vegetables in each packet. Fold foil over chicken and vegetables, bringing edges together; fold edges over to seal securely. Pleat and crimp edges to make an airtight seal. Bake at 375° for 30 minutes.
4. Remove chicken mixture from packets, and transfer to individual serving plates. Or, if desired, place packets on individual serving plates; cut an opening in the top of each packet, and fold aluminum foil back. Sprinkle each serving with 1 tablespoon Parmesan cheese. Yield: 4 servings (serving size: about 5 ounces chicken, ¾ cup vegetable mixture, and 1 tablespoon cheese).

CALORIES 282; FAT 8.3g (sat 2.1g); PROTEIN 42.9g; CARBOHYDRATE 7.8g; FIBER 1.8g; CHOLESTEROL 102mg; IRON 2.1mg; SODIUM 219mg; CALCIUM 113mg

(pictured on page 233)

► carbo rating: 6

Chicken with Artichokes and Olives

Artichoke hearts, Dijon mustard, and olives all help punch up the flavor of simple pan-seared chicken.

    1   tablespoon olive oil
    4   (6-ounce) skinless, boneless chicken breast halves
    ¼   teaspoon salt
    ¼   teaspoon pepper
    ½   cup dry white wine
    ¼   cup fat-free, less-sodium chicken broth
    2   teaspoons Dijon mustard
    1   teaspoon cornstarch
    ⅓   cup pitted kalamata olives
    1   (14-ounce) can quartered artichoke hearts, drained
    2   tablespoons minced fresh parsley

1. Heat oil in a large nonstick skillet over medium-high heat. Sprinkle chicken with salt and pepper. Add chicken to pan; cook 5 minutes on each side. Remove chicken from pan; keep warm.
2. Combine wine, broth, mustard, and cornstarch. Add to pan, scraping pan to loosen browned bits. Bring to a boil; cook 1 minute. Stir in olives and artichokes; cook 1 minute. Spoon sauce over chicken; sprinkle with parsley. Yield: 4 servings (serving size: 1 chicken breast half and ¼ cup sauce).

CALORIES 323; FAT 10.1g (sat 1.6g); PROTEIN 42.4g; CARBOHYDRATE 10.1g; FIBER 3.8g; CHOLESTEROL 99mg; IRON 2.1mg; SODIUM 788mg; CALCIUM 50mg

► carbo rating: 6

Brie-and-Caramelized Onion-Stuffed Chicken Breasts

This elegant dish features a buttery-tasting melted Brie-and-onion stuffing.

    1   teaspoon olive oil, divided
    1½   cups sliced onion
    4   garlic cloves, thinly sliced
    ⅔   cup dry white wine, divided
    2   ounces Brie cheese, rind removed and cheese cut into small pieces
    ⅛   teaspoon salt
    ⅛   teaspoon black pepper
    4   (6-ounce) skinless, boneless chicken breast halves
    2   tablespoons minced onion
    1   tablespoon chopped fresh sage
    2   garlic cloves, minced
    1   (10½-ounce) can low-sodium chicken broth

1. Heat ½ teaspoon oil in a large nonstick skillet over medium heat. Add sliced onion; cook 30 minutes or until golden, stirring often. Add sliced garlic, and sauté 5 minutes. Stir in ⅓ cup wine; cook 5 minutes or until liquid almost evaporates. Spoon onion mixture into a bowl; cool. Stir in Brie, salt, and pepper.
2. Cut a horizontal slit through thickest portion of each chicken breast half to form a pocket. Stuff about 1½ tablespoons onion mixture into pockets.
3. Heat ½ teaspoon oil in pan over medium-high heat. Add chicken; cook 6 minutes on each side or until done. Remove chicken from pan; keep warm.
4. Add ⅓ cup wine, minced onion, sage, and minced garlic to pan. Cook over medium-high heat 2 minutes; stir in broth. Bring mixture to a boil, and cook 7 minutes or until sauce is reduced to ¾ cup. Return chicken to pan; cover and simmer 2 minutes or until thoroughly heated. Serve sauce with chicken. Yield: 4 servings (serving size: 1 stuffed chicken breast half and 3 tablespoons sauce).

CALORIES 285; FAT 7.9g (sat 3.5g); PROTEIN 44.4g; CARBOHYDRATE 7g; FIBER 1g; CHOLESTEROL 114mg; IRON 1.7mg; SODIUM 321mg; CALCIUM 75mg

► carbo rating: 6
Zesty Barbecued Chicken

Many commercial barbecue sauces are very high in sugar, so this low-carb, tangy-sweet sauce recipe is a good one to keep on hand.

1½	cups no-salt-added tomato sauce
6	tablespoons lemon juice
1½	tablespoons "measures-like-sugar" calorie-free brown sugar sweetener (such as Brown Sugar Twin)
3	tablespoons cider vinegar
2	tablespoons low-sodium Worcestershire sauce
2	teaspoons minced garlic
1½	teaspoons prepared mustard
¾	teaspoon ground red pepper
¼	teaspoon black pepper
6	(8-ounce) skinless, bone-in chicken breast halves

Cooking spray

1. Combine first 9 ingredients in a saucepan. Bring to a boil; cover, reduce heat, and simmer 20 minutes.
2. Pour 1 cup tomato sauce mixture into a heavy-duty zip-top plastic bag. Set aside remaining tomato sauce mixture. Add chicken to bag; seal bag, and shake until chicken is well coated. Marinate in refrigerator 8 hours, turning bag occasionally.
3. Prepare grill.
4. Remove chicken from marinade; discard marinade. Place chicken on grill rack coated with cooking spray; cover and grill 8 minutes on each side or until chicken is done, basting frequently with reserved tomato sauce mixture. Yield: 6 servings (serving size: 1 chicken breast half).

CALORIES 190; FAT 2g (sat 0.5g); PROTEIN 35g; CARBOHYDRATE 7g;
FIBER 1.1g; CHOLESTEROL 86mg; IRON 1.7mg; SODIUM 130mg; CALCIUM 34mg

► carbo rating: 6
Broiled Tandoori Chicken

Traditional tandoori dishes get their name from being cooked in a tandoori oven. Used throughout India, a tandoori oven is made of clay and brick and withstands extremely high temperatures. The meat or chicken is often coated before baking with a spicy yogurt mixture.

1	(8-ounce) carton plain low-fat yogurt
¼	cup chopped fresh cilantro
1	tablespoon paprika
1	tablespoon minced peeled fresh ginger
1	tablespoon fresh lemon juice
1½	teaspoons curry powder
½	teaspoon ground cumin
¼	teaspoon ground red pepper
1	garlic clove, minced
1½	pounds skinless, boneless chicken breasts, cut into 1-inch pieces

Cooking spray

1. Combine first 9 ingredients in a bowl. Stir in chicken; cover and marinate in refrigerator 30 minutes.
2. Preheat broiler.
3. Remove chicken from marinade, discarding marinade. Thread chicken evenly onto 4 (8-inch) skewers. Place chicken on a broiler pan coated with cooking spray. Broil 6 minutes; turn skewers, and broil 6 minutes or until done. Yield: 4 servings (serving size: 1 skewer).

CALORIES 231; FAT 2.6g (sat 0.7g); PROTEIN 43g; CARBOHYDRATE 6.7g;
FIBER 0.8g; CHOLESTEROL 100mg; IRON 2mg; SODIUM 156mg;
CALCIUM 143mg

▶ **carbo rating: 6**

Garlic-Roasted Chicken and Onions

When you roast garlic, it gets soft and has a mellow, buttery flavor.

12	garlic cloves

Cooking spray

4	chicken drumsticks (about 1 pound), skinned
4	chicken thighs (about 1½ pounds), skinned
½	cup finely chopped onion
¾	teaspoon salt, divided
½	teaspoon dried oregano
¼	teaspoon dried thyme
¼	teaspoon pepper

1. Preheat oven to 425°.
2. Sprinkle garlic into a 13 x 9-inch baking dish coated with cooking spray. Arrange chicken over garlic; sprinkle onion, ½ teaspoon salt, oregano, thyme, and pepper over chicken. Cover and bake at 425° for 30 minutes.
3. Uncover chicken; bake 30 more minutes or until chicken is done. Remove chicken from dish, and add ¼ teaspoon salt to drippings. Drizzle drippings over chicken. Yield: 4 servings (serving size: 1 drumstick and 1 thigh).

CALORIES 221; FAT 6.1g (sat 1.5g); PROTEIN 33.2g; CARBOHYDRATE 6.8g; FIBER 1.1g; CHOLESTEROL 129mg; IRON 2.2mg; SODIUM 582mg; CALCIUM 47mg

▶ **carbo rating: 6**

Baked Buffalo Chicken

These chicken thighs may remind you of the spicy chicken wings served at your local sports grill. You'll need the cool blue cheese dressing to tame the heat.

Cooking spray

1½	teaspoons vegetable oil
12	small bone-in chicken thighs (about 2¼ pounds), skinned
¼	cup hot sauce
3	tablespoons fat-free margarine, melted
2	tablespoons water
1	tablespoon white vinegar
1	teaspoon celery seeds
⅛	teaspoon pepper
½	cup reduced-fat blue cheese dressing

1. Preheat oven to 400°.
2. Heat oil in a nonstick skillet coated with cooking spray over medium-high heat. Add chicken; cook 4 minutes on each side. Transfer chicken to an 11 x 7-inch baking dish coated with cooking spray.
3. Combine hot sauce and next 5 ingredients; pour over chicken. Bake, uncovered, at 400° for 25 minutes. Serve with blue cheese dressing. Yield: 4 servings (serving size: 3 thighs and 2 tablespoons dressing).

CALORIES 299; FAT 14.8g (sat 2.8g); PROTEIN 30.4g; CARBOHYDRATE 7.4g; FIBER 1.2g; CHOLESTEROL 133mg; IRON 2mg; SODIUM 535mg; CALCIUM 66mg

► carbo rating: 7

Chicken Kebabs with Salsa

Be sure not to crowd the pieces of chicken on the skewer because all the pieces might not get done.

¾ cup chopped seeded tomato
¼ cup chopped avocado
2 tablespoons fresh lime juice
1 tablespoon chopped green onions
1 tablespoon chopped fresh cilantro
1 teaspoon finely chopped jalapeño pepper
¼ teaspoon minced garlic
¾ pound skinless, boneless chicken breast halves, cut into 1-inch pieces
2 tablespoons fresh lime juice
2 teaspoons low-sodium soy sauce
1 teaspoon minced garlic
Cooking spray
Jalapeño pepper (optional)
Lime slices (optional)
Cilantro sprig (optional)

1. Combine first 7 ingredients. Cover and chill.
2. Place chicken in a shallow dish. Combine 2 tablespoons lime juice, soy sauce, and garlic. Pour over chicken. Cover and marinate in refrigerator 1 hour.
3. Prepare grill.
4. Remove chicken from marinade, reserving marinade. Place marinade in a small saucepan; bring to a boil, and remove from heat. Thread chicken onto 2 (10-inch) skewers. Place chicken on grill rack coated with cooking spray; grill, covered, 6 to 8 minutes or until chicken is done, turning occasionally, and basting with reserved marinade.
5. Spoon tomato mixture onto a serving plate; place chicken kebabs over tomato mixture. If desired, garnish with jalapeño pepper, lime slices, and cilantro sprig. Yield: 2 servings (serving size: 1 skewer and about ½ cup tomato mixture).

CALORIES 247; FAT 5.3g (sat 1.1g); PROTEIN 40.8g; CARBOHYDRATE 8.6g; FIBER 2g; CHOLESTEROL 99mg; IRON 1.9mg; SODIUM 298mg; CALCIUM 34mg

► carbo rating: 7

Pecan Chicken Fingers

Instead of a flour coating, these chicken fingers are dredged in a spicy mixture of pecans and wheat germ. The nuts and wheat germ not only add a toasted, nutty flavor to the chicken, they also create a crust with extra crunch. These chicken fingers are high in fat and calories because of the pecans, but it's the heart-healthy type of fat. The serving size is 4 ounces instead of 6 because, in addition to the chicken, the pecans, wheat germ, and buttermilk all provide protein.

1½ cups chopped pecans, toasted and coarsely ground
½ cup toasted wheat germ
¼ cup sesame seeds
1 tablespoon Creole or Cajun seasoning
½ teaspoon garlic powder
½ teaspoon salt
¼ teaspoon pepper
1 cup low-fat buttermilk
1½ pounds chicken tenders
3 tablespoons light butter, melted
Cooking spray

1. Preheat oven to 400°.
2. Combine first 7 ingredients in a shallow dish. Pour buttermilk into a second shallow dish. Dip chicken in buttermilk; dredge in pecan mixture.
3. Place chicken on a jelly roll pan coated with cooking spray. Drizzle butter evenly over chicken. Bake at 400° for 20 minutes or until chicken is done. Serve warm. Yield: 6 servings (serving size: about 4 ounces).

CALORIES 436; FAT 29.7g (sat 4.4g); PROTEIN 33.5g; CARBOHYDRATE 10.8g; FIBER 4.3g; CHOLESTEROL 76mg; IRON 11.1mg; SODIUM 420mg; CALCIUM 50mg

Santa Fe Grilled Chicken

Lime juice adds tanginess to the chicken and jalapeño pepper adds heat to the fresh tomato salsa.

4	(6-ounce) skinless, boneless chicken breast halves
¼	teaspoon salt
¼	teaspoon pepper
⅓	cup fresh lime juice
2	teaspoons olive oil
1¾	cups diced plum tomato (about ¾ pound)
⅓	cup chopped onion
3	tablespoons minced fresh cilantro
2	tablespoons red wine vinegar
1	tablespoon minced seeded jalapeño pepper

Cooking spray

1. Place chicken between 2 sheets of heavy-duty plastic wrap, and flatten to ½-inch thickness, using a meat mallet or rolling pin. Sprinkle chicken with salt and pepper; place in a shallow dish.
2. Combine lime juice and olive oil in a small bowl; stir well, and pour over chicken. Cover chicken, and marinate in refrigerator 3 hours, turning occasionally.
3. Combine tomato and next 4 ingredients in a small bowl. Cover and chill thoroughly.
4. Prepare grill.
5. Remove chicken from marinade, discarding marinade. Place chicken on grill rack coated with cooking spray; cover and grill 5 to 6 minutes on each side or until done. Serve with chilled tomato mixture. Yield: 4 servings (serving size: 1 chicken breast half and about ½ cup tomato mixture).

CALORIES 240; FAT 4.7g (sat 0.9g); PROTEIN 40.4g; CARBOHYDRATE 8g; FIBER 1.5g; CHOLESTEROL 99mg; IRON 1.8mg; SODIUM 266mg; CALCIUM 32mg

Grilled Firecracker Chicken

With just a touch of sweetness from the low-sugar jelly, this fiery hot sauce brings plain ol' grilled chicken breasts to life.

⅓	cup no-salt-added tomato sauce
¼	cup sugar-free apple jelly (such as Smucker's Light)
2	tablespoons lemon juice
⅛	teaspoon garlic powder

Dash of salt
6	slices canned jalapeño peppers
4	(6-ounce) skinless, boneless chicken breast halves

Cooking spray

1. Combine first 6 ingredients in a blender or food processor; process until smooth.
2. Place chicken in a heavy-duty zip-top plastic bag. Add ¼ cup tomato sauce mixture, reserving remaining tomato sauce mixture. Seal bag, and shake until chicken is well coated. Marinate in refrigerator at least 15 minutes.
3. Prepare grill.
4. Remove chicken from marinade, discarding marinade. Place chicken on grill rack coated with cooking spray; cover and grill 5 minutes on each side or until done. Remove chicken from grill, and serve with reserved tomato sauce mixture. Yield: 4 servings (serving size: 1 chicken breast half and about 2 tablespoons tomato sauce mixture).

CALORIES 215; FAT 2.4g (sat 0.6g); PROTEIN 39.6g; CARBOHYDRATE 8.6g; FIBER 1.1g; CHOLESTEROL 99mg; IRON 2mg; SODIUM 742mg; CALCIUM 27mg

▶ carbo rating: 8
Cajun Fire Chicken

The thick and chunky tomato sauce gets its fire from the hot sauce and a little pungency from the fresh cilantro.

Cooking spray
- 2 teaspoons olive oil
- 4 (6-ounce) skinless, boneless chicken breast halves
- 1 (14½-ounce) can stewed tomatoes, undrained and chopped
- 1 green bell pepper, coarsely chopped
- ⅓ cup chopped fresh cilantro, divided
- 2 teaspoons hot sauce
- ½ teaspoon dried thyme

Hot sauce (optional)
Thyme sprigs (optional)

1. Heat oil in a large nonstick skillet coated with cooking spray over medium-high heat. Add chicken to pan, and cook 4 to 5 minutes on each side or until chicken is done.
2. Add tomatoes, bell pepper, ¼ cup cilantro, 2 teaspoons hot sauce, and thyme to pan. Bring to a boil; cover, reduce heat, and simmer 5 minutes. Uncover and simmer 5 minutes.
3. Stir in remaining cilantro. If desired, serve with additional hot sauce and garnish with thyme sprigs. Yield: 4 servings (serving size: 1 chicken breast half and one-fourth of tomato mixture).

CALORIES 248; FAT 4.6g (sat 0.9g); PROTEIN 40.7g; CARBOHYDRATE 9.8g; FIBER 1.9g; CHOLESTEROL 99mg; IRON 2.3mg; SODIUM 354mg; CALCIUM 60mg

(pictured on page 234)

▶ carbo rating: 8
Chicken with Tomato-Vinegar Sauce

Fines herbes, *pronounced "FEEN erb," is a mixture of very finely chopped herbs, usually chervil, chives, parsley, and tarragon.*

- 2 cups coarsely chopped peeled tomato
- 1 cup red wine vinegar
- ¾ cup fat-free, less-sodium chicken broth
- 2 tablespoons no-salt-added tomato paste
- 15 garlic cloves
- 4 (8-ounce) skinless, bone-in chicken breast halves
- 1 teaspoon fines herbes
- 1 bay leaf

1. Combine first 5 ingredients in a medium saucepan; stir well. Cover and simmer over medium-low heat 20 minutes. Add chicken, fines herbes, and bay leaf. Cover and simmer 25 minutes or until chicken is tender. Transfer chicken to a serving platter, and keep warm.
2. Bring tomato mixture to a boil; cook, uncovered, over medium heat 20 minutes or until mixture is reduced to 1⅓ cups. Remove and discard bay leaf and, if desired, garlic.
3. Spoon tomato mixture over chicken. Yield: 4 servings (serving size: 1 chicken breast half and ⅓ cup tomato mixture).

CALORIES 247; FAT 2.7g (sat 0.7g); PROTEIN 44.3g; CARBOHYDRATE 10.1g; FIBER 1.6g; CHOLESTEROL 105mg; IRON 2.6mg; SODIUM 258mg; CALCIUM 53mg

4. Place leek and hens, meaty sides up, in an 11 x 7-inch baking dish. Combine tomatoes and next 9 ingredients; pour over hens. Cover and bake at 375° for 20 minutes. Uncover and bake 10 more minutes or until a meat thermometer registers 180°. Remove and discard bay leaf. Yield: 4 servings (serving size: ½ hen and one-fourth of vegetable mixture).

CALORIES 261; FAT 10.2g (sat 2g); PROTEIN 31.2g; CARBOHYDRATE 10.6g; FIBER 2.3g; CHOLESTEROL 133mg; IRON 3.4mg; SODIUM 478mg; CALCIUM 81mg

▶ carbo rating: 8
Cornish Hens Provençale

Tomatoes, garlic, and olive oil are the key ingredients of Provençale cooking, and ideal for low-carb eating.

2	(1½-pound) Cornish hens, skinned
Cooking spray	
1	tablespoon olive oil
1¾	cups chopped leek
1	(14½-ounce) can no-salt-added whole tomatoes, drained and chopped
½	cup fat-free, less-sodium chicken broth
¼	cup dry white wine
1	(2¼-ounce) can sliced ripe olives, drained
1	teaspoon dried thyme
1	teaspoon ground turmeric
½	teaspoon garlic powder
¼	teaspoon salt
¼	teaspoon pepper
1	bay leaf

1. Preheat oven to 375°.
2. Remove and discard giblets and neck from hens. Rinse hens under cold water; pat dry. Split each hen in half lengthwise. Trim excess fat.
3. Heat oil in a large nonstick skillet coated with cooking spray over medium-high heat. Add hens; cook until hens are lightly browned on both sides, turning occasionally. Remove hens from pan. Add leek; sauté until tender.

▶ carbo rating: 9
Chicken with 40 Cloves of Garlic

This is a classic Provençale-style dish in which the thighs and drumsticks are baked with garlic cloves. The garlic cooks in its own skin, becoming very soft and creamy.

2½	cups chopped onion
1	teaspoon dried tarragon
6	parsley sprigs
4	celery stalks, each cut into 3 pieces
8	chicken thighs (about 3 pounds), skinned
8	chicken drumsticks (about 2 pounds), skinned
½	cup dry vermouth
1½	teaspoons salt
½	teaspoon pepper
⅛	teaspoon ground nutmeg
40	garlic cloves (about 3 heads), unpeeled

1. Preheat oven to 375°.
2. Combine first 4 ingredients in a 4-quart casserole or shallow roasting pan. Arrange chicken over vegetables. Drizzle with vermouth; sprinkle with salt, pepper, and nutmeg. Nestle garlic around chicken. Cover casserole with foil, and bake at 375° for 1½ hours. Yield: 8 servings (serving size: 1 thigh, 1 drumstick, 5 tablespoons vegetable mixture, and 5 garlic cloves).

CALORIES 238; FAT 6.2g (sat 1.5g); PROTEIN 33.9g; CARBOHYDRATE 10.5g; FIBER 1.6g; CHOLESTEROL 129mg; IRON 2.3mg; SODIUM 602mg; CALCIUM 68mg

▶ carbo rating: 9

Boston Beach Jerk Chicken

Jerk is the Jamaican method of barbecue. Add oak, pecan, or hickory wood to a charcoal fire to make your jerk more authentic. Be sure to wear gloves when handling the chiles and packing on the rub; the oil in the chiles will burn your skin.

4   cups (1-inch) pieces green onions
¼   cup fresh thyme
1   tablespoon freshly ground black pepper
1   tablespoon freshly ground coriander seeds
3   tablespoons grated peeled fresh ginger
2   tablespoons fresh lime juice
2   tablespoons vegetable oil
2   teaspoons salt
2   teaspoons freshly ground allspice
1   teaspoon freshly ground nutmeg
1   teaspoon ground cinnamon
5   garlic cloves, peeled and halved
3   bay leaves
1   to 2 Scotch bonnet or habanero peppers, halved and seeded
1   (3½-pound) roasting chicken
    Cooking spray

1. Place first 14 ingredients in a food processor; process until a thick paste forms, scraping sides of bowl once.
2. Remove and discard giblets and neck from chicken. Rinse chicken with cold water; pat dry. Remove skin, and trim excess fat; split chicken in half lengthwise. Place chicken in a large shallow dish. Spread 1¼ cups spice mixture over both sides of chicken. Cover and marinate in refrigerator 1 to 4 hours.
3. Prepare grill.
4. Place chicken on grill rack coated with cooking spray; cover and grill 45 minutes or until done, turning frequently and basting with remaining ¼ cup spice mixture. Yield: 4 servings (serving size: about 5 ounces).

CALORIES 353; FAT 13.4g (sat 2.1g); PROTEIN 44.1g; CARBOHYDRATE 14.3g; FIBER 5.3g; CHOLESTEROL 132mg; IRON 4.7mg; SODIUM 1344mg; CALCIUM 143mg

▶ carbo rating: 9

Turkey Breast Cutlets in Port Wine Sauce

Slicing the tenderloins ensures even cooking.

1   pound turkey tenderloins
⅔   cup low-salt beef broth, divided
¼   cup port wine
2   tablespoons chopped dried cherries
2   teaspoons black cherry fruit spread (such as Polaner)
1   teaspoon Worcestershire sauce
½   teaspoon balsamic vinegar
¼   teaspoon pepper
1   teaspoon cornstarch
1   teaspoon butter
3   tablespoons chopped shallots
1   teaspoon chopped fresh rosemary

1. Heat a large nonstick skillet over medium-high heat.
2. Cut tenderloins diagonally across grain into 1-inch-thick slices. Pound each slice to ½-inch thickness, using a meat mallet or rolling pin. Combine ½ cup broth, wine, and next 5 ingredients. Combine remaining broth and cornstarch, stirring with a whisk.
3. Melt butter in pan. Add shallots and rosemary; sauté 3 minutes. Add turkey; cook 3 minutes. Turn turkey over; cook 1 minute. Add wine mixture; bring to a boil. Cook 2 minutes. Add cornstarch mixture; boil 1 minute. Yield: 4 servings (serving size: about 3 ounces turkey and about ¼ cup sauce).

CALORIES 194; FAT 2g (sat 0.9g); PROTEIN 29.3g; CARBOHYDRATE 9.7g; FIBER 0.5g; CHOLESTEROL 73mg; IRON 1.8mg; SODIUM 195mg; CALCIUM 22mg

▶ carbo rating: 10

Marinated Greek Kebabs

The feta with basil and tomatoes adds a distinctive flavor, but the recipe is just as good with plain feta because it's such a sharp cheese.

1	(8-ounce) carton plain fat-free yogurt
⅓	cup (1.3 ounces) crumbled feta cheese with basil and sun-dried tomatoes
½	teaspoon grated lemon rind
2	tablespoons fresh lemon juice
2	teaspoons dried oregano
½	teaspoon salt
¼	teaspoon black pepper
¼	teaspoon dried rosemary, crushed
1½	pounds skinless, boneless chicken breast halves, cut into 1-inch pieces
1	large red onion, cut into 8 wedges
1	large green bell pepper, cut into 1½-inch pieces
Cooking spray	

1. Combine first 8 ingredients in a medium bowl, stirring well with a whisk. Add chicken, tossing to coat; cover and marinate in refrigerator 3 hours.
2. Prepare grill.
3. Cut onion wedges in half crosswise. Remove chicken from yogurt mixture, discarding yogurt mixture. Thread chicken, onion chunks, and bell pepper pieces evenly onto 4 (12-inch) skewers, alternating chicken and vegetables.
4. Place skewers on grill rack coated with cooking spray. Cover and grill 15 minutes or until done, turning twice. Yield: 4 servings (serving size: 1 skewer).

CALORIES 276; FAT 4.7g (sat 2.1g); PROTEIN 45.1g; CARBOHYDRATE 11.5g; FIBER 1.8g; CHOLESTEROL 106mg; IRON 2mg; SODIUM 562mg; CALCIUM 183mg

▶ carbo rating: 11

Paillard of Chicken

*A **paillard** is a thin slice of meat or chicken that is quickly sautéed. In this version, the slices of chicken are dredged and coated in an herbed, whole wheat breadcrumb mixture.*

5	slices whole wheat bread
2	tablespoons grated Parmesan cheese
2	tablespoons chopped fresh parsley
8	(6-ounce) skinless, boneless chicken breast halves
¼	cup fresh lemon juice
⅓	cup whole wheat flour
1	teaspoon cracked black pepper
1	teaspoon dried thyme
1	teaspoon dried rubbed sage
¼	teaspoon dried rosemary, crushed
¼	teaspoon salt
3	large egg whites, lightly beaten
2	tablespoons olive oil, divided

1. Place bread in a food processor; process 30 seconds or until crumbly. Combine breadcrumbs, cheese, and parsley; set aside.
2. Place each chicken breast half between 2 sheets of heavy-duty plastic wrap; flatten to ¼-inch thickness using a meat mallet or rolling pin. Brush both sides of chicken with lemon juice. Combine flour and next 4 ingredients in a large zip-top plastic bag. Add chicken, and seal bag; shake to coat.
3. Sprinkle both sides of chicken with salt. Dip chicken in egg white; dredge in breadcrumb mixture.
4. Heat 2 teaspoons oil in a large nonstick skillet over medium heat. Add 3 chicken breast halves; cook 4 minutes on each side or until done. Remove from pan; keep warm. Repeat procedure with remaining oil and chicken. Yield: 8 servings (serving size: 1 chicken breast half).

CALORIES 295; FAT 6.9g (sat 1.5g); PROTEIN 43.6g; CARBOHYDRATE 13g; FIBER 2.1g; CHOLESTEROL 100mg; IRON 2.3mg; SODIUM 321mg; CALCIUM 58mg

▶ carbo rating: 12

Turkey Sausage with Peppers

You can substitute any type of low-fat turkey sausage for Italian-style. Italian turkey sausages often have a strong taste of fennel seeds, a spice with a licorice-like flavor. If you prefer, use a reduced-fat smoked sausage or a full-fat smoked sausage.

8	ounces Italian turkey sausage
Cooking spray	
1	onion, sliced
1	green bell pepper, sliced
1	red bell pepper, sliced
⅓	cup dry white wine

1. Remove and discard casings from sausage. Cut sausage into 1½-inch pieces.
2. Coat a large nonstick skillet with cooking spray; place over medium-high heat until hot. Add sausage, onion, and peppers; cook 8 to 10 minutes or until sausage is browned and vegetables are tender, stirring occasionally.
3. Add wine to pan. Bring to a boil; reduce heat, and simmer 2 to 3 minutes or until sauce is slightly thickened, stirring occasionally. Yield: 2 servings (serving size: 3 ounces sausage and 1½ cups vegetable mixture).

CALORIES 245; FAT 10.8g (sat 3.2g); PROTEIN 22.3g; CARBOHYDRATE 15.2g; FIBER 3.8g; CHOLESTEROL 95mg; IRON 2mg; SODIUM 813mg; CALCIUM 34mg

(pictured on page 234)

▶ carbo rating: 13

Ivory Coast Chicken

This traditional slow-cooked dish, **kedjenou,** *adapts easily to American kitchens. A terra-cotta pot called a* **canari** *is used in the Ivory Coast, but a Dutch oven does the job perfectly. Cover the pot with a tight lid to prevent steam from escaping. To keep the moisture in, shake the pan periodically. This dish is normally served over cooked rice, so use brown rice if you wish. Rice is not included in the analysis.*

4	chicken breast halves (about 2 pounds), skinned
4	chicken leg quarters (about 2 pounds), skinned
6	cups coarsely chopped onion (about 3 pounds)
5	cups chopped seeded plum tomato
1	cup water
1	tablespoon grated peeled fresh ginger
1½	teaspoons finely chopped seeded jalapeño pepper
1	teaspoon salt
½	teaspoon freshly ground black pepper
5	garlic cloves, minced
1	bay leaf

1. Combine all ingredients in a large Dutch oven. Cover and bring to a simmer over medium heat. Reduce heat to medium-low; cook 1 hour or until chicken is done, gently shaking pan every 10 minutes. Remove and discard bay leaf. Yield: 8 servings (serving size: about 4 ounces chicken and ¾ cup vegetable mixture).

CALORIES 250; FAT 4.1g (sat 1g); PROTEIN 36.4g; CARBOHYDRATE 16.5g; FIBER 3.5g; CHOLESTEROL 104mg; IRON 2.1mg; SODIUM 422mg; CALCIUM 51mg

▶ carbo rating: 14

Rum-Marinated Chicken Breasts with Pineapple Relish

The hot sauce we tested with was Pickapeppa Sauce.

½ cup dark rum
¼ cup barbecue sauce
3 tablespoons fresh lime juice
1 tablespoon Caribbean hot sauce
1 teaspoon sea or kosher salt
2 teaspoons vegetable oil
4 (8-ounce) bone-in chicken breast halves
1 small pineapple, peeled, cored, and cut into
    ½-inch-thick rings (about 12 ounces)
Cooking spray
½ cup finely chopped red bell pepper
1 teaspoon grated lime rind
2 tablespoons fresh lime juice
1 teaspoon dark rum
¼ teaspoon Caribbean hot sauce
⅛ teaspoon sea or kosher salt
4 lime wedges

1. Combine first 6 ingredients in a zip-top plastic bag. Add chicken to bag; seal. Marinate in refrigerator 1 to 2 hours, turning bag occasionally. Remove chicken from bag, reserving marinade; set chicken aside. Let marinade stand at room temperature 10 minutes. Strain through a sieve into a bowl; discard solids.
2. Prepare grill.
3. Place pineapple on grill rack coated with cooking spray; grill 3 minutes on each side or until soft and browned around edges. Cool slightly; chop. Combine pineapple, bell pepper, and next 5 ingredients; set aside.
4. Place chicken on grill rack coated with cooking spray; grill 30 minutes or until done, turning occasionally. Remove and discard skin, if desired (analysis does not include skin).
5. Bring marinade to a boil in a saucepan; cook 1 minute. Drizzle over chicken. Serve with relish and lime. Yield: 4 servings (serving size: 1 chicken breast half, ½ cup relish, 2 tablespoons sauce, and 1 lime wedge).

CALORIES 288; FAT 4.5g (sat 0.6g); PROTEIN 29.6g; CARBOHYDRATE 15.6g; FIBER 1.9g; CHOLESTEROL 72mg; IRON 1.5mg; SODIUM 971mg; CALCIUM 28mg

▶ carbo rating: 17

Chicken with Fruit and Olives

This dish really marinates twice. The chicken soaks in a vinegar-oil-garlic mixture before it's cooked, then it chills in the cooking juices, making for very tender meat.

¼ cup red wine vinegar
3 tablespoons extravirgin olive oil
½ teaspoon salt
¼ teaspoon freshly ground black pepper
4 garlic cloves, minced
½ cup pitted prunes, chopped
½ cup dried apricots, chopped
½ cup pitted green olives, halved
3 pounds skinless, bone-in chicken breasts
1 cup dry white wine
½ cup finely chopped fresh flat-leaf parsley

1. Combine first 5 ingredients in a 13 x 9-inch baking dish, stirring with a whisk. Add prunes, apricots, and olives; toss well to coat. Add chicken; turn to coat. Cover and chill at least 6 hours or overnight.
2. Preheat oven to 450°.
3. Pour wine around, but not over, chicken; let stand 15 minutes. Bake at 450° for 35 minutes or until chicken is done; let stand 15 minutes. Sprinkle with parsley. Cover and refrigerate at least 2 hours or overnight. Remove chicken from bones; discard bones. Return chicken to fruit mixture; let stand 15 minutes. Serve with a slotted spoon. Yield: 6 servings (serving size: about 4 ounces chicken and about ¼ cup fruit mixture).

CALORIES 328; FAT 9.6g (sat 1.7g); PROTEIN 38.2g; CARBOHYDRATE 19g; FIBER 2.4g; CHOLESTEROL 102mg; IRON 2.7mg; SODIUM 393mg; CALCIUM 42mg

salads

There's a whole world of interesting low-carb salads out there, so don't just settle for a little chopped lettuce and a few tomato slices. Check out *Green Bean Salad with Blue Cheese Dressing* (page 285), *Gazpacho Salad* (page 286), *Greek Salad Bowl* (page 288), and *Chicken Salad with Asparagus* (page 291).

▶ carbo rating: 1
Blue Cheese Dressing

This homemade blue cheese dressing is low in carbs, plus it's thicker and cheesier than many commercial brands. (See the chart below.)

⅓   cup light mayonnaise
⅓   cup low-fat buttermilk
¼   cup (1 ounce) crumbled blue cheese
1   tablespoon white wine vinegar
2   teaspoons prepared horseradish
1   teaspoon white Worcestershire sauce
½   teaspoon salt
¼   teaspoon pepper

1. Combine all ingredients in a bowl; stir well with a whisk. Cover and chill 1 hour. Serve with salad greens or fresh vegetables. Yield: 1 cup plus two tablespoons (serving size: 2 tablespoons).

CALORIES 48; FAT 4.1g (sat 1.2g); PROTEIN 1.2g; CARBOHYDRATE 1.6g; FIBER 0.1g; CHOLESTEROL 6mg; IRON 0.1mg; SODIUM 272mg; CALCIUM 33mg

▶ carbo rating: 2
Creamy Feta Dressing

We've used light mayonnaise and reduced-fat sour cream to keep the total fat down, but you can use the full-fat products if you prefer.

1   garlic clove
⅓   cup light mayonnaise
¼   cup (1 ounce) crumbled feta cheese
⅓   cup reduced-fat sour cream
½   cup low-fat buttermilk
¼   teaspoon salt
⅛   teaspoon pepper

1. Drop garlic through food chute with food processor on; process until minced. Add mayonnaise and remaining ingredients. Process until well blended, scraping sides of food processor bowl once. Cover and chill 1 hour. Serve with salad greens or summer tomatoes. Yield: 1 cup (serving size: 2 tablespoons).

CALORIES 65; FAT 5.5g (sat 2.1g); PROTEIN 1.5g; CARBOHYDRATE 2.4g; FIBER 0g; CHOLESTEROL 12mg; IRON 0.1mg; SODIUM 214mg; CALCIUM 53mg

salad dressing comparison
Compare the carbohydrate content and carbo ratings in these popular salad dressings.

Salad Dressing (2 tablespoons)	Calories	Carbohydrate (grams)	Fiber (grams)	Carbo Rating
Blue Cheese	154	2.3	0.0	2
Blue Cheese, reduced-fat	28	4.2	0.0	4
Blue Cheese, fat-free	39	8.7	1.2	8
French	143	4.9	0.0	5
French, fat-free	42	10.3	0.7	10
Italian	137	3.0	0.0	3
Italian, reduced-fat	56	1.9	0.1	2
Italian, fat-free	13	2.5	0.2	2
Ranch	150	1.0	0.0	1
Ranch, fat-free	48	10.7	0.2	10
Thousand Island	115	4.6	0.0	5
Thousand Island, reduced-fat	62	6.8	0.4	6
Thousand Island, fat-free	42	9.4	1.1	8

▶ **carbo rating: 2**

Sliced Cucumber Salad

The English cucumber is ideal for this salad because it is seedless. You can also use pickling cucumbers or salad cucumbers, but they contain seeds. (See information below on seeding cucumbers.)

2	cups thinly sliced peeled English cucumber (about 2)
1	tablespoon minced fresh chives
2	teaspoons minced fresh cilantro
2	tablespoons rice vinegar
1	teaspoon sugar
⅛	teaspoon salt
⅛	teaspoon crushed red pepper

1. Combine cucumber, chives, and cilantro in a medium bowl. Combine vinegar and next 3 ingredients in a small bowl, stirring until sugar dissolves. Pour vinegar mixture over cucumber mixture; stir gently. Yield: 4 servings (serving size: ½ cup).

CALORIES 12; FAT 0.1g (sat 0g); PROTEIN 0.4g; CARBOHYDRATE 2.6g; FIBER 0.5g; CHOLESTEROL 0mg; IRON 0.1mg; SODIUM 74mg; CALCIUM 9mg

seeding cucumbers

It's not too much trouble to seed cucumbers if you can't find the seedless variety. Just cut the cucumber in half lengthwise, and scrape the seeds out with a spoon. Then slice or chop the cucumber as called for in the recipe.

▶ **carbo rating: 3**

Orange-Avocado Salad

If you can't find watercress, use 2 more cups of torn fresh spinach.

¼	teaspoon grated orange rind
2	tablespoons fresh orange juice
2	tablespoons red wine vinegar
2	teaspoons olive oil
⅛	teaspoon salt
⅛	teaspoon pepper
2	cups torn fresh watercress
1	cup torn fresh spinach
2	oranges, peeled and sectioned
1	small avocado, peeled and thinly sliced

1. Combine first 6 ingredients in a small bowl, stirring well with a whisk.
2. Combine watercress and spinach. Pour orange juice mixture over greens; toss gently.
3. Divide watercress mixture evenly among salad plates. Arrange orange sections and avocado slices evenly over each salad. Yield: 6 servings (serving size: about 1 cup).

CALORIES 60; FAT 4.5g (sat 0.7g); PROTEIN 1.1g; CARBOHYDRATE 5.1g; FIBER 1.9g; CHOLESTEROL 0mg; IRON 0.4mg; SODIUM 63mg; CALCIUM 40mg

▶ carbo rating: 3

Mixed Greens with Bacon-Horseradish Dressing

Turkey bacon is slightly lower in fat than regular bacon, but you can use regular if you prefer. The carbo rating will be the same.

6 turkey bacon slices
½ cup low-fat buttermilk
2 tablespoons light mayonnaise
1 teaspoon prepared horseradish
⅛ teaspoon salt
⅛ teaspoon freshly ground black pepper
6 cups torn mixed salad greens
1 cup sliced mushrooms
Freshly ground black pepper (optional)

1. Place bacon on a microwave-safe plate lined with paper towels. Microwave at HIGH 5 minutes. Remove from microwave, and crumble bacon.
2. Combine buttermilk and next 4 ingredients, stirring well with a whisk.
3. Combine salad greens and mushrooms; arrange evenly on salad plates. Spoon 2 tablespoons buttermilk dressing over each salad; sprinkle evenly with bacon. Sprinkle with freshly ground black pepper, if desired. Yield: 6 servings (serving size: 1 cup).

CALORIES 72; FAT 4.8g (sat 1.1g); PROTEIN 4.2g; CARBOHYDRATE 3.8g; FIBER 1.2g; CHOLESTEROL 15mg; IRON 1mg; SODIUM 288mg; CALCIUM 51mg

storing greens

Store leafy greens unwashed in plastic bags in the refrigerator; any added moisture will cause them to spoil more rapidly. When you're ready to use them, remove unwanted stems, and tear the leaves into smaller pieces.

▶ carbo rating: 3

Mexican Napa Slaw

Jicama *(HEE-ka-ma) is a brown-skinned vegetable with a crisp, white flesh similar to a turnip. It takes on the flavor of other ingredients and adds a crunchy texture. There are 8 grams of carbohydrate and 4.4 grams of fiber in a ¾-cup portion of sliced jicama.*

6 cups shredded napa (Chinese) cabbage
2 cups alfalfa sprouts
¾ cup peeled and very thinly sliced jicama
¼ cup chopped fresh cilantro
1 red bell pepper, sliced
1 Anaheim chile pepper, seeded and minced
2 green onions, finely chopped
2 tablespoons "measures-like-sugar" calorie-free sweetener
2 tablespoons fresh lime juice
1 tablespoon olive oil
½ teaspoon freshly ground black pepper
¼ teaspoon salt
2 garlic cloves, crushed

1. Combine first 7 ingredients in a large bowl. Combine sweetener and next 5 ingredients in a small bowl; add to vegetables, and toss well. Cover and chill 1 hour, stirring occasionally. Yield: 8 servings (serving size: about 1 cup).

CALORIES 43; FAT 1.9g (sat 0.3g); PROTEIN 1.4g; CARBOHYDRATE 5.1g; FIBER 2g; CHOLESTEROL 0mg; IRON 0.3mg; SODIUM 83mg; CALCIUM 40mg

Sliced Tomato Salad with Capers and Basil

This salad is best if you make it with juicy, sweet, summertime tomatoes.

2	tomatoes (about ¾ pound)
2	tablespoons coarsely chopped fresh basil
1	teaspoon capers
1	tablespoon balsamic vinegar
1	tablespoon water
2	teaspoons extravirgin olive oil
1	small garlic clove, minced
¼	teaspoon freshly ground black pepper
⅛	teaspoon salt

1. Cut each tomato vertically into 6 slices. Arrange on a serving plate; sprinkle with basil and capers.
2. Combine vinegar and next 5 ingredients in a small bowl; stir with a whisk. Pour vinegar mixture over tomatoes. Yield: 4 servings (serving size: 3 tomato slices).

CALORIES 37; FAT 2.5g (sat 0.3g); PROTEIN 0.7g; CARBOHYDRATE 3.8g; FIBER 0.9g; CHOLESTEROL 0mg; IRON 0.4mg; SODIUM 106mg; CALCIUM 8mg

Shrimp Salad

Instead of cooking your own shrimp, you can buy steamed shrimp at the seafood counter of the supermarket. You'll need about ½ pound of steamed shrimp. This makes a great low-carb main-dish salad that's perfect for lunch or a light supper.

1	pound unpeeled medium shrimp
3	cups water
⅓	cup reduced-fat sour cream
2	tablespoons finely chopped celery
1	tablespoon finely chopped onion
2	teaspoons lemon juice
⅛	teaspoon salt
⅛	teaspoon curry powder
2	green lettuce leaves

1. Peel and devein shrimp. Bring water to a boil; add shrimp, and cook 3 to 5 minutes or until shrimp are done. Drain well; rinse with cold water. Cut each shrimp in half crosswise, and place in a small bowl.
2. Combine sour cream and next 5 ingredients, stirring well. Add sour cream mixture to shrimp, and toss gently. Cover and chill thoroughly. Serve on lettuce-lined plates. Yield: 2 servings (serving size: 1 cup).

CALORIES 231; FAT 6.7g (sat 3.5g); PROTEIN 37.5g; CARBOHYDRATE 3.1g; FIBER 0.3g; CHOLESTEROL 352mg; IRON 5.5mg; SODIUM 554mg; CALCIUM 116mg

guide to salad greens

Mild, tender salad greens are nutritional powerhouses. They're dense with vitamins A and C and contribute calcium, iron, and fiber. But it's their captivating flavors and wonderful versatility that make greens such a joy. Here are some of the greens you can select as you experiment with colors and textures to create a variety of salads.

Arugula This peppery, pungent leafy green is often found in mesclun salad mixes, where it behaves like a cross between lettuce and herb. Spring is arugula's prime time. Leaves that grow in cool weather are more tender and mellow than those suffering the heat of summer. Most arugula from grocery stores has short, tender stems. If you buy yours in bulk or from a farmers' market, however, it may have longer, thicker stems. Trim these away by cutting them off at the base of the leaf.

Bibb This tender lettuce is also called limestone lettuce. It has very tender pale green leaves that are loosely gathered in a small head.

Butter lettuce This lettuce is also called Boston lettuce. It has a loose head with soft, textured, light green leaves, and is similar to Bibb lettuce, but larger.

Curly Endive This lettucelike salad green has an off-white, compact center and loose, lacy, green-rimmed outer leaves that curl at the tips. It has a prickly texture and a slightly bitter taste. Use it in salads, or stir into soups and bean dishes.

Dandelion Greens The slender, saw-toothed leaves have a slightly bitter taste. You may find these greens more often as part of a mix of greens called mesclun.

Escarole Escarole has broad bright green leaves that grow in loose heads. It's a variety of endive but is not as bitter as Belgian endive or chicory.

Green leaf (or red leaf) An all-purpose salad green, green leaf lettuce has large ruffled leaves that are gathered at the stem into a loose head. It has a very

selecting and storing greens

Selecting Choose heads of greens that are densely packed and heavy for their size. Don't buy heads with brown or wilted leaves. If you are buying salad greens packed in cellophane bags, check the freshness date and make sure that there are no leaves in the bottom of the bag that are brown, wet, or wilted.

Storing Store salad greens unwashed in plastic bags. (If you wash them, then store them, moisture will collect on the leaves and cause them to wilt or discolor before you're ready to use them.) Tender-leaved lettuces will keep for about 4 days in the crisper compartment of the refrigerator; firm lettuces such as iceberg and romaine will keep for up to 10 days.

mild flavor. Red leaf lettuce is similar, but has a deep red blush on the edges of the leaves.

Iceberg Also known as crisphead lettuce, this variety features bland, sturdy leaves that are pale green on the outside of the head, and pale yellow or ivory at the center. The heads are round and tightly layered.

Mesclun This term applies to a mixture of salad greens such as arugula, dandelion, frisée, oak leaf, radicchio, and sorrel. It's often packaged as "gourmet salad greens" and is best eaten raw.

Radicchio This bitter-flavored member of the chicory family has burgundy-red leaves with white ribs. Most often used in salads, radicchio can also be grilled or roasted. Escarole, another member of the chicory family, is a good substitute.

Romaine This lettuce comes in an elongated head of crisp, sturdy leaves. The head has pale and crunchy inner leaves called romaine hearts, which are sometimes sold separately. Romaine leaves are juicy and sweet, and are traditionally used for Caesar salads.

Spinach Spinach has dark green leaves that may be curled or smooth, depending on the variety. Choose leaves that are crisp and dark green with a fresh fragrance. Spinach is usually very gritty and must be thoroughly washed. Like other dark, leafy greens, spinach is rich in beta carotene, vitamin A, potassium, and folic acid. And while we know from Popeye that spinach is high in iron, the form of iron is not as well absorbed as that found in meats.

Watercress This member of the mustard family has small, crisp, dark green leaves with a sharp, peppery flavor. It's best eaten raw. Choose leaves with a deep green color. A good substitute for watercress is another pungent-flavored green, such as arugula. If you don't care for the sharp flavor, you can use spinach.

Carbo Ratings for Greens

Most salad greens contain about the same amount of carbohydrate and fiber, so a 1-cup serving of any of the above greens will have the same carbo rating. (One cup of chopped salad greens has about 1.3 grams of carbohydrate and about 1.1 grams of fiber, so the carbo rating is 0.) If you substitute one for another in a salad recipe, it won't affect the salad's carbo rating.

▶ carbo rating: 4

Mediterranean Tossed Salad

If tomato-basil feta cheese isn't available, substitute peppercorn feta or plain feta.

6	cups torn green leaf lettuce
½	cup thinly sliced red onion (about 1 small)
¼	cup sliced ripe olives
2	ounces crumbled feta cheese with basil and tomato
1	teaspoon dried oregano
⅓	cup fat-free vinaigrette

1. Combine lettuce, onion, olives, cheese, and oregano in a large bowl; pour vinaigrette over salad, and toss gently. Serve immediately. Yield: 4 servings (serving size: 1½ cups).

CALORIES 67; FAT 4.1g (sat 2.1g); PROTEIN 3.3g; CARBOHYDRATE 4.9g; FIBER 1.3g; CHOLESTEROL 10mg; IRON 1.1mg; SODIUM 222mg; CALCIUM 45mg

▶ carbo rating: 4

Avocado-Cucumber Toss

This cool salad is a low-carb addition to Mexican food, and it's much healthier than refried beans covered in cheese.

4	teaspoons cider vinegar
1	tablespoon extravirgin olive oil
½	teaspoon salt
¼	teaspoon pepper
2	cups chopped cucumber
1	cup cherry tomatoes, quartered (about 12 tomatoes)
1	diced peeled avocado (about 1 cup)

1. Combine first 4 ingredients in a jar; cover tightly, and shake vigorously.
2. Place cucumber, tomato, and avocado in a bowl; add vinegar mixture, and toss gently to coat. Serve immediately. Yield: 4 servings (serving size: 1 cup).

CALORIES 129; FAT 11.3g (sat 1.7g); PROTEIN 1.8g; CARBOHYDRATE 7.9g; FIBER 3.5g; CHOLESTEROL 0mg; IRON 1mg; SODIUM 304mg; CALCIUM 17mg

▶ carbo rating: 4

Spinach Salad with Strawberries and Pecans

This poppy seed dressing has only 2 grams of carbohydrate per 2 tablespoons; the same amount of a commercial poppy seed dressing has 8 grams of carbohydrate. (See the chart on page 276 for other salad dressing comparisons.)

2	tablespoons "measures-like-sugar" calorie-free sweetener
3	tablespoons cider vinegar or white vinegar
3	tablespoons vegetable oil
½	small onion, coarsely chopped
1½	teaspoons Dijon mustard
½	teaspoon salt
¼	teaspoon pepper
1	teaspoon poppy seeds
1	(10-ounce) package fresh spinach, torn
1	cup halved strawberries
⅓	cup pecan halves, toasted

1. Combine first 7 ingredients in a blender; process until smooth, stopping once to scrape down sides. Stir in poppy seeds.
2. Combine spinach, strawberries, and pecans; drizzle with poppy seed dressing. Yield: 6 servings (serving size: 1 cup).

CALORIES 132; FAT 11.8g (sat 0.9g); PROTEIN 2.5g; CARBOHYDRATE 6.4g; FIBER 2.3g; CHOLESTEROL 0mg; IRON 1.7mg; SODIUM 265mg; CALCIUM 64mg

(pictured on page 235)

---

heart smart salad

The spinach salad above just might keep your heart healthy. Spinach is a top source of beta-carotene, which appears to reduce the risk of heart disease. Strawberries contain vitamin C, which also can help prevent heart disease. And pecans are packed with heart-healthy monounsaturated fat.

▶ carbo rating: 5

Tossed Salad with Buttermilk Dressing

This low-fat buttermilk dressing is lower in carbohydrate than most commercial low-fat salad dressings because in many of those low-fat dressings, sugar or other sweeteners are added to take the place of fat.

2	cups tightly packed torn romaine lettuce
2	cups tightly packed torn leaf lettuce
1¼	cups halved cherry tomatoes
½	cup sliced red onion
¼	cup chopped celery
½	cup low-fat buttermilk
1	tablespoon grated Parmesan cheese
6	tablespoons light mayonnaise
1	teaspoon dried parsley flakes
¼	teaspoon cracked black pepper
1	garlic clove, minced

1. Combine first 5 ingredients in a large bowl; toss well.
2. Combine buttermilk and next 5 ingredients in a small bowl; stir well. Spoon buttermilk dressing over salad; toss gently to coat. Serve immediately. Yield: 6 servings (serving size: ½ cup).

CALORIES 81; FAT 5.6g (sat 1g); PROTEIN 2g; CARBOHYDRATE 6.3g; FIBER 1.3g; CHOLESTEROL 7mg; IRON 0.6mg; SODIUM 164mg; CALCIUM 53mg

(pictured on page 236)

▶ **carbo rating: 5**

Chunky Asian Slaw

You'll find hoisin sauce in the Asian section of the supermarket. One tablespoon of hoisin sauce has 7 grams of carbohydrate, and you only need to use a small amount to get a big flavor boost.

4 cups coarsely shredded napa (Chinese) cabbage
1 cup sugar snap peas, trimmed and halved
⅓ cup thinly sliced red bell pepper
¼ cup diagonally sliced green onions (about 2)
2 tablespoons rice vinegar
1 tablespoon hoisin sauce
½ teaspoon dark sesame oil
2 tablespoons chopped unsalted peanuts

1. Combine first 4 ingredients in a large bowl.
2. Combine vinegar, hoisin sauce, and oil, stirring well. Pour vinegar mixture over cabbage mixture; toss well.
3. Serve immediately, or cover and chill. Sprinkle with peanuts just before serving. Yield: 5 servings (serving size: 1 cup).

CALORIES 53; FAT 2.4g (sat 0.3g); PROTEIN 2.3g; CARBOHYDRATE 6.6g; FIBER 1.6g; CHOLESTEROL 0mg; IRON 1.1mg; SODIUM 134mg; CALCIUM 58mg

make your own hoisin sauce

It's easy to make your own hoisin sauce with ingredients you probably already have on hand: Mix 3 tablespoons brown sugar, 3 tablespoons reduced-sodium soy sauce, and ¼ teaspoon garlic powder.

▶ **carbo rating: 5**

Caraway Coleslaw

Instead of shredding your own cabbage, buy a package of preshredded cabbage or coleslaw mix (without the dressing packet). A 10-ounce package of preshredded cabbage or coleslaw contains about 6 cups.

3 cups shredded cabbage
½ cup chopped green bell pepper
⅓ cup light mayonnaise
1 tablespoon white vinegar
½ teaspoon sugar
½ teaspoon caraway seeds
¼ teaspoon seasoned salt

1. Combine cabbage and bell pepper. Combine mayonnaise and next 4 ingredients, stirring well. Pour mayonnaise mixture over cabbage. Toss well. Cover and chill. Yield: 6 servings (serving size: ½ cup).

CALORIES 63; FAT 4.6g (sat 0.9g); PROTEIN 0.5g; CARBOHYDRATE 5.3g; FIBER 0.8g; CHOLESTEROL 4mg; IRON 0.3mg; SODIUM 171mg; CALCIUM 20mg

► carbo rating: 5

Crunchy Coleslaw

If you don't eat carrots, leave them out and add another ¾ cup of chopped red bell pepper. The carbo rating will be the same. (See the chart below for information about the carb content of honey Dijon mustard.)

3	cups packaged finely shredded green cabbage
¾	cup packaged preshredded carrot
½	cup chopped onion
¼	cup finely chopped red bell pepper
½	cup plain fat-free yogurt
1	tablespoon honey Dijon mustard
½	teaspoon salt
¼	teaspoon pepper

1. Combine first 4 ingredients in a medium bowl; toss well. Combine yogurt and next 3 ingredients; pour over cabbage mixture. Toss gently to coat. Cover and chill 1 hour. Stir just before serving. Yield: 6 servings (serving size: ½ cup).

CALORIES 34; FAT 0.3g (sat 0g); PROTEIN 1.8g; CARBOHYDRATE 6.6g; FIBER 1.4g; CHOLESTEROL 0mg; IRON 0.4mg; SODIUM 269mg; CALCIUM 59mg

---

carb content of mustards

Compare the carbohydrate content in 2 tablespoons of these different types of mustard.
- Yellow mustard, 1.2g
- Dijon mustard, 3.0g
- Stone-ground brown mustard, 3.4g
- Honey Dijon mustard, 7.1g

► carbo rating: 5

Tomatillo Salsa Salad

In addition to being a great salad, this tangy fresh salsa mixture is also great spooned over chicken or fish. Try it with Grilled Caribbean Chicken (page 244), Grilled Herbed Chicken (page 248), or Quick Seared Tuna Steaks (page 104).

2	cups chopped tomatillos (about 12)
⅓	cup chopped fresh cilantro
¼	cup chopped green onions
½	teaspoon salt
½	teaspoon ground cumin
2	(4½-ounce) cans sliced ripe olives, drained and chopped
1	red bell pepper, chopped
1	(15-ounce) can black beans, rinsed and drained

1. Combine first 7 ingredients in a medium bowl, stirring well. Add beans, and toss gently. Yield: 10 servings (serving size: ½ cup).

CALORIES 75; FAT 4.3g (sat 0g); PROTEIN 1.9g; CARBOHYDRATE 7.8g; FIBER 2.4g; CHOLESTEROL 0mg; IRON 0.8mg; SODIUM 326mg; CALCIUM 13mg

▶ carbo rating: 5

Green Bean Salad with Blue Cheese Dressing

Here's your salad and your side all in one dish. This blue cheese and green bean combo is delicious served with the Beef Tenderloin au Poivre on page 191.

¼ cup low-fat sour cream
2   tablespoons low-fat buttermilk
2   tablespoons crumbled blue cheese
1   tablespoon light mayonnaise
½   teaspoon fresh lemon juice
⅛   teaspoon salt
⅛   teaspoon pepper
2   cups trimmed and halved green beans (about 8 ounces)
⅓   cup finely chopped red onion
2   slices 40%-less-fat bacon (such as Gwaltney), cooked and crumbled

1. Combine first 7 ingredients in a small bowl; stir with a whisk.
2. Steam green beans, covered, 14 minutes or until crisp-tender. Rinse with cold water. Drain well, and pat dry with paper towels.
3. Combine beans and onion in a large bowl; add dressing, and stir gently. Sprinkle evenly with crumbled bacon. Yield: 4 servings (serving size: ½ cup).

CALORIES 89; FAT 5.2g (sat 2.5g); PROTEIN 4.3g; CARBOHYDRATE 7g;
FIBER 2.2g; CHOLESTEROL 15mg; IRON 0.7mg; SODIUM 256mg; CALCIUM 79mg

▶ carbo rating: 6

Minted Cucumber Salad

This cool, crisp salad is a low-carb variation of a traditional, high-sugar, marinated cucumber salad. Some traditional marinated cucumber salads have as much as ¾ cup sugar. We used a calorie-free sweetener and reduced the amount to 2 teaspoons. The fresh mint also contributes a bit of a sweet sensation.

½   cup vanilla low-fat yogurt
3   tablespoons chopped fresh mint
2   tablespoons white wine vinegar
2   teaspoons "measures-like-sugar" calorie-free sweetener
Dash of hot sauce
3   cucumbers, peeled and thinly sliced
1   small red onion, sliced and separated into rings
Boston lettuce leaves (optional)

1. Combine first 5 ingredients in a small bowl; stir well with a whisk.
2. Place cucumber and onion slices in a shallow dish. Spoon yogurt mixture over vegetables. Cover and chill at least 30 minutes. Serve over lettuce leaves, if desired. Yield: 6 servings (serving size: 1 cup).

CALORIES 39; FAT 0.4g (sat 0.2g); PROTEIN 1.9g; CARBOHYDRATE 7.5g;
FIBER 1.4g; CHOLESTEROL 1mg; IRON 0.7mg; SODIUM 18mg; CALCIUM 51mg

▶ carbo rating: 7

Gazpacho Salad

Gazpacho—a chilled soup of pureed tomatoes, bell peppers, and onions—traditionally has breadcrumbs in the mixture. This quick and easy salad version of gazpacho has the vegetables, but not the bread.

1   cup thinly sliced peeled cucumber (about 1 medium)
¾   cup chopped yellow bell pepper (about 1 small)
3   tablespoons Italian dressing
3   ripe tomatoes, cut into wedges
2   garlic cloves, crushed

1. Combine all ingredients in a medium bowl, stirring well. Serve immediately, or cover and chill up to 8 hours. Yield: 4 servings (serving size: about 1 cup).

CALORIES 85; FAT 5.8g (sat 0.8g); PROTEIN 1.4g; CARBOHYDRATE 8.5g; FIBER 1.5g; CHOLESTEROL 0mg; IRON 0.6mg; SODIUM 97mg; CALCIUM 16mg

crushing garlic

If you don't have a garlic press to crush the garlic, place the flat edge of a large knife over unpeeled cloves, and press firmly. Remove the papery skin, and crush again. When you crush garlic, rather than slice or mince it, you release much more of its aromatic oils.

high flavor cheese

A great way to add a lot of low-carb flavor to a recipe without adding a lot of fat is to use a small amount of a high-flavored cheese such as blue cheese, feta, goat cheese, gorganzola, or Parmesan. You don't need much for a flavor punch.

▶ carbo rating: 7

Broccoli-and-Cauliflower Salad with Blue Cheese Dressing

Make this salad two to three hours ahead and refrigerate to intensify the flavors.

1   (16-ounce) package fresh broccoli and cauliflower florets
3   tablespoons low-fat mayonnaise
3   tablespoons low-fat buttermilk
2   tablespoons finely diced red onion
2   tablespoons crumbled blue cheese
¼   teaspoon salt
⅛   teaspoon freshly ground black pepper
1   tablespoon finely chopped fresh parsley

1. Steam broccoli and cauliflower, covered, 3 to 4 minutes or until crisp-tender. Rinse under cold water, and drain well. Set aside.
2. Combine mayonnaise, buttermilk, onion, blue cheese, salt, and pepper in a small bowl.
3. Combine broccoli and cauliflower with dressing in a large bowl. Sprinkle with parsley; stir well. Yield: 4 servings (serving size: 1 cup).

CALORIES 69; FAT 2.2g (sat 0.8g); PROTEIN 4.1g; CARBOHYDRATE 10.2g; FIBER 3.3g; CHOLESTEROL 3mg; IRON 0.8mg; SODIUM 345mg; CALCIUM 74mg

▶ carbo rating: 7

Mixed Greens with Parmesan Walnuts

While you're toasting the nuts, go ahead and toast extra and keep them on hand for snacks. (See page 384 for information on toasting nuts.)

¾   cup walnut pieces
Butter-flavored cooking spray
  2   tablespoons grated Parmesan cheese
  2   cups loosely packed torn iceberg lettuce
  2   cups loosely packed torn leaf lettuce
  2   cups loosely packed torn curly endive
  2   cups loosely packed torn fresh spinach
  ⅓   cup fat-free balsamic vinaigrette

1. Preheat oven to 350°.
2. Place walnuts in an 8-inch square baking pan. Coat walnuts with cooking spray. Bake at 350° for 5 minutes. Sprinkle with cheese, tossing to coat. Bake an additional 4 to 5 minutes or until cheese is lightly browned. Cool completely.
3. Combine iceberg lettuce and next 3 ingredients; toss. Drizzle with vinaigrette, and toss gently to coat. Top with walnuts. Yield: 4 servings (serving size: 2 cups).

CALORIES 191; FAT 15.8g (sat 1.9g); PROTEIN 5.9g; CARBOHYDRATE 9.6g;
FIBER 2.8g; CHOLESTEROL 2mg; IRON 2.1mg; SODIUM 321mg; CALCIUM 94mg

▶ carbo rating: 7

Carrot-Cabbage Coleslaw

You can leave out the carrot and add another ¾ cup of shredded cabbage if your low-carb plan does not allow carrots. The carbo rating will be the same. (See page 221 for information on including carrots in a low-carb diet.)

1¼   cups shredded cabbage
  ¾   cup shredded carrot
  ¼   cup grated Red Delicious apple
  ¼   cup crushed pineapple in juice, drained
  ¼   cup light mayonnaise
  1   tablespoon lemon juice
Cabbage leaves (optional)

1. Combine first 6 ingredients in a medium bowl; toss well. Cover and chill thoroughly.
2. Spoon coleslaw into a cabbage-lined bowl before serving, if desired. Yield: 4 servings (serving size: ½ cup).

CALORIES 76; FAT 5g (sat 0.8g); PROTEIN 0.8g; CARBOHYDRATE 7.6g;
FIBER 1.1g; CHOLESTEROL 5mg; IRON 0.3mg; SODIUM 138mg; CALCIUM 21mg

bags vs. heads

Prewashed, bagged salad greens are widely available in supermarkets, and we think they're fine to use when convenience and speed are crucial. However, we prefer to use fresh heads of greens whenever possible because the heads seem to stay crisp longer.

If you're buying bagged greens, check the expiration date stamped on the package, and buy the freshest greens possible. Once the bag is opened, store the greens in a salad crisper or other airtight container in the refrigerator instead of the original plastic package because moisture will collect in the plastic bag and cause the greens to become limp and soggy.

▶ carbo rating: 7

Sweet Yellow Peppers and Tomatoes with Feta Cheese

Because they are just a more mature stage of green bell peppers, yellow bell peppers are sweeter than the green ones.

3	tablespoons red wine vinegar
1	tablespoon water
1½	teaspoons olive oil
¾	teaspoon dried oregano
½	teaspoon Dijon mustard
⅛	teaspoon salt
1	garlic clove, minced
¾	cup thinly sliced red onion
6	plum tomatoes, cut lengthwise into ⅛-inch-thick slices
2	yellow bell peppers, cut into ⅛-inch-thick rings
¼	cup (1 ounce) crumbled feta cheese

Freshly ground black pepper

1. Combine first 7 ingredients in a small bowl, stirring well with a whisk.

2. Combine 1 tablespoon vinegar mixture and onion in a small bowl, tossing well.

3. Spoon onion mixture evenly onto a serving platter. Arrange tomato around edge of platter; place pepper rings in center of platter on top of onion. Drizzle remaining vinegar mixture over vegetables. Top with cheese; sprinkle with black pepper. Yield: 6 servings (serving size: 2 tablespoons onion mixture, 1 tomato, ⅓ bell pepper, and 2 teaspoons cheese).

CALORIES 69; FAT 3.2g (sat 1.3g); PROTEIN 2.4g; CARBOHYDRATE 9.1g; FIBER 2.2g; CHOLESTEROL 6mg; IRON 1.2mg; SODIUM 147mg; CALCIUM 49mg

▶ carbo rating: 8

Greek Salad Bowl

If your cucumber is large, slice it in half lengthwise, remove the seeds, if desired, and then cut crosswise into thin slices.

1	(14-ounce) can quartered artichoke hearts, drained
1	cup sliced cucumber
⅓	cup crumbled feta cheese
12	kalamata olives, pitted
1	large tomato, cut into thin wedges
⅓	cup fresh lemon juice
1	tablespoon olive oil
½	teaspoon dried oregano
½	teaspoon lemon pepper seasoning
1	garlic clove, crushed

Freshly ground black pepper

1. Combine first 5 ingredients in a large bowl. Combine lemon juice and next 4 ingredients in a small bowl; stir with a whisk until blended. Pour over vegetable mixture; toss to coat. Sprinkle with pepper. Yield: 6 servings (serving size: ¾ cup).

CALORIES 97; FAT 5.9g (sat 1.3g); PROTEIN 3.1g; CARBOHYDRATE 10.2g; FIBER 2g; CHOLESTEROL 6mg; IRON 1.1mg; SODIUM 236mg; CALCIUM 63mg

(pictured on page 237)

► carbo rating: 8

Marinated Three-Tomato Salad

Fresh herbs and white wine vinegar (both with practically zero carbs) flavor this colorful salad. Yellow cherry tomatoes are seasonal, so if you can't find them at your supermarket, add 2 additional cups of red cherry tomatoes.

2	cups halved red cherry tomatoes
2	cups halved yellow cherry tomatoes
½	cup chopped cucumber
½	cup chopped red onion
¼	cup white wine vinegar
1	tablespoon dried tomato sprinkles
1	tablespoon minced fresh basil
1	tablespoon minced fresh oregano
1	tablespoon olive oil
¼	teaspoon salt
¼	teaspoon pepper
1	garlic clove, minced
2	cups shredded romaine lettuce

1. Combine red and yellow tomatoes, cucumber, and onion in a large bowl.

2. Combine vinegar and next 7 ingredients in a small bowl; stir with a whisk until combined. Pour over tomato mixture, stirring gently to coat. Cover and chill 1 hour.

3. Divide shredded lettuce among 4 salad plates; spoon tomato mixture over lettuce. Yield: 4 servings (serving size: ½ cup lettuce and 1 cup tomato mixture).

CALORIES 81; FAT 4g (sat 0.6g); PROTEIN 2.4g; CARBOHYDRATE 10.9g; FIBER 2.8g; CHOLESTEROL 0mg; IRON 1.4mg; SODIUM 200mg; CALCIUM 31mg

(pictured on page 238)

► carbo rating: 8

Chicken Salad

This chunky chicken salad is good over greens or in a sandwich with whole-grain bread.

3	cups chopped cooked chicken breast
1	cup thinly sliced celery
2	tablespoons lemon juice
1	tablespoon minced onion
½	cup light mayonnaise
½	teaspoon pepper
¼	teaspoon salt
½	cup seedless green grapes, halved lengthwise
½	cup seedless red grapes, halved lengthwise
1	(2-ounce) package sliced almonds, toasted

Bibb lettuce (optional)

1. Combine first 4 ingredients; cover and chill at least 1 hour.

2. Combine mayonnaise, pepper, and salt. Add mayonnaise mixture, grapes, and almonds to chilled chicken mixture; toss gently. Serve chicken salad on lettuce leaves, if desired. Yield: 6 servings (serving size: 1 cup).

CALORIES 254; FAT 13.7g (sat 2g); PROTEIN 22.8g; CARBOHYDRATE 9.7g; FIBER 1.7g; CHOLESTEROL 61mg; IRON 1mg; SODIUM 319mg; CALCIUM 51mg

(pictured on page 239)

chicken choices for salads

A salad such as the one above is a great use of leftover chicken. You'll need about a pound of cooked chicken (meat only) to get 3 cups of chopped. But if you don't have leftover chicken, here are some other options.

• Frozen cooked diced chicken
• Refrigerated grilled chicken strips
• Deli-roasted chicken (remove skin; use white meat)

▶ carbo rating: 9

Layered Vegetable Salad

For bacon in a flash, cook it in the microwave. Place bacon slices on a microwave-safe plate or bacon rack, cover with paper towels, and microwave at HIGH about 1 minute per slice until crisp.

    4   cups torn iceberg lettuce
    1   cup chopped celery
    1   (10-ounce) package frozen green peas, thawed
    1   cup chopped red onion
    1   cup chopped green bell pepper
    ¾   cup light mayonnaise
    ¾   cup reduced-fat sour cream
    3   bacon slices, cooked and crumbled
    ½   cup (2 ounces) shredded reduced-fat Cheddar
        cheese

1. Layer lettuce, celery, peas, onion, and green bell pepper in a 2-quart bowl.
2. Combine mayonnaise and sour cream, stirring well. Spread mixture over top of salad. Sprinkle bacon around edges of mayonnaise mixture, and sprinkle cheese in center. Cover and chill. Toss before serving. Yield: 8 servings (serving size: 1 cup).

CALORIES 185; FAT 12.8g (sat 4.2g); PROTEIN 6g; CARBOHYDRATE 11.8g; FIBER 2.4g; CHOLESTEROL 24mg; IRON 0.8mg; SODIUM 359mg; CALCIUM 94mg

▶ carbo rating: 10

Mozzarella-Tomato Salad

This simple salad is best in the summer when juicy, fresh-from-the-garden tomatoes are available. When selecting tomatoes, look for those that are firm and well-shaped, and have brightly colored skin. They should be heavy for their size and blemish-free.

     2   large red tomatoes, each cut into 4 slices
     2   large yellow tomatoes, each cut into 4 slices
     6   (1-ounce) slices part-skim mozzarella cheese,
         each cut in half
    12   large basil leaves
     3   tablespoons fat-free balsamic vinaigrette
     1   teaspoon freshly ground black pepper

1. Stack 4 tomato slices, 3 cheese slices, and 3 basil leaves in each of 4 stacks, alternating tomato, cheese, and basil.
2. Drizzle stacks evenly with vinaigrette. Cover and chill. Sprinkle with pepper before serving. Yield: 4 servings (serving size: 1 tomato stack and about ¾ tablespoon vinaigrette).

CALORIES 165; FAT 7.9g (sat 4.7g); PROTEIN 14g; CARBOHYDRATE 11.4g; FIBER 1.9g; CHOLESTEROL 23mg; IRON 0.7mg; SODIUM 407mg; CALCIUM 333mg

(pictured on page 240)

▶ **carbo rating: 10**
Roasted Vegetable Salad

Make sure the vegetables have enough room on the jelly roll pan and are arranged in a single layer when roasting. If they're piled up on the pan, all of the pieces won't get cooked completely. (See page 295 for more information on roasting vegetables.)

2	small yellow squash, cut into 1-inch pieces (about 2½ cups)
1	green bell pepper, cut into ¼-inch strips
½	onion, cut into 6 wedges and separated
2	teaspoons extravirgin olive oil, divided

Cooking spray

1	cup halved grape tomatoes
16	pitted kalamata olives, chopped
1	tablespoon balsamic vinegar
1	tablespoon chopped fresh basil
1½	teaspoons chopped fresh oregano
¼	teaspoon salt
¼	teaspoon freshly ground black pepper

1. Preheat oven to 450°.
2. Combine first 3 ingredients on a large jelly roll pan. Drizzle with 1 teaspoon oil; toss well. Coat squash mixture with cooking spray; arrange in a single layer. Bake at 450° for 15 minutes. Add tomatoes; turn vegetables with a spatula. Bake 5 minutes or until lightly browned. Remove from oven; cool on a wire rack 10 minutes.
3. Combine squash mixture, 1 teaspoon oil, olives, and remaining 5 ingredients in a bowl; toss gently. Serve immediately. Yield: 4 servings (serving size: ¾ cup).

CALORIES 116; FAT 6.8g (sat 0.9g); PROTEIN 2.5g; CARBOHYDRATE 13.3g; FIBER 3.5g; CHOLESTEROL 0mg; IRON 0.9mg; SODIUM 397mg; CALCIUM 40mg

(pictured on page 305)

▶ **carbo rating: 10**
Chicken Salad with Asparagus

Instead of adding fruit to the chicken salad, we stirred in asparagus pieces, radishes, tomatoes, and green onions to reduce the carbs.

⅓	cup low-fat mayonnaise
3	tablespoons plain fat-free yogurt
1	teaspoon curry powder
1	teaspoon lemon juice
¼	teaspoon salt
⅛	teaspoon pepper
2½	cups (2-inch) sliced asparagus (about 1¾ pounds)
½	teaspoon salt
2	cups shredded cooked chicken breast
¼	cup thinly sliced radishes
2	tablespoons thinly sliced green onions
2	tablespoons finely chopped fresh cilantro

Boston lettuce leaves

12	cherry tomatoes, halved

1. Combine first 6 ingredients in a small bowl; set aside.
2. Boil asparagus in water and ½ teaspoon salt 2 minutes or until crisp-tender; drain. Plunge into ice water; drain.
3. Combine asparagus, chicken, radishes, onions, and mayonnaise mixture in a large bowl. Sprinkle with cilantro, and toss gently. Cover and chill.
4. Serve over lettuce leaves, and top each serving with 6 tomato halves. Yield: 4 servings (serving size: 1¼ cups).

CALORIES 161; FAT 3.8g (sat 0.7g); PROTEIN 20.1g; CARBOHYDRATE 12g; FIBER 1.9g; CHOLESTEROL 48mg; IRON 1.4mg; SODIUM 685mg; CALCIUM 43mg

(pictured on page 306)

► carbo rating: 10

Warm Blue Cheese and Pear Salad

Blue cheese and pear always make a pleasing flavor combination.

- ¼ cup water
- 1 tablespoon sugar
- 1 tablespoon red wine vinegar
- ½ teaspoon beef-flavored bouillon granules
- 2 cups finely shredded red cabbage
- 1 cup chopped peeled pear (about ½ pound)
- 4 teaspoons crumbled blue cheese

1. Combine water, sugar, vinegar, and bouillon granules in a large skillet over high heat. Cover, reduce heat, and simmer 1 minute. Add cabbage to pan, and cook 2 minutes, stirring frequently.
2. Add chopped pear, and sauté 2 minutes or until pear is crisp-tender; remove from heat. Sprinkle salad with crumbled blue cheese, and serve immediately. Yield: 4 servings (serving size: ½ cup).

CALORIES 58; FAT 1.3g (sat 0.7g); PROTEIN 1.3g; CARBOHYDRATE 11.1g; FIBER 1.6g; CHOLESTEROL 3mg; IRON 0.3mg; SODIUM 172mg; CALCIUM 39mg

► carbo rating: 10

Turkey Club Salad

This hearty salad is simply a club sandwich without the bread. You can substitute any creamy dressing, such as Thousand Island or ranch, for the blue cheese dressing.

- 8 cups thinly sliced romaine lettuce
- 8 ounces smoked turkey, cut into thin strips
- 1 cup halved cherry tomatoes
- 2 bacon slices, cooked and crumbled
- ½ cup reduced-fat blue cheese dressing

1. Combine first 4 ingredients in a large bowl; add dressing, and toss well. Yield: 4 servings (serving size: about 2½ cups).

CALORIES 198; FAT 10.1g (sat 2g); PROTEIN 14g; CARBOHYDRATE 12.8g; FIBER 3.3g; CHOLESTEROL 37mg; IRON 1.9mg; SODIUM 833mg; CALCIUM 89mg

► carbo rating: 11

Mixed Antipasto Salad

*An **antipasto** ("before the meal") appetizer usually has cold cuts, smoked meats, cheese, olives, and marinated vegetables. This salad version is served over romaine lettuce. Look for convenient 16-ounce packages of torn romaine lettuce in the produce section of your local supermarket.*

- 4 cups torn romaine lettuce
- 1½ cups sliced mushrooms
- ⅓ cup sliced red onion
- ¼ cup sliced ripe olives
- 2 ounces part-skim mozzarella cheese, cut into cubes
- 1 (14-ounce) can artichoke hearts, drained and quartered
- 1 (7-ounce) jar roasted red bell peppers, drained and coarsely chopped
- ¼ cup fat-free Italian herb and cheese dressing
- ¼ teaspoon coarsely ground black pepper

1. Combine first 7 ingredients in a large bowl. Add dressing; toss well. Sprinkle evenly with pepper. Yield: 5 servings (serving size: 1½ cups).

CALORIES 93; FAT 2.8g (sat 1.3g); PROTEIN 5.9g; CARBOHYDRATE 12.9g; FIBER 1.5g; CHOLESTEROL 7mg; IRON 1.7mg; SODIUM 510mg; CALCIUM 118mg

(pictured on page 307)

▶ **carbo rating: 11**

Citrus-Salmon Salad

Not only does this salad taste great, it's good for your heart because of the antioxidants in the citrus fruit and spinach, and the omega-3 fats in the salmon.

2	navel oranges
2	pink grapefruit
1	tablespoon olive oil
1	tablespoon Dijon mustard
1	teaspoon honey
¼	teaspoon salt
¼	teaspoon pepper
2	tablespoons Jamaican jerk seasoning
1	(1½-pound) skinless salmon fillet

Cooking spray

5	cups torn spinach
½	cup thinly sliced red onion
2	tablespoons sunflower seeds

1. Grate ½ teaspoon rind from orange; set rind aside.
2. Peel oranges and grapefruit. Cut out citrus sections over a bowl, reserving juice. Set citrus sections aside. Squeeze membranes over bowl to extract additional juice. Discard membranes.
3. Combine 6 tablespoons citrus juice, grated rind, olive oil, and next 4 ingredients in a small bowl; stir well with a whisk. Cover dressing, and chill. Reserve remaining citrus juice for another use.
4. Preheat broiler.
5. Rub jerk seasoning over fish. Place fish on a broiler pan coated with cooking spray. Broil 14 minutes or until fish flakes easily when tested with a fork. Flake into bite-sized pieces; cover and chill 30 minutes.
6. Combine citrus sections, spinach, and onion. Drizzle dressing over salad; toss gently to coat. Divide salad evenly among 5 plates; top each salad evenly with fish, and sprinkle with sunflower seeds. Yield: 5 servings (serving size: 2 cups salad, 4 ounces salmon, and 1 teaspoon seeds).

CALORIES 333; FAT 16g (sat 2.6g); PROTEIN 31g; CARBOHYDRATE 15.7g; FIBER 5.1g; CHOLESTEROL 89mg; IRON 3mg; SODIUM 797mg; CALCIUM 105mg

(pictured on page 308)

▶ **carbo rating: 12**

Grilled Chicken and Raspberry Salad

Italian salad mix is a combination of romaine lettuce and radicchio. One 10-ounce bag contains about 6 cups of greens.

¼	cup balsamic vinegar
3	tablespoons raspberry fruit spread
4	(4-ounce) skinless, boneless chicken breast halves

Cooking spray

1	(10-ounce) package ready-to-eat Italian salad mix
1	cup raspberries

Freshly ground black pepper

1. Prepare grill.
2. Combine vinegar and fruit spread in a small bowl, stirring with a whisk until smooth. Reserve 3 tablespoons vinegar mixture. Brush remaining ¼ cup vinegar mixture evenly over chicken breast halves. Place chicken on grill rack coated with cooking spray; grill, covered, 5 minutes on each side or until chicken is done. Set chicken aside.
3. Place salad mix in a large bowl; pour reserved 3 tablespoons vinegar mixture over lettuce, and toss well. Arrange lettuce mixture evenly on each of 4 individual serving plates.
4. Cut chicken crosswise into thin strips; arrange chicken strips evenly on lettuce mixture. Top evenly with raspberries. Sprinkle with pepper. Yield: 4 servings (serving size: 1½ cups lettuce, 3 ounces chicken, and ¼ cup raspberries).

CALORIES 190; FAT 1.8g (sat 0.4g); PROTEIN 27.7g; CARBOHYDRATE 15.1g; FIBER 3.3g; CHOLESTEROL 66mg; IRON 1.9mg; SODIUM 83mg; CALCIUM 50mg

(pictured on page 309)

▶ carbo rating: 12
Yogurt-Topped Fruit Salad

The sweetness in this creamy dressing is from the vanilla yogurt. Be sure to look for a brand of yogurt that does not have added sugar.

1½	cups sliced strawberries
2	small bananas, peeled and sliced
1	orange, peeled and sectioned
6	green leaf lettuce leaves
¼	cup vanilla low-fat yogurt sweetened with aspartame
1	tablespoon creamy peanut butter
1	tablespoon chopped salted, roasted peanuts

1. Combine first 3 ingredients in a bowl; toss gently. Spoon ½ cup fruit mixture onto each of 6 lettuce-lined salad plates.
2. Combine yogurt and peanut butter, stirring well. Spoon yogurt mixture evenly over fruit. Sprinkle evenly with peanuts. Yield: 6 servings (serving size: ½ cup).

CALORIES 89; FAT 3g (sat 0.6g); PROTEIN 2.6g; CARBOHYDRATE 14.8g; FIBER 3g; CHOLESTEROL 0mg; IRON 0.6mg; SODIUM 40mg; CALCIUM 38mg

▶ carbo rating: 13
Waldorf Salad

Red grapes contain an antioxidant called resveratrol that may help lower cholesterol and reduce the risk of heart disease. Red wine contains resveratrol, too.

1½	cups coarsely chopped apple (about 1 medium)
1	cup coarsely chopped pear (about 1 medium)
1	cup seedless red grapes
½	cup thinly sliced celery
⅓	cup vanilla fat-free yogurt
1	tablespoon apple juice
¼	teaspoon ground ginger

1. Combine first 4 ingredients in a bowl. Combine yogurt, apple juice, and ginger; pour over apple mixture, tossing to coat. Yield: 6 servings (serving size: ⅔ cup).

CALORIES 63; FAT 0.5g (sat 0.2g); PROTEIN 1g; CARBOHYDRATE 15.2g; FIBER 1.8g; CHOLESTEROL 1mg; IRON 0.2mg; SODIUM 15mg; CALCIUM 29mg

▶ carbo rating: 13
Spicy Chicken Finger Salad

These oven-fried chicken fingers have a crispy coating of whole wheat cereal flakes instead of corn flakes or a flour mixture. You'll need ⅔ cup cereal flakes to get ⅓ cup of crushed. Place cereal flakes in a zip-top plastic bag and crush with a rolling pin.

⅓	cup crushed whole wheat cereal flakes (such as Total)
2	teaspoons chili powder
½	teaspoon garlic powder
1	pound chicken breast tenderloins
Cooking spray	
6	cups torn romaine lettuce
1	cup sliced celery
1	cup grape tomatoes
½	cup sliced red onion
½	cup reduced-fat olive oil vinaigrette
¼	cup crumbled blue cheese

1. Preheat oven to 375°.
2. Combine first 3 ingredients in a heavy-duty zip-top plastic bag; add chicken. Seal bag, and shake until chicken is well coated. Place chicken on a baking sheet coated with cooking spray. Bake at 375° for 15 minutes or until chicken is done.
3. Combine lettuce, celery, tomatoes, and onion. Pour vinaigrette over lettuce mixture, and toss well.
4. Place lettuce mixture evenly on 4 individual serving plates. Arrange chicken evenly over salads; sprinkle each serving with 1 tablespoon cheese. Yield: 4 servings (serving size: about 2 cups lettuce mixture, 3 ounces chicken, and 1 tablespoon cheese).

CALORIES 276; FAT 10.6g (sat 2.6g); PROTEIN 30.5g; CARBOHYDRATE 16.5g; FIBER 3.9g; CHOLESTEROL 72mg; IRON 6.2mg; SODIUM 521mg; CALCIUM 328mg

(pictured on page 310)

► carbo rating: 13

Grecian Pork Tenderloin Salad

This succulent pork tenderloin also stands alone as an easy five-ingredient entrée. Follow steps 1, 3, and 4, and use the first five ingredients.

1½ tablespoons red wine vinegar
1½ teaspoons olive oil
 1 teaspoon chopped fresh oregano
 1 garlic clove, crushed
 1 pound pork tenderloin, trimmed
1½ cups sliced peeled cucumber, divided
 1 tablespoon chopped fresh dill
 1 (8-ounce) carton plain fat-free yogurt
Cooking spray
 4 cups tightly packed torn romaine lettuce
 ½ cup thinly sliced onion, separated into rings
 ½ cup thinly sliced radishes
 2 tablespoons crumbled feta cheese
 2 teaspoons chopped fresh mint
 2 tomatoes, each cut into 8 wedges
 1 green bell pepper, cut crosswise into 12 rings
 8 pitted ripe olives

1. Combine first 4 ingredients in a large heavy-duty zip-top plastic bag; add pork, turning to coat. Seal bag, and marinate in refrigerator 30 minutes, turning bag occasionally.
2. Place ½ cup cucumber, dill, and yogurt in a food processor; process 10 seconds or until smooth, scraping sides of processor bowl once. Set aside.
3. Prepare grill.
4. Remove pork from bag, discarding marinade. Place on a grill rack coated with cooking spray. Cover and grill 25 minutes or until a meat thermometer registers 155°, turning pork occasionally. Remove pork from grill; let stand 10 minutes or until thermometer registers 160°. Cut pork into thin slices.
5. Divide lettuce among 4 plates; top evenly with remaining cucumber, onion, and next 6 ingredients. Divide pork evenly among plates; top each with 6 tablespoons yogurt dressing. Yield: 4 servings.

CALORIES 256; FAT 8g (sat 2.3g); PROTEIN 30.6g; CARBOHYDRATE 16g; FIBER 3.3g; CHOLESTEROL 82mg; IRON 3.4mg; SODIUM 197mg; CALCIUM 186mg

► carbo rating: 13

Roasted Winter Vegetable Salad

Applying high heat to vegetables locks in their natural flavors while caramelizing the outer layers. With little effort and no added sugar, vegetables become beautifully glazed side dishes. (See page 291 for more information on roasting vegetables.)

 ½ cup fat-free Italian dressing, divided
 1 teaspoon dried rosemary
3½ teaspoons olive oil, divided
 ¾ teaspoon salt, divided
 ¼ teaspoon ground red pepper
 7 cups cubed peeled acorn squash (about 2½ pounds)
 4 cups chopped fennel bulb (about 4 small bulbs)
 2 onions, cut into ½-inch-thick wedges
Cooking spray
 12 cups mixed baby salad greens
 2 tablespoons balsamic vinegar

1. Preheat oven to 450°.
2. Combine ¼ cup dressing, rosemary, 2 teaspoons olive oil, ½ teaspoon salt, and ground red pepper, stirring well with a whisk. Combine acorn squash, fennel, and onion in a large bowl. Add dressing mixture, tossing to coat. Spread vegetable mixture evenly in a roasting pan coated with cooking spray. Roast at 450° for 45 minutes or until vegetables are tender, stirring occasionally. Set aside.
3. Place salad greens in a bowl. Add ¼ cup salad dressing, 1½ teaspoons olive oil, ¼ teaspoon salt, and balsamic vinegar; toss well. Add roasted vegetable mixture, tossing gently. Yield: 12 servings (serving size: 1 cup).

CALORIES 77; FAT 1.7g (sat 0.2g); PROTEIN 2.5g; CARBOHYDRATE 14.8g; FIBER 2g; CHOLESTEROL 0mg; IRON 1.6mg; SODIUM 299mg; CALCIUM 103mg

When it comes to selecting olive oil, there are a lot of choices in the markets, and sometimes it's hard to know whether to opt for the 3-liter tin or the boutique bottle. Perhaps you often choose something in between: You don't buy the cheapest or the most expensive. Instead, you settle for a mid-priced oil and then use it for everything. But that strategy may actually be giving you the least taste for your money.

Olive oil is used for two very different purposes: as a fat for cooking and as a condiment to add flavor to a dish. If you use the same mid-range oil for both purposes, you're paying too much for cooking oil and aren't getting enough flavor as a condiment. When you heat olive oil, it loses much of its taste, so it's a waste to use extravirgin olive oil that way. Besides, "pure" oil, a less expensive grade, is actually better to cook with because it's refined, with no olive particles at the bottom of the bottle that can burn at high heat.

But when you're using olive oil for its flavor—when tossing it with roasted vegetables or adding it to pasta, for example—a higher-priced extravirgin oil will usually produce a much better result than a mid-priced one.

▶ carbo rating: 13

Lemon-Dill White Bean Salad

Beans are a terrific source of folate, the nutrient that helps prevent certain birth defects. It also lowers homocysteine levels (high levels are linked to heart disease and heart attack).

1   (16-ounce) can navy beans, rinsed and drained
½   cup chopped green onions
2   tablespoons chopped fresh dill
1   tablespoon extravirgin olive oil
1   tablespoon lemon juice
½   teaspoon salt
8   slices tomato (about 1 large)
1   lemon, quartered (optional)

1. Combine first 6 ingredients in a medium bowl, tossing gently.
2. Place 2 tomato slices on each of 4 individual salad plates; top each with ½ cup bean mixture. Serve with a lemon wedge, if desired. Yield: 4 servings (serving size: 2 tomato slices and ½ cup bean mixture).

CALORIES 122; FAT 3.9g (sat 0.6g); PROTEIN 5.7g; CARBOHYDRATE 17.4g; FIBER 4g; CHOLESTEROL 0mg; IRON 1.7mg; SODIUM 541mg; CALCIUM 43mg

(pictured on page 311)

▶ **carbo rating: 13**

Smoked Turkey Mango Salad

Mangoes are ripe and sweet when they're as soft as a ripe banana. If you can't find fresh mango, you can use a jar of refrigerated mango slices. Measure out 1 cup and save the rest for another use. The grapefruit-vinegar dressing provides a delicious flavor contrast to the sweet fruit.

6	ounces smoked turkey breast, cut into thin strips
4	cups thinly sliced savoy cabbage
1	cup finely chopped mango (about 1 large)
½	cup chopped fresh cilantro
½	red onion, slivered
3	tablespoons grapefruit juice
2	tablespoons cider vinegar
1	tablespoon olive oil
½	teaspoon pepper
¼	teaspoon salt

1. Combine first 5 ingredients in a large bowl.
2. Combine grapefruit juice and next 4 ingredients in a small jar; cover tightly, and shake vigorously. Pour dressing over salad, and toss gently. Serve immediately. Yield: 4 servings (serving size: 1½ cups).

CALORIES 135; FAT 4.6g (sat 1.1g); PROTEIN 11.5g; CARBOHYDRATE 14.2g; FIBER 1.7g; CHOLESTEROL 24mg; IRON 1.1mg; SODIUM 491mg; CALCIUM 36mg

(pictured on page 312)

▶ **carbo rating: 14**

Greek Spinach Salad

Try a flavored feta cheese like tomato-basil or black peppercorn for variety.

¼	cup red wine vinegar
1	tablespoon water
2	teaspoons olive oil
½	teaspoon dried oregano
1	or 2 garlic cloves, minced
1	(15-ounce) can chickpeas (garbanzo beans), rinsed and drained
1½	cups sliced cucumber (about 1 medium)
1½	cups chopped plum tomato (about 5)
5	cups loosely packed torn spinach
⅓	cup crumbled feta cheese

Freshly ground black pepper (optional)

1. Combine first 5 ingredients, stirring well with a whisk. Combine chickpeas, cucumber, and tomato in a large bowl; add vinegar mixture, tossing well.
2. Add spinach and feta cheese; toss salad gently. Sprinkle salad with pepper, if desired. Yield: 6 servings (serving size: 1½ cups).

CALORIES 126; FAT 4.2g (sat 1.3g); PROTEIN 6.3g; CARBOHYDRATE 17.2g; FIBER 3.4g; CHOLESTEROL 5mg; IRON 2.3mg; SODIUM 186mg; CALCIUM 86mg

▶ carbo rating: 17

Tabbouleh with Feta

Feta cheese gives this classic Middle Eastern salad a tangy twist.

¾	cup uncooked bulgur
1¼	cups boiling water
¼	teaspoon salt
1½	cups chopped English cucumber
1	cup chopped plum tomato
1	cup finely chopped fresh parsley
½	cup finely chopped fresh mint
⅓	cup (1.3 ounces) crumbled feta cheese
¼	cup minced red onion
2	garlic cloves, minced
3	tablespoons fresh lemon juice
1½	tablespoons extravirgin olive oil
¼	teaspoon freshly ground black pepper

1. Combine first 3 ingredients in a large bowl. Cover and let stand 30 minutes or until water is absorbed. Add cucumber and next 6 ingredients; toss gently.
2. Combine lemon juice, olive oil, and pepper in a small bowl; stir well with a whisk. Pour dressing over salad; toss gently to coat. Cover and chill at least 8 hours. Yield: 5 servings (serving size: 1 cup).

CALORIES 160; FAT 6.7g (sat 2g); PROTEIN 5.2g; CARBOHYDRATE 22.5g; FIBER 5.8g; CHOLESTEROL 8mg; IRON 2.7mg; SODIUM 231mg; CALCIUM 96mg

▶ carbo rating: 17

Green Bean-and-Yellow Tomato Salad

The yellow of the tomatoes and the green of the beans make a colorful salad presentation, but you can use red tomatoes if you wish. The carbo rating will be the same.

½	pound green beans, trimmed and cut into 2-inch pieces
2	yellow tomatoes, each cut into 8 wedges
⅓	cup vertically sliced red onion
2	tablespoons red wine vinegar
2	teaspoons minced fresh or ½ teaspoon dried thyme
1	teaspoon olive oil
⅛	teaspoon salt
	Dash of black pepper
1	garlic clove, minced

1. Steam green beans, covered, 3 minutes or until tender. Rinse with water; drain.
2. Combine beans, tomato wedges, and onion in a bowl. Combine vinegar and next 5 ingredients in a bowl; stir well with a whisk. Pour vinegar mixture over bean mixture; toss. Serve at room temperature. Yield: 2 servings (serving size: 1 cup).

CALORIES 118; FAT 3.2g (sat 0.5g); PROTEIN 4.4g; CARBOHYDRATE 22.2g; FIBER 5.5g; CHOLESTEROL 0mg; IRON 2.4mg; SODIUM 177mg; CALCIUM 60mg

best uses for bulgur

Here are our suggestions for using the different grinds of bulgur in a variety of recipes.

Coarse-grind is good for low-fat stuffings, casseroles, and vegetarian tacos. It can also be used in pilafs, soups, salads, and artisan breads.

Medium-grind is an all-purpose size used in salads, stews, soups, multigrain bakery goods, and especially in meatless burgers and chili.

Fine-grind makes a nutritious breakfast cereal and is perfect for breads and even desserts. Fine and medium grinds are both used in tabbouleh salads, pilafs, and in any recipe as a substitute for rice.

▶ **carbo rating: 18**

Three-Bean Salad with Roasted Onion

Three-bean salads are often loaded with sugar. This savory version get its flavor from sherry vinegar, olive oil, mustard seeds, and fresh rosemary. The roasted onion adds a touch of sweetness.

1	large red onion, peeled and halved (about ¾ pound)

Cooking spray

¾	pound wax beans (about 3 cups)
1½	cups frozen black-eyed peas
1½	cups frozen lima beans
¼	cup sherry vinegar
2	tablespoons olive oil
1	teaspoon mustard seeds, crushed
1	teaspoon minced fresh rosemary
½	teaspoon salt
¼	teaspoon black pepper
1	garlic clove, minced

1. Preheat oven to 450°.
2. Place onion halves, cut sides down, in a baking dish coated with cooking spray. Bake, uncovered, at 450° for 30 minutes or until tender. Cool slightly; coarsely chop, and set aside.
3. Trim ends from wax beans, and remove strings. Cook black-eyed peas and lima beans in boiling water 4 minutes. Add wax beans; cook 8 minutes or until tender. Drain.
4. Combine vinegar and next 6 ingredients in a large bowl; stir well with a whisk. Add onion, peas, and beans; toss to coat. Cover and marinate in refrigerator at least 8 hours. Yield: 7 servings (serving size: 1 cup).

CALORIES 157; FAT 4.6g (sat 0.6g); PROTEIN 6.6g; CARBOHYDRATE 21.9g; FIBER 3.5g; CHOLESTEROL 0mg; IRON 1.9mg; SODIUM 270mg; CALCIUM 55mg

▶ **carbo rating: 18**

Beans and Greens Salad

If you can't find the convenient package of mixed baby salad greens, use a 4-cup mixture of salad greens like escarole, radicchio, endive, and romaine lettuce. If you're looking for a light supper, serve this salad with Fresh Tomato Soup (page 352) or a Tuna-Cheese Melt (page 354).

1	(5-ounce) package mixed baby salad greens
1	(16-ounce) can red kidney beans, rinsed and drained
1	(15-ounce) can cannellini beans, rinsed and drained
1	onion, cut in half lengthwise and thinly sliced crosswise
¼	cup chopped fresh basil
2	tablespoons fresh lemon juice
1	tablespoon prepared mustard
1	tablespoon white wine vinegar
1	tablespoon olive oil
½	teaspoon pepper
¼	teaspoon salt

1. Combine first 5 ingredients in a bowl; toss gently.
2. Combine lemon juice and next 5 ingredients in a jar; cover tightly, and shake vigorously. Pour over salad, and toss gently. Yield: 4 servings (serving size: about 2 cups).

CALORIES 160; FAT 4.2g (sat 0.5g); PROTEIN 7.2g; CARBOHYDRATE 24.4g; FIBER 6.5g; CHOLESTEROL 0mg; IRON 2.5mg; SODIUM 558mg; CALCIUM 75mg

(pictured on page 313)

▶ carbo rating: 23
White Bean-and-Tomato Salad

Lemon juice, olive oil, and sage perk up the flavor of canned beans in this simple, rustic salad. It also makes a great lunch. We recommend serving it with Quick Pita Chips (page 63).

1	(15.8-ounce) can Great Northern beans, rinsed and drained
3	cups chopped seeded tomato
3	tablespoons chopped celery
2	tablespoons sliced green onions
1	tablespoon extravirgin olive oil
1	tablespoon fresh lemon juice
1½	teaspoons chopped fresh sage
¼	teaspoon salt
¼	teaspoon pepper

Sage sprigs (optional)

1. Combine first 9 ingredients in a bowl; toss gently. Garnish with sage sprigs, if desired. Yield: 4 servings (serving size: 1 cup).

CALORIES 188; FAT 4.3g (sat 0.7g); PROTEIN 9.5g; CARBOHYDRATE 30.4g; FIBER 7.6g; CHOLESTEROL 0mg; IRON 2.7mg; SODIUM 322mg; CALCIUM 83mg

(pictured on page 314)

▶ carbo rating: 28
Frozen Fruit Salad

This frozen fruit salad contains no sugar other than the natural sugar of the fruits. Most traditional frozen fruit salads have ¼ to ½ cup of granulated sugar.

1½	cups seedless red grapes, halved
1½	cups sliced ripe banana (about 3)
1½	cups grapefruit sections (about 2 large)
1½	cups chopped fresh pineapple
1¾	cups pineapple juice
⅓	cup thawed orange juice concentrate

1. Combine all ingredients in a large bowl. Pour mixture into a 13 x 9-inch baking dish. Cover and freeze 4 hours or until firm.
2. Let stand at room temperature 30 minutes or until slightly thawed before cutting into 8 equal pieces. Yield: 8 servings (serving size: 1 piece).

CALORIES 121; FAT 0.5g (sat 0.1g); PROTEIN 1.2g; CARBOHYDRATE 30.2g; FIBER 1.8g; CHOLESTEROL 0mg; IRON 0.5mg; SODIUM 2mg; CALCIUM 25mg

fruit purchasing guide

How much do I need to buy? What do I do with it? Here's what you need to know about buying and preparing fresh fruits, plus the carbo rating for a serving of each fruit.

Fruit	Approximate Servings	Preparation*	Carbo Rating
Apples	3 to 4 servings per pound	Wash. Peel and core as required, and cut as desired.	1 medium: 17
Apricots	3 to 4 servings per pound	Wash. Cut in half, remove pit, and slice as desired.	1 medium: 4
Bananas	3 to 4 servings per pound	Peel, and cut as desired.	1 medium: 25
Blackberries	4 servings per pound	Rinse lightly just before serving.	½ cup: 7
Blueberries	4 servings per pound	Wash and drain; sort and remove stems.	½ cup: 9
Cherries	4 servings per pound	Wash; sort and remove stems and pits.	½ cup: 3
Cranberries	8 servings per pound	Sort, wash, and drain.	½ cup: 4
Figs	6 servings per pound	Rinse gently just before serving. Peel, if desired.	1 medium: 8
Grapefruit	2 servings per pound	Cut into halves, or peel and cut into sections.	½ medium: 10
Grapes	4 servings per pound	Wash thoroughly. Remove stems; leave whole or halve.	½ cup: 14
Kiwifruit	3 to 4 servings per pound	Peel and slice. Or cut off top and use a spoon to scoop out flesh.	1 medium: 9
Lemons	4 lemons per pound	Wash. Slice or cut into wedges. Grate rind, if desired.	1 medium: 10
Oranges	2 servings per pound	Wash. Cut into halves, peel and cut into sections, or slice.	1 medium: 12
Peaches	4 servings per pound	Blanch to remove skin. Cut to remove seed. Chop or slice.	1 medium: 8
Pears	4 servings per pound	Wash. Peel and core as required, and cut as desired.	1 medium: 21
Pineapple	3 servings per pound	Cut off top, bottom, and skin. Chop or slice as desired.	½ cup diced: 9
Plums	4 to 5 servings per pound	Wash. Keep whole, or cut in half and remove pit.	1 medium: 8
Raspberries	4 servings per pound	Rinse lightly just before serving.	½ cup: 3
Rhubarb	4 to 8 pieces per pound	Remove leaf and hard area at base of stem. Wash and cut across stem into desired width.	½ cup diced: 2
Strawberries	2 to 3 servings per pound	Rinse and remove stems. Leave whole, slice, or chop.	½ cup sliced: 5

*The preparation instructions are general; refer to your recipe for more detailed directions.

side dishes

Don't settle for plain ol' steamed vegetables to go with your meats. Move the sides to the center of the plate with high-flavor dishes such as *Garlicky Sautéed Spinach* (page 322), *Broccoli with Caraway-Cheese Sauce* (page 325), and *Spicy Black-Eyed Peas* (page 338). And if you're tired of vegetables, we've got some brown rice recipes on pages 340, 342, and 343.

▶ carbo rating: 0

Beet Greens with Oregano and Feta

Even if you've given up beets in your low-carb plan, you don't want to miss out on the vitamin-packed, mild-flavored beet greens.

11	cups coarsely chopped beet greens (about 1 pound beets with greens attached)
1	teaspoon olive oil
¼	teaspoon dried oregano, crushed
⅛	teaspoon pepper
1	teaspoon fresh lemon juice
2	tablespoons crumbled feta cheese

1. Rinse beet greens; drain well. Heat oil in a large nonstick skillet over medium-high heat. Add beet greens; cover and cook, stirring occasionally, 1½ to 2 minutes or until greens wilt. Reduce heat to low; add oregano and pepper.

2. Cook, uncovered, 5 minutes or until tender, stirring occasionally. Remove from heat; add lemon juice, and stir gently. Sprinkle each serving with feta cheese. Yield: 6 servings (serving size: ½ cup greens and 1 teaspoon feta cheese).

CALORIES 29; FAT 1.5g (sat 0.6g); PROTEIN 1.7g; CARBOHYDRATE 3g; FIBER 2.6g; CHOLESTEROL 3mg; IRON 2.4mg; SODIUM 175mg; CALCIUM 100mg

beet basics

• When you buy beets, remove the greens as soon as you get home. Trim stems of roots to about 1 inch. Cover and store both the roots and the greens in the refrigerator. Use the greens within 1 or 2 days. The roots will keep for up to 2 weeks.

• For another side dish, you can roast the beet roots. Wash them whole and place on a foil-lined baking sheet. Bake at 425° for 45 minutes or until tender. After cooking, trim off about ¼ inch of the beet roots. Rub off the skins. They should slip off easily after cooking.

• One beet (about 2 inches in diameter) has 7.8 grams of carbohydrate and 2.3 grams of fiber for a carbo rating of 6.

preparing asparagus

Gently snap off the tough ends of asparagus where they seem to break naturally, or use the shortcut on page 323.

▶ carbo rating: 2

Lemon Roasted Asparagus

Sprinkling fresh vegetables with lemon juice and fresh herbs is a simple low-carb way to add flavor.

1	pound asparagus (about 40 spears)
	Cooking spray
2	teaspoons olive oil
2	tablespoons finely chopped fresh cilantro
½	teaspoon grated lemon rind
2	teaspoons fresh lemon juice (about ½ lemon)
½	teaspoon salt
¼	teaspoon pepper

1. Preheat oven to 450°.

2. Snap off tough ends of asparagus. Place asparagus on a jelly roll pan coated with cooking spray. Drizzle with oil, turning to coat.

3. Bake at 450° for 8 to 10 minutes or until asparagus is tender, shaking pan often to roast asparagus evenly. Sprinkle remaining ingredients over asparagus. Yield: 5 servings (serving size: 8 spears).

CALORIES 28; FAT 1.4g (sat 0.2g); PROTEIN 1.9g; CARBOHYDRATE 3.3g; FIBER 1.2g; CHOLESTEROL 0mg; IRON 0.6mg; SODIUM 154mg; CALCIUM 16mg

Roasted Vegetable Salad
▶ carbo rating: 10
page 291

Chicken Salad with Asparagus

▶ carbo rating: 10

page 291

Mixed Antipasto Salad
▶ carbo rating: 11
page 292

Citrus-Salmon Salad
▶ carbo rating: 11
page 293

Grilled Chicken and
Raspberry Salad
► carbo rating: 12
page 293

Spicy Chicken Finger Salad
▶ carbo rating: 13
page 294

Lemon-Dill White Bean Salad
▶ carbo rating: 13
page 296

Smoked Turkey Mango Salad
▶ carbo rating: 13
page 297

Beans and Greens Salad
▶ carbo rating: 18
page 299

White Bean-and-Tomato Salad
▶ carbo rating: 23
page 300

314

Sesame Steamed Broccoli
▶ carbo rating: 2
page 321

Lemony Asparagus with Parsley
▶ carbo rating: 3
page 323

**Summer Squash with
Tomatoes and Basil**

▶ carbo rating: 5

page 329

**Tomatoes with Green
Onions and Basil**
▶ carbo rating: 6
page 330

Mexican Black Beans
▶ carbo rating: 10
page 336

Artichokes with Browned Garlic and Lemon Dipping Sauce
▶ carbo rating: 10
page 337

Broccoli and Cauliflower au Gratin
▶ carbo rating: 12
page 339

▶ **carbo rating: 2**
Sesame Steamed Broccoli

Steaming broccoli for a short time is the best way to preserve all of its disease-fighting nutrients; overcooking can destroy those nutrients.

  1   (12-ounce) package broccoli florets (about 4½ cups)
  2   tablespoons low-sodium soy sauce
  2   teaspoons sesame seeds, toasted
1½   teaspoons dark sesame oil
  ¼   teaspoon freshly ground black pepper
  ⅛   teaspoon salt

1. Steam broccoli, covered, 6 minutes or until crisp-tender.
2. Combine soy sauce and next 4 ingredients. Pour soy sauce mixture over broccoli; toss. Yield: 4 servings (serving size: 1 cup).

CALORIES 54; FAT 2g (sat 0.3g); PROTEIN 3.1g; CARBOHYDRATE 5g; FIBER 2.6g; CHOLESTEROL 0mg; IRON 2.9mg; SODIUM 398mg; CALCIUM 41mg

(pictured on page 315)

▶ **carbo rating: 2**
Cauliflower with Chives and Lemon

The simple addition of butter and fresh lemon juice brings out the cauliflower's best flavor.

  3   cups fresh cauliflower florets (about ¾ pound)
  2   tablespoons finely chopped fresh chives
1½   tablespoons light butter, melted
  1   tablespoon fresh lemon juice (about ½ lemon)
  ¼   teaspoon salt
  ¼   teaspoon freshly ground black pepper

1. Place cauliflower in a medium saucepan, and add water to cover. Bring to a boil, and cook 5 minutes or until crisp-tender.
2. Transfer cauliflower florets to a bowl; add chives and remaining ingredients. Yield: 4 servings (serving size: about ¾ cup).

CALORIES 39; FAT 2.4g (sat 1.5g); PROTEIN 1.9g; CARBOHYDRATE 4.3g; FIBER 2g; CHOLESTEROL 8mg; IRON 0.4mg; SODIUM 196mg; CALCIUM 19mg

convenient cauliflower

You'll find prepackaged cauliflower florets in the produce section of the supermarket. If the bagged florets aren't available, use 1 head of cauliflower to get 3 cups of florets.

▶ carbo rating: 2

Garlicky Sautéed Spinach

This five-minute side is one of our favorites. It goes with just about anything.

1   tablespoon butter
1   small garlic clove, minced
½   (10-ounce) package fresh spinach
1   tablespoon lemon juice
⅛   teaspoon crushed red pepper

1. Melt butter in a large nonstick skillet over medium heat. Add garlic, and sauté 30 seconds. Add spinach, lemon juice, and red pepper. Sauté 2 to 3 minutes or until spinach wilts. Yield: 2 servings (serving size: 1 cup).

CALORIES 71; FAT 6g (sat 3.6g); PROTEIN 2.2g; CARBOHYDRATE 3.5g; FIBER 2g; CHOLESTEROL 16mg; IRON 2mg; SODIUM 116mg; CALCIUM 76mg

removing garlic odor

To remove the garlic smell from your fingers after mincing garlic, rub your fingers along the flat sides of a stainless steel knife (be careful not to touch the sharp edge) or a stainless steel sink.

▶ carbo rating: 2

Cumin-Scented Squash

Pungent, sharp, and slightly bitter, cumin is a common ingredient in Indian spice blends and Mexican foods. Like other spices, it should be stored in a cool place and away from heat.

2   yellow squash, halved lengthwise
1   tablespoon olive oil
¼   teaspoon ground cumin
¼   teaspoon salt
⅛   teaspoon ground red pepper

1. Preheat oven to 450°.
2. Place squash halves, cut sides up, on a baking sheet; drizzle with oil. Bake at 450° for 20 minutes.
3. Cook cumin in a small nonstick skillet over medium heat, stirring and shaking often, 3 to 4 minutes or until fragrant. Combine cumin, salt, and red pepper in a small bowl. Sprinkle over squash. Yield: 4 servings (serving size: 1 squash half).

CALORIES 48; FAT 3.6g (sat 0.5g); PROTEIN 1.1g; CARBOHYDRATE 3.9g; FIBER 1.7g; CHOLESTEROL 0mg; IRON 0.5mg; SODIUM 149mg; CALCIUM 19mg

► carbo rating: 3

Roasted Asparagus

Roasting really brings out the flavor of fresh asparagus. Once you've tried the tender spears roasted, you may never prepare them another way.

1¼   pounds asparagus spears, rinsed and trimmed
1   tablespoon olive oil
¼   teaspoon salt
¼   teaspoon pepper
Cooking spray

1. Preheat oven to 400°.
2. Toss asparagus with olive oil, salt, and pepper. Arrange asparagus in a single layer on a foil-lined baking sheet coated with cooking spray. Bake at 400° for 8 to 10 minutes or until tender, shaking pan often to roast asparagus evenly. Yield: 5 servings (serving size: about 4 ounces).

CALORIES 56; FAT 2.8g (sat 0.4g); PROTEIN 2.5g; CARBOHYDRATE 5g; FIBER 2.5g; CHOLESTEROL 0mg; IRON 0.5mg; SODIUM 118mg; CALCIUM 25mg

asparagus shortcut

Leave the rubber bands on the bunch of asparagus, and use a sharp knife to cut off the ends of the stalks about where the stalk begins to turn green. Remove bands, and then rinse well. Try this quick approach and you'll never go back to the traditional method of snapping off the tough ends.

► carbo rating: 3

Lemony Asparagus with Parsley

It does not matter whether you use pencil-thin asparagus spears or thicker ones in this recipe. Although many people believe that the thin spears are younger and more tender than the thicker ones, that is not really true.

1   teaspoon olive oil
3   cups (2-inch) diagonally sliced asparagus (about 1 pound)
2   tablespoons finely chopped fresh flat-leaf parsley
1   tablespoon fresh lemon juice (about ½ lemon)
¼   teaspoon salt
¼   teaspoon coarsely ground black pepper

1. Heat oil in a large nonstick skillet over medium-high heat. Add asparagus; cook, stirring occasionally, 7 minutes or until crisp-tender. Remove from heat; stir in parsley and remaining ingredients. Yield: 4 servings (serving size: ½ cup).

CALORIES 35; FAT 1.4g (sat 0.2g); PROTEIN 2.4g; CARBOHYDRATE 5g; FIBER 2.2g; CHOLESTEROL 0mg; IRON 1mg; SODIUM 151mg; CALCIUM 25mg

(pictured on page 315)

▶ carbo rating: 3
Balsamic Pan-Roasted Broccoli

Instead of steaming broccoli, roast it quickly in a skillet to brown the florets and add flavor. The balsamic vinegar offers a hint of sweetness.

  1   teaspoon olive oil
Cooking spray
  1   (12-ounce) package fresh broccoli florets
  1   tablespoon balsamic vinegar
  ¼   teaspoon salt
  ¼   teaspoon freshly ground black pepper

1. Heat oil in a large nonstick skillet coated with cooking spray over medium heat. Add broccoli; cook, turning occasionally, 8 minutes or until lightly browned and crisp-tender. Remove from heat; add vinegar, salt, and pepper, and stir. Yield: 4 servings (serving size: ¾ cup).

CALORIES 37; FAT 1.4g (sat 0.2g); PROTEIN 2.6g; CARBOHYDRATE 5.1g; FIBER 2.5g; CHOLESTEROL 0mg; IRON 0.8mg; SODIUM 171mg; CALCIUM 43mg

balsamic vinegar basics

Balsamic vinegar is made from the juice of Trebblano grapes (a sweet white Italian grape) and gets its characteristic dark color and tangy sweetness from being aged in oak barrels for long periods of time. Some imported balsamic vinegars have been aged as long as 25 years and are quite expensive, but you can find reasonably priced bottles on the shelves with other vinegars at the supermarket.

▶ carbo rating: 3
Pesto-Tossed Cauliflower

Pesto has a very concentrated flavor, so a small amount goes a long way. You can find bottled pesto on the shelves with other sauces and condiments or in the refrigerated section with the fresh pasta sauces.

  4   cups cauliflower florets
  ½   cup water
  2½ tablespoons commercial pesto
  ¼   teaspoon salt
  ¼   teaspoon freshly ground black pepper

1. Place cauliflower in a microwave-safe bowl; pour water over cauliflower. Cover with plastic wrap; vent. Microwave at HIGH 6 minutes or until done.
2. Drain cauliflower, and return to dish. Add pesto, salt, and pepper; toss well. Cover; microwave at HIGH 1 minute or until hot. Yield: 4 servings (serving size: 1 cup).

CALORIES 74; FAT 4.7g (sat 1.2g); PROTEIN 3.8g; CARBOHYDRATE 5.9g; FIBER 2.8g; CHOLESTEROL 3mg; IRON 0.8mg; SODIUM 252mg; CALCIUM 92mg

▶ **carbo rating: 4**

Broccoli with Caraway-Cheese Sauce

Caraway seeds have a distinct nutty flavor. Store the seeds in an airtight container in a cool, dark place up to six months to maintain this flavor.

2	pounds fresh broccoli (about 8 cups)
2	teaspoons margarine or butter
¾	cup fat-free milk
1½	tablespoons all-purpose flour
¼	teaspoon salt
⅛	teaspoon pepper
¼	cup (1 ounce) shredded Gruyère or Swiss cheese
½	teaspoon caraway seeds
1	(2-ounce) jar diced pimiento, drained

1. Remove and discard broccoli leaves; cut off and discard tough ends of stalks. Wash broccoli; cut into spears. Arrange spears in a steamer basket over boiling water. Cover and steam 8 minutes or until broccoli is crisp-tender. Drain and place on a serving platter; set aside, and keep warm.

2. Melt margarine in a saucepan over medium heat. Add milk and next 3 ingredients; cook, stirring constantly with a whisk, until smooth. Add cheese and caraway seeds; cook, stirring constantly, until cheese melts and mixture is thickened and bubbly.

3. Pour sauce over broccoli. Sprinkle with pimiento, and serve immediately. Yield: 8 servings (serving size: 1 cup).

CALORIES 58; FAT 2.4g (sat 0.9g); PROTEIN 4.2g; CARBOHYDRATE 6.3g; FIBER 2.3g; CHOLESTEROL 4mg; IRON 0.8mg; SODIUM 128mg; CALCIUM 100mg

▶ **carbo rating: 4**

Green Beans with Cilantro

If you're tired of plain ol' beans, spice them up by adding hot pepper and cilantro.

1½	teaspoons olive oil
	Cooking spray
3	cups (2-inch) diagonally cut green beans (about ¾ pound)
1	tablespoon minced fresh cilantro
1	small jalapeño pepper, seeded and minced
¼	teaspoon salt

1. Heat oil in a large nonstick skillet coated with cooking spray over medium-high heat. Add green beans; sauté 10 minutes or until tender and browned in spots.

2. Stir in cilantro, minced pepper, and salt. Yield: 4 servings (serving size: ½ cup).

CALORIES 43; FAT 1.9g (sat 0.3g); PROTEIN 1.6g; CARBOHYDRATE 6.5g; FIBER 2.8g; CHOLESTEROL 0mg; IRON 0.9mg; SODIUM 151mg; CALCIUM 31mg

▶ carbo rating: 4
Zucchini with Garlic

It's hard to beat the flavor of garden-fresh zucchini, simply seasoned with butter and garlic.

1   tablespoon light butter
3   garlic cloves, minced
2   cups cubed zucchini (about ¾ pound)
¼   teaspoon salt
¼   teaspoon freshly ground black pepper

1. Melt butter in a large nonstick skillet over medium-high heat. Add garlic, and sauté 1 minute. Add zucchini; cook, stirring occasionally, 6 to 7 minutes or until crisp-tender. Stir in salt and pepper. Yield: 2 servings (serving size: ¾ cup).

CALORIES 55; FAT 3.3g (sat 2.1g); PROTEIN 2.2g; CARBOHYDRATE 6.6g; FIBER 2.3g; CHOLESTEROL 10mg; IRON 0.7mg; SODIUM 331mg; CALCIUM 32mg

selecting zucchini

Fresh zucchini is available year-round in most supermarkets, but it's at its peak in late spring and early summer. Select small zucchini about 1½ inches in diameter and 6 inches in length. They're younger, have thinner skins, and are more tender than the larger ones.

coleslaw mix

Look for cabbage-and-carrot coleslaw mix in the produce section with prepackaged lettuce and salads. Buy a coleslaw mix without a seasoning packet, and without carrots, if you prefer.

▶ carbo rating: 5
Sautéed Cabbage with Dill

This cabbage is good either warm or at room temperature. If you have any left over, try it as a lower-sodium substitute for sauerkraut.

2   teaspoons butter
4   cups cabbage-and-carrot coleslaw mix (about 8 ounces)
1   cup thinly sliced leek (about 1 large)
2   tablespoons chopped fresh dill
2   teaspoons fresh lemon juice (about ½ lemon)
¼   teaspoon salt
⅛   teaspoon freshly ground black pepper

1. Melt butter in a large nonstick skillet over medium heat. Stir in coleslaw and leek. Cover and cook 4 minutes or until cabbage wilts, stirring twice.
2. Remove cabbage mixture from heat. Add dill and remaining ingredients. Serve warm or at room temperature. Yield: 4 servings (serving size: ½ cup).

CALORIES 49; FAT 2.2g (sat 1.2g); PROTEIN 1.4g; CARBOHYDRATE 7.2g; FIBER 2g; CHOLESTEROL 5mg; IRON 0.9mg; SODIUM 184mg; CALCIUM 48mg

holiday menu

White wine

Garlic-Herb Cheese Spread (page 52)
with raw vegetables

Mixed Greens with Bacon-Horseradish Dressing
(page 278)

Stuffed Turkey Breast (page 261)

Brown Rice with Peas (page 342)

Roasted Snap Beans (below)

Quick Berry Whips (page 372)

▶ carbo rating: 37

▶ carbo rating: 5
Roasted Snap Beans

To get the beans nicely browned, be sure to spread them evenly in a single layer on the pan, and roast them on the top rack of the oven.

Cooking spray
1   pound whole snap or string beans, trimmed
2   teaspoons extravirgin olive oil
¼   teaspoon salt, divided
⅛   teaspoon pepper

1. Preheat oven to 500°.
2. Coat a jelly roll pan with cooking spray. Place beans on pan, and arrange in a single layer. Drizzle with oil, and toss gently to coat. Sprinkle with ⅛ teaspoon salt. Bake at 500° for 12 minutes or until beans are tender and beginning to brown, stirring once. Sprinkle with ⅛ teaspoon salt and pepper. Yield: 4 servings (serving size: ½ cup).

CALORIES 54; FAT 2.5g (sat 0.4g); PROTEIN 1.9g; CARBOHYDRATE 7.5g;
FIBER 2.2g; CHOLESTEROL 0mg; IRON 1.1mg; SODIUM 153mg; CALCIUM 39mg

▶ carbo rating: 5
Garlic-Roasted Green Beans

An easy way to prepare green beans is to rinse them in a colander under running water, gather them into small bunches with like ends together, and cut off the ends with a sharp knife. When you finish, you'll have a neat stack of green beans ready to cook.

1   pound green beans, trimmed
2   garlic cloves, sliced
Olive oil-flavored cooking spray
2   teaspoons lemon juice
1   teaspoon olive oil
1   teaspoon salt-free lemon pepper seasoning

1. Preheat oven to 450°.
2. Place beans and garlic in a single layer on a foil-lined baking sheet. Coat beans and garlic with cooking spray; toss well. Drizzle lemon juice and olive oil over beans and garlic; sprinkle with lemon pepper seasoning.
3. Bake, uncovered, at 450° for 8 to 10 minutes or until beans are crisp-tender, stirring once. Yield: 4 servings (serving size: 1 cup).

CALORIES 48; FAT 1.3g (sat 0.2g); PROTEIN 2.2g; CARBOHYDRATE 8.8g;
FIBER 3.9g; CHOLESTEROL 0mg; IRON 1.2mg; SODIUM 8mg; CALCIUM 45mg

► carbo rating: 5

Roasted Onions and Peppers

Instead of potatoes, offer this savory low-carb side dish with the Seared Steaks with Creamy Horseradish Sauce on page 208.

1   Vidalia or other sweet onion, thinly sliced
1   green bell pepper, seeded and cut into thin strips
1   red bell pepper, seeded and cut into thin strips
Cooking spray
2   teaspoons olive oil
2   teaspoons Creole seasoning

1. Preheat oven to 475°.
2. Place first 3 ingredients in a single layer in a large roasting pan. Coat vegetables with cooking spray; drizzle with olive oil. Sprinkle with Creole seasoning. Bake at 475° for 15 to 17 minutes or until lightly browned. Yield: 4 servings (serving size: about ½ cup).

CALORIES 46; FAT 2.4g (sat 0.3g); PROTEIN 0.9g; CARBOHYDRATE 6.2g; FIBER 1.6g; CHOLESTEROL 0mg; IRON 0.3mg; SODIUM 302mg; CALCIUM 11mg

(pictured on page 160)

► carbo rating: 5

Marinated Portobellos

Be sure to keep the flavorful juices that accumulate on the mushrooms as they cook. This dish is the perfect accompaniment for grilled beef or pork.

¼   cup low-sodium teriyaki sauce
2   tablespoons orange juice
2   teaspoons minced garlic
1   teaspoon sesame oil
¼   teaspoon crushed red pepper
4   (4-inch) portobello mushroom caps
Cooking spray
Sesame seeds (optional)

1. Combine first 5 ingredients in a small bowl; stir well. Place mushroom caps, gills up, in a shallow dish. Pour teriyaki mixture evenly over gills. Cover and chill at least 1 hour.
2. Prepare grill.
3. Place mushroom caps, gills down, on grill rack coated with cooking spray. Grill, covered, 5 minutes on each side or until tender. Cut mushroom caps into ½-inch-thick slices. Sprinkle with sesame seeds, if desired. Yield: 4 servings (serving size: 1 mushroom cap).

CALORIES 56; FAT 1.2g (sat 0.2g); PROTEIN 1.2g; CARBOHYDRATE 6.3g; FIBER 1.1g; CHOLESTEROL 0mg; IRON 0.1mg; SODIUM 265mg; CALCIUM 5mg

portobello mushrooms

Let cremini mushrooms grow a few days longer, and you end up with portobellos. This flying saucer-like disk, which often measures from 3 to 6 inches across, is firm, meaty, and intensely flavorful. The portobello stands up to such gutsy flavors as acidic marinades, fresh rosemary and basil, and chile peppers. Grilling and roasting are the best cooking methods for preserving the mushroom's steaklike texture.

▶ **carbo rating: 5**

Summer Squash with Tomatoes and Basil

When your summer garden bounty is coming in, this simple skillet dish is an ideal way to cook all the squash, tomatoes, and basil.

1	teaspoon olive oil
	Cooking spray
5	cups cubed yellow squash (about 1¼ pounds)
1	cup grape tomatoes, halved
2	tablespoons chopped fresh basil
¼	teaspoon salt
¼	teaspoon freshly ground black pepper

1. Heat oil in a large nonstick skillet coated with cooking spray over medium heat. Add squash; cook, stirring occasionally, 6 minutes or until tender.
2. Add tomato and remaining ingredients; cook 1 minute or until thoroughly heated. Yield: 4 servings (serving size: 1 cup).

CALORIES 49; FAT 1.7g (sat 0.3g); PROTEIN 1.9g; CARBOHYDRATE 8.4g; FIBER 3.6g; CHOLESTEROL 0mg; IRON 1mg; SODIUM 153mg; CALCIUM 39mg

(pictured on page 316)

---

flavor variations

You can use zucchini instead of yellow squash, and fresh oregano or rosemary instead of basil.

▶ **carbo rating: 5**

Turnip Greens with Canadian Bacon

Some cooks add a pinch of sugar to their greens to balance the bitterness. This recipe doesn't have sugar, but the balsamic vinegar and roasted bell peppers add a touch of tangy sweetness. We replaced the traditional fat back or ham hock with Canadian bacon to reduce the overall fat and sodium.

1	(6-ounce) package Canadian bacon, cut into ½-inch pieces
	Olive oil-flavored cooking spray
2	(16-ounce) packages fresh turnip greens, coarsely chopped
¼	cup water
1	cup chopped bottled roasted red bell peppers, drained
2	tablespoons balsamic vinegar
½	teaspoon salt
¼	teaspoon freshly ground black pepper

1. Cook Canadian bacon in a large Dutch oven coated with cooking spray 3 to 4 minutes or until lightly browned. Add greens and water; cover, and reduce heat to low. Steam 10 minutes or until greens are tender. Stir in bell peppers and remaining ingredients. Simmer 3 minutes. Yield: 8 servings (serving size: ½ cup).

CALORIES 69; FAT 2g (sat 0.6g); PROTEIN 6.3g; CARBOHYDRATE 7.9g; FIBER 2.9g; CHOLESTEROL 11mg; IRON 1.6mg; SODIUM 819mg; CALCIUM 227mg

▶ carbo rating: 6
Lemony Green Beans

The light lemon flavor of these fresh beans is a nice complement to roasted turkey, chicken, or pork tenderloin.

2 tablespoons light butter
1 teaspoon grated lemon rind
2 teaspoons fresh lemon juice (about ½ lemon)
¼ teaspoon salt
¼ teaspoon freshly ground black pepper
4 cups green beans, trimmed (about 1 pound)
2 tablespoons water

1. Place butter in a microwave-safe bowl; microwave at HIGH 20 seconds or until melted. Stir in lemon rind and next 3 ingredients. Set aside.
2. Place beans in a large microwave-safe bowl; add water. Cover and microwave at HIGH 3 to 4 minutes or until crisp-tender. Drain well. Toss beans with butter mixture. Yield: 4 servings (serving size: 1 cup).

CALORIES 53; FAT 3.1g (sat 2g); PROTEIN 2.1g; CARBOHYDRATE 6.5g; FIBER 1g; CHOLESTEROL 10mg; IRON 0.9mg; SODIUM 187mg; CALCIUM 33mg

buying green beans

Buy about 1 pound of green beans to get 4 cups trimmed beans. A good rule of thumb for green beans is to count on about ¼ pound of fresh beans per serving.

winter tomatoes

Although winter is not really the season for tomatoes, some are better than others in winter. The best bets are vine-ripened, Roma, and cherry tomatoes.

Vine-ripened tomatoes are small to medium in size and are often sold in clusters still attached to a vine.

Oval Roma or plum tomatoes have firmer pulp and fewer seeds than other varieties, so they hold their shape well.

Cherry and grape tomatoes are always flavorful because their size, shape, and packaging protects them; they have less need to be hybridized to stand up to the rigors of mechanical harvesting and shipping.

▶ carbo rating: 6
Tomatoes with Green Onions and Basil

Delight in the sweetness of grape or cherry tomatoes.

1½ teaspoons olive oil
1 pint grape or cherry tomatoes
1½ tablespoons thinly sliced green onions
1 tablespoon minced fresh basil
2 teaspoons balsamic vinegar
¼ teaspoon salt
⅛ teaspoon pepper

1. Heat oil in a large nonstick skillet over medium-high heat. Add tomatoes; sauté 1 to 2 minutes or until tomatoes are heated. Remove from heat, and stir in green onions and remaining ingredients; toss gently. Serve immediately. Yield: 2 servings (serving size: about ¾ cup).

CALORIES 67; FAT 3.9g (sat 0.5g); PROTEIN 1.3g; CARBOHYDRATE 8.2g; FIBER 1.9g; CHOLESTEROL 0mg; IRON 0.8mg; SODIUM 309mg; CALCIUM 12mg

(pictured on page 317)

► carbo rating: 7
Cauliflower Puttanesca

A puttanesca sauce is a spicy mixture of tomatoes, onions, capers, olives, garlic, and oregano. It's often served over pasta, but in this recipe, it perks up the flavor of mild cauliflower.

2	teaspoons olive oil
⅓	cup diced onion
⅓	cup chopped green bell pepper
1	garlic clove, minced
1	(14½-ounce) can diced tomatoes, undrained
¼	cup water
1	tablespoon chopped pitted kalamata olives
1	tablespoon red wine vinegar
1	teaspoon sugar
1	teaspoon capers
2	teaspoons tomato paste
⅛	teaspoon black pepper
4½	cups cauliflower florets

1. Heat oil in a large nonstick skillet over medium heat. Add onion and green bell pepper; sauté 6 minutes or until tender. Add garlic; cook 30 seconds. Add tomatoes and next 7 ingredients; stir well. Bring to a boil; reduce heat, and simmer, uncovered, 10 minutes or until thick. Set aside, and keep warm.
2. Steam cauliflower 4 minutes or until crisp-tender. Spoon cauliflower onto serving plates; top with sauce. Yield: 6 servings (serving size: ⅔ cup cauliflower and ⅓ cup sauce).

CALORIES 66; FAT 2.3g (sat 0.3g); PROTEIN 2.6g; CARBOHYDRATE 10.4g; FIBER 3.6g; CHOLESTEROL 0mg; IRON 0.7mg; SODIUM 167mg; CALCIUM 34mg

► carbo rating: 7
Italian Eggplant

In this variation of eggplant Parmesan, instead of coating the eggplant slices in breadcrumbs, you simply coat them with cooking spray and brown them before topping the slices with a tomato mixture and cheese.

	Olive oil-flavored cooking spray
1	small eggplant, peeled and thinly sliced into 6 slices (about 1 pound)
	Freshly ground black pepper
1½	cups canned whole tomatoes, chopped
1	tablespoon minced onion
2	teaspoons dried basil
3	garlic cloves, minced
½	cup (2 ounces) shredded part-skim mozzarella cheese
2	tablespoons minced fresh parsley
1	tablespoon grated Parmesan cheese

1. Preheat broiler.
2. Coat a jelly roll pan with cooking spray. Arrange eggplant in pan in a layer; coat with cooking spray. Broil 6 to 7 minutes, or until lightly browned. Turn and lightly coat with cooking spray; season with pepper. Broil an additional 6 to 7 minutes, or until lightly browned.
3. Combine tomato and next 3 ingredients in a bowl.
4. Arrange eggplant in an 11 x 7-inch baking dish coated with cooking spray. Top eggplant with mozzarella cheese and tomato mixture. Reduce oven temperature to 375°. Bake, uncovered, 12 to 15 minutes, or until cheese melts. Sprinkle parsley and Parmesan over eggplant mixture. Serve immediately. Yield: 6 servings (serving size: 1 topped eggplant slice).

CALORIES 72; FAT 2.4g (sat 1.2g); PROTEIN 4.2g; CARBOHYDRATE 9.5g; FIBER 2.2g; CHOLESTEROL 6mg; IRON 0.9mg; SODIUM 215mg; CALCIUM 110mg

▶ carbo rating: 7

Peppers Braised with Herbs

If you don't have fresh tomatoes, substitute 2 cups of canned no-salt-added plum tomatoes, drained and chopped.

Cooking spray
1 teaspoon olive oil
2 onions, thinly sliced
½ cup dry white wine
2 tomatoes, peeled, seeded, and coarsely chopped
1 large red bell pepper, seeded and cut into strips
1 large green bell pepper, seeded and cut into strips
1 large yellow bell pepper, seeded and cut into strips
¼ teaspoon salt
½ cup fat-free, less-sodium chicken broth
9 mint or basil sprigs, divided

1. Coat a nonstick skillet with cooking spray, and add oil; place over medium-high heat until hot. Add onion, and cook 5 to 7 minutes or until tender, stirring often. Add wine; cook 2 to 3 minutes. Stir in tomato, bell pepper strips, and salt; bring to a boil. Reduce heat to low; cover and simmer 15 minutes.
2. Add broth and 1 mint sprig; cover and simmer 15 minutes. Remove from heat, and allow to cool to room temperature. Remove mint sprig, and discard. Garnish with remaining mint sprigs. Yield: 8 servings (serving size: ¾ cup).

CALORIES 60; FAT 1.1g (sat 0.2g); PROTEIN 1.5g; CARBOHYDRATE 9.8g; FIBER 2.4g; CHOLESTEROL 0mg; IRON 1.1mg; SODIUM 81mg; CALCIUM 18mg

▶ carbo rating: 7

Roasted Squash and Peppers

You can use this basic roasted vegetable recipe for any of your favorite vegetables. The baking time might vary slightly, depending on the size of the pieces.

3 small yellow squash
3 small zucchini
2 red bell peppers
Olive oil-flavored cooking spray
1 teaspoon dried oregano
¼ teaspoon salt
¼ teaspoon pepper
1 tablespoon balsamic vinegar

1. Preheat oven to 500°.
2. Cut squash and zucchini in half crosswise. Cut halves lengthwise into ½-inch-thick wedges. Cut bell peppers into 2-inch-long strips. Set pepper strips aside.
3. Coat a large baking sheet with cooking spray. Place squash and zucchini in a single layer on baking sheet; coat vegetables with cooking spray. Sprinkle with oregano, salt, and pepper.
4. Bake at 500° for 5 minutes. Turn squash and zucchini gently; add pepper strips. Bake an additional 8 minutes or to desired degree of doneness. Transfer vegetables to a serving bowl. Add vinegar to vegetables, and toss gently. Yield: 4 servings (serving size: 1 cup).

CALORIES 50; FAT 1g (sat 0.1g); PROTEIN 2.5g; CARBOHYDRATE 10.1g; FIBER 3g; CHOLESTEROL 0mg; IRON 1.8mg; SODIUM 153mg; CALCIUM 39mg

▶ carbo rating: 7
Roasted Vegetables

Roasting is one of the simplest cooking methods and one of the best ways to preserve the vitamin content in vegetables. It also brings out a vegetable's natural sweetness.

Olive oil-flavored cooking spray
  2   tomatoes, seeded and cut into 1-inch cubes
  1   red bell pepper, cut into 1-inch pieces
  1   yellow bell pepper, cut into 1-inch pieces
  1   small yellow onion, cut into ½-inch wedges and separated
  1   zucchini, cut into ½-inch-thick slices
  1   chipotle pepper in adobo sauce, drained, seeded, and finely chopped
  1   tablespoon extravirgin olive oil
  ¼   teaspoon salt
  ¼   teaspoon freshly ground black pepper

1. Preheat broiler.
2. Cover baking sheet with foil; coat with cooking spray. Arrange tomato, bell peppers, onion, and zucchini on baking sheet; coat vegetables with cooking spray. Broil 16 minutes, stirring once. Remove vegetables from baking sheet; transfer to a large serving bowl.
3. Combine chipotle pepper and next 3 ingredients in a small bowl; stir with a whisk until blended. Pour over warm vegetables; toss gently to coat. Serve warm or chilled. Yield: 6 servings (serving size: ½ cup).

CALORIES 60; FAT 2.7g (sat 0.4g); PROTEIN 1.6g; CARBOHYDRATE 8.8g; FIBER 2.2g; CHOLESTEROL 0mg; IRON 0.7mg; SODIUM 247mg; CALCIUM 18mg

▶ carbo rating: 7
Baked Tomatoes Tapenade

Bake this savory olive topping on top of fresh juicy tomatoes for a quick and easy side dish.

  ½   cup pitted kalamata olives, chopped
  2   teaspoons capers
  2   teaspoons olive oil
  1   teaspoon balsamic vinegar
  ½   teaspoon lemon juice
  1   garlic clove, minced
Cooking spray
  2   large tomatoes, sliced in half horizontally

1. Preheat oven to 400°.
2. Combine first 6 ingredients. Arrange tomato halves on a baking sheet coated with cooking spray. Bake at 400° for 6 minutes. Remove from oven. Top evenly with olive mixture. Bake at 400° for 6 minutes. Yield: 4 servings (serving size: 1 tomato half).

CALORIES 110; FAT 8.2g (sat 1g); PROTEIN 1.6g; CARBOHYDRATE 9.1g; FIBER 1.8g; CHOLESTEROL 0mg; IRON 0.8mg; SODIUM 392mg; CALCIUM 17mg

tomato tips

There's more to tomatoes than just their juicy freshness and bright red color. Tomatoes are packed full of good-for-you nutrients and are a very low-calorie food. One medium tomato can provide up to 20 percent of your daily recommended vitamin A and 40 percent of your daily recommended vitamin C, while packing in only about 30 calories. In addition to being a good source of soluble fiber and potassium, tomatoes have been shown to reduce the incidence of several cancers.

▶ **carbo rating: 8**

Buttery Herbed Green Beans

You can use any other dried herbs such as oregano, basil, or thyme for the tarragon for a flavor variation.

½   cup water
2   (9-ounce) packages frozen whole green beans
     (about 5 cups)
2   teaspoons butter
2   tablespoons finely chopped fresh parsley
2   teaspoons cider or balsamic vinegar
½   teaspoon salt
½   teaspoon dried tarragon
Parsley sprigs (optional)

1. Bring water to a boil over high heat in a large non-stick skillet; add green beans. Cover and cook 8 minutes or until beans are crisp-tender; drain.
2. Combine beans and butter in pan; cook over low heat until butter melts. Add chopped parsley, vinegar, salt, and tarragon; toss well. Garnish with parsley, if desired. Yield: 3 servings (serving size: 1 cup).

CALORIES 81; FAT 2.9g (sat 1.4g); PROTEIN 3.2g; CARBOHYDRATE 13.4g; FIBER 4.9g; CHOLESTEROL 7mg; IRON 1.7mg; SODIUM 412mg; CALCIUM 79mg

▶ **carbo rating: 8**

Buttery Baby Limas with Tarragon Mustard

The yogurt-based spread adds a sweet, buttery flavor to the baby limas.

1¼   cups water
1   (10-ounce) package frozen baby lima beans,
     thawed
2   tablespoons yogurt-based spread (such as
     Brummel & Brown)
1   tablespoon Dijon mustard
¼   teaspoon salt
¼   teaspoon dried tarragon
⅛   teaspoon pepper

1. Bring water to a boil in a small saucepan; add beans. Cover and simmer 8 minutes. Drain well.
2. Add yogurt-based spread and next 4 ingredients to beans; stir well. Yield: 5 servings (serving size: ⅓ cup).

CALORIES 85; FAT 2.5g (sat 0.5g); PROTEIN 4.2g; CARBOHYDRATE 12g; FIBER 3.6g; CHOLESTEROL 0mg; IRON 1.3mg; SODIUM 245mg; CALCIUM 22mg

► carbo rating: 8

Herbed Green Peas with Mushrooms

If you don't have tarragon, use the same amount of any savory herb like oregano or basil. If fresh herbs are in season, substitute 1 tablespoon of a minced fresh herb for each teaspoon of any dried herb.

1	teaspoon vegetable oil
½	cup thinly sliced onion
1½	cups sliced mushrooms
1½	cups frozen green peas, thawed
2	tablespoons water
1	teaspoon dried tarragon
¼	teaspoon salt
⅛	teaspoon freshly ground black pepper

1. Heat oil in a large nonstick skillet over medium heat until hot. Add onion; cook 4 minutes or until tender, stirring often. Add mushrooms; cook 4 minutes or until tender, stirring often. Stir in peas and remaining ingredients; cover and cook 4 minutes or just until peas are tender. Serve immediately. Yield: 4 servings (serving size: about ¾ cup).

CALORIES 69; FAT 1.3g (sat 0.2g); PROTEIN 3.6g; CARBOHYDRATE 10g; FIBER 2.5g; CHOLESTEROL 0mg; IRON 1.3mg; SODIUM 212mg; CALCIUM 17mg

► carbo rating: 9

Old-World Cabbage and Onions with Bacon

To shred cabbage, start by slicing the head into fourths; remove core of each wedge. Then turn over and thinly slice into shreds using a sharp knife.

2	bacon slices
1	cup thinly sliced Vidalia or other sweet onion
5	cups shredded cabbage
1	teaspoon "measures-like-sugar" calorie-free sweetener
¼	teaspoon salt
⅛	teaspoon pepper

1. Cook bacon in a large nonstick skillet over medium-high heat until crisp; remove bacon from pan, reserving 1 tablespoon drippings in pan. Crumble bacon.
2. Add onion to hot drippings; sauté 5 minutes or until tender. Add cabbage and sweetener; sauté 10 minutes. Stir in reserved bacon, salt, and pepper; remove from heat. Cover; let stand 2 minutes. Yield: 4 servings (serving size: ½ cup).

CALORIES 77; FAT 2g (sat 0.6g); PROTEIN 3.5g; CARBOHYDRATE 13.1g; FIBER 4g; CHOLESTEROL 3mg; IRON 0.9mg; SODIUM 220mg; CALCIUM 69mg

"I get tired of eating the same vegetable side dishes, so **it's great to have some new ones to jazz up my dinners.**"

Jenni Lawrence

▶ carbo rating: 9

Texas Caviar

This Texas "caviar" is made from black-eyed peas. It's better if you make it one to three days ahead so the flavors will blend. Serve this flavorful pea and vegetable medley with grilled chicken or pork.

1½ cups chopped tomato, seeded
⅓ cup thinly sliced green onions
2 tablespoons canned chopped green chiles
2 tablespoons white wine vinegar
1 tablespoon minced seeded jalapeño pepper
1 tablespoon chopped fresh cilantro
1 teaspoon olive oil
¼ teaspoon salt
¼ teaspoon ground cumin
⅛ teaspoon pepper
1 garlic clove, minced
1 (15.8-ounce) can black-eyed peas, rinsed and drained

1. Combine all ingredients in a bowl. Cover and chill. Yield: 6 servings (serving size: about ½ cup).

CALORIES 62; FAT 1.2g (sat 0.2g); PROTEIN 4g; CARBOHYDRATE 10g; FIBER 1.4g; CHOLESTEROL 0mg; IRON 1mg; SODIUM 210mg; CALCIUM 20mg

▶ carbo rating: 10

Mexican Black Beans

Slice green onions using kitchen scissors. There's less to clean up than if you slice them with a knife on a cutting board.

2 (15-ounce) cans black beans, rinsed and drained
1 (14½-ounce) can Mexican-style stewed tomatoes, undrained
1 tablespoon red wine vinegar
1 teaspoon "measures-like-sugar" calorie-free sweetener
¼ cup sliced green onions (about 2 large)

1. Combine first 4 ingredients in a large saucepan, stirring well. Cook over medium heat 10 minutes, stirring occasionally. Ladle beans into serving bowls; sprinkle each serving with sliced green onions. Yield: 7 servings (serving size: ¾ cup).

CALORIES 80; FAT 0.2g (sat 0.1g); PROTEIN 4.7g; CARBOHYDRATE 15.9g; FIBER 5.8g; CHOLESTEROL 0mg; IRON 1.5mg; SODIUM 346mg; CALCIUM 36mg

(pictured on page 318)

"Texas Caviar is also good to serve as an appetizer dip.
Scoop it up with Quick Pita Chips (page 63)."

Laurl Self

► carbo rating: 10

Creamed Spinach

If you can't find garlic-flavored light cream cheese, use plain light cream cheese and stir in ⅛ teaspoon garlic powder.

  1   (10-ounce) package frozen chopped spinach
  3   tablespoons roasted garlic-flavored light cream cheese
Cooking spray
  ¼   cup chopped onion (about ¼ small)
  ¼   cup chopped red bell pepper (about ¼ small)
  ¼   teaspoon salt
Dash of black pepper
  ¾   cup evaporated fat-free milk

1. Cook spinach according to package directions, omitting salt; drain well. Combine spinach and cream cheese in a bowl, stirring well.
2. Coat a medium saucepan with cooking spray; place over medium-high heat until hot. Add onion and red bell pepper, and cook 3 minutes or until tender, stirring often. Stir in spinach mixture, salt, and black pepper.
3. Reduce heat to medium-low. Gradually add milk, stirring until smooth. Cook, stirring constantly, 3 to 5 minutes or until mixture is creamy. Yield: 3 servings (serving size: ½ cup).

CALORIES 117; FAT 3.2g (sat 1.9g); PROTEIN 9.3g; CARBOHYDRATE 13.7g; FIBER 3.4g; CHOLESTEROL 10mg; IRON 2.3mg; SODIUM 430mg; CALCIUM 294mg

► carbo rating: 10

Artichokes with Browned Garlic and Lemon Dipping Sauce

Fresh artichokes with a dipping sauce are an elegant low-carb indulgence. Since you eat the artichoke piece by piece, you can eat slowly and enjoy the flavor of every bite.

  4   large artichokes
  2   teaspoons butter or margarine
  1   garlic clove, minced
  ¼   cup water
  2   tablespoons fresh lemon juice (about 1 lemon)
  1   tablespoon white wine Worcestershire sauce
  1   tablespoon Dijon mustard
Dash of ground white pepper

1. Wash artichokes by plunging up and down in cold water. Cut off stem ends; trim about ½ inch from top of each artichoke. Cut off artichoke stems; remove bottom leaves.
2. Place artichokes, stem ends down, in an 11 x 7-inch baking dish; add water to depth of 1 inch. Cover with heavy-duty plastic wrap, and vent. Microwave at HIGH 10 minutes or until a leaf near the center of each artichoke pulls out easily. Drain. Remove fuzzy choke from center of each artichoke with a spoon.
3. Melt butter in a small saucepan; stir in garlic. Cook over medium heat, stirring constantly, until garlic is lightly browned. Add water and next 4 ingredients; cook just until hot. Serve as a dipping sauce with whole artichokes. Yield: 4 servings (serving size: 1 artichoke and 2 tablespoons sauce).

CALORIES 91; FAT 2.4g (sat 1.3g); PROTEIN 3.5g; CARBOHYDRATE 16.7g; FIBER 6.5g; CHOLESTEROL 5mg; IRON 2mg; SODIUM 28mg; CALCIUM 66mg

(pictured on page 319)

► carbo rating: 11
Grilled Vegetable Skewers

Spoon these vegetables over mixed greens for a hearty salad, or wrap them in a whole wheat tortilla for a meat-free sandwich. Or if you want to cook the whole meal on the grill, serve them with the All-American Grilled Steak on page 207.

¼ cup olive oil
2 tablespoons tarragon or balsamic vinegar
¾ teaspoon dried thyme
½ teaspoon salt
¼ teaspoon pepper
1 clove garlic, crushed
2 large yellow squash, cut into ¾-inch-thick slices
1 large zucchini, cut into ¾-inch-thick slices
1 large green bell pepper, cut into 1-inch squares
1 large yellow bell pepper, cut into 1-inch squares
1 large red bell pepper, cut into 1-inch squares
¾ pound fresh mushrooms
Cooking spray

1. Combine oil and next 5 ingredients in a large bowl, stirring with a wire whisk. Add vegetables; toss gently. Cover and let stand 1 hour, tossing occasionally.
2. Prepare grill.
3. Drain vegetables, reserving marinade. Thread vegetables alternately on 5 (10-inch) skewers. Place skewers on grill rack coated with cooking spray; cover and grill 12 to 14 minutes or until vegetables are tender, turning once and basting with reserved marinade. Yield: 5 servings (serving size: 1 skewer or about 1 cup vegetables).

CALORIES 172; FAT 11.8g (sat 1.7g); PROTEIN 5.7g; CARBOHYDRATE 14.7g; FIBER 4.2g; CHOLESTEROL 0mg; IRON 1.7mg; SODIUM 244mg; CALCIUM 44mg

► carbo rating: 11
Spicy Black-Eyed Peas

If you're trying to cut back on sodium, use reduced-sodium bacon and omit the salt.

2 bacon slices
1 (16-ounce) can whole tomatoes, undrained and chopped
1 (15.8-ounce) can black-eyed peas, rinsed and drained
2 cups frozen chopped pepper, onion, and celery blend (such as McKenzie's)
1 teaspoon ground cumin
½ teaspoon dry mustard
½ teaspoon salt
½ teaspoon black pepper
½ teaspoon curry powder
½ teaspoon chili powder
1 garlic clove, minced
2 tablespoons chopped fresh parsley

1. Cook bacon in a large nonstick skillet over medium heat until crisp. Remove bacon; crumble and set aside. Drain pan.
2. Combine tomatoes and next 9 ingredients in pan. Bring to a boil; reduce heat, and simmer 20 minutes, stirring occasionally. Pour mixture into a serving dish; sprinkle with bacon and parsley. Yield: 6 servings (serving size: ½ cup).

CALORIES 79; FAT 2.1g (sat 0.6g); PROTEIN 3.4g; CARBOHYDRATE 13.4g; FIBER 2.7g; CHOLESTEROL 5mg; IRON 2mg; SODIUM 504mg; CALCIUM 42mg

▶ **carbo rating: 12**

Broccoli and Cauliflower au Gratin

The breadcrumb topping for the cheesy vegetables is made with whole wheat bread. Use 1½ (1-ounce) slices of whole wheat bread to get 1 cup of fresh breadcrumbs.

  2 cups coarsely chopped fresh broccoli florets
  2 cups coarsely chopped fresh cauliflower florets
  1 cup fresh whole wheat breadcrumbs
  1 teaspoon olive oil
  ½ teaspoon paprika
  ¼ teaspoon salt
  ¼ teaspoon pepper
  2 small garlic cloves, minced
  1 tablespoon all-purpose flour
  ½ cup fat-free milk
  1 cup (4 ounces) shredded reduced-fat sharp
     Cheddar cheese
  Cooking spray

1. Preheat oven to 375°.
2. Steam broccoli and cauliflower, covered, 5 minutes or until crisp-tender. Drain well; set aside.
3. Combine breadcrumbs and next 5 ingredients; stir well, and set aside.
4. Place flour in a small saucepan. Gradually add milk, stirring with a whisk until blended. Bring to a boil over medium-high heat, and cook 1 minute or until thick, stirring constantly. Remove from heat, and add cheese, stirring until cheese melts.
5. Combine vegetables and cheese sauce, stirring well to coat. Spoon mixture into a 1-quart baking dish coated with cooking spray. Sprinkle with breadcrumb mixture. Bake at 375° for 25 minutes or until breadcrumbs are lightly browned. Let stand 5 minutes before serving. Yield: 4 servings (serving size: about 1 cup).

CALORIES 153; FAT 6.2g (sat 2.7g); PROTEIN 10.7g; CARBOHYDRATE 15g; FIBER 2.9g; CHOLESTEROL 1.5mg; IRON 1.2mg; SODIUM 411mg; CALCIUM 270mg

(pictured on page 320)

▶ **carbo rating: 12**

Ratatouille

Ratatouille *is a traditional dish from the Provençe region of France and is a mixture of eggplant, tomatoes, onions, bell peppers, and garlic that is simmered in olive oil. You can serve it as a side dish with meats and poultry, or as an appetizer with whole wheat crackers.*

  2 teaspoons olive oil
  1 small onion, vertically sliced
  1 small eggplant, cut into ¾-inch cubes
  1 (14-ounce) can stewed tomatoes
  1 small yellow squash, cut in half lengthwise and
     thinly sliced
  1 zucchini, cut in half lengthwise and thinly sliced
  1 small green bell pepper, thinly sliced
  4 garlic cloves, minced
  1 teaspoon dried thyme
  1 teaspoon dried basil
  ¼ teaspoon freshly ground black pepper

1. Heat oil in a large nonstick skillet over medium heat. Add onion, and sauté 5 minutes. Add eggplant; sauté 5 minutes.
2. Add stewed tomatoes and next 5 ingredients to skillet; stir well. Cover, reduce heat, and simmer 15 minutes. Add basil and black pepper; cook 2 minutes. Serve warm or at room temperature. Yield: 5 servings (serving size: 1 cup).

CALORIES 85; FAT 2.3g (sat 0.3g); PROTEIN 2.7g; CARBOHYDRATE 15.4g; FIBER 3.3g; CHOLESTEROL 0mg; IRON 1.6mg; SODIUM 208mg; CALCIUM 60mg

▶ carbo rating: 13

Grilled Vegetable Salsa

Serve this smoky salsa with grilled shrimp or chicken. The flavor and color of the salsa are best when all three colors of bell pepper are used, but it's still good if you use only one type of pepper. The carbo rating will essentially be the same.

1	pound red bell peppers
1	pound yellow bell peppers
1	pound green bell peppers

Cooking spray

2	portobello mushroom caps (about 8 ounces)
1	red onion, cut into ½-inch-thick slices
1	tablespoon chopped fresh thyme
1	tablespoon balsamic vinegar
½	teaspoon salt
¼	teaspoon black pepper

1. Prepare grill.
2. Cut each bell pepper in half; discard stems, seeds, and membranes.
3. Place bell pepper halves, skin sides down, on grill rack coated with cooking spray. Add mushroom caps and onion slices to rack; cover and grill 20 minutes or until vegetables are tender, turning mushroom caps and onions after 10 minutes (do not turn bell pepper halves). Remove vegetables from grill rack. Set mushroom caps and onions aside. Place bell pepper halves in a large zip-top plastic bag immediately; seal bag, and let stand 15 minutes.
4. Peel bell pepper halves, and coarsely chop. Coarsely chop mushroom caps and onion slices. Combine chopped vegetables, thyme, and remaining ingredients in a bowl; stir well. Serve warm or at room temperature. Yield: 6 servings (serving size: ½ cup).

CALORIES 70; FAT 0.5g (sat 0.1g); PROTEIN 3g; CARBOHYDRATE 15.5g; FIBER 2.6g; CHOLESTEROL 0mg; IRON 1.1mg; SODIUM 202mg; CALCIUM 29mg

▶ carbo rating: 13

Stir-Fried Brown Rice

There's no need to give up stir-fried rice when you're watching carbs. Just switch to high-fiber brown rice. Brown rice has five times more fiber than white rice.

Cooking spray

1	teaspoon olive oil
¾	cup chopped celery
½	cup chopped onion
¼	cup thinly sliced carrot
1	teaspoon ground cumin
1	teaspoon minced peeled fresh ginger
1¼	cups fat-free, less-sodium chicken broth
1	cup uncooked instant brown rice
3	tablespoons dried tomato sprinkles
1	cup frozen green peas, thawed

1. Coat a large nonstick skillet with cooking spray; add oil, and place over medium-high heat until hot. Add celery, onion, and carrot; cook 4 minutes or until vegetables are tender, stirring often. Stir in cumin and ginger; cook, stirring constantly, 1 minute. Add broth, rice, and tomato sprinkles; bring to a boil. Cover, reduce heat, and simmer 15 minutes or until liquid is absorbed and rice is tender. Stir in peas. Yield: 7 servings (serving size: about ½ cup).

CALORIES 90; FAT 1.3g (sat 0.1g); PROTEIN 3.9g; CARBOHYDRATE 15.8g; FIBER 2.4g; CHOLESTEROL 0mg; IRON 0.7mg; SODIUM 313mg; CALCIUM 17mg

(pictured on page 385)

▶ **carbo rating: 16**

Stuffed Zucchini and Yellow Squash

To save time, you can use packaged angel hair coleslaw instead of shredding the cabbage yourself.

2	zucchini, halved lengthwise (about 6 ounces each)
2	yellow squash, halved lengthwise (about 6 ounces each)

Cooking spray

2	cups shredded green cabbage
1	cup finely chopped onion
1	cup finely chopped green bell pepper
1	teaspoon dried oregano
2	garlic cloves, minced

Dash of crushed red pepper

2	(1-ounce) slices whole wheat bread
¾	cup (3 ounces) shredded part-skim mozzarella cheese
¼	cup chopped fresh parsley
2	tablespoons Parmesan cheese
½	teaspoon salt
⅛	teaspoon black pepper

1. Preheat oven to 350°.
2. Scoop pulp out of zucchini and yellow squash, leaving a ¼-inch shell. Place squash and zucchini shells on a baking sheet, and set aside. Coarsely chop pulp.
3. Coat a large nonstick skillet with cooking spray; place over medium-high heat. Add pulp, cabbage, and next 5 ingredients. Cook 10 minutes or until liquid is absorbed and vegetables are tender, stirring constantly. Remove from heat.
4. Place bread in a food processor; pulse 5 to 7 times or until coarse crumbs form.
5. Add breadcrumbs, cheese, and next 4 ingredients to vegetable mixture; stir well. Spoon vegetable mixture evenly into squash and zucchini shells, pressing firmly. Bake at 350° for 25 to 30 minutes or until shells are tender. Yield: 4 servings (serving size: 1 squash half and 1 zucchini half).

CALORIES 171; FAT 5.7g (sat 3g); PROTEIN 12.4g; CARBOHYDRATE 20.7g; FIBER 4.9g; CHOLESTEROL 14mg; IRON 2.1mg; SODIUM 545mg; CALCIUM 277mg

▶ **carbo rating: 18**

Mushroom Barley

Look for barley on the same aisle in the supermarket as rice and other grains. Cooked barley has more than 1½ times the fiber of cooked brown rice.

1	(14¼-ounce) can low-salt beef broth
1	tablespoon low-sodium Worcestershire sauce
¼	teaspoon salt
¼	teaspoon pepper
1	cup uncooked quick-cooking barley

Cooking spray

1	(8-ounce) package sliced mushrooms
¾	cup frozen chopped onion, thawed
½	cup finely chopped celery (about 1 rib)

1. Combine first 4 ingredients in a medium saucepan; bring to a boil. Add barley; cover, reduce heat, and simmer 10 minutes. Remove from heat; let stand 5 minutes.
2. Coat a nonstick skillet with cooking spray; place over medium-high heat until hot. Add mushrooms, onion, and celery; cook 3 minutes or until tender, stirring often. Stir into cooked barley. Yield: 8 servings (serving size: ¾ cup).

CALORIES 109; FAT 0.5g (sat 0.1g); PROTEIN 3.4g; CARBOHYDRATE 23g; FIBER 4.7g; CHOLESTEROL 0mg; IRON 1.1mg; SODIUM 93mg; CALCIUM 15mg

(pictured on page 386)

mushroom know-how

Choosing: Mushrooms should have a mushroomy aroma. If they don't smell good, chances are they won't taste good. Avoid wet spots; dry, cracking edges; flattened gills (under the cap); splayed-out caps; wrinkled flesh; telltale insect holes; and white mold.
Cleaning: Some mushrooms carry little sand or dirt and only need a quick wipe with a damp paper towel to clean. Others, especially wild varieties, attract ferns, pine needles, dirt, and other cling-ons, so it may take longer to clean them. Remove the stems, discarding or saving for later use. Use a damp paper towel or a soft brush to wipe both sides of the cap.

▶ carbo rating: 20

Brown Rice with Peas

Make nutty-tasting brown rice a staple in your kitchen—it has five times more fiber than white rice, so the carbo rating is lower than that of white rice.

1⅓	cups water
1	cup uncooked instant brown rice
1	cup frozen green peas
2	tablespoons thinly sliced green onions
1½	tablespoons preshredded fresh Parmesan cheese
1	teaspoon butter
⅛	teaspoon salt
⅛	teaspoon freshly ground black pepper

1. Combine water and rice in a medium saucepan. Bring to a boil; cover, reduce heat, and simmer 10 minutes or until water is absorbed and rice is tender.
2. Stir in green peas and remaining ingredients. Yield: 4 servings (serving size: ¾ cup).

CALORIES 130; FAT 2.4g (sat 1g); PROTEIN 4.6g; CARBOHYDRATE 22.3g; FIBER 2.8g; CHOLESTEROL 4mg; IRON 0.8mg; SODIUM 161mg; CALCIUM 32mg

▶ carbo rating: 21

Roasted Sweet Potatoes and Onions

Sweet potatoes are one of nature's most nutrient-dense foods. Sweet potatoes are rich in beta carotene, vitamin C, and vitamin E. One cup has more than six times the recommended amount of beta carotene and 50 percent of the Recommended Dietary Allowance (RDA) for vitamin C.

1	large sweet potato, peeled and cut into ½-inch cubes
1	onion, cut into ½-inch wedges
2	teaspoons extravirgin olive oil
¼	teaspoon salt
⅛	teaspoon pepper
	Cooking spray

1. Preheat oven to 400°.
2. Combine first 5 ingredients in a large bowl; toss well.
3. Arrange potato mixture in a single layer on a non-stick baking sheet. Coat potato mixture lightly with cooking spray. Bake at 400° for 20 to 25 minutes or until potato is tender, stirring once. Serve immediately. Yield: 4 servings (serving size: ½ cup).

CALORIES 121; FAT 2.6g (sat 0.4g); PROTEIN 1.8g; CARBOHYDRATE 23.2g; FIBER 2.2g; CHOLESTEROL 0mg; IRON 0.6mg; SODIUM 158mg; CALCIUM 26mg

▶ **carbo rating: 26**

Sesame-Garlic Brown Rice

Pump up the flavor of your meal with this Asian-inspired brown rice recipe.

1⅓	cups water
1	cup uncooked instant brown rice
2	teaspoons dark sesame oil
1	cup shredded carrot
1	tablespoon bottled minced garlic
¼	cup thinly sliced green onions (about 2 large)
1	tablespoon low-sodium soy sauce
¼	teaspoon salt
¼	teaspoon coarsely ground black pepper

1. Combine water and rice in a medium saucepan; bring to a boil over medium heat. Cover, reduce heat, and simmer 10 minutes or until water is absorbed.
2. Heat sesame oil in a small nonstick skillet; add carrot, and sauté 2 to 3 minutes or until crisp-tender.
3. Remove rice from heat; stir in sautéed carrot, garlic, and remaining ingredients. Yield: 4 servings (serving size: ¾ cup).

CALORIES 155; FAT 3.1g (sat 0.3g); PROTEIN 2.9g; CARBOHYDRATE 29g; FIBER 2.8g; CHOLESTEROL 0mg; IRON 0.9mg; SODIUM 295mg; CALCIUM 30mg

---

simple substitutions

If you have leftover brown rice, the Sesame-Garlic Brown Rice recipe (above) is a great way to use it. Just reheat the rice in the skillet, and stir in the other ingredients. You'll need about 2 cups of cooked rice.

▶ **carbo rating: 26**

Brown Rice Pilaf

Instead of carrot and celery, you can sauté bell peppers and squash to stir into the rice.

1	teaspoon olive oil
½	cup diced carrot
⅓	cup diced celery
¼	cup chopped onion
1	cup uncooked long-grain brown rice
½	cup water
¼	teaspoon salt
⅛	teaspoon pepper
1	(14-ounce) can fat-free, less-sodium chicken broth
¾	cup frozen green peas, thawed
1½	to 2 tablespoons chopped fresh dill

1. Heat oil in a large saucepan over medium heat. Add carrot, celery, and onion; sauté 4 minutes or until tender. Add rice and next 4 ingredients; stir well. Bring to a boil; reduce heat, and simmer, covered, 45 minutes or until rice is tender.
2. Add peas, and stir gently. Remove from heat, and let stand 5 minutes. Add dill, and stir gently. Yield: 6 servings (serving size: ½ cup).

CALORIES 152; FAT 1.8g (sat 0.3g); PROTEIN 4.9g; CARBOHYDRATE 29.4g; FIBER 3.4g; CHOLESTEROL 0mg; IRON 0.9mg; SODIUM 327mg; CALCIUM 25mg

vegetable purchasing guide

How much do I need to buy? What do I do with it? Here's what you need to know about buying and preparing fresh vegetables, plus the carbo rating for one serving of each vegetable.

Vegetable	Approximate Servings	Preparation*	Carbo Rating
Artichoke, globe	2 servings per pound (2 artichokes)	Wash; cut off stem and ½ inch off top. Remove loose bottom leaves. Cut off thorny tips with scissors. Rub cut surfaces with lemon.	1 medium: 7
Asparagus	3 to 4 servings per pound	Snap off tough ends. Remove scales, if desired.	4 ounces: 2
Beans, dried	6 to 8 servings per pound	Sort and wash. Cover with water 2 inches above beans; soak overnight. Drain. Or cover with water, bring to a boil, and cook 2 minutes. Remove from heat, and let stand 1 hour. Drain.	½ cup, cooked: 14
Beans, green	4 servings per pound	Wash; trim ends, and remove strings.	½ cup: 1
Beans, lima	2 servings per pound unshelled 4 servings per pound shelled	Shell and wash.	½ cup, cooked: 14
Beets	3 to 4 servings per pound	Leave root and 1 inch of stem; scrub with vegetable brush.	1 medium: 6
Broccoli	3 to 4 servings per pound	Remove outer leaves and tough ends of lower stalks. Wash. Cut into spears or chop.	½ cup: 1
Brussels sprouts	4 servings per pound	Wash; remove discolored leaves. Cut off stem ends.	½ cup: 2
Cabbage	4 servings per pound	Remove outer leaves; wash. Shred, chop, or cut into wedges.	½ cup: 1
Carrots	4 servings per pound	Scrape; remove ends, and rinse. Leave tiny carrots whole; large: slice, chop, or cut into strips.	½ cup: 4
Cauliflower	4 servings per head	Remove outer leaves and stalk; wash. Leave whole, or break into florets.	½ cup: 1
Celery	4 servings per bunch	Separate stalks; trim off leaves and base. Rinse. Slice diagonally, or chop.	½ cup: 1
Cucumbers	2 servings per cucumber	Peel, if desired; slice or chop.	½ cup: 1
Eggplant	2 to 3 servings per pound	Wash and peel, if desired. Cut into cubes, or cut crosswise into slices.	½ cup, cooked: 3

Note: All carbo ratings are for raw vegetables unless otherwise indicated.

Vegetable	Approximate Servings	Preparation*	Carbo Rating
Greens	3 to 4 servings per pound	Remove stems; wash thoroughly. Tear into bite-sized pieces.	½ cup, cooked: 1
Leeks	3 servings per pound	Remove root, tough outer leaves, and tops, leaving 2 inches of dark leaves. Wash thoroughly. Slice, if desired.	½ cup, cooked: 3
Mushrooms	4 servings per pound	Wipe with damp paper towels, or wash gently and pat dry. Cut off tips of stems. Slice, if desired.	½ cup: 1
Okra	4 servings per pound	Wash and pat dry. Trim ends.	½ cup, cooked: 2
Onions	4 servings per pound	Peel; cut large onions into quarters or slices, or leave small onions whole.	½ cup: 7
Parsnips	4 servings per pound	Scrape; cut off ends. Slice or chop.	½ cup, cooked: 10
Peas, black-eyed, fresh	2 servings per pound unshelled 4 servings per pound shelled	Shell and wash.	½ cup, cooked: 12
Peas, snow	4 servings per pound	Wash; trim ends, and remove tough strings.	½ cup: 2
Peppers, bell	1 serving per pepper	Cut off top, and remove seeds and membranes. Leave whole to stuff, slice into thin strips, or chop.	½ cup: 2
Potatoes, sweet	2 to 3 servings per pound	Scrub potatoes. Leave whole to bake, or peel, if desired, and slice or cut into chunks.	1 small: 19
Pumpkin	4½ to 5 cups cooked, mashed per 5-pound pumpkin	Slice in half crosswise. Remove seeds.	½ cup, cooked: 5
Rutabagas	2 to 3 servings per pound	Wash; peel, and slice or cube.	½ cup, cooked: 6
Squash, spaghetti	2 servings per pound	Rinse; cut in half lengthwise, and discard seeds.	½ cup, cooked: 4
Squash, summer	3 to 4 servings per pound	Wash; trim ends. Slice or chop.	½ cup: 1
Squash, winter (acorn, butternut, hubbard)	2 servings per pound	Rinse; cut in half, and remove seeds.	½ cup, cooked: 10
Tomatoes	4 servings per pound	Wash; peel, if desired. Slice or chop.	½ cup: 2
Turnips	3 servings per pound	Wash; peel, and slice or cube.	½ cup, cooked: 2

*The preparation instructions are general; refer to your recipe for more detailed directions.

soups & sandwiches

If you think you have to give up the comfort of a soup and sandwich combo because of your low-carb diet, think again. Simmer a pot of hearty *Slow-Cooker Chili* (page 362) and sink your teeth into a *Grilled Three-Cheese Sandwich* (page 351) without going over your carb limit.

▶ carbo rating: 6
Creole Shrimp Stew

If you're buying unpeeled shrimp, you'll need to buy ½ pound to get 6 ounces of peeled and deveined shrimp.

    Cooking spray
- 1   teaspoon vegetable oil
- ½   cup chopped onion
- ½   cup chopped celery
- 1½   teaspoons minced fresh or ½ teaspoon dried thyme
- ½   teaspoon salt
- ¼   teaspoon freshly ground black pepper
- 1   (14.5-ounce) can no-salt-added diced tomatoes, undrained
- 2   tablespoons dry red wine
- 6   ounces peeled and deveined medium shrimp
- 6   ounces halibut fillets, cut into bite-sized pieces

1. Coat a Dutch oven with cooking spray; add oil. Place over medium-high heat until hot. Add onion and next 4 ingredients; sauté 5 minutes. Add tomato and wine. Bring to a boil; reduce heat, and simmer, uncovered, 5 minutes.
2. Add shrimp and fillets to Dutch oven. Cover and simmer 5 minutes or until shrimp are done and fish flakes easily when tested with a fork. Yield: 4 servings (serving size: 1 cup).

CALORIES 132; FAT 3g (sat 0.5g); PROTEIN 18.7g; CARBOHYDRATE 7.3g; FIBER 1.4g; CHOLESTEROL 85mg; IRON 1.9mg; SODIUM 406mg; CALCIUM 71mg

tomato benefits

Eating tomatoes, especially canned tomato products such as diced or whole tomatoes, tomato sauce, and tomato paste, may help prevent cancer. These products contain lycopene, an antioxidant that has been shown to reduce the risk of prostate, colon, and bladder cancers.

▶ carbo rating: 7
Fresh Tomato Soup with Cilantro

Cilantro adds an assertive flavor to dishes and is used frequently in the cuisines of Mexico, the Caribbean, India, and Thailand. It's best to add cilantro at the end of cooking because it loses its flavor when heated for a long time.

- 1   cup vertically sliced onion
- 1   teaspoon olive oil
- ¼   cup thinly sliced celery
- 1   small garlic clove, minced
- 1   teaspoon ground cumin
- ½   teaspoon salt
- ⅛   to ¼ teaspoon pepper
- 4   cups coarsely chopped peeled tomato (about 2½ pounds)
- 2   cups fat-free, less-sodium chicken broth
- ⅓   cup water
- 2   tablespoons chopped fresh cilantro

    Cilantro sprigs (optional)

1. Cut onion slices in half. Heat oil in a large saucepan over medium heat. Add onion, celery, and garlic; sauté 4 minutes or until tender. Add cumin, salt, and pepper; cook 2 minutes, stirring constantly. Add tomato, chicken broth, and water; bring to a boil. Reduce heat, and simmer, uncovered, 10 minutes.
2. Place 2½ cups tomato mixture in a blender; process until smooth. Return tomato puree to pan, and stir well. Stir in chopped cilantro. Serve warm or chilled. Garnish with cilantro sprigs, if desired. Yield: 6 cups (serving size: 1 cup).

CALORIES 52; FAT 1.3g (sat 0.2g); PROTEIN 1.7g; CARBOHYDRATE 9.1g; FIBER 2g; CHOLESTEROL 0mg; IRON 1mg; SODIUM 352mg; CALCIUM 18mg

▶ **carbo rating: 8**

Shrimp and Crab Bouillabaisse

Traditionally, a bouillabaisse is served over thick slices of French bread. This low-carb version omits the bread and highlights the rich blend of flavors from the spiced broth, savory vegetables, and fresh seafood.

1	pound unpeeled medium shrimp
6	cups water

Olive oil-flavored cooking spray

1	teaspoon olive oil
2	cups chopped tomato
1	cup chopped onion
1	teaspoon ground coriander
1	teaspoon ground cumin
½	teaspoon pepper
3	garlic cloves, minced
3	cups fat-free, less-sodium chicken broth
½	pound fresh lump crabmeat, drained
½	cup chopped fresh cilantro
¼	cup dry white wine

1. Peel and devein shrimp. Bring water to a boil in a large saucepan; add shrimp, and cook 3 to 5 minutes or until shrimp are done. Drain well, and set aside.
2. Coat a Dutch oven with cooking spray; add oil. Place over medium-high heat until hot. Add tomato and next 5 ingredients; sauté 5 minutes or until onion is tender. Add broth; bring to a boil. Add shrimp, crabmeat, cilantro, and wine. Reduce heat, and simmer 2 minutes. Yield: 5 servings (serving size: 1½ cups).

CALORIES 188; FAT 3.4g (sat 0.5g); PROTEIN 29.5g; CARBOHYDRATE 9.3g; FIBER 2g; CHOLESTEROL 165mg; IRON 3.1mg; SODIUM 652mg; CALCIUM 92mg

▶ **carbo rating: 9**

Thai Hot-and-Sour Soup

A lot of Thai foods are high in carbs because they include noodles or a sweet peanut or coconut sauce. This soup features the heat of Thai food without the sweet.

1	pound unpeeled medium shrimp
1	teaspoon olive oil

Olive oil-flavored cooking spray

4	garlic cloves, minced
1	teaspoon crushed red pepper
1	cup chopped onion
1	cup sliced mushrooms
1	cup chopped seeded peeled tomato
½	cup drained canned bamboo shoots, cut into thin strips
1	teaspoon ground ginger
1	teaspoon hot sauce
¼	teaspoon dried lemon peel
4½	cups fat-free, less-sodium chicken broth
2	tablespoons low-sodium soy sauce
2	tablespoons lime juice

1. Peel and devein shrimp; set aside.
2. Heat oil in a large saucepan coated with cooking spray over medium-high heat. Add garlic and red pepper; sauté 1 minute. Add onion and next 6 ingredients; sauté until onion is tender. Add chicken broth and soy sauce; bring to a boil. Cover, reduce heat, and simmer 25 minutes.
3. Stir in shrimp and lime juice. Cook 3 minutes or until shrimp are done. Yield: 5 servings (serving size: 1½ cups).

CALORIES 156; FAT 2.8g (sat 0.5g); PROTEIN 23.2g; CARBOHYDRATE 9.8g; FIBER 1.4g; CHOLESTEROL 138mg; IRON 2.8mg; SODIUM 917mg; CALCIUM 67mg

what's the difference?

Chowder, bisque, chili, stew: these various dishes all warm you up on a cold day, are served in a soup bowl, and are eaten with a spoon. But what's the real difference between these dishes, and which ones are better low-carb choices? Here are some general definitions and some tips on how each might fit into a low-carb plan.

Bisque: a thick, rich soup made of pureed food and cream or milk. It may contain vegetables, seafood, or poultry. The cream mixture in a bisque is usually thickened with a few tablespoons of flour, but the source of most of the carbohydrate will be the cream or milk and the vegetables. A seafood bisque will probably have slightly less carbohydrate than a vegetable bisque.

Chowder: a thick, rich, chunky soup made with seafood or vegetables. Chowders often have potatoes, so this type of soup is usually not the best low-carb choice.

Chili: a blend of diced or ground beef, tomatoes, chiles, chili powder, and often beans. Vegetarian and chicken chilis are also options. Chili is usually a good choice because, even though it does contain carbohydrate, most of that carbohydrate is from beans and tomatoes. Top your chili with cheese, sour cream, or onions instead of crackers.

Gumbo: a thick, stewlike dish that begins with a dark roux (a mixture of cooked fat and flour), which lends a rich flavor and adds thickness. Vegetables found in a gumbo include tomatoes, onions, and okra, which also serves as a thickener. Gumbo also includes a variety of meats or shellfish, such as chicken, sausage, and shrimp. Gumbo almost always has rice, so if you're making your own, use brown rice.

Soup: a combination of vegetables and meat cooked in a broth; it may be served hot or cold. Select soups without pasta or potatoes.

Stew: a combination of meat, vegetables, and a thick broth created from the stewing liquid and the natural juices of the food being cooked. Choose stews with vegetables other than potatoes.

▶ carbo rating: 9

Pork and Vegetable Stew

Briefly freeze the pork to make it easier to cut into pieces.

Cooking spray
2   teaspoons olive oil
1½ pounds boneless pork loin, cut into 2-inch pieces
1   cup finely chopped onion
3   cups (1-inch) cubed peeled butternut squash (about 14 ounces)
1½ cups matchstick-cut carrot
1¼ cups finely chopped celery
1   teaspoon dried rubbed sage
¾   teaspoon pepper
½   teaspoon salt
1   (28-ounce) can diced tomatoes, undrained
1   (14-ounce) can fat-free, less-sodium chicken broth
1   garlic clove, minced
1   tablespoon grated orange rind

1. Heat oil in Dutch oven coated with cooking spray over medium-high heat. Add pork; cook 5 minutes, stirring occasionally. Add onion; sauté 5 minutes. Stir in squash and next 8 ingredients. Bring to a boil; cover, reduce heat, and simmer 45 minutes or until squash and pork are tender. Stir in orange rind. Yield: 9 servings (serving size: 1 cup).

CALORIES 172; FAT 5.5g (sat 1.7g); PROTEIN 18.6g; CARBOHYDRATE 12.6g; FIBER 3.3g; CHOLESTEROL 45mg; IRON 1.6mg; SODIUM 537mg; CALCIUM 74mg

► carbo rating: 9

Cream of Cauliflower Soup with Curry

Fresh cauliflower may be substituted for frozen. Just steam 1 pound of fresh cauliflower florets before they're added in the second step.

Cooking spray
- 1 cup chopped onion
- ½ cup chopped celery
- ½ cup chopped carrot
- 1 (16-ounce) package frozen cauliflower florets, thawed
- 1 (14-ounce) can fat-free, less-sodium chicken broth
- ½ teaspoon curry powder
- ¼ teaspoon pepper
- 2 cups fat-free milk, divided
- ¾ teaspoon salt
- 2 tablespoons light butter

Celery leaves (optional)

1. Heat a Dutch oven coated with cooking spray over medium-high heat. Add onion, celery, and carrot; sauté 4 minutes.
2. Add cauliflower, broth, curry powder, and pepper; bring to a boil over high heat. Cover, reduce heat, and simmer 20 minutes or until carrot is tender.
3. Remove from heat; stir in 1 cup milk. Place 1 cup cauliflower mixture in a blender; process 10 seconds or until smooth, and pour into a large bowl. Repeat procedure with remaining cauliflower mixture.
4. Return cauliflower mixture to pan; stir in 1 cup milk and salt. Cook over medium heat until thoroughly heated, stirring frequently. Remove soup from heat; add butter, stirring until butter melts. Garnish with celery leaves, if desired. Yield: 6 servings (serving size: 1 cup).

CALORIES 85; FAT 2.5g (sat 1.5g); PROTEIN 6.1g; CARBOHYDRATE 11.7g; FIBER 2.8g; CHOLESTEROL 8mg; IRON 0.7mg; SODIUM 577mg; CALCIUM 131mg

(pictured on page 387)

► carbo rating: 9

Grilled Three-Cheese Sandwiches

You can use other cheeses in place of the Swiss and Cheddar, but keep the blue cheese because of the sharp flavor and crumbly texture it contributes to the mixture. The carbo rating will remain the same, no matter which cheeses you use. Because of all the cheese, this sandwich provides about one-third of your daily calcium requirement.

- ½ cup (2 ounces) shredded reduced-fat Swiss cheese
- ½ cup (2 ounces) shredded reduced-fat sharp Cheddar cheese
- ½ cup (2 ounces) crumbled blue cheese
- ¼ cup fat-free mayonnaise
- 1 tablespoon finely chopped green onions
- 8 (1-ounce) slices low-carb multigrain bread
- 2 tablespoons yogurt-based spread (such as Brummel & Brown)

1. Preheat griddle.
2. Combine first 5 ingredients; stir well. Spread cheese mixture evenly over 4 bread slices. Top with remaining bread slices.
3. Spread tops of sandwiches evenly with half of yogurt-based spread. Place sandwiches, spread side down, on a medium-hot griddle (325°). Cook 5 minutes or until bottom bread slices are lightly browned. Spread remaining yogurt-based spread on tops of sandwiches; turn sandwiches. Cook 5 minutes or until bottom bread slices are lightly browned and cheese melts. Yield: 4 servings (serving size: 1 sandwich).

Note: These sandwiches were analyzed with a multigrain bread that has 7 grams of carbohydrate and 4 grams of fiber per 1-ounce slice.

CALORIES 329; FAT 18.2g (sat 8g); PROTEIN 25.5g; CARBOHYDRATE 17.5g; FIBER 8.5g; CHOLESTEROL 34mg; IRON 0.1mg; SODIUM 554mg; CALCIUM 340mg

▶ carbo rating: 10
Veal and Artichoke Stew

The small amount of flour (about 2 teaspoons per serving) adds to the browning of the veal and helps thicken the stew.

3	tablespoons all-purpose flour
½	teaspoon salt
1½	pounds lean boned veal shoulder roast, cut into 1-inch cubes
1	tablespoon vegetable oil
1	cup chopped onion
2½	cups fat-free, less-sodium chicken broth
2	tablespoons lemon juice
½	teaspoon lemon pepper
½	teaspoon dried tarragon
2	(9-ounce) packages frozen artichoke hearts

1. Combine flour and salt in a shallow dish; stir well. Dredge veal in flour mixture.
2. Heat oil in a Dutch oven over medium-high heat; add veal, and cook 6 minutes, stirring occasionally. Add onion; sauté 2 minutes.
3. Stir in broth, lemon juice, lemon pepper, and tarragon; bring to a boil. Cover, reduce heat, and simmer 1 hour.
4. Add artichoke hearts; bring to a boil. Reduce heat, and simmer, uncovered, 10 minutes or until veal and artichoke hearts are tender and sauce thickens. Yield: 6 servings (serving size: 1 cup).

CALORIES 205; FAT 6.1g (sat 1.5g); PROTEIN 26g; CARBOHYDRATE 11g; FIBER 1.1g; CHOLESTEROL 98mg; IRON 1.6mg; SODIUM 621mg; CALCIUM 36mg

▶ carbo rating: 11
Fresh Tomato Soup

Make the most out of summertime's sweet and juicy garden-fresh tomatoes.

1⅓	pounds fresh tomatoes (about 4 medium)
⅔	cup water
⅓	cup chopped onion
1¼	cups fat-free, less-sodium chicken broth
1	(8-ounce) can no-salt-added tomato sauce
½	teaspoon sugar
¼	teaspoon salt
⅛	teaspoon pepper
1	tablespoon chopped fresh basil
1	teaspoon chopped fresh thyme

1. With a knife, make a shallow X on bottom of each tomato. Dip tomatoes into a large pot of boiling water to blanch 30 seconds or just until skins begin to crack. Plunge immediately into ice water. Remove from water, and pull skin away, using a sharp paring knife. Gently remove seeds, and chop tomato.
2. Combine water and onion in a large saucepan. Bring to a boil; reduce heat, and simmer, uncovered, 5 minutes. Stir in tomato, chicken broth, and next 4 ingredients. Bring to a boil; reduce heat, and simmer, covered, 25 minutes.
3. Stir in basil and thyme. Simmer, uncovered, 5 minutes. Remove from heat; cool 10 minutes.
4. Place half of mixture in a blender; process until smooth. Repeat with remaining mixture. Return to saucepan. Cook 3 to 4 minutes or until thoroughly heated. Serve immediately. Yield: 4 servings (serving size: 1 cup).

CALORIES 66; FAT 0.6g (sat 0.1g); PROTEIN 2.2g; CARBOHYDRATE 13.9g; FIBER 2.9g; CHOLESTEROL 0mg; IRON 1.3mg; SODIUM 349mg; CALCIUM 30mg

► carbo rating: 11

Butternut Squash and Caramelized Onion Soup with Pesto

Savory pesto is a great low-carb way to add another level of flavor to cream soups. The butternut squash and caramelized onions add a subtle sweet flavor to the soup.

1	butternut squash (about 1¾ pounds), halved lengthwise
2	teaspoons olive oil
3	cups sliced Vidalia or other sweet onion (about 1 large)
½	cup Sauternes or other sweet white wine
2	(14-ounce) cans fat-free, less-sodium chicken broth
2	tablespoons commercial pesto

1. Preheat oven to 375°.

2. Place butternut squash, cut side down, in a baking dish. Pour water to a depth of ½ inch. Bake at 375° for 45 minutes or until very tender. Scoop out pulp; set aside.

3. Heat oil in a large skillet over medium heat. Add onion; cook 30 minutes or until golden brown, stirring frequently. Stir in wine and chicken broth. Bring to a boil; cover, reduce heat, and simmer 10 minutes or until onion is tender. Cool 5 minutes.

4. Place half of onion mixture and half of squash in a blender; process at low speed until smooth. Return soup to pan; repeat procedure with remaining squash and onion. Bring to a boil; reduce heat, and simmer, uncovered, 5 minutes or until thoroughly heated. Ladle into bowls; spoon 1 teaspoon pesto into center of each bowl. Swirl soup and pesto together using the tip of a knife. Yield: 6 servings (serving size: ¾ cup soup and 1 teaspoon pesto).

CALORIES 104; FAT 4g (sat 0.9g); PROTEIN 4.2g; CARBOHYDRATE 14.8g; FIBER 3.5g; CHOLESTEROL 2mg; IRON 0.9mg; SODIUM 421mg; CALCIUM 83mg

► carbo rating: 12

Egg Drop Soup

The egg drop soups that are served in most Chinese restaurants are fairly similar to this homemade one. If you're eating out, you can count on this same amount of carbohydrate.

¾	cup hot water
¼	ounce dried wood ear mushrooms
2	tablespoons fresh lemon juice
1	tablespoon low-sodium soy sauce
2	teaspoons grated peeled fresh ginger
⅛	teaspoon pepper
1	garlic clove, halved
3	(14-ounce) cans fat-free, less-sodium chicken broth
2	large eggs, lightly beaten
3	green onions, thinly sliced

1. Combine water and mushrooms in a small bowl; cover and let stand 30 minutes.

2. Drain mushrooms, reserving ½ cup liquid. Discard mushroom stems. Cut mushroom caps into thin slices. Combine mushroom caps, reserved ½ cup liquid, lemon juice, soy sauce, ginger, pepper, garlic, and broth in a medium saucepan; bring to a boil. Slowly drizzle egg into soup, stirring constantly with a fork. Reduce heat to low, and cook 1 minute, stirring constantly. Remove and discard garlic. Ladle soup into bowls, and sprinkle evenly with green onions. Yield: 6 servings (serving size: 1 cup).

CALORIES 90; FAT 1.8g (sat 0.6g); PROTEIN 4.1g; CARBOHYDRATE 13.5g; FIBER 1.7g; CHOLESTEROL 71mg; IRON 0.6mg; SODIUM 659mg; CALCIUM 13mg

► carbo rating: 12
Tuna-Cheese Melt

Instead of provolone cheese, you can use Swiss, Cheddar, or any other type of sliced cheese. (See page 34 for information on selecting the best low-carb breads.)

1   small red bell pepper
1   small yellow bell pepper
1   (6-ounce) can white tuna in spring water, drained and flaked
4   (¾-ounce) slices reduced-calorie seven-grain bread, toasted
½   cup torn fresh watercress
2   teaspoons Italian dressing
¼   teaspoon coarsely ground black pepper
2   (1-ounce) slices provolone cheese, cut into thin strips

1. Cut tops off bell peppers; remove and discard seeds and membranes. Cook bell peppers in boiling water 5 minutes; drain. Rinse with cold water until cool, and drain. Cut bell peppers into ¼-inch-wide slices. Set aside.
2. Preheat broiler.
3. Spoon tuna evenly over toasted bread slices; arrange 2 tablespoons watercress over each. Drizzle ½ teaspoon Italian dressing over each sandwich. Top evenly with bell pepper slices, and sprinkle evenly with black pepper. Top with cheese strips. Broil 2 to 3 minutes or until cheese melts. Serve warm with assorted fresh vegetables, if desired (vegetables not included in analysis). Yield: 4 servings (serving size: 1 open-faced sandwich).

CALORIES 161; FAT 6.4g (sat 2.5g); PROTEIN 13.9g; CARBOHYDRATE 13.6g; FIBER 1.2g; CHOLESTEROL 19mg; IRON 1.3mg; SODIUM 340mg; CALCIUM 132mg

► carbo rating: 13
Thai-Style Pumpkin Soup

Cilantro, ginger, and red pepper are all typical ingredients in Thai-style recipes and really pump up the flavor in this creamy pumpkin soup.

2   (14-ounce) cans fat-free, less-sodium chicken broth
1   (15-ounce) can pumpkin
1   (12-ounce) can mango nectar
¼   cup creamy peanut butter
2   tablespoons rice vinegar
1½   tablespoons minced green onions
1   teaspoon grated peeled fresh ginger
½   teaspoon grated orange rind
¼   teaspoon crushed red pepper
1   garlic clove, crushed
Chopped fresh cilantro (optional)

1. Combine first 3 ingredients in a large saucepan, and bring to a boil. Cover, reduce heat, and simmer 10 minutes.
2. Combine 1 cup pumpkin mixture and peanut butter in a blender or food processor; process until smooth. Add mixture to pan. Stir in vinegar and next 5 ingredients; cook 3 minutes or until thoroughly heated. Ladle into soup bowls. Sprinkle with cilantro, if desired. Yield: 7 servings (serving size: 1 cup).

CALORIES 115; FAT 4.9g (sat 1.1g); PROTEIN 4.7g; CARBOHYDRATE 15.7g; FIBER 2.8g; CHOLESTEROL 0mg; IRON 1.1mg; SODIUM 358mg; CALCIUM 24mg

► carbo rating: 14
Smoked Turkey-Bean Soup

Look for smoked turkey legs in the refrigerated meats/poultry section of the grocery store, near the roasted chickens. Be sure to rinse the beans under cold running water and drain well before adding to the soup.

2	cups water
1	cup chopped onion
¼	cup chopped carrot
½	cup chopped celery
¼	teaspoon pepper
1	bay leaf
3	(15.8-ounce) cans Great Northern beans, rinsed and drained
1	(14-ounce) can fat-free, less-sodium chicken broth
1	(10-ounce) whole smoked turkey leg
2	teaspoons white wine vinegar

1. Combine all ingredients except vinegar in a Dutch oven. Bring to a boil; reduce heat, and simmer, uncovered, 1 hour and 15 minutes.
2. Stir in vinegar; discard bay leaf. Remove turkey leg from soup; discard skin. Remove meat from bone; discard bone. Shred meat into bite-sized pieces, and add to soup. Yield: 6 servings (serving size: 1 cup).

CALORIES 190; FAT 3.3g (sat 0.9g); PROTEIN 16.3g; CARBOHYDRATE 22.3g; FIBER 8.1g; CHOLESTEROL 23mg; IRON 2.3mg; SODIUM 461mg; CALCIUM 61mg

(pictured on page 388)

tips for freezing

One great thing about soup is that you can make a large batch and freeze it for later use. To ensure quality in your frozen foods, use the following checklist.

☐ The container or packaging is moisture-proof, airtight, and odorless

☐ Food is packaged in small portions

☐ Food is packaged in shallow containers

☐ Container or packaging fits the shape and size of the food to be frozen

☐ Food is packed tightly to eliminate as much air space as possible

☐ Container or packaging is almost full, leaving only a little space for the food to expand as it freezes

☐ Excess air is pressed from freezer bags

☐ Container or bag is tightly sealed

☐ Contents of freezer are organized so wrappings don't become loose or pierced

☐ Packages are labeled with a freezer marker indicating the contents, number of servings, and date of storage

☐ Food is placed in a single layer on freezer shelves until frozen

☐ Freezer is set to and maintains 0° or below

☐ Freezer is not freezing too much food at a time

☐ An inventory identifying each food in the freezer and its "use by" date is posted on the outside of the freezer and is updated each time an item is removed

☐ Thaw soups in the refrigerator

☐ Thick soups and stews get thicker when frozen; add more liquid—water, broth, or milk—as the soup reheats if it seems too thick

☐ Soups and stews that contain potatoes don't freeze well

▶ carbo rating: 14

Quick Vegetable Soup

This recipe is easily doubled or tripled, so make extra to freeze. (See the tips for freezing on page 355.)

2	cups frozen vegetable soup mix with tomatoes
¾	cup bottled home-style savory beef gravy
½	cup water
¼	cup dry red wine
¼	teaspoon pepper
1	(14.5-ounce) can diced tomatoes with garlic and onion, undrained

1. Combine all ingredients in a large saucepan; bring to a boil. Cover, reduce heat, and simmer 30 minutes. Yield: 4 servings (serving size: 1 cup).

CALORIES 99; FAT 1.5g (sat 0g); PROTEIN 6.3g; CARBOHYDRATE 16.2g; FIBER 2.3g; CHOLESTEROL 0mg; IRON 1.4mg; SODIUM 941mg; CALCIUM 44mg

---

shrink your stomach with soup

New research indicates that starting each meal with a small cup of soup may actually help you lose weight. How? The warm soup fills your stomach and curbs your appetite so that you consume fewer calories during the rest of the meal. For best results, choose a soup low in fat and sodium, such as a broth or a vegetable-based soup.

▶ carbo rating: 14

Shrimp and Tomato Soup

This brothy soup is a quick and easy version of traditional **cioppino,** *an Italian seafood stew. (See the more traditional recipe for cioppino on the next page.)*

1	(14.5-ounce) can no-salt-added stewed tomatoes, undrained
1	(14-ounce) can fat-free, less-sodium chicken broth
½	teaspoon dried Italian seasoning
¼	to ½ teaspoon hot sauce
⅛	teaspoon salt
⅛	teaspoon pepper
½	pound peeled and deveined medium shrimp

1. Combine first 6 ingredients in a large saucepan; bring to a boil. Reduce heat; simmer, uncovered, 5 minutes.
2. Add shrimp, and simmer 4 minutes or until shrimp are done. Yield: 2 servings (serving size: 2 cups).

CALORIES 193; FAT 2.1g (sat 0.4g); PROTEIN 27.4g; CARBOHYDRATE 17.2g; FIBER 3.6g; CHOLESTEROL 172mg; IRON 3.7mg; SODIUM 948mg; CALCIUM 104mg

► **carbo rating: 15**

Senatorial Bean Soup

For decades this soup has been served in the cafeteria of our nation's Capitol. Close to the end of the cooking time, we pureed half the soup and added it back to the remaining soup. This is a good way to thicken vegetable soups without adding flour.

1	cup dried navy beans
2	tablespoons margarine or butter
2½	cups chopped leek
2	cups sliced carrot
1	cup thinly sliced celery
1	cup diced cooked ham
4	garlic cloves, minced
8	cups water
2	teaspoons chicken-flavored bouillon granules
1	teaspoon beef-flavored bouillon granules
1	teaspoon dried rubbed sage
¼	teaspoon salt
2	bay leaves

1. Sort and wash beans; place in a large Dutch oven. Cover with water to 2 inches above beans. Bring to a boil; cook 2 minutes. Remove from heat; cover and let stand 1 hour. Drain; set aside.
2. Melt margarine or butter in Dutch oven over medium-high heat. Add leek, carrot, celery, ham, and garlic; sauté 10 minutes. Add beans, 8 cups water, and remaining ingredients; bring to a boil. Cover, reduce heat, and simmer 2 hours or until beans are very tender. Discard bay leaves.
3. Place half of soup in a blender; pulse on low speed 8 times or until smooth. Return pureed mixture to pan; cook, uncovered, over medium-low heat 30 minutes. Yield: 10 servings (serving size: 1 cup).

CALORIES 132; FAT 3.6g (sat 0.9g); PROTEIN 7.9g; CARBOHYDRATE 18g; FIBER 3.1g; CHOLESTEROL 9mg; IRON 1.9mg; SODIUM 566mg; CALCIUM 57mg

► **carbo rating: 16**

Cioppino

Cioppino *is a traditional Italian seafood stew with a tomato base and a mixture of different types of fish and shellfish. This one features clams, mussels, shrimp, and crabmeat.*

2	tablespoons olive oil
2	cups chopped onion
1¾	cups chopped fennel bulb (about 1 small)
1	cup chopped green bell pepper
4	garlic cloves, minced
3	tablespoons red wine vinegar
1	teaspoon saffron threads
¼	teaspoon crushed red pepper
3	(14.5-ounce) cans diced tomatoes, undrained
1	cup dry white wine
1	(8-ounce) bottle clam juice
1	tablespoon chopped fresh or 1 teaspoon dried thyme
2	pounds small clams in shells (about 24), scrubbed
1	pound mussels (about 16), scrubbed and debearded
1	pound medium shrimp, peeled and deveined
8	ounces lump crabmeat, shell pieces removed

1. Heat oil in a large nonstick skillet over medium-high heat. Add onion and next 3 ingredients; sauté 5 minutes or until crisp-tender. Add vinegar, saffron, and red pepper; cook 3 minutes or until vinegar evaporates.
2. Add tomatoes and next 3 ingredients; bring to a boil. Reduce heat, and simmer 15 minutes. Add clams; cover and cook 10 minutes or until shells open. Discard any unopened shells. Add mussels; cook 5 minutes or until shells open. Discard any unopened shells. Add shrimp and crabmeat; cook 4 minutes or until shrimp are done. Yield: 8 servings (serving size: 2 cups).

CALORIES 252; FAT 7g (sat 1g); PROTEIN 29g; CARBOHYDRATE 18g; FIBER 2.1g; CHOLESTEROL 130mg; IRON 8.7mg; SODIUM 631mg; CALCIUM 162mg

(pictured on page 389)

wild about rice

Wild rice isn't rice at all—it's the seed of an annual water grass that is natural to the cold waters of Minnesota and Canada. This kind of "wild" wild rice accounts for only a small part of the wild rice sold in supermarkets—the kind you're likely to find is cultivated wild rice, grown primarily in paddies in Minnesota and California.

All forms of wild rice, however, can live up to the "wild" in the name in one way: an unmistakable earthy, bold flavor—simultaneously herblike and buttery. Cooked, its grains retain a slight springiness, to the point of chewiness, which adds texture.

Rice and wild rice are not the same thing, and while the former is perfect as the base of many a dish, wild rice is more wisely used as a flavoring mixed with other ingredients. A ½-cup serving of wild rice has 17.5 grams of carbohydrate and 1.5 grams of fiber (carbo rating: 16). The same amount of long-grain white rice has 22.3 grams of carbohydrate and 0.3 grams of fiber (carbo rating: 22).

▶ **carbo rating: 16**

Creamy Wild Rice-Turkey Chowder

Regular wild rice can take over an hour to cook fully; we've shaved off some time by using the quick-cooking version. Smoked turkey adds a nice flavor, but you can use any kind of cooked turkey.

Cooking spray
- 4 ounces smoked turkey, diced
- 1 cup chopped green onions (about 4)
- ½ cup chopped carrot
- 1½ cups 1% low-fat milk
- 1 (10¾-ounce) can condensed reduced-fat, reduced-sodium cream of mushroom soup
- ⅓ cup quick-cooking wild rice
- ¼ teaspoon pepper

1. Coat a medium saucepan with cooking spray, and place over medium-high heat until hot. Add turkey, green onions, and carrot to pan; sauté 3 minutes.

2. Add milk and soup, stirring well; bring mixture to a boil. Stir in rice; bring to a boil. Cover, reduce heat to medium-low, and simmer 5 minutes or until rice is tender. Stir in pepper. Yield: 4 servings (serving size: 1 cup).

CALORIES 167; FAT 4.6g (sat 1.7g); PROTEIN 12.7g; CARBOHYDRATE 17.5g; FIBER 2g; CHOLESTEROL 26mg; IRON 1mg; SODIUM 550mg; CALCIUM 199mg

(pictured on page 390)

▶ **carbo rating: 17**

White Bean-Chicken Chili

We've used convenience products such as frozen chopped cooked chicken, frozen onion, and bottled garlic as timesavers, but you can use fresh products if you prefer. To get 3 cups of frozen chopped cooked chicken, buy a 20-ounce package. You'll have about 2 cups of chicken left over.

- 1 teaspoon olive oil
- 1 cup frozen chopped onion
- 2 teaspoons bottled minced garlic
- 2 (15.5-ounce) cans cannellini beans, undrained
- 3 cups frozen chopped cooked chicken
- 1 (14-ounce) can fat-free, less-sodium chicken broth
- 1½ teaspoons salt-free Mexican seasoning
- ¼ teaspoon salt
- 1 cup (4 ounces) shredded Monterey Jack cheese with jalapeño peppers

1. Heat oil in a Dutch oven over medium-high heat. Add onion and garlic; sauté 2 minutes.
2. Mash 1 can of beans in a small bowl with a fork. Add mashed beans, remaining can of beans, and next 4 ingredients to pan; bring to a boil. Reduce heat, and simmer 15 minutes. Add cheese; simmer 5 minutes, stirring constantly. Yield: 6 servings (serving size: 1½ cups).

CALORIES 284; FAT 8g (sat 4.2g); PROTEIN 28.3g; CARBOHYDRATE 23.5g; FIBER 6.1g; CHOLESTEROL 58mg; IRON 2.1mg; SODIUM 920mg; CALCIUM 187mg

(pictured on page 391)

▶ **carbo rating: 17**

Roasted Tomato-and-Red Pepper Soup

The key step in roasting bell peppers is to seal them in a bag immediately after taking them out of the oven. The steam produced in the bag makes the skins slide off easily.

1½	pounds red bell peppers
2	pounds tomatoes, halved and seeded
2	tablespoons olive oil
1	cup chopped onion
4	garlic cloves, minced
1½	cups tomato juice
1	tablespoon chopped fresh marjoram
½	teaspoon salt
¼	teaspoon black pepper

1. Preheat broiler.

2. Cut bell peppers in half lengthwise; discard seeds and membranes. Place bell peppers and tomatoes, skin sides up, on a foil-lined baking sheet; flatten peppers with hand. Broil 15 minutes or until vegetables are blackened. Place peppers in a zip-top plastic bag; seal and let stand 10 minutes. Peel peppers and tomato; chop. Place half of chopped peppers and half of chopped tomatoes in a blender; process until smooth.

3. Heat oil in a saucepan over medium-low heat. Add onion and garlic; cover and cook 5 minutes. Add pureed vegetables, remaining chopped bell peppers and tomato, tomato juice, 1 tablespoon marjoram, salt, and black pepper; cook over medium heat until thoroughly heated. Yield: 5 servings (serving size: 1 cup).

CALORIES 126; FAT 4g (sat 0.6g); PROTEIN 3.9g; CARBOHYDRATE 22.7g; FIBER 5.6g; CHOLESTEROL 0mg; IRON 3.4mg; SODIUM 521mg; CALCIUM 42mg

▶ **carbo rating: 18**

Dump-and-Stir Chili

This chili takes about 25 minutes to make—start to finish—and feeds a crowd. If you need some toppings, choose low-carb options such as sour cream, shredded Cheddar cheese, or chopped onion.

2	(15-ounce) cans 99%-fat-free turkey chili without beans
2	(15-ounce) cans no-salt-added pinto beans, undrained
2	(14.5-ounce) cans no-salt-added diced tomatoes, undrained
1	(10-ounce) can diced tomatoes and green chiles, undrained
3	tablespoons instant minced onion
1	tablespoon chili powder

1. Combine all ingredients in a large Dutch oven, and bring to a boil. Cover, reduce heat, and simmer 10 minutes. Uncover; simmer 10 minutes, stirring occasionally. Yield: 11 servings (serving size: 1 cup).

CALORIES 170; FAT 1.2g (sat 0.4g); PROTEIN 14.1g; CARBOHYDRATE 25.6g; FIBER 7.3g; CHOLESTEROL 0mg; IRON 2.5mg; SODIUM 591mg; CALCIUM 95mg

the bean bonus

Don't panic when you see a high carbohydrate value for a recipe with beans. Yes, beans are sources of carbohydrate, but it's high-fiber carbohydrate. In addition to fiber, beans are packed with protein, iron, and B vitamins. Because they have so many nutrients, and are sources of both soluble and insoluble fiber, beans may help reduce the risk of heart disease, type 2 diabetes, and some types of cancer.

▶ **carbo rating: 18**

Chili

Low-carb topping options for this basic beefy chili are chopped sweet onion, shredded Cheddar cheese, chopped bell pepper, or low-fat yogurt.

Cooking spray
1	pound ground round
1	cup chopped onion
4	garlic cloves, minced
1	tablespoon dried oregano
1½	teaspoons chili powder
1½	teaspoons ground cumin
½	teaspoon salt
½	teaspoon pepper
¼	to ½ teaspoon ground cinnamon
2	(8-ounce) cans no-salt-added tomato sauce
1	(15-ounce) can no-salt-added kidney beans, undrained
1	(14.5-ounce) can no-salt-added stewed tomatoes, undrained
7	tablespoons fat-free sour cream

Sliced green onions (optional)

1. Coat a large saucepan or Dutch oven with cooking spray; place over medium-high heat until hot. Add beef, onion, and garlic; cook until meat is browned, stirring to crumble. Drain well; return mixture to pan.
2. Add oregano and next 8 ingredients to pan; stir well. Cover, reduce heat, and simmer 20 minutes. Ladle into bowls. Serve with sour cream. Garnish with sliced green onions, if desired. Yield: 7 servings (serving size: 1 cup chili and 1 tablespoon sour cream).

CALORIES 204; FAT 4.5g (sat 1.5g); PROTEIN 19.7g; CARBOHYDRATE 21.3g; FIBER 3.4g; CHOLESTEROL 40mg; IRON 4mg; SODIUM 241mg; CALCIUM 83mg

▶ **carbo rating: 18**

Spicy Chicken Pockets

A (6-inch) whole wheat pita has 3 more grams of fiber than a plain pita, even though they both have about the same amount of carbohydrate. Because of the fiber, whole wheat pitas have a lower carbo rating than regular pitas. (See page 5 for information on the role of fiber in a low-carb diet.)

6	(4-ounce) skinless, boneless chicken breast halves
3½	tablespoons salt-free Creole seasoning
1	tablespoon vegetable oil

Cooking spray
8	lettuce leaves
4	(6-inch) whole wheat pita bread rounds, cut in half crosswise
1	small red onion, thinly sliced and separated into rings
1	cup alfalfa sprouts
¾	cup chopped cucumber
¾	cup chopped tomato

1. Rub both sides of chicken with Creole seasoning, and place in a large shallow dish. Cover and refrigerate at least 30 minutes.
2. Prepare grill.
3. Brush both sides of chicken evenly with oil. Place chicken on grill rack coated with cooking spray; grill, covered, 5 to 6 minutes on each side or until chicken is done.
4. Place 1 lettuce leaf in each pita half. Layer onion and next 3 ingredients evenly into pita halves. Cut chicken into strips, and arrange evenly over vegetables. Serve warm. Yield: 8 servings (serving size: 1 filled pita half).

CALORIES 217; FAT 4.2g (sat 0.6g); PROTEIN 23.8g; CARBOHYDRATE 21.9g; FIBER 4.3g; CHOLESTEROL 49mg; IRON 2.4mg; SODIUM 230mg; CALCIUM 33mg

► carbo rating: 19
Smoked Turkey and Barley Stew

Quick-cooking barley can be found in either the breakfast cereal or soup section of the grocery store. (See page 144 for more information on barley.)

1	tablespoon olive oil
2	cups chopped onion
1½	cups sliced carrot (about 3 medium)
1½	cups sliced celery
1	(8-ounce) package sliced mushrooms
1	cup uncooked quick-cooking barley
1	(32-ounce) carton fat-free, less-sodium chicken broth, divided
2	cups water
2	cups cubed smoked turkey (about 12 ounces)
1½	tablespoons chopped fresh thyme
1	bay leaf
1	(0.88-ounce) package turkey gravy mix (such as French's)
⅓	cup dry sherry
½	teaspoon freshly ground black pepper

1. Heat oil in a 4-quart Dutch oven over medium-high heat. Add onion, carrot, and celery; cook 6 minutes, stirring frequently. Add mushrooms; cook 2 minutes. Stir in barley, 3 cups broth, water, and next 3 ingredients; bring to a boil. Reduce heat, and simmer, uncovered, 20 minutes or until barley is tender.
2. Combine gravy mix, 1 cup broth, and sherry, stirring with a whisk. Stir gravy mixture into barley mixture; bring to a boil. Reduce heat, and simmer, uncovered, 10 minutes. Stir in pepper. Discard bay leaf. Yield: 10 servings (serving size: 1 cup).

CALORIES 191; FAT 4.5g (sat 1g); PROTEIN 14.6g; CARBOHYDRATE 24g; FIBER 5g; CHOLESTEROL 26mg; IRON 1.7mg; SODIUM 407mg; CALCIUM 40mg

► carbo rating: 19
Lamb Pockets with Cucumber Topping

If you don't care for lamb, you can use the same amount of ground round or lean ground beef. The carbo rating will be the same.

1	cup grated cucumber
½	cup plain low-fat yogurt
¼	teaspoon seasoned salt
¼	teaspoon dried dill
1	pound ground lamb
¼	cup chopped onion
1	garlic clove, minced
¼	teaspoon salt
¼	teaspoon pepper
¾	cup chopped tomato
¼	cup sliced green onions
4	(6-inch) whole wheat pita bread rounds, cut in half crosswise
8	green leaf lettuce leaves

1. Press cucumber between layers of paper towels to remove excess moisture. Combine cucumber, yogurt, seasoned salt, and dill; cover and chill.
2. Cook meat, chopped onion, and garlic in a large nonstick skillet over medium-high heat until meat is browned, stirring until it crumbles. Drain, if necessary. Stir in ¼ teaspoon salt and pepper. Set aside.
3. Combine tomato and green onions. Line each pita half with a lettuce leaf; top evenly with meat mixture, cucumber mixture, and tomato mixture. Serve immediately. Yield: 8 servings (serving size: 1 filled pita half).

CALORIES 195; FAT 4.9g (sat 1.7g); PROTEIN 16.8g; CARBOHYDRATE 20g; FIBER 1.3g; CHOLESTEROL 41mg; IRON 2.1mg; SODIUM 346mg; CALCIUM 53mg

> "My love of bread is a challenge for me when it comes to cutting back on carbs. It's nice to know that there are some sandwiches that are okay to eat."
>
> *Stacey Hill*

▶ carbo rating: 20
Roast Beef-Feta Pita Pockets

For a lower-sodium sandwich, use leftover cooked roast beef instead of sliced deli meat.

⅔ cup chopped seeded cucumber
⅓ cup light ranch dressing
¼ cup (1 ounce) crumbled feta cheese
4 green leaf lettuce leaves
2 (6-inch) whole wheat pitas, cut in half
6 ounces very thinly sliced deli roast beef

1. Combine cucumber, dressing, and cheese in a small bowl; stir well. Place 1 lettuce leaf into each pita half; add 1½ ounces roast beef to each pita pocket. Spoon cucumber mixture evenly into each pocket. Serve immediately. Yield: 4 servings (serving size: 1 filled pita half).

CALORIES 210; FAT 8.2g (sat 2.3g); PROTEIN 12.4g; CARBOHYDRATE 22.4g; FIBER 2.8g; CHOLESTEROL 29mg; IRON 1.7mg; SODIUM 793mg; CALCIUM 62mg

▶ carbo rating: 20
Slow-Cooker Chili

The chili can be made on the stovetop if you don't have a slow cooker. After adding beans and tomatoes, bring to a boil. Reduce heat; simmer, partially covered, 1½ hours.

1 pound ground round
1 cup chopped onion
½ cup chopped green bell pepper
¼ cup dry red wine or water
1 tablespoon chili powder
1 teaspoon sugar
1 teaspoon ground cumin
¼ teaspoon salt
1 garlic clove, minced
1 (15-ounce) can kidney beans, undrained
1 (14.5-ounce) can Mexican-style stewed tomatoes with jalapeño peppers and spices, undrained
6 tablespoons (1½ ounces) shredded reduced-fat extrasharp Cheddar cheese

1. Cook beef in a large nonstick skillet over medium-high heat until browned, stirring to crumble. Add onion and next 7 ingredients; cook 7 minutes or until onion is tender.
2. Place meat mixture in an electric slow cooker, and stir in beans and tomatoes. Cover with lid, and cook on low-heat setting for 4 hours. Ladle into bowls; sprinkle with cheese. Yield: 6 servings (serving size: 1¼ cups chili and 1 tablespoon cheese).

CALORIES 243; FAT 5.6g (sat 2.3g); PROTEIN 25.5g; CARBOHYDRATE 22.9g; FIBER 3.1g; CHOLESTEROL 49mg; IRON 4.1mg; SODIUM 637mg; CALCIUM 154mg

▶ carbo rating: 21
Chicken and Barley Soup

To make this soup even more hearty, stir in some chopped smoked sausage. The sausage will not change the carbo rating.

1   pound skinless, boneless chicken breasts, cut into bite-sized pieces
1½   cups chopped onion (about 1 large)
1½   cups chopped celery (about 4 large ribs)
1   cup chopped red bell pepper (about 1)
½   cup uncooked barley
1   teaspoon crushed red pepper
½   teaspoon dried oregano
½   teaspoon dried thyme
¼   teaspoon pepper
¼   teaspoon turmeric
⅛   teaspoon salt
3   (14-ounce) cans fat-free, less-sodium chicken broth

1. Combine all ingredients in a large saucepan. Bring to a boil; cover, reduce heat, and simmer 15 minutes. **2.** Uncover, and simmer 15 minutes or until barley is tender. Yield: 4 servings (serving size: 2 cups).

CALORIES 265; FAT 3.5g (sat 0.9g); PROTEIN 31.1g; CARBOHYDRATE 28g; FIBER 6.8g; CHOLESTEROL 63mg; IRON 2.5mg; SODIUM 983mg; CALCIUM 58mg

▶ carbo rating: 22
Bacon, Ham, and Lentil Soup

Most legume soups benefit from being made a day ahead so their flavors meld. Substitute green split peas for the lentils, if you prefer; they take less time to cook, so monitor the soup accordingly.

5   slices thick-sliced bacon, cut crosswise into ½-inch strips
1½   cups (½-inch) cubed ham (about 8 ounces)
1   cup chopped onion
1   cup chopped fennel bulb
1   cup chopped celery
½   cup chopped leek
½   cup chopped carrot
3   (14-ounce) cans fat-free, less-sodium chicken broth
2   cups water
1   cup canned diced tomatoes with basil, garlic, and oregano
1   pound dried lentils
1   teaspoon chopped fresh or ¼ teaspoon dried thyme
½   teaspoon freshly ground black pepper
2   bay leaves
¼   cup chopped fresh chives

1. Cook bacon strips in a Dutch oven over medium heat until crisp. Remove from pan, reserving 2 tablespoons drippings in pan; set bacon aside. Add ham to drippings in pan; cook 2 minutes, stirring frequently. Add onion and next 4 ingredients; cover and cook 10 minutes, stirring occasionally. Add broth and next 6 ingredients. Bring to a boil; cover, reduce heat, and simmer 30 minutes or until lentils are tender. Discard bay leaves; sprinkle with bacon and chives just before serving. Yield: 8 servings (serving size: 1¾ cups).

CALORIES 359; FAT 11g (sat 4g); PROTEIN 25.2g; CARBOHYDRATE 40.6g; FIBER 18.9g; CHOLESTEROL 21mg; IRON 6.1mg; SODIUM 956mg; CALCIUM 72mg

► carbo rating: 24
Spicy Two-Bean Soup

Mashing a portion of the beans makes the soup thicker without adding flour. (See page 359 for more information on the value of beans in a low-carb diet.)

1	teaspoon olive oil
1	cup frozen chopped onion
½	teaspoon garlic powder
1	(19-ounce) can cannellini beans, rinsed and drained
1	(16-ounce) can kidney beans, rinsed and drained
1	(14-ounce) can fat-free, less-sodium chicken broth
2	(4.5-ounce) cans chopped green chiles
1	tablespoon ground cumin
¼	teaspoon salt
½	cup (2 ounces) shredded Monterey Jack cheese with jalapeño peppers

1. Heat oil in a large saucepan over medium-high heat. Add onion and garlic powder; sauté until tender.
2. Mash half of cannellini beans; add to onion mixture. Add remaining cannellini beans and kidney beans. Stir in broth and next 3 ingredients. Bring to a boil; cover, reduce heat, and simmer 8 minutes. Sprinkle each serving with 2 tablespoons cheese. Yield: 4 servings (serving size: 1½ cups).

CALORIES 235; FAT 6.6g (sat 3.2g); PROTEIN 14g; CARBOHYDRATE 30.6g; FIBER 6.5g; CHOLESTEROL 15mg; IRON 3.8mg; SODIUM 974mg; CALCIUM 210mg

► carbo rating: 24
Thai Clam Pot

Somen *are delicate noodles made with wheat flour, a dash of oil, and water. Look for them on the shelves with other noodles, or in an Asian food market. Vermicelli or angel hair pasta can be substituted for the somen, and the carbo rating will actually stay the same.*

6	ounces uncooked somen (wheat noodles)
1	teaspoon vegetable oil
1	teaspoon crushed red pepper
8	garlic cloves, thinly sliced
8	green onions, cut into 2-inch pieces
1½	cups water
¾	cup mirin (sweet rice wine)
3	pounds small clams in shells (about 48), scrubbed
1	cup thinly sliced basil
2	tablespoons fish sauce

1. Cook somen in boiling water 5 minutes; drain. Rinse with cold water. Drain; set aside.
2. Heat oil in a large Dutch oven over medium-high heat. Add pepper, garlic, and green onions; stir-fry 30 seconds. Add 1½ cups water and mirin; bring to a boil. Add clams; cover, reduce heat, and simmer 10 minutes or until clams open. Discard any unopened shells. Stir in sliced basil and fish sauce, and cook 1 minute.
3. Divide noodles and clams evenly among 6 bowls; top each with ½ cup cooking liquid. Yield: 6 servings.

CALORIES 150; FAT 1.4g (sat 0.2g); PROTEIN 8.9g; CARBOHYDRATE 25.1g; FIBER 1.6g; CHOLESTEROL 13mg; IRON 5.9mg; SODIUM 1,011mg; CALCIUM 54mg

▶ carbo rating: 24

Peppered Turkey-Watercress Burgers

If you don't care for the sharp peppery flavor of watercress, you can use 1½ cups of finely chopped fresh spinach. Cracked black pepper is the secret ingredient in this recipe. Substituting ground black pepper for the cracked pepper will make the burgers too spicy hot.

1	pound ground turkey breast
1½	cups chopped trimmed watercress
¾	cup plain low-fat yogurt, divided
2	teaspoons cracked black pepper, divided
½	teaspoon salt
½	teaspoon Worcestershire sauce

Cooking spray

4	(1½-ounce) whole wheat hamburger buns, toasted
1	cup trimmed watercress
4	(¼-inch-thick) slices tomato

1. Prepare grill.

2. Combine turkey, chopped watercress, ¼ cup yogurt, 1 teaspoon cracked pepper, salt, and Worcestershire sauce in a bowl. Divide mixture into 4 equal portions, shaping each portion into a ½-inch-thick patty. Press 1 teaspoon pepper onto both sides of patties.

3. Place patties on grill rack coated with cooking spray; cover and grill 5 minutes on each side or until done.

4. Spread 2 tablespoons yogurt over top half of each bun. Line bottom half of each bun with ¼ cup trimmed watercress; top each with a patty, a tomato slice, and top half of bun. Yield: 4 servings (serving size: 1 burger).

CALORIES 300; FAT 6.8g (sat 2.2g); PROTEIN 32.3g; CARBOHYDRATE 26.5g; FIBER 2.5g; CHOLESTEROL 76mg; IRON 2.6mg; SODIUM 656mg; CALCIUM 154mg

▶ carbo rating: 24

Grilled Vegetable Pita Sandwiches

If you don't want a sandwich, just serve these tasty grilled veggies over mixed greens. (The carbo rating will decrease to 21.) Sprinkle with sprouts and cheese, and top with dressing.

1	tablespoon olive oil
1	teaspoon dried Italian seasoning
1	teaspoon dried parsley flakes
¼	teaspoon salt
¼	teaspoon pepper
1	zucchini, cut lengthwise into ¼-inch-thick slices
1	eggplant, cut lengthwise into ¼-inch-thick slices
1	yellow squash, cut lengthwise into ¼-inch-thick slices
1	small red onion, cut into ¼-inch-thick slices

Cooking spray

1	tomato, thinly sliced
4	(6-inch) whole wheat pitas, cut in half
1	cup alfalfa sprouts
1	cup (4 ounces) shredded reduced-fat Monterey Jack cheese
½	cup light ranch dressing

1. Prepare grill.

2. Combine first 5 ingredients in a small bowl. Brush zucchini, eggplant, yellow squash, and onion with oil mixture. Place vegetables on grill rack coated with cooking spray; cover and grill 6 minutes or until tender, turning once.

3. Layer grilled vegetables and tomato evenly in pita halves. Fill each pita half with 2 tablespoons sprouts; top with 1 tablespoon each of cheese and dressing. Yield: 8 servings (serving size: 1 filled pita half).

CALORIES 213; FAT 9.3g (sat 2.7g); PROTEIN 8.6g; CARBOHYDRATE 27.5g; FIBER 3.6g; CHOLESTEROL 14mg; IRON 1.6mg; SODIUM 524mg; CALCIUM 133mg

▶ carbo rating: 25
Lentil Soup

This fiber-rich, meat-free soup uses vegetable broth, but if you prefer to use chicken or beef broth, either will work fine. (See page 175 for more information on lentils.)

7½   cups vegetable broth
1½   cups dried lentils
  1   cup chopped onion
  1   cup chopped carrot
  ½   cup chopped celery
  ½   cup chopped parsnip
  2   tablespoons low-sodium soy sauce
  2   teaspoons dried oregano
  ½   teaspoon salt

1. Combine broth and lentils in a 4½-quart Dutch oven; bring to a boil. Cover, reduce heat, and simmer 30 minutes. Add chopped onion and remaining ingredients; cover and simmer 15 minutes. Yield: 8 servings (serving size: 1 cup).

CALORIES 166; FAT 0.6g (sat 0.1g); PROTEIN 11.4g; CARBOHYDRATE 30.8g; FIBER 6.3g; CHOLESTEROL 0mg; IRON 4mg; SODIUM 595mg; CALCIUM 56mg

broth basics

Compare the carbohydrate and sodium in these different canned broths from Swanson.

Type of broth (½ cup)	Carbohydrate (g)	Sodium (mg)
Beef	0.5	410
Chicken	0.5	500
Chicken, fat-free, less-sodium	0.5	310
Vegetable	1.5	500

▶ carbo rating: 26
Tuna Salad Sandwiches

You can use pimiento in place of roasted red bell peppers in this quick and easy sandwich.

  2   (6-ounce) cans chunk white tuna in water, drained and flaked
  ¾   cup diced celery
  ½   cup minced onion
  ⅓   cup light mayonnaise
  2   tablespoons minced fresh parsley
  2   tablespoons chopped bottled roasted red bell peppers
  2   tablespoons lemon juice
  ⅛   teaspoon ground white pepper
  8   (1-ounce) slices whole wheat bread
  8   romaine lettuce leaves

1. Combine first 8 ingredients in a medium bowl; stir well.
2. Spread tuna mixture evenly on 4 bread slices. Top each with 2 lettuce leaves and 1 bread slice. Yield: 4 servings (serving size: 1 sandwich).

CALORIES 283; FAT 9.1g (sat 1.6g); PROTEIN 20.6g; CARBOHYDRATE 29.9g; FIBER 3.6g; CHOLESTEROL 30mg; IRON 2.6mg; SODIUM 664mg; CALCIUM 90mg

▶ carbo rating: 26

Fiesta Burgers

These hamburgers feature whole wheat buns and a salsa topping that adds not only a punch of flavor, but also extra fiber. This recipe can easily be cut in half to make four burgers.

1⅓	cups chopped seeded tomato
¼	cup finely chopped onion
¼	cup taco sauce
1	(4.5-ounce) can chopped green chiles, drained
2	pounds ground round
2	tablespoons low-sodium Worcestershire sauce
½	teaspoon ground cumin
¼	teaspoon onion powder
¼	teaspoon garlic powder
8	green leaf lettuce leaves
8	whole wheat hamburger buns, split and toasted

1. Combine first 4 ingredients; cover mixture and chill 30 minutes.

2. Combine meat and next 4 ingredients; divide mixture into 8 equal portions, shaping each into a 4-inch patty. Broil 3 inches from heat 4 minutes on each side or until done.

3. Place a lettuce leaf on bottom half of each bun; top each with a patty. Top evenly with tomato mixture, and cover with bun tops. Yield: 8 servings (serving size: 1 burger).

CALORIES 322; FAT 8.3g (sat 2.4g); PROTEIN 31.7g; CARBOHYDRATE 30.33g; FIBER 4.1g; CHOLESTEROL 61mg; IRON 4.2mg; SODIUM 365mg; CALCIUM 72mg

▶ carbo rating: 27

Shrimp Melts

Ask the seafood department at your local grocery store to steam your fresh shrimp to keep preparation time to a minimum. Use whole-grain English muffins because they have more fiber and help keep the carbo rating down.

1	pound cooked peeled small shrimp
¾	cup minced onion
½	cup low-fat sour cream
1½	tablespoons fresh lemon juice (about ½ lemon)
½	teaspoon dried dill
½	teaspoon prepared mustard
½	teaspoon Worcestershire sauce
¼	teaspoon celery seeds
4	whole-grain English muffins, split and lightly toasted
4	(¾-ounce) slices reduced-fat sharp Cheddar cheese, cut in half diagonally

1. Preheat broiler.

2. Combine first 8 ingredients in a bowl; stir well.

3. Place muffin halves on a baking sheet. Spoon shrimp mixture onto muffin halves; broil 3 minutes. Top each muffin half with 1 cheese slice half; broil 3 minutes or until cheese melts. Yield: 4 servings (serving size: 2 muffin halves).

CALORIES 310; FAT 7.6g (sat 3.3g); PROTEIN 27.7g; CARBOHYDRATE 32.1g; FIBER 5.5g; CHOLESTEROL 144mg; IRON 3.7mg; SODIUM 822mg; CALCIUM 366mg

▶ carbo rating: 29

Chipotle-Black Bean Chili

You need only 1 teaspoon of the chipotle chile in adobo sauce, so place the rest in an airtight container and store in the refrigerator or freezer for another use.

  1   teaspoon olive oil
  1   cup finely chopped onion
  6   garlic cloves, minced
  2   tablespoons chili powder
  1   teaspoon minced drained canned chipotle chile in adobo sauce
  ¼   teaspoon pepper
  ⅛   teaspoon salt
  2   (15-ounce) cans black beans, drained
  2   (14.5-ounce) cans no-salt-added whole tomatoes, undrained and chopped
  1   (4.5-ounce) can chopped green chiles, drained
     Cilantro sprigs (optional)

1. Heat oil in a large saucepan over medium-high heat. Add onion and garlic; sauté 3 minutes or until tender.
2. Add chili powder and next 6 ingredients; bring to a boil. Reduce heat; cover and simmer 15 minutes, stirring occasionally. Ladle chili into individual bowls, and garnish with cilantro sprigs, if desired. Yield: 6 servings (serving size: 1 cup).

CALORIES 190; FAT 2g (sat 0.3g); PROTEIN 10.9g; CARBOHYDRATE 35.5g; FIBER 6.8g; CHOLESTEROL 0mg; IRON 3.3mg; SODIUM 423mg; CALCIUM 93mg

▶ carbo rating: 30

Twenty-Minute Chili

This hearty high-fiber chili is one of the easiest—and tastiest—around. Hot beans, salsa, and chili powder provide the heat, while tomatoes and peppers add garden-fresh appeal. For even more heat, add a small amount of chopped fresh pepper such as habanero, jalapeño, banana, serrano, or Scotch bonnet.

  1   (16-ounce) can chili hot beans, undrained
  1   (15-ounce) can black beans, rinsed and drained
  1   (14.5-ounce) can Mexican-style stewed tomatoes, undrained
  ½   cup chunky salsa
  1   tablespoon ground cumin
  2   teaspoons chili powder
  1   yellow bell pepper, coarsely chopped (about 1 cup)
  1   green bell pepper or red bell pepper, coarsely chopped (about 1 cup)
  ¼   cup reduced-fat sour cream
  ½   cup (2 ounces) shredded reduced-fat Monterey Jack cheese

1. Combine first 8 ingredients in a large saucepan; cover. Bring to a boil. Reduce heat; simmer 10 minutes, stirring occasionally. Ladle chili into individual bowls; top each serving with 1 tablespoon sour cream and 2 tablespoons cheese. Yield: 4 servings (serving size: 1½ cups).

Note: The sodium in this chili is high because of the canned beans and canned tomatoes. If you need to decrease the sodium in your diet, use no-salt-added canned vegetables.

CALORIES 301; FAT 8g (sat 4.4g); PROTEIN 15.2g; CARBOHYDRATE 43.1g; FIBER 13.1g; CHOLESTEROL 18mg; IRON 3.9mg; SODIUM 1,116mg; CALCIUM 203mg

(pictured on page 391)

▶ **carbo rating: 30**

Egg-and-Tuna Salad Sandwiches

See page 49 for tips on making perfect hard-cooked eggs.

4	hard-cooked large eggs, chopped
1	(6-ounce) can chunk light tuna in water, drained
3	tablespoons light mayonnaise
2	tablespoons minced red onion
2	tablespoons Dijon mustard
½	teaspoon freshly ground black pepper
10	(1-ounce) slices whole wheat bread
5	large red leaf lettuce leaves
5	(¼-inch-thick) slices tomato
1¼	cups alfalfa sprouts

1. Combine first 6 ingredients in a medium bowl. Spread ½ cup egg mixture over each of 5 bread slices. Top each with 1 lettuce leaf, 1 tomato slice, ¼ cup alfalfa sprouts, and 1 bread slice. Yield: 5 servings (serving size: 1 sandwich).

CALORIES 294; FAT 9.8g (sat 2.3g); PROTEIN 19.5g; CARBOHYDRATE 34.8g; FIBER 4.8g; CHOLESTEROL 184mg; IRON 4mg; SODIUM 697mg; CALCIUM 176mg

▶ **carbo rating: 32**

Spicy Black Bean-and-Sausage Soup

You can use any type of smoked sausage in place of the turkey kielbasa without changing the carbo rating.

2	(15-ounce) cans black beans, rinsed, drained, and divided
2½	cups water, divided
1	tablespoon olive oil
2	cups diced onion
1	teaspoon chili powder
½	teaspoon ground cumin
¼	to ½ teaspoon hot sauce
¼	teaspoon pepper
1	garlic clove, minced
6	ounces turkey kielbasa, diced

1. Place 1 cup beans and ½ cup water in a food processor or blender, and process until smooth.
2. Heat oil in a large Dutch oven over medium-high heat. Add onion; sauté 4 minutes or until onion is soft.
3. Add bean puree, remaining beans, 2 cups water, chili powder, and next 4 ingredients; bring to a boil. Cover, reduce heat, and simmer 5 minutes, stirring occasionally. Stir in kielbasa; cook 1 minute or until thoroughly heated. Yield: 4 servings (serving size: 1½ cups).

CALORIES 291; FAT 8.3g (sat 2.6g); PROTEIN 17.8g; CARBOHYDRATE 38.9g; FIBER 7g; CHOLESTEROL 23mg; IRON 7.8mg; SODIUM 789mg; CALCIUM 72mg

desserts

If desserts are your downfall, **satisfy your sweet tooth with low-carb treats** such as *Chocolate-Almond Cookies* (page 372), *Homemade Peach Ice Cream* (page 377), and *No-Bake Cherry Cheesecake* (page 410). Also, check out "10 Low-Carb Ways to Satisfy Your Sweet Tooth" on page 379.

▶ **carbo rating: 2**

Quick Berry Whips

You can also make this quick and easy dessert with sugar-free lemon-, orange-, or cherry-flavored gelatin.

1 (0.3-ounce) package sugar-free strawberry-flavored gelatin
¾ cup boiling water
½ cup low-calorie cranberry juice
½ cup frozen reduced-calorie whipped topping, thawed

1. Prepare gelatin with ¾ cup boiling water according to package directions using steps 1 and 2 of speed-set method and substituting cranberry juice for cold water.
2. Pour gelatin mixture into a blender; process 10 seconds, stopping once to scrape down sides. Add whipped topping; process 15 seconds.
3. Pour gelatin mixture evenly into 6 dessert glasses. Cover and chill 1 hour or until set. Yield: 6 servings (serving size: 1 cup).

CALORIES 20; FAT 0.7g (sat 0g); PROTEIN 1.1g; CARBOHYDRATE 2.2g; FIBER 0g; CHOLESTEROL 0mg; IRON 0mg; SODIUM 15mg; CALCIUM 2mg

▶ **carbo rating: 3**

Chocolate-Almond Cookies

Enjoy one of these little cookies with a steaming cup of chocolate-flavored coffee.

1 (8-ounce) package sugar-free chocolate-flavored snack cake mix (such as Sweet'N Low)
1 large egg, lightly beaten
2½ tablespoons water
1 tablespoon almond extract
½ teaspoon vanilla extract
Cooking spray
50 almond slices, toasted (2 to 3 tablespoons)

1. Preheat oven to 350°.
2. Combine first 5 ingredients in a bowl, stirring until blended.
3. Drop dough by level teaspoonfuls onto baking sheets coated with cooking spray. Press 1 almond slice into top of each cookie. Bake at 350° for 8 minutes. Transfer cookies to wire racks, and cool completely. Yield: about 4 dozen cookies (serving size: 1 cookie).

CALORIES 18; FAT 0.4g (sat 0.3g); PROTEIN 0.4g; CARBOHYDRATE 3.6g; FIBER 0.1g; CHOLESTEROL 4mg; IRON 0.2mg; SODIUM 4mg; CALCIUM 3mg

almond advice

Eating 1½ ounces of almonds (about ⅓ cup or 34 almonds) may reduce the risk of heart disease when they're part of a diet low in saturated fat and cholesterol. Eating almonds can also help reduce the risk of developing type 2 diabetes and possibly even Alzheimer's disease. The health benefits of almonds are due to the fact that these nuts contain monounsaturated fat and fiber and are a leading source of the antioxidant vitamin E.

▶ **carbo rating: 4**
Peanut Butter Cookies

For the best results, use regular stick margarine instead of a reduced-calorie or tub-style margarine, and regular peanut butter rather than a low-carb or natural peanut butter.

¾ cup plus 2 tablespoons peanut butter
2 tablespoons margarine, softened
¾ cup all-purpose flour
⅓ cup "measures-like-sugar" calorie-free sweetener
1 large egg, lightly beaten
¼ teaspoon vanilla extract

1. Preheat oven to 350°.
2. Beat peanut butter and margarine with a mixer at medium speed until blended.
3. Lightly spoon flour into dry measuring cups; level with a knife. Combine flour and sweetener in a medium bowl. Add flour mixture to peanut butter mixture, beating well. Add egg and vanilla; beat well.
4. Shape dough into 24 (1-inch) balls. Place balls, 2 inches apart, on ungreased baking sheets; flatten cookies in a crisscross pattern with a fork. Bake at 350° for 12 minutes. Cool completely on baking sheets. Yield: 2 dozen cookies (serving size: 1 cookie).

CALORIES 84; FAT 6g (sat 1.2g); PROTEIN 3.4g; CARBOHYDRATE 5.1g; FIBER 0.7g; CHOLESTEROL 9mg; IRON 0.4mg; SODIUM 63mg; CALCIUM 6mg

▶ **carbo rating: 5**
Chocolate-Peanut Butter Balls

These chocolate treats are great to pack in a brown bag lunch or for a portable snack. It's not necessary to keep them refrigerated if you pack them for lunch.

¼ cup nutlike cereal nuggets (such as Grape-Nuts)
2 tablespoons extracrunchy peanut butter
1 (0.75-ounce) package chocolate sugar-free dairy shake mix (such as Alba)
1 packet sugar substitute with aspartame (such as Equal)
1½ tablespoons water
½ teaspoon honey
½ teaspoon vanilla extract

1. Combine all ingredients in a medium bowl, stirring until moist and well blended.
2. Shape mixture into 8 (1-inch) balls. Cover and chill. Yield: 8 servings (serving size: 1 ball).

CALORIES 48; FAT 2g (sat 0.4g); PROTEIN 2.3g; CARBOHYDRATE 5.5g; FIBER 0.7g; CHOLESTEROL 1mg; IRON 1.2mg; SODIUM 61mg; CALCIUM 23mg

(pictured on page 393)

how sweet it is

Compare the carbo ratings for these various types of sugars and sweeteners.

Sweetener (1 tablespoon)	Carbohydrate (grams)	Fiber (grams)	Carbo Rating
Splenda	1.5g	0g	2
Powdered Sugar	7.5g	0g	8
Brown Sugar	8.8g	0g	9
Equal	9.1g	0g	9
Granulated Sugar	12.5g	0g	13
Maple Syrup	13.4g	0g	13
Corn Syrup	16.3g	0g	16
Honey	17.5g	0g	17

► carbo rating: 6
Grapefruit Sorbet

If you don't want to squeeze your own grapefruit juice, you can use juice from the carton or a bottled grapefruit juice.

1½ cups water
½ cup "measures-like-sugar" calorie-free sweetener
Orange rind strips from 2 oranges
1½ cups fresh pink or red grapefruit juice (about 3 medium grapefruit)
1 tablespoon lemon juice

1. Combine water and sweetener in a saucepan; bring to a boil. Add orange rind; reduce heat, and simmer 5 minutes. Strain mixture, discarding rind. Cool completely.
2. Add grapefruit juice and lemon juice to water mixture; stir well. Pour into a 9-inch square baking pan; cover and freeze until firm.
3. Break frozen mixture into pieces. Add frozen mixture to a blender or food processor, in batches, and process until smooth but not thawed. Serve immediately. Yield: 8 servings (serving size: ½ cup).

CALORIES 25; FAT 0.1g (sat 0g); PROTEIN 0.2g; CARBOHYDRATE 5.9g; FIBER 0g; CHOLESTEROL 0mg; IRON 0.1mg; SODIUM 0mg; CALCIUM 4mg

► carbo rating: 7
Vanilla-Roasted Strawberries

It's best to use unsalted butter in this recipe so that the flavor of the fruit and the vanilla is not masked by a salty butter mixture. Serve these spiced berries over vanilla low-carb ice cream, if desired.

2 tablespoons unsalted butter
1 vanilla bean, split lengthwise
24 strawberries, tops removed
2 tablespoons "measures-like sugar" calorie-free sweetener
3 tablespoons dry red wine
1½ tablespoons balsamic vinegar
1 tablespoon chilled unsalted butter, cut into small pieces

1. Preheat oven to 400°.
2. Melt 2 tablespoons butter in a 9-inch square baking pan in oven. Scrape seeds from vanilla bean into melted butter; stir well. Place strawberries, cut sides down, in pan. Sprinkle with sweetener. Add vanilla bean halves to pan. Bake at 400° for 10 minutes or until berries are soft. Cool 20 minutes.
3. Remove berries from pan, and transfer pan juices to a small skillet. Discard vanilla bean halves. Add wine and vinegar to pan; bring to a simmer over medium heat. Remove from heat, and whisk in 1 tablespoon chilled butter. Drizzle wine mixture over berries. Serve immediately. Yield: 4 servings (serving size: ⅓ cup berries and 3 tablespoons sauce).

CALORIES 118; FAT 8.9g (sat 5.3g); PROTEIN 0.8g; CARBOHYDRATE 9.5g; FIBER 2.5g; CHOLESTEROL 23mg; IRON 0.5mg; SODIUM 5mg; CALCIUM 20mg

using vanilla beans

• Vanilla beans freeze well; just pop them into the microwave for 15 to 30 seconds to plump and thaw.
• Revive a dry vanilla bean by wrapping it in a damp paper towel and microwaving at HIGH 5 to 8 seconds.
• The bean is easier to cut and more seeds can be scraped when moist, so scrape the seeds after steeping the bean in liquid.

► **carbo rating: 8**

Creamy Yogurt Cups

The flavor of this creamy dessert will remind you of a creamsicle, but you can make these cups with any flavor of sugar-free gelatin.

1 (0.3-ounce) package sugar-free orange-flavored gelatin
¾ cup boiling water
½ cup orange juice
1 (8-ounce) carton vanilla fat-free yogurt with aspartame
2 teaspoons vanilla extract

1. Prepare gelatin with ¾ cup boiling water according to package directions using steps 1 and 2 of speed-set method and substituting orange juice for cold water. Stir in yogurt and vanilla.

2. Pour gelatin mixture evenly into individual glasses. Cover and chill 1 hour or until set. Yield: 4 servings (serving size: ¾ cup).

CALORIES 52; FAT 0g (sat 0g); PROTEIN 3.6g; CARBOHYDRATE 7.7g; FIBER 0.1g; CHOLESTEROL 1mg; IRON 0.1mg; SODIUM 41mg; CALCIUM 85mg

► **carbo rating: 8**

Banana-Nut Cookies

Instead of sugar, these nutty cookies are sweetened with mashed banana.

2 cups uncooked regular oats
1 cup raisins
1 cup chopped walnuts
½ teaspoon salt
1½ cups mashed banana (about 3 medium)
⅓ cup vegetable oil
1 teaspoon vanilla extract

1. Preheat oven to 350°.

2. Combine first 4 ingredients in a large bowl; stir well. Combine banana, oil, and vanilla; stir well. Add banana mixture to dry ingredients, stirring to combine. Let stand 15 minutes.

3. Drop dough by rounded tablespoonfuls onto ungreased baking sheets. Bake at 350° for 15 minutes or until lightly golden. Transfer cookies to wire racks; cool completely. Yield: 3 dozen cookies (serving size: 1 cookie).

CALORIES 77; FAT 4.3g (sat 0.4g); PROTEIN 1.8g; CARBOHYDRATE 8.8g; FIBER 1.1g; CHOLESTEROL 0mg; IRON 0.4mg; SODIUM 33mg; CALCIUM 8mg

ripe bananas

The riper the bananas, the sweeter they'll be and the easier they'll be to mash. The best bananas to use are those with skins that have turned almost completely dark. Let bananas ripen at room temperature until the skin is covered with brown speckles. At this point of ripeness, you can use them or store them in the refrigerator. In the refrigerator, the skins will continue to darken, but the fruit will not be affected. (See page 90 for a shortcut for ripening bananas.)

▶ carbo rating: 8

Banana Ice Cream

Cool, creamy, and delicious—just the way you remember all the homemade ice cream you used to eat at backyard cookouts. A ½-cup serving of commercial banana ice cream has 22 grams of carbohydrate.

2	cups 2% reduced-fat milk
¾	cup egg substitute
¾	cup evaporated fat-free milk
⅓	cup "measures-like-sugar" calorie-free sweetener
3	large ripe bananas, peeled and mashed
1	tablespoon lemon juice
1½	teaspoons vanilla extract

1. Combine first 4 ingredients in a large bowl. Add mashed banana, lemon juice, and vanilla, stirring well.
2. Pour mixture into the freezer can of an ice-cream freezer; freeze according to manufacturer's instructions. Spoon ice cream into a freezer-safe container; cover and freeze 1 hour or until firm. Yield: 16 servings (serving size: ½ cup).

CALORIES 54; FAT 0.6g (sat 0.4g); PROTEIN 3g; CARBOHYDRATE 9.1g; FIBER 0.8g; CHOLESTEROL 3mg; IRON 0.3mg; SODIUM 53mg; CALCIUM 69mg

▶ carbo rating: 9

Piña Colada Granita

Granita *is the Italian word for an ice, a frozen mixture of water, sugar, and some type of flavoring. This one is sweetened with pineapple juice instead of sugar, and tastes like a frozen piña colada.*

1	(8-ounce) can pineapple chunks in juice, undrained
3	cups pineapple juice
½	cup cream of coconut
⅓	cup dark rum
2	tablespoons fresh lemon juice
1	teaspoon coconut extract

Mint sprigs (optional)

1. Place pineapple chunks in a blender or food processor; process until smooth. Combine pineapple, 3 cups pineapple juice, and next 4 ingredients in a 13 x 9-inch baking dish; cover and freeze at least 8 hours or until firm.
2. Remove frozen pineapple mixture from freezer. Scrape entire mixture with a fork until fluffy. Spoon mixture into a freezer-safe container; cover and freeze up to 1 month. Garnish with mint sprigs, if desired. Yield: 16 servings (serving size: ½ cup).

CALORIES 64; FAT 1.7g (sat 1.5g); PROTEIN 0.5g; CARBOHYDRATE 9.7g; FIBER 0.4g; CHOLESTEROL 0mg; IRON 0.2mg; SODIUM 5mg; CALCIUM 10mg

▶ **carbo rating: 10**

Roasted Pineapple with Cilantro

Roasting fruit brings out even more of its natural sweetness.

1	large pineapple, peeled and cored
2	tablespoons pineapple juice
1	tablespoon chopped fresh cilantro
1	tablespoon honey
½	teaspoon ground ginger
⅛	teaspoon ground cloves

1. Preheat oven to 425°.
2. Cut pineapple into 10 wedges; place wedges on a jelly roll pan.
3. Combine juice and next 4 ingredients in a bowl; stir with a whisk. Drizzle juice mixture over pineapple. Bake at 425° for 20 minutes; broil 2 minutes or until pineapple is browned. Yield: 5 servings (serving size: 2 pineapple wedges).

CALORIES 40; FAT 0.2g (sat 0g); PROTEIN 0.2g, CARBOHYDRATE 10.2g, FIBER 0.7g; CHOLESTEROL 0mg; IRON 0.3mg; SODIUM 1mg; CALCIUM 6mg

---

sweet as honey

Honey has about 6 grams of carbohydrate per teaspoon and is sweeter than granulated sugar (4 grams of carbohydrate per teaspoon), so you won't need as much honey to sweeten foods. But tablespoon for tablespoon, honey has more carbohydrate than sugar: 17.5 grams for honey compared to 12.5 grams for sugar. Either way, they're both concentrated sources of carbohydrate, so use sparingly.

▶ **carbo rating: 10**

Homemade Peach Ice Cream

What better way to enjoy the taste of summer than with a bowl of homemade peach ice cream? Traditional peach ice cream has 20 grams of carbohydrate per ½-cup serving.

2	cups evaporated fat-free milk
1	cup fat-free milk
⅔	cup "measures-like-sugar" calorie-free sweetener
½	cup egg substitute
¼	teaspoon almond extract (or ½ teaspoon vanilla extract)
1	cup chopped fresh or frozen peaches (about 2 medium)

1. Combine first 5 ingredients in a large bowl; beat with a mixer at medium speed until blended. Stir in peaches.
2. Pour mixture into the freezer can of a 2-quart ice-cream freezer; freeze according to manufacturer's instructions. Spoon ice cream into a freezer-safe container; cover and freeze 1 hour or until firm. Yield: 12 servings (serving size: ½ cup).

CALORIES 58; FAT 0.1g (sat 0.1g); PROTEIN 5.1g; CARBOHYDRATE 10.5g; FIBER 0.5g; CHOLESTEROL 2mg; IRON 0.2mg; SODIUM 75mg; CALCIUM 136mg

(pictured on page 395)

▶ carbo rating: 10
Chocolate Mousse

For a low-carb garnish, sift a bit of unsweetened cocoa over the top of each mousse.

1   envelope unflavored gelatin
1   cup cold water
2   tablespoons unsweetened cocoa
6   tablespoons sugar-free chocolate syrup
2¾ cups frozen reduced-calorie whipped topping, thawed and divided

1. Sprinkle gelatin over cold water in a small saucepan; let stand 1 minute. Cook over low heat, stirring constantly, about 3 minutes or until gelatin dissolves. Remove from heat; cool.
2. Add cocoa and chocolate syrup to gelatin mixture, stirring with a whisk until smooth. Fold in 2 cups whipped topping. Spoon evenly into 6 individual dessert dishes. Cover and chill 2 hours or until firm.
3. Spoon into individual dessert bowls. Top each serving with 2 tablespoons whipped topping. Yield: 6 servings (serving size: ½ cup).

CALORIES 91; FAT 3.9g (sat 3.8g); PROTEIN 1.9g; CARBOHYDRATE 11.3g; FIBER 1.1g; CHOLESTEROL 0mg; IRON 1mg; SODIUM 13mg; CALCIUM 3mg

(pictured on page 394)

▶ carbo rating: 11
Strawberries with Chocolate Sauce

Here's a quick and easy chocolate sauce that you can serve with any fruit or drizzle over low-carb ice cream.

24 strawberries
8   (2-ounce) sugar-free milk chocolate candy bars
2   tablespoons evaporated fat-free milk

1. Wash strawberries; drain well. Do not remove caps. Insert a wooden pick into the center of each strawberry cap.
2. Place chocolate in a small bowl. Microwave at HIGH 2 minutes, stirring every 30 seconds until chocolate melts. Add milk, stirring well with a whisk until smooth.
3. Serve sauce with strawberries. Yield: 6 servings (serving size: 4 strawberries and 1 tablespoon sauce).

CALORIES 72; FAT 3.5g (sat 0g); PROTEIN 1.1g; CARBOHYDRATE 13.1g; FIBER 2.5g; CHOLESTEROL 3mg; IRON 0.4mg; SODIUM 7mg; CALCIUM 23mg

▶ carbo rating: 11
Strawberry Whip

To partially thaw strawberries, place all three unopened packages in a large bowl, cover them with hot water, and let stand for 5 minutes.

3   (10-ounce) packages frozen strawberries in light syrup, partially thawed
2   tablespoons fresh lime juice
1   cup frozen reduced-calorie whipped topping, thawed

1. Place strawberries and lime juice in a food processor; process until smooth, stopping once to scrape down sides. Fold in whipped topping, and serve immediately. Yield: 10 servings (serving size: ½ cup).

CALORIES 57; FAT 0.9g (sat 0.4g); PROTEIN 0.2g; CARBOHYDRATE 12g; FIBER 0.6g; CHOLESTEROL 0mg; IRON 0.3mg; SODIUM 5mg; CALCIUM 5mg

▶ carbo rating: 11
Berry Sorbet

The sorbets you can buy at the grocery store, while low in fat, are usually very high in sugar. In addition to the fruit, this one is sweetened with white grape juice and a bit of calorie-free sweetener.

1   (16-ounce) package frozen unsweetened strawberries, thawed
1   (14-ounce) package frozen unsweetened raspberries, thawed
½   cup white grape juice
3   tablespoons "measures-like-sugar" calorie-free sweetener

1. Place strawberries and raspberries in a blender or food processor; process 30 seconds or until smooth, stopping once to scrape down sides.
2. Pour fruit mixture into a wire-mesh strainer; press with the back of a spoon against sides of strainer to squeeze out juice. Discard pulp and seeds remaining in strainer.
3. Combine fruit juice, grape juice, and sweetener; stir well. Pour mixture into an 8-inch square baking pan. Cover and freeze until mixture is almost firm.
4. Break frozen mixture into large pieces, and place in blender or food processor; process until fluffy but not thawed. Serve immediately, or cover and freeze. Yield: 6 servings (serving size: ½ cup).

CALORIES 63; FAT 0.4g (sat 0g); PROTEIN 0.8g; CARBOHYDRATE 15.5g; FIBER 4.7g; CHOLESTEROL 0mg; IRON 0.9mg; SODIUM 2mg; CALCIUM 18mg

10 low-carb ways to satisfy your sweet tooth

Here are a few secret weapons to use when you're craving sweets.

1. If you're a coffee drinker, indulge in a cup of flavored coffee after your meal. Chocolate-almond and hazelnut are two examples.

2. Finish off your meal with a piece of sweet, juicy fruit—not only will the fruit tingle your taste buds, it's good for you, too!

3. Dump a can of peaches, pineapple, or pears (packed in juice) into a shallow dish and freeze. When you're ready for dessert, plop the frozen fruit in your blender, and you've got a quick fruit sorbet.

4. Blend fresh berries in a food processor for a quick fruit sauce. Spoon it over vanilla low-carb ice cream.

5. Put a single layer of seedless grapes on a baking sheet and freeze for about 20 minutes. It's almost like eating candy!

6. Top a piece of angel food cake with fresh strawberries and a spoonful of reduced-calorie whipped topping.

7. Make mini ice cream sandwiches with about 2 tablespoons softened low-carb ice cream sandwiched between 2 ginger snaps or sugar-free cookies.

8. Top lemon yogurt with a few fresh berries, and serve in a fancy dessert glass.

9. Add a splash of fruit-flavored liqueur to mixed fresh fruit, and serve in a stemmed glass.

10. Crumble a sugar-free sandwich cream cookie over a scoop of low-carb ice cream.

► carbo rating: 11
Fig Bars

The flavor may remind you of a Fig Newton without the outer cookie layer.

1½   cups chopped dried figs
1   tablespoon all-purpose flour
½   cup water
¾   cup flaked unsweetened coconut
½   cup reduced-calorie margarine
⅓   cup "measures-like-sugar" calorie-free sweetener
1¾   cups quick-cooking oats, toasted
½   teaspoon vanilla extract
Cooking spray

1. Combine figs and flour in a medium bowl; toss lightly to coat.
2. Bring water to a boil in a medium saucepan. Add fig mixture, coconut, margarine, and sweetener to pan, stirring well. Cook, uncovered, over medium heat 5 to 7 minutes or until mixture is thickened, stirring often. Add oats and vanilla, stirring until oats are moistened.
3. Press mixture into bottom of a 9-inch square baking pan coated with cooking spray. Cover and chill thoroughly. Cut into bars. Yield: 2 dozen bars (serving size: 1 bar).

Microwave Instructions: Place ½ cup water in a 1-cup liquid measure. Microwave at HIGH 2 to 3 minutes or until water boils; pour water over fig mixture. Add coconut, margarine, and sweetener to fig mixture, stirring well. Microwave, uncovered, at HIGH 2 to 3 minutes or until mixture is thickened, stirring after every minute. Add oats and vanilla, stirring until oats are moistened. Proceed with recipe as directed.

CALORIES 91; FAT 4.3g (sat 2.1g); PROTEIN 1.5g; CARBOHYDRATE 13.3g; FIBER 2.5g; CHOLESTEROL 0mg; IRON 0.6mg; SODIUM 48mg; CALCIUM 23mg

► carbo rating: 12
Strawberry-Banana Ice Cream

When the ice cream mixture is packed with fruit, you don't have to use as much sweetener to achieve the perfect flavor.

2   cups strawberries, mashed
1   ripe banana, mashed
1   quart fat-free half-and-half or evaporated fat-free milk
½   cup egg substitute
½   cup "measures-like-sugar" calorie-free sweetener
1½   teaspoons vanilla extract

1. Combine all ingredients.
2. Pour mixture into the freezer can of a 2-quart ice-cream freezer; freeze according to manufacturer's instructions. Spoon ice cream into a freezer-safe container; cover and freeze 1 hour or until firm. Yield: 13 servings (serving size: ½ cup).

CALORIES 73; FAT 0.1g (sat 0g); PROTEIN 1.2g; CARBOHYDRATE 12.2g; FIBER 0.7g; CHOLESTEROL 0mg; IRON 0.3mg; SODIUM 93mg; CALCIUM 56mg

ice cream caution

There are quite a number of low-carb and sugar-free ice creams on the market today, so if you're picking up a carton, be sure to read the label to know what you're getting. Generally, the carbohydrate content of the no-sugar-added products and the low-carb products don't differ significantly, although some of the low-carb products do have more fiber (from gels and gums), resulting in a lower net carb value.

If you're concerned about total calories, however, watch out for the fat in some of the low-carb products. Just because they are low in carbs does not mean that they are low in fat. Many of these ice creams have more fat than premium ice creams. Look on the nutrition label to determine not only the carbohydrate content, but the fiber and fat content as well.

▶ carbo rating: 13
Grapefruit Ice

This frozen treat is the perfect combination of tangy and sweet flavors. And while the recipe calls for a jar of grapefruit sections as a shortcut, it works great with fresh grapefruit sections, too. A 26-ounce jar of grapefruit sections is equivalent to 2½ cups, or about 2 large grapefruit.

1   large orange
1   tablespoon "measures-like-sugar" calorie-free
    sweetener
1   (26-ounce) jar grapefruit sections, undrained
Mint sprigs (optional)

1. Peel and section orange over a bowl; squeeze membranes to extract juice. Reserve juice for another use; discard membranes.
2. Combine orange sections, sweetener, and grapefruit in a blender or food processor; process until smooth. Pour mixture into a 13 x 9-inch baking pan. Cover and freeze 2 hours, stirring every 30 minutes with a fork. Let stand 5 minutes before serving. Garnish with mint sprigs, if desired. Yield: 6 servings (serving size: 1 cup).

CALORIES 63; FAT 0.3g (sat 0g); PROTEIN 0.8g; CARBOHYDRATE 14.6g;
FIBER 1.2g; CHOLESTEROL 0mg; IRON 0.3mg; SODIUM 3mg; CALCIUM 29mg

"This dessert has excellent flavor—clean and rich. I loved it! I also like that it's easy to prepare."
Brad Sims

▶ carbo rating: 13
Pineapple-Mint Freeze

When you've enjoyed a big, hearty meal, sometimes you need a refreshingly light dessert to cleanse your palate. This pineapple freeze will do just that.

1   (20-ounce) can pineapple chunks in juice, chilled
2   tablespoons chopped fresh mint
Mint sprigs (optional)

1. Place pineapple chunks and juice in an 8-inch square baking dish. Freeze 1½ to 2 hours or until almost frozen.
2. Place frozen pineapple and chopped mint in a blender or food processor; process until smooth, but not melted.
3. Spoon ½ cup pineapple mixture into each of 5 dessert dishes. Garnish with mint sprigs, if desired. Yield: 5 servings (serving size: ½ cup).

CALORIES 57; FAT 0g (sat 0g); PROTEIN 0.1g; CARBOHYDRATE 14.1g;
FIBER 1.1g; CHOLESTEROL 0mg; IRON 0.6mg; SODIUM 10mg; CALCIUM 5mg

(pictured on page 396)

► carbo rating: 13

Rocky Road Fudge Pops

Look for the plastic holders at specialty kitchen shops, or use 3-ounce paper cups and craft sticks.

1 (1.4-ounce) package sugar-free, fat-free chocolate instant pudding mix
2 tablespoons "measures-like-sugar" calorie-free sweetener
1 cup fat-free milk
1 (12-ounce) can evaporated fat-free milk
¾ cup miniature marshmallows
⅓ cup chopped sugar-free milk chocolate bar (2 ounces)
¼ cup plus 3 tablespoons coarsely chopped unsalted, dry roasted peanuts, divided

1. Combine pudding mix and sweetener in a large bowl. Gradually add fat-free milk and evaporated milk, stirring with a whisk until smooth. Stir in marshmallows, chocolate, and ¼ cup peanuts.
2. Sprinkle 3 tablespoons peanuts evenly among 12 plastic holders. Pour pudding mixture into holders, and add sticks. Freeze 3 hours or until firm. Yield: 12 servings (serving size: 1 pop).

CALORIES 107; FAT 4.2g (sat 1.2g); PROTEIN 4.6g; CARBOHYDRATE 13.6g; FIBER 0.7g; CHOLESTEROL 2mg; IRON 0.2mg; SODIUM 157mg; CALCIUM 106mg

(pictured on page 397)

► carbo rating: 14

Roasted Spiced Plums

Roast fresh plums in a spiced juice mixture for a classy fruit dessert.

4 plums, halved
Cooking spray
½ cup orange juice
¼ cup "measures-like-sugar" calorie-free sweetener
½ teaspoon ground cinnamon
⅛ teaspoon freshly grated whole nutmeg
⅛ teaspoon ground cumin
⅛ teaspoon ground cardamom
2 tablespoons slivered almonds, toasted

1. Preheat oven to 450°.
2. Place plum halves, cut sides up, in an 11 x 7-inch baking dish coated with cooking spray. Combine orange juice and next 5 ingredients. Drizzle orange juice mixture over plums. Bake at 450° for 20 minutes. Top with almonds. Yield: 4 servings (serving size: 2 plum halves and ½ tablespoon almonds).

CALORIES 89; FAT 3g (sat 0.2g); PROTEIN 1.6g; CARBOHYDRATE 15.4g; FIBER 1.7g; CHOLESTEROL 0mg; IRON 0.3mg; SODIUM 1mg; CALCIUM 17mg

▶ carbo rating: 14

Mint Chocolate Chip Ice Cream

The touch of bittersweet chocolate is a nice balance for the mint flavor. Ounce per ounce, bittersweet chocolate has a little less carbohydrate than milk chocolate (see chart below).

2 cups evaporated fat-free milk
1 cup fat-free milk
⅔ cup "measures-like-sugar" calorie-free sweetener
½ cup egg substitute
½ teaspoon peppermint extract
6 drops green food coloring (optional)
4 ounces bittersweet chocolate, coarsely chopped

1. Combine first 5 ingredients and food coloring, if desired, in a large bowl; beat with a mixer at medium speed until well blended. Stir in chocolate.
2. Pour mixture into the freezer can of a 2-quart ice-cream freezer; freeze according to manufacturer's instructions. Spoon ice cream into a freezer-safe container; cover and freeze 1 hour or until firm. Yield: 12 servings (serving size: ½ cup).

CALORIES 96; FAT 2.5g (sat 1.4g); PROTEIN 4.8g; CARBOHYDRATE 14.2g; FIBER 0.1g; CHOLESTEROL 4mg; IRON 0.4mg; SODIUM 87mg; CALCIUM 138mg

▶ carbo rating: 15

Banana Pops

These are great to keep on hand in the freezer for those times when you need a quick "sweet fix."

2 cups mashed ripe banana (about 5 medium)
1 cup orange juice
1 teaspoon lemon juice

1. Combine all ingredients in a medium bowl; divide mixture evenly among popsicle molds. Cover and freeze 8 hours. Yield: 8 servings (serving size: 1 pop).

Note: For testing purposes only, we used 8 (½-cup) popsicle molds. The yield may vary depending on size of molds.

CALORIES 66; FAT 0.3g (sat 0.1g); PROTEIN 0.8g; CARBOHYDRATE 16.5g; FIBER 1.4g; CHOLESTEROL 0mg; IRON 0.2mg; SODIUM 1mg; CALCIUM 7mg

chocolate comparisons

Compare the carbo ratings for different types of chocolate.

Chocolate (1 ounce)	Carbohydrate (grams)	Fiber (grams)	Carbo Rating
Unsweetened Chocolate	8.5g	4.7g	4
Bittersweet Chocolate	14.2g	2.0g	12
Milk Chocolate	16.8g	1.0g	16
Dark Chocolate	17.6g	1.4g	16

► carbo rating: 15
Chocolate-Pecan Parfaits

Instead of topping the parfaits with plain chopped pecans, you can use the Spiced Pecans on page 58.

2	cups vanilla fat-free, no-sugar-added ice cream
½	cup sugar-free chocolate syrup
¼	cup chopped pecans

1. Spoon ¼ cup ice cream into each of 4 parfait glasses; top each with 1 tablespoon chocolate syrup. Repeat procedure with remaining ice cream and chocolate syrup. Sprinkle 1 tablespoon chopped pecans over each serving. Yield: 4 servings (serving size: ½ cup ice cream, 2 tablespoons syrup, and 1 tablespoon pecans).

CALORIES 116; FAT 5.4g (sat 0.5g); PROTEIN 3.2g; CARBOHYDRATE 16.5g; FIBER 1.7g; CHOLESTEROL 0mg; IRON 1.6mg; SODIUM 45mg; CALCIUM 45mg

toasting pecans

Toast pecans and other nuts to bring out their flavor. To toast pecans, spread them in a shallow pan and bake for 10 to 15 minutes at 350°, stirring occasionally. Watch them carefully because they burn easily.

You can also toast them in the microwave in a shallow dish for 1 to 2 minutes at HIGH, stopping every 30 seconds to stir and check to see if they're toasted.

► carbo rating: 15
Marinated Strawberries

Add a tangy, spicy bite to sweet strawberries with fresh lime juice and a sprinkling of black pepper.

2	tablespoons fresh lime juice
2	tablespoons honey
½	teaspoon olive oil
½	teaspoon cracked black pepper
1	quart strawberries, cut into thick slices

Grated lime rind (optional)

1. Combine first 4 ingredients; stir with a whisk. Add strawberries; toss. Cover and chill. Sprinkle with lime rind, if desired. Yield: 4 servings (serving size: ¾ cup).

CALORIES 174; FAT 1.0g (sat 0.1g); PROTEIN 0.8g; CARBOHYDRATE 17.5g; FIBER 2.7g; CHOLESTEROL 0mg; IRON 0.6mg; SODIUM 2mg; CALCIUM 21mg

(pictured on cover, bottom center)

► carbo rating: 16
Red Grape Sorbet

Red grape juice, like red wine, may offer protection from heart disease because of a compound in the skins of red grapes.

2½	cups red grape juice, divided
1	envelope unflavored gelatin

Mint sprigs (optional)

1. Combine ½ cup grape juice and gelatin in a medium saucepan; cook over low heat, stirring until gelatin dissolves. Remove from heat; stir in 2 cups grape juice. Pour mixture into an 8-inch square baking pan. Freeze until almost firm.
2. Break frozen mixture into pieces, and place in a food processor; process several seconds or until fluffy but not thawed. Return to freezer, and freeze until firm.
3. Scoop sorbet into individual dessert dishes using an ice cream scoop. Garnish with mint sprigs, if desired. Yield: 6 servings (serving size: ½ cup).

CALORIES 68; FAT 0.1g (sat 0g); PROTEIN 1.6g; CARBOHYDRATE 15.8g; FIBER 0.1g; CHOLESTEROL 0mg; IRON 0.3mg; SODIUM 5mg; CALCIUM 10mg

Stir Fried Brown Rice
▶ carbo rating: 13
page 340

Mushroom Barley
▶ carbo rating: 18
page 341

Cream of Cauliflower Soup with Curry
▶ carbo rating: 9
page 351

Smoked Turkey-Bean Soup
▶ carbo rating: 14
page 355

Cioppino
▶ carbo rating: 16
page 357

Creamy Wild Rice-Turkey Chowder
▶ carbo rating: 16
page 358

White Bean-Chicken Chili
▶ carbo rating: 17
page 358

Twenty-Minute Chili
▶ carbo rating: 30
page 368

Chocolate-Peanut Butter Balls
▶ carbo rating: 5
page 373

Chocolate Mousse
▶ carbo rating: 10
page 378

Homemade Peach Ice Cream
▶ carbo rating: 10
page 377

Pineapple-Mint Freeze
▶ carbo rating: 13
page 381

Rocky Road Fudge Pops
▶ carbo rating: 13
page 382

Peaches in Red Wine
▶ carbo rating: 17
page 401

Chocolate Chunk Ice Cream
▶ carbo rating: 25
page 407

Ice Cream Sandwich Dessert
▶ carbo rating: 26
page 408

▶ carbo rating: 17
Fudgy Peanut Butter Ice Cream

We tested this recipe with a package of mini sugar-free chocolate peanut butter cups. If you want to use the larger ones, you'll need to use 2½ (1.5-ounce) packages (5 pieces).

1	(1.4-ounce) package sugar-free, fat-free chocolate instant pudding mix
1½	cups fat-free milk
1	(12-ounce) can evaporated fat-free milk
1	(3.5-ounce) package mini sugar-free chocolate peanut butter cups (such as Russell Stover), chopped

1. Combine first 3 ingredients in a large bowl, stirring with a whisk until smooth. Stir in chopped candy.
2. Pour chocolate mixture into the freezer can of a 2-quart ice-cream freezer; freeze according to manufacturer's instructions. Spoon ice cream into a freezer-safe container; cover and freeze 1 hour or until firm. Yield: 8 servings (serving size: ½ cup).

CALORIES 130; FAT 4.7g (sat 2.2g); PROTEIN 6.2g; CARBOHYDRATE 17.5g; FIBER 0.7g; CHOLESTEROL 1mg; IRON 0.5mg; SODIUM 157mg; CALCIUM 246mg

what is malitol?

If you look at the tiny print of the ingredient list on a package of sugar-free chocolate candy, you're likely to see the word *malitol*. What is it? Malitol is a natural sugar substitute based on a malt extract that allows chocolate to have a sweet taste without containing sugar. Malitol has become a popular sugar substitute in many sugar-free chocolate products.

Malitol is just one sweetener in a family of sweeteners called polyols, or sugar alcohols. (A sugar alcohol does not contain alcohol; it's called an alcohol because of its chemical structure.) Sugar alcohols have fewer calories than sugars, and, because they are absorbed more slowly than other sugars, don't cause as big a rise in blood glucose. One drawback of sugar alcohols is that excess consumption can have a laxative effect.

▶ carbo rating: 18
Wheat and Carrot Cake

For all of the carrot cake fans who've given it up for the low-carb lifestyle, the joy is back! This snack cake is sweetened with a small amount of calorie-free sweetener and honey, and has a fair amount of fiber because of the whole wheat flour and the carrot. Because it's sweet and tender on its own, we liked it fine without a cream cheese frosting, but if you want one, see the recipe on the next page.

½	cup egg substitute
½	cup vanilla fat-free yogurt sweetened with aspartame
¼	cup "measures-like-sugar" calorie-free sweetener
¼	cup honey
¼	cup vegetable oil
2	cups whole wheat flour
1	teaspoon baking soda
1½	teaspoons ground cinnamon
1½	cups grated carrot
½	cup raisins
	Cooking spray
	Cream Cheese Frosting (optional)

1. Preheat oven to 400°.
2. Combine first 5 ingredients in a bowl; stir well. Lightly spoon flour into dry measuring cups; level with a knife. Combine flour and next 4 ingredients, stirring well. Add egg substitute mixture to flour mixture, stirring well.
3. Pour batter into an 8-inch square baking pan coated with cooking spray. Bake at 400° for 30 to 35 minutes or until a wooden pick inserted in center comes out clean. Cool in pan 10 minutes on a wire rack. Spread Cream Cheese Frosting on top of cooled cake, if desired (frosting not included in analysis). Yield: 16 servings (serving size: 1 square).

CALORIES 124; FAT 3.8g (sat 0.3g); PROTEIN 3.3g; CARBOHYDRATE 21g; FIBER 2.6g; CHOLESTEROL 0mg; IRON 0.9mg; SODIUM 108mg; CALCIUM 25mg

▶ carbo rating: 17

Peaches in Red Wine

If your carb allowance is high enough, serve these tangy peaches over vanilla no-sugar-added or low-carb ice cream.

1	(750-milliliter) bottle dry red wine
¼	cup "measures-like-sugar" calorie-free sweetener
¼	cup orange rind strips
¼	cup lemon rind strips
⅛	teaspoon ground cardamom
7	whole cloves
4	black peppercorns
1	cinnamon stick
6	cups fresh peach slices

1. Combine first 8 ingredients in a large saucepan. Bring to a boil over medium-high heat; cook 15 minutes or until wine mixture is reduced to 1½ cups. Cool to room temperature.
2. Strain mixture through a sieve over a bowl; discard solids. Combine wine mixture and peaches in a bowl; cover and chill 4 hours, stirring occasionally. Yield: 6 servings (serving size: 1 cup).

CALORIES 81; FAT 0.2g (sat 0g); PROTEIN 1.3g; CARBOHYDRATE 20.8g; FIBER 3.4g; CHOLESTEROL 0mg; IRON 0.5mg; SODIUM 5mg; CALCIUM 13mg

(pictured on page 398)

---

peach preparation

Leaving the peels on peaches helps them retain their shape and texture during cooking and cuts down on preparation time. Wash the fuzz off the peel before proceeding with your recipe.

▶ carbo rating: 17

Ruby Peach Melba

This is a quick and easy low-carb version of a Peach Melba—a dessert created in the late 1800s for Dame Nellie Melba, an Australian opera singer. In the traditional version, the peach halves are poached in syrup, placed on a scoop of ice cream, and topped with a sweet raspberry sauce.

1½	cups raspberries
2	tablespoons "measures-like-sugar" calorie-free sweetener
2	teaspoons lemon juice
1	(16-ounce) can peach halves in juice, drained
1½	cups vanilla fat-free, no-sugar-added ice cream

1. Combine first 3 ingredients in a small bowl, tossing lightly to coat. Let stand 5 minutes.
2. Spoon raspberry mixture evenly into individual dessert dishes. Place 1 peach half, cut side up, in each dish, and spoon ¼ cup ice cream over each serving. Serve immediately. Yield: 6 servings (serving size: ¼ cup raspberries, 1 peach half, and ¼ cup ice cream).

CALORIES 84; FAT 0.2g (sat 0g); PROTEIN 1.7g; CARBOHYDRATE 20.4g; FIBER 3.3g; CHOLESTEROL 0mg; IRON 0.5mg; SODIUM 17mg; CALCIUM 34mg

Cream Cheese Frosting:

This recipe makes enough frosting to cover an 8-inch square cake such as the Wheat and Carrot Cake on the previous page.

1½ (8-ounce) packages ⅓-less-fat cream cheese, softened
2 tablespoons pineapple juice
½ teaspoon vanilla
½ cup "measures-like-sugar" calorie-free sweetener

1. Combine first 3 ingredients in a medium bowl. Beat cheese mixture with a mixer at medium speed until creamy. Add sweetener; beat until blended. Yield: 1¾ cups (serving size: 2 tablespoons).

CALORIES 66; FAT 5.2g (sat 0g); PROTEIN 2.6g; CARBOHYDRATE 2.1g; FIBER 0g; CHOLESTEROL 17mg; IRON 0mg; SODIUM 0mg; CALCIUM 18mg

▶ **carbo rating: 18**
Coeur à la Crème with Goat Cheese

Coeur à la crème *is French for "heart with cream" and is a classic dessert made in a special heart-shaped pan with holes. The mixture firms as it's chilled and the liquid from the cream cheese drains out through the holes. It's served unmolded and garnished with fresh berries or other fruit. Our low-fat, low-carb version features reduced-fat cheeses and sour cream and calorie-free sweetener. The extra kick of flavor comes from the goat cheese.*

1⅓ cups ⅓-less-fat cream cheese, softened
1 cup part-skim ricotta cheese
1 cup reduced-fat sour cream
½ cup "measures-like-sugar" calorie-free sweetener
2 ounces goat cheese
1 envelope unflavored gelatin
¼ cup cold water
2½ cups berries (such as raspberries, blueberries, or sliced strawberries)
20 gingersnaps

1. Line a 4-cup coeur à la crème mold with a double layer of damp cheesecloth; allow cheesecloth to extend over edge of mold.
2. Combine first 5 ingredients in a food processor; process until smooth.
3. Sprinkle gelatin over cold water in a saucepan; let stand 1 minute. Cook over low heat, stirring until gelatin dissolves, about 2 minutes. Remove from heat; cool slightly. Add ¼ cup cheese mixture to gelatin mixture, stirring with a whisk; add to remaining cheese mixture in processor, and process 1 minute.
4. Spoon cheese mixture into prepared mold. Fold cheesecloth over top of cheese mixture; place mold in a shallow dish, and chill at least 12 hours.
5. Unfold cheesecloth, and invert cheese mixture onto a serving plate; remove cheesecloth. Serve with berries and gingersnaps. Yield: 10 servings (serving size: ⅓ cup crème, ¼ cup berries, and 2 gingersnaps).

CALORIES 253; FAT 14.1g (sat 4.1g); PROTEIN 11.2g; CARBOHYDRATE 20.3g; FIBER 1.8g; CHOLESTEROL 42mg; IRON 1.3mg; SODIUM 153mg; CALCIUM 139mg

cheese course

When dining out, the cheese course is a great low-carb option for dessert. Most cheese courses come with a variety of cheeses, along with a few crackers and pieces of fruit that complement the flavors of the cheeses. You can sample the cheeses without the crackers or fruit, or just nibble on the fruit. Either way, you'll get fewer carbs than if you'd ordered a fruit dessert, sorbet, or ice cream. Ask your server about the amounts of cheese that come with the course—usually one course is plenty for a couple of people to share.

▶ carbo rating: 19

Berries Jubilee

If you don't want to have a flaming dessert, just leave off the brandy and spoon the warm berry mixture over ice cream. The cooked alcohol contributes only a negligible amount of carbohydrate, so the carbo rating is the same without the brandy.

2	tablespoons "measures-like-sugar" calorie-free sweetener
1	tablespoon cornstarch
⅛	teaspoon salt
½	teaspoon grated orange rind
½	cup orange juice
½	cup water
1½	cups blueberries
1½	cups raspberries
2	tablespoons brandy
4	cups vanilla reduced-fat, no-sugar-added ice cream

1. Combine first 3 ingredients in a large skillet. Stir in rind, juice, and water; bring to a boil. Cook 1 minute or until slightly thickened. Add berries; cook 3 minutes or until thoroughly heated.

2. Add brandy; cook 3 minutes. Spoon warm berry sauce over ice cream. Yield: 8 servings (serving size: ½ cup ice cream and ⅓ cup sauce).

CALORIES 146; FAT 4.5g (sat 2.4g); PROTEIN 3.4g; CARBOHYDRATE 21.7g; FIBER 2.4g; CHOLESTEROL 11mg; IRON 0.2mg; SODIUM 96mg; CALCIUM 136mg

---

low-carb ice cream

If you prefer to use low-carb ice cream for your desserts, it works fine. In Berries Jubilee (above), we used a reduced-fat, no-sugar-added ice cream that has 99 calories, 12 grams carbohydrate, 0 grams fiber, and 4 grams fat per ½-cup serving (carbo rating 12). Breyer's Carb Smart Vanilla Ice Cream has 130 calories, 10 grams carbohydrate, 3 grams fiber, and 9 grams fat per ½-cup serving (carbo rating 7).

▶ carbo rating: 21

Cookies 'n' Cream Crunch

When you combine the creaminess of ice cream and the crunch of cookies, you get a dessert that's out of this world.

1	(6½-ounce) package sugar-free chocolate sandwich cookies, crushed
⅓	cup chopped pecans
3	tablespoons light butter, melted
1	quart vanilla low-carb ice cream, softened

1. Combine first 3 ingredients; set aside 1 cup cookie crumb mixture. Press remaining crumb mixture firmly into bottom of a 9-inch square baking pan. Freeze 10 minutes.

2. Spread ice cream over crumb mixture in pan. Sprinkle reserved crumb mixture over ice cream; gently press mixture into ice cream. Cover and freeze at least 8 hours.

3. Let stand at room temperature 5 minutes before serving; cut into squares. Yield: 9 servings (serving size: 1 square).

CALORIES 175; FAT 10.3g (sat 3.1g); PROTEIN 3.5g; CARBOHYDRATE 22.2g; FIBER 0.8g; CHOLESTEROL 7mg; SODIUM 126mg; IRON 0.9mg; CALCIUM 39mg

▶ carbo rating: 22
Chocolate-Peanut Butter Bread Pudding

Bread and pudding are two words you wouldn't normally associate with a low-carb diet, but you can enjoy bread pudding without any guilt if you use a multigrain bread and a calorie-free sweetener.

4	(1-ounce) slices multigrain, low-calorie, high-fiber bread, cut into 1-inch cubes
¼	cup semisweet chocolate minichips
1	cup fat-free milk
¼	cup "measures-like-sugar" brown sugar calorie-free sweetener (such as Brown Sugar Twin)
¼	cup egg substitute
¼	cup natural creamy-style peanut butter

Cooking spray

1. Preheat oven to 350°.
2. Place bread cubes in a large bowl; sprinkle with chocolate minichips.
3. Combine milk and next 3 ingredients in a blender; process until smooth. Pour milk mixture over bread mixture; stir to coat. Let stand 10 minutes.
4. Transfer mixture to a 1-quart baking dish coated with cooking spray. Bake at 350° for 30 minutes or until pudding is firm. Serve immediately. Yield: 4 servings (serving size: ¾ cup).

CALORIES 236; FAT 12g (sat 3.2g); PROTEIN 10.4g; CARBOHYDRATE 27.2g; FIBER 5.1g; CHOLESTEROL 4mg; IRON 1.8mg; SODIUM 256mg; CALCIUM 127mg

▶ carbo rating: 22
Chocolate Milkshake

Because it is a source of calcium and contains chocolate, this milkshake is actually good for you. (See the information below about the health benefits of chocolate.)

1½	cups vanilla fat-free, no-sugar-added ice cream
¾	cup fat-free milk
1	tablespoon no-sugar-added chocolate drink mix
1	tablespoon sugar-free chocolate syrup
¼	teaspoon vanilla extract
3	ice cubes

1. Combine all ingredients except ice in a blender; process until smooth. Add ice; process mixture until smooth. Serve immediately. Yield: 2 servings (serving size: 1 cup).

CALORIES 115; FAT 0.4g (sat 0.2g); PROTEIN 5.9g; CARBOHYDRATE 22g; FIBER 0.5g; CHOLESTEROL 2mg; IRON 0.8mg; SODIUM 112mg; CALCIUM 173mg

the truth about chocolate

Research has shown that chocolate and cocoa contain some of the same antioxidants found in fruit, vegetables, tea, and red wine. But it's still not known just what chocolate's antioxidants do in the body. There are a multitude of studies showing a link between fruits and vegetables and a decreased risk of cancer, but no direct studies show the same link for chocolate.

Peach Crisp

If fresh peaches are not in season, you can use 2 cups canned or thawed frozen sliced peaches as a substitute.

2 cups peach slices (about 2 medium)
2 tablespoons "measures-like-sugar" brown sugar calorie-free sweetener (such as Brown Sugar Twin), divided
3 tablespoons all-fruit peach spread (such as Simply Fruit)
1 tablespoon fresh lemon juice
½ teaspoon ground cinnamon
¼ teaspoon ground nutmeg
Cooking spray
¾ cup regular oats
2 tablespoons chilled butter, cut into small pieces
Vanilla low-carb ice cream or frozen whipped topping, thawed (optional)

1. Preheat oven to 475°.
2. Combine peaches, 1 tablespoon sweetener, and next 4 ingredients. Place in a 2-quart baking dish coated with cooking spray.
3. Combine 1 tablespoon sweetener, oats, and butter; stir until crumbly. Sprinkle over peach mixture. Bake, uncovered, at 475° for 15 minutes or until golden. Serve warm. Top with ice cream or whipped topping, if desired (ice cream or topping not included in analysis). Yield: 4 servings (serving size: ½ cup).

CALORIES 160; FAT 6.9g (sat 3.1g); PROTEIN 2.8g; CARBOHYDRATE 23.4g;
FIBER 1.6g; CHOLESTEROL 15mg; IRON 0.9mg; SODIUM 44mg; CALCIUM 22mg

Spiced Bananas

If you can't find the brown sugar substitute, it's fine to use another calorie-free sweetener.

Butter-flavored cooking spray
3 tablespoons butter
3 tablespoons "measures-like-sugar" brown sugar calorie-free sweetener (such as Brown Sugar Twin)
½ teaspoon vanilla extract
Dash of ground cinnamon
2 very ripe bananas, split lengthwise
2 cups vanilla fat-free, no-sugar-added ice cream

1. Melt butter in a medium nonstick skillet coated with cooking spray over medium heat. Add brown sugar substitute, vanilla, and cinnamon; cook 1 minute or until sugar substitute dissolves.
2. Arrange banana in pan; cook over medium-high heat 2 minutes or until thoroughly heated, turning once. Spoon banana mixture evenly over ½-cup portions of ice cream. Yield: 4 servings (serving size: ½ banana and ½ cup ice cream).

CALORIES 178; FAT 8.7g (sat 4.4g); PROTEIN 2.2g; CARBOHYDRATE 23.9g;
FIBER 1.6g; CHOLESTEROL 23mg; IRON 0.2mg; SODIUM 92mg; CALCIUM 55mg

▶ carbo rating: 23

Cookies and Cream Dessert

This superfast dessert is a variation of the Ice Cream Sandwich Dessert on page 408—it's basically the cookies and cream mixture without the ice cream sandwiches.

¼ cup brewed coffee
2 teaspoons "measures-like-sugar" calorie-free sweetener
1 (1-ounce) sugar-free milk chocolate bar, melted
1 (12-ounce) container frozen fat-free whipped topping, thawed
14 sugar-free chocolate sandwich cookies (such as Murray), crumbled

1. Combine coffee, sweetener, and melted chocolate, stirring well to combine.
2. Add coffee mixture to whipped topping, stirring well. Fold crumbled cookies into whipped topping, reserving about ¼ cup crumbled cookies.
3. Spoon whipped topping mixture into an 8-inch square baking pan. Sprinkle with reserved crumbled cookies. Cover and freeze until firm. Cut into squares. Yield: 9 servings (serving size: 1 square).

CALORIES 139; FAT 4.7g (sat 1g); PROTEIN 1.1g; CARBOHYDRATE 23.9g; FIBER 0.4g; CHOLESTEROL 1mg; IRON 0.6mg; SODIUM 78mg; CALCIUM 0mg

"Yum! This does not taste low-carb at all!"

Christina Argo

▶ carbo rating: 25

Chocolate Chunk Ice Cream

Because of the gelatin and the lack of sugar and fat, this ice cream freezes hard. Let it sit out at room temperature a few minutes to soften before you spoon it into dishes.

2 envelopes unflavored gelatin
4 cups evaporated fat-free milk, divided
¾ cup egg substitute
1 tablespoon vanilla extract
⅓ cup unsweetened cocoa
24 packets (or 7¼ teaspoons) calorie-free sweetener with aspartame (such as Equal)
1 (2.8-ounce) sugar-free milk chocolate bar, chopped

1. Sprinkle gelatin over 2 cups evaporated milk in a medium saucepan; let stand 5 minutes.
2. Cook over medium heat until gelatin dissolves and mixture just comes to a boil. Gradually stir about 1 cup of hot milk mixture into egg substitute; add to remaining hot milk mixture, stirring constantly. Cook, stirring constantly, 2 minutes (do not boil). Remove from heat. Stir in 2 cups milk and vanilla.
3. Combine cocoa and sweetener in a large bowl. Gradually add hot milk mixture, stirring until smooth. Stir in chopped candy. Chill approximately 30 minutes or just until cold, stirring occasionally (do not overchill).
4. Pour chocolate mixture into the freezer can of a 4-quart ice-cream freezer; freeze according to manufacturer's instructions. Spoon ice cream into a freezer-safe container; cover and freeze 1 hour or until firm. Yield: 8 servings (serving size: ½ cup).

CALORIES 183; FAT 4g (sat 2.4g); PROTEIN 13.2g; CARBOHYDRATE 26.8g; FIBER 1.4g; CHOLESTEROL 12mg; IRON 0.9mg; SODIUM 218mg; CALCIUM 333mg

(pictured on page 399)

► carbo rating: 26
Ice Cream Sandwich Dessert

This make-ahead dessert is quite a crowd-pleaser, even for people who aren't counting carbs. Look for the rectangular no-sugar-added or low-carb ice cream sandwiches instead of the round ones because the rectangles will fit better in the baking dish.

2   tablespoons brewed coffee
1   (1-ounce) sugar-free milk chocolate bar
1   (8-ounce) container frozen fat-free whipped topping, thawed
14 (0.3-ounce) sugar-free fudge-dipped wafers (such as Murray), chopped and divided
6   (2.3-ounce) reduced-fat, no-sugar-added ice cream sandwiches

1. Combine coffee and chocolate bar in a microwave-safe dish; microwave at LOW 1 minute or until chocolate melts, stirring once. (Even if the chocolate does not appear to be completely melted, remove the mixture from the microwave oven and stir until the chocolate melts. The chocolate might burn if it is heated much longer than 1 minute.)
2. Spoon whipped topping into a bowl, and fold chocolate mixture into whipped topping. Stir in half of chopped wafer bars.
3. Arrange ice cream sandwiches in an 11 x 7-inch baking dish. Spread whipped topping mixture evenly over ice cream sandwiches. Sprinkle with remaining chopped wafer bars. Cover and freeze at least 2 hours or until firm. Cut into squares. Yield: 12 servings (serving size: 1 square).

CALORIES 163; FAT 5.8g (sat 3g); PROTEIN 2.5g; CARBOHYDRATE 26.7g; FIBER 0.4g; CHOLESTEROL 5.4mg; IRON 0.2mg; SODIUM 90mg; CALCIUM 10mg

(pictured on page 400)

ice cream sandwich dessert options

This versatile recipe has a lot of options, and it's great just about any way you make it.
• Use 2 tablespoons sugar-free chocolate syrup instead of the milk chocolate bar.
• Use any type of sugar-free or low-carb chocolate cookies you wish in place of the fudge-dipped wafers. The carbohydrate content may vary slightly, depending on the type of cookies you use. The wafers we tested with have 19 grams of carbohydrate per 4 bars.
• Leave both the coffee and the chocolate out of the whipped topping, and just stir the chopped cookies into the plain fat-free topping.
• Use only half the amount of cookies, and top the dessert with chopped nuts.

"This is an excellent dessert! I'm not a big 'sweets person,' but I love my daily latte and this is quite reminiscent of it. Loved it!"

Brenda Howe

► carbo rating: 27

Creamy Fruit Ambrosia

A traditional ambrosia is a chilled mixture of oranges and banana mixed with coconut, and can be served as either a salad or dessert. This one has peaches instead of banana, and is topped with a creamy yogurt mixture and toasted pecans for some crunch.

4	cups cubed fresh pineapple
2	cups coarsely chopped peeled peaches
1	(8-ounce) carton vanilla fat-free yogurt sweetened with aspartame
¼	cup no-sugar-added peach spread
2	tablespoons shredded unsweetened coconut, toasted
2	tablespoons finely chopped pecans, toasted

1. Combine pineapple and peaches in a large bowl; cover and chill.

2. Combine yogurt and peach spread in a small bowl; stir well.

3. Spoon fruit mixture evenly into 6 dessert dishes. Top with yogurt mixture; sprinkle with coconut and pecans. Yield: 6 servings (serving size: about 1 cup).

CALORIES 152; FAT 3.5g (sat 1.3g); PROTEIN 2.3g; CARBOHYDRATE 30.1g; FIBER 2.9g; CHOLESTEROL 1mg; IRON 0.6mg; SODIUM 23mg; CALCIUM 71mg

► carbo rating: 28

Raspberry Smoothies

A fruit smoothie is also a good option for breakfast on the run.

1½	cups fresh or frozen raspberries
1½	cups frozen reduced-calorie whipped topping, thawed
1	(8-ounce) carton lemon low-fat yogurt

1. Combine all ingredients in a blender. Add ice cubes to reach 4-cup level. Process until smooth. Serve immediately. Yield: 4 servings (serving size: 1 cup).

CALORIES 144; FAT 0.7g (sat 0g); PROTEIN 2.5g; CARBOHYDRATE 30.8g; FIBER 3.1g; CHOLESTEROL 0mg; IRON 0.3mg; SODIUM 52mg; CALCIUM 107mg

Strawberry Smoothies: Use 1½ cups sliced strawberries instead of raspberries; proceed with recipe as directed.

Blueberry Smoothies: Use 1½ cups blueberries instead of raspberries; proceed with recipe as directed.

Peach Smoothies: Use 1½ cups fresh or frozen sliced peaches instead of raspberries, use vanilla low-fat yogurt instead of lemon, and proceed with recipe as directed.

calcium and weight loss

Some new research shows that eating low-fat calcium-containing foods may help you burn fat. Because it has both milk and ice cream, this shake is a yummy way to get your calcium. One serving provides 173 milligrams of calcium, which is about 14 percent of the daily requirement for men and women over 50 years of age.

▶ carbo rating: 30

No-Bake Cherry Cheesecake

Most of the carbohydrate in this cheesecake comes from the crust and the fruit topping. If you like plain cheesecake, leave off the cherry pie filling and the carbo rating will be 27.

1	(8-ounce) package fat-free cream cheese, softened
½	(8-ounce) package ⅓-less-fat cream cheese, softened
¾	cup evaporated fat-free milk
2½	tablespoons lemon juice
2	packets sugar substitute with aspartame (such as Equal)
½	(8-ounce) container frozen fat-free whipped topping, thawed
1	(9-inch) graham cracker crust
½	cup light cherry pie filling

1. Beat cheeses with a mixer at medium speed 2 minutes or until blended (do not overbeat). Add milk, lemon juice, and sugar substitute; beat 1 minute or just until smooth. Fold in whipped topping.
2. Spoon cream cheese mixture into crust; cover and chill until firm. Cut into 8 slices, and top each slice with 1 tablespoon cherry pie filling. Yield: 8 servings (serving size: 1 slice).

CALORIES 250; FAT 10g (sat 1.6g); PROTEIN 8.2g; CARBOHYDRATE 30.5g; FIBER 0.8g; CHOLESTEROL 14mg; IRON 0.6mg; SODIUM 344mg; CALCIUM 128mg

▶ carbo rating: 31

Orange-Pumpkin Tarts

Offer these individual tarts as an alternative to pumpkin pie at your next holiday meal.

1	cup crumbled sugar-free oatmeal cookies (5 cookies)
2	tablespoons butter or margarine, melted
	Cooking spray
1	teaspoon all-purpose flour
½	cup canned pumpkin
½	cup evaporated fat-free milk
¼	cup "measures-like-sugar" calorie-free sweetener
¼	cup egg substitute
2	tablespoons orange juice
½	teaspoon pumpkin pie spice
¼	cup frozen reduced-calorie whipped topping, thawed

1. Preheat oven to 375°.
2. Combine cookie crumbs and butter, stirring well. Coat 4 (4-inch) tartlet pans with cooking spray. Sprinkle flour evenly over bottoms of pans. Press crumb mixture into bottoms and three-fourths way up sides of pans. Bake at 375° for 5 minutes.
3. Combine pumpkin and next 5 ingredients, stirring well with a whisk. Pour evenly into prepared crusts.
4. Bake at 375° for 25 minutes or until set. Cool completely on a wire rack. Top each tart with 1 tablespoon whipped topping. Yield: 4 servings (serving size: 1 tart).

CALORIES 261; FAT 12.7g (sat 4.9g); PROTEIN 6.9g; CARBOHYDRATE 32.6g; FIBER 1.5g; CHOLESTEROL 18mg; IRON 1.4mg; SODIUM 224mg; CALCIUM 147mg

▶ carbo rating: 31
Chocolate-Peppermint Parfaits

To crush the peppermints, place the candies in a heavy-duty zip-top plastic bag. Seal the bag, and crush the candy by pounding it with a meat mallet or heavy rolling pin.

⅓   cup finely crushed sugar-free hard peppermint candies (about 11 candies), divided
2¼ cups frozen fat-free whipped topping, thawed
1   (1.4-ounce) package sugar-free chocolate instant pudding mix
1¾ cups fat-free milk

1. Set aside 1 tablespoon crushed candies. Fold remaining crushed candies into whipped topping; set aside ½ cup plus 2 tablespoons topping mixture. Spoon half of remaining whipped topping mixture evenly into 5 parfait glasses.
2. Prepare pudding mix according to package directions, using fat-free milk. Layer half of pudding evenly over topping mixture in glasses. Repeat layers.
3. Top each parfait with 2 tablespoons reserved topping mixture; sprinkle evenly with 1 tablespoon crushed candies. Yield: 5 servings (serving size: 1 parfait).

CALORIES 132; FAT 0.2g (sat 0.1g); PROTEIN 3.4g; CARBOHYDRATE 30.5g; FIBER 0g; CHOLESTEROL 2mg; IRON 0.9mg; SODIUM 262mg; CALCIUM 123mg

▶ carbo rating: 32
Chocolate-Macadamia Nut Pie

This impressive pie is sure to please everyone, whether they're "low-carbers" or not. And it has the added benefit of being a make-ahead dessert.

1   (6.5-ounce) package sugar-free chocolate sandwich cookies, crushed (about 1⅔ cup)
3   tablespoons butter, melted
Cooking spray
2   cups chocolate fat-free, no-sugar-added ice cream, softened
1   (3½-ounce) jar unsalted macadamia nuts, coarsely chopped
2   (8-ounce) cartons frozen fat-free whipped topping, thawed
Shaved sugar-free chocolate bars (optional)
Toasted macadamia nuts (optional)
Whipped topping (optional)

1. Combine crushed cookies and butter. Press mixture firmly in bottom of a 9-inch springform pan coated with cooking spray.
2. Combine softened ice cream and nuts, stirring well. Fold in whipped topping. Pour mixture into prepared crust. Cover and freeze until firm.
3. Remove sides of springform pan; let pie stand 10 minutes before serving. Top with chocolate shavings, toasted nuts, and whipped topping, if desired. Yield: 10 servings (serving size: 1 slice).

CALORIES 276; FAT 15.6g (sat 4.2g); PROTEIN 2.9g; CARBOHYDRATE 32.7g; FIBER 1.1g; CHOLESTEROL 9mg; IRON 1mg; SODIUM 134mg; CALCIUM 8mg

recipe index

carbo rating index

subject index